# The New York Times

# TOUGHEST CROSSWORD PUZZLE MEGAOMNIBUS

## Volume 1

Edited by Eugene T. Maleska

Random House
Puzzles & Games

SOLUTIONS TO THE PUZZLES ARE FOUND AT THE BACK OF THE BOOK


Published in the United States by Random House, Inc., New York, and simultaneously in Canada by Random House of Canada Limited, Toronto.



Random House Puzzles & Games Web site address:
www.puzzlesatrandom.com

ISBN 0-8129-3652-3

Manufactured in the United States of America

1 2 3 4 5 6 7 8 9 10

First Edition

**ACROSS**

1. Knocks
5. Queen of the Greek gods
9. Fix
13. ___ the Red
14. Pindar, e.g.
16. On top of
17. At the vital moment
20. Trim
21. Hide out
22. Lena or Marilyn
23. Hawk
24. Office worker, for short
26. Tongue ___
31. Neoteric
33. Plumbum
34. W.W. II battle site
35. Stravinsky
36. Strange
38. Morsel
39. Greek letter
40. Spur
41. Meat cuts
43. Where the tides meet the currents
46. Bore
47. Bridge unit
48. Small pies
50. Expression of disinterest
53. End of the line
56. Last possible time
58. Ace
59. Hop
60. Prefix with blast or carp
61. Chinese cooking dishes
62. Ending with young or old
63. Fathoms below

**DOWN**

1. U.S. flag designer: 1818
2. He composed "Rule, Britannia"
3. Deliberately threw wide to the batter
4. Hesperus, for one
5. Pongee fabric
6. Prepared for publication
7. Jambalaya ingredient
8. Interrogate
9. Highway inns
10. Three monkeys' subject
11. Verne's captain
12. Pearson
15. Forbearing
18. Booboo
19. Registered as a candidate
23. Graf ___
24. Strike, as with 28 Down
25. Roman robes
27. Suppress, as a vowel
28. David's ammunition
29. TV Western
30. Della or Peewee
32. Told
37. Piece of beef
38. Marine "carport"
40. Kind of cross or knight
42. Slip for a ship
44. Members of the wedding
45. Posture at the plate
49. Showy flower
50. Lade
51. Cry of shocked disbelief
52. Half a fortnight
53. Easter ends it
54. ___ Rijn, Utrecht's stream
55. Fulcrum
57. Corporeal duct

# 2

**ACROSS**

1. Magi's guide
5. Ivy Leaguers
9. Roundup item
14. Relative of bingo
15. Kind of weed
16. Companion of Pan
17. The last of "Hamlet"
18. First fratricide victim
19. Student's mark
20. Early O'Neill play
23. Book of the Apocrypha
24. Coarse tobacco
25. "____ Smile Be Your Umbrella"
28. Pictures
32. "____ diem!"
36. Prolific author
38. Joint familiar to a botanist
39. Hero of 2,327 performances
40. Pepper-pot ingredient
41. Dunce cap
42. "____ no money"
43. "Arrivederci ____"
44. Palanquin
45. Mass exodus
47. Russian mountain range
49. "____ la vie!"
51. Hobby of George V and F.D.R.
56. Late O'Neill play
61. Word with cropper or holder
62. Twenty quires
63. Space
64. Mummified, in a way
65. Polynesian cloth
66. Monastic's room
67. Author of "Steppenwolf"
68. British machine gun
69. Being

**DOWN**

1. Emulate Hamill
2. Cal and Carnegie
3. Sweetened the pot
4. Rolling stone
5. Pass, as time
6. Spot for an earring
7. Champagne bucket
8. Lonely flights
9. Congestion
10. "The ____ of age . . .": Burke
11. Playwright O'Casey
12. Libertine Marquis de ____
13. Keats's specialty
21. Stag or ram
22. Lorelei's river
26. Elephant's-ear
27. Soul
29. Word of approval
30. Novelist Ferber
31. Perceived
32. Item on the barrelhead
33. ____ in one's bonnet
34. Call on the phone
35. Chiropodists
37. Form of silica
40. Worthless stuff
44. Developer's interest
46. Ebb
48. Clinker collector
50. Lawyer's business, at times
52. Quickly
53. Folkways
54. Strips
55. Trite
56. He wrote "The Nazarene"
57. Quaker pronoun
58. Members of a crew
59. Achievement
60. Foot racer's goal

# 3

**ACROSS**

1. Hit
5. Show disdain
10. Hamburg housewife
14. Wahine's dance
15. Infamous Frenchman
16. "Gigi" playwright
17. Over
18. Heights
20. Cut the ___ (refute)
22. Begin
23. Fissure
24. Track figures
28. News bulletin
32. L.S.U. site
38. Preminger
39. Eagerly expecting
40. Mail
41. Muse
42. Ooze
43. Garb for 14 Across
45. King of Judea
47. Huntley
48. U.S. journalist
51. Japanese city
56. Words symbolizing good sense
62. Kind of revolution
63. Kind of code
64. Laurel
65. Washer cycle
66. Nest noise
67. Kind of rule
68. Of a cereal
69. Residue

**DOWN**

1. Chases flies
2. Unconventional
3. Cork-removal sound
4. Done for
5. Jack jumper
6. Cowboy's concern
7. Beyond
8. Boon
9. Sweetheart
10. Pioneer's piece
11. Cross
12. Tops
13. Red letters
19. Volcanic rock
21. "High ___"
25. Go slow
26. R.I. rebel: 1842
27. Roadside plant
29. King of the Huns
30. Budge
31. Owl's sound
32. Party
33. To ___ (exactly)
34. Layer
35. Timely
36. Exclamation
37. Gaelic
44. Kind of battery: Abbr.
46. Diablo's opposite
49. Musical vamp
50. Narrow streak
52. Afternoon TV fare
53. Roman coins
54. Truckle
55. Modify to suit
56. Perch
57. Within: Prefix
58. Cheese
59. Cue
60. Comfort
61. Hollow

# 4

**ACROSS**

1. Et ___
7. How this word goes
13. Ludicrous
14. Records kept by Evelyn and Frank
16. Fawn upon
17. In ___ (basically)
18. Part of R.S.V.P.
19. Gape
21. "Bear" in C.B. lingo
22. Military sch.
24. Aware of
25. Dwelling in a Valentino film
26. Mineral: Comb. form
27. Ruminate
28. Avant-___
29. Smoothest
31. Most wan
32. War-plane maneuver
34. Trees used in making cabinets
37. With importunacy
41. Della from Detroit
42. One-spots
43. The Fates, e.g.
44. Milk: Comb. form
45. Ski resort in Utah
46. Emulate Hancock
47. Suffix with favor or labor
48. Red Cross supply
51. Rotten
52. Brighter
54. Declaim
56. Wake-up time for many
57. He has tales
58. V-shaped fieldworks
59. Oozed

**DOWN**

1. Will supplement
2. Strive to equal
3. Sesame
4. Organism modified by environment
5. Be in good standing
6. Pub
7. "___ Fideles"
8. Fish or "Kid"
9. Scratch out
10. Galena, for one
11. Heartfelt
12. Endorses
13. Late Spanish cellist
15. Rhyme royal
20. Teaches
23. Most profound
25. Certain gifts
27. Gulls
28. Showed resiliency
30. Persephone
31. Greedy ones
33. Builders of castles in the air
34. Actor who played Disraeli
35. Fourth-anniversary gift
36. Mislead
38. Kind of tax
39. Tied, in surgery
40. Over there
42. Causes fear
45. ". . . Cassius has ___ and hungry look"
48. Mexican fruit or drink
49. Opposite of aweather
50. Dover ___ (fish dish)
53. Someone to raise besides Cain
55. Small explosive device

# 5

**ACROSS**

1. Salute
5. Old Testament book
9. Colleague of Freud
14. Armbone
15. Form of "Hosea"
16. Orange Bowl site
17. Anthropologist Margaret
18. Felicitations
20. Some teeth
22. Pied-____ (lodging)
23. Frauds
24. "Do you take ____ woman . . ."
25. Where an Ens. serves
26. Short solo
29. Mrs. Humphrey
32. Garrets
34. Algerian port
35. ". . . nothing like ____"
37. Starr of Green Bay
38. Wraps around
40. Nobelist Lagerlöf et al.
42. Eerie sittings
43. Immerse
44. Article
45. Marooned
49. Click beetle
52. Imprecation
53. Light-blue items in a nest
55. River to the Elbe
56. Sacred figures
57. Fun affair
58. Kind of cone
59. Burn slightly
60. City on the Oka
61. Angry-dog sound

**DOWN**

1. Vaporous
2. Coeur d'____ (resort lake)
3. Faulty
4. Palace help
5. Mechanical man
6. Customers
7. Dick Tracy's wife
8. ____ up (excited)
9. Friendships
10. Withdrawing support, as from a church
11. Comic Bert
12. Retired: Abbr.
13. Stand up
19. Hilo girls
21. Function, in trig
24. Cable car
26. Gather
27. Tyrannizes
28. Port of Spain
29. One of the "Stooges"
30. Coffeemakers
31. Cavalry, of old
33. Aves.
36. Think
39. Fierce
41. Redact
45. "Worn Earth" poet
46. Twangy
47. City of old Syria
48. He bells the cat
49. Apple-tossing goddess
50. Points; places
51. ____ marché (cheap)
52. Solidifying agent
54. Kind of trip

6

## ACROSS

1. Light-switch position
4. Bridegroom's buss fare
8. Apportion
13. Ne ___ ultra (acme)
15. Part of Q.E.D.
16. Silly one
17. Anthony's female counterpart
18. Star that brightens, then fades
19. Frome or Allen
20. Tchaikovsky hero
23. Stretch (with "out")
24. Italian composer Riccardo
25. Dispatch
26. Turner or Cole
27. Kind of market
30. Famed puppeteer
32. Make limp and soiled
37. Lorelei
40. Thine: Fr.
41. Gratings
43. Relative of a 'copter
44. Sharpened
46. Implications
48. Double CCII
50. Yule song
51. Half a dance
53. Weak-eyed worm hunter
56. Pierre's dreams
60. "Leave ___ to heaven . . .": Hamlet's father's ghost
61. Rossini hero
64. Chou ___
66. Totals
67. Server
68. Derisive sound
69. Liquefy
70. Bone: Prefix
71. Chores
72. Alaska's is 585,412 sq. mi.
73. Poet's "forever"

## DOWN

1. Chose
2. Cooking staple
3. Mushrooms, e.g.
4. Bingo's relative
5. Shackle
6. Makes a bank deposit
7. Actors' milieu
8. Orders of business
9. Destiny
10. Wagner hero
11. Honshu city
12. Belief
14. Wagner hero
21. Popular piano number
22. Those elected
28. Breakfast item
29. Field: Comb. form
31. Verdi hero
32. Scrooge utterance
33. Ike's command
34. Verdi hero
35. Ullmann of films
36. Idyllic place
38. "Maid of Athens, ___ we part . . ."
39. 1, 2, etc.: Abbr.
42. Producer's favorite letters
45. Fools; blockheads
47. School session
49. "___, che sapete" (Mozart aria)
51. Word with hope or treasure
52. Hair rinse
54. Andean denizen
55. Church official
57. Frost forte
58. Puff up
59. Not so straightforward
62. Inactive
63. ___ de bandera (Spanish flagstaff)
65. Noah's refuge

# 7

## ACROSS

1. Hammarskjöld
4. Smile lovingly
8. Gentle rain
12. Author of the withholding-tax plan
13. Wife of "Hagar the Horrible"
14. "Tell ___ Sweeney!"
15. Verdi's "caro nome" is one
16. Like big planes in flight
17. "How ___ Is Love?"
18. Apocalypse quartet
20. Versailles event: 1919
22. Editor's note
23. Before IX
24. Where to find 13 Across
27. Aircraft statistic
31. Notre Dame "fighters"
32. Gift-bearing trio
33. Hawaiian city
34. Word with board or lights
35. Performs alone
36. Landed
37. Lanchester
38. Breakwater
39. Between win and show
40. Land brokers
42. The "Big Bad Wolf" did it
43. Court judgment
44. Figure on a shoe box
45. Not quite with it
48. Rare
52. Site of Waikiki Beach
53. Fanfare
55. Glass unit
56. Single
57. Brings up
58. Test-paper choice
59. Comedian Mort ___
60. "Auld Lang ___"
61. Proposal response, perhaps

## DOWN

1. Mexican's silver dollar
2. Afghan bigwig
3. Optimist: "My ___"
4. Basque headgear
5. Esau's father-in-law
6. ___ Khan
7. Cocktails
8. Pessimist's reply to 3 Down
9. Graceful tree
10. Photocopy, for short
11. British politico
12. Pep-rally sound
13. Harness parts
19. Draw with acid
21. Oil-drilling equipment
23. Stamina
24. Autumn libation
25. Papal cape
26. Beethoven's "___ Solemnis"
27. Homeland of Dylan Thomas
28. Rice dish
29. Kind of "Blue Gown"
30. In the public eye
32. Watered fabric
35. Habitual freeloaders
39. "The Godfather" author
41. Andalusian uncle
42. People of early Britain
44. Kind of drum
45. Certain chits
46. London child's nursemaid
47. Mother's admonition
48. ___ Bator, Mongolia
49. ___ Island, site of a U.S. navy yard
50. Burden
51. Maiden-name denoter
54. Dodgers' clean-up hitter, once

8

## ACROSS

1. Taylor nickname
4. Anderson's "High ___"
7. Treat shabbily
10. Kitchen abbr.
13. Name meaning "watchful"
14. Suffix with verb or herb
15. Ballroom favorite
17. Year in Trajan's reign
18. Part of the French Alps
19. "___ washes the other"
20. Haifa is here: Abbr.
21. "Camino ___"
23. Prize for "Annie": 1977
24. Singing siblings
28. Dad's or Gramp's
29. Closefisted
30. G.S.A. founder
33. Start of a Nichols title
36. "Très ___, merci"
37. ___-Çoburg
38. Storyland siblings
41. Have contiguity
42. Party in Gomorrah
43. Flip head over heels
44. First name from 1776
45. Singer from Texas
46. "What Kind of Fool ___?"
47. Singing siblings
53. Home of Baylor U.
54. Sills, e.g.
55. The whole ball of wax
56. Kind of 20's gin
59. Go on an angle
60. Nabors or Backus
61. Make ___ scarce (flee)
62. Top card
63. Alias: Abbr.
64. Canceled, with "out"
65. Sparks's "Help!"
66. Size between sml. and lge.
67. Farm femme

## DOWN

1. Lawful
2. Kind of coffee or stew
3. Scene of Mailer's "The Fight"
4. ". . . to bury Caesar, not ___ him"
5. Almond willows
6. Newsy digest
7. Out-of-this-world object
8. Any man but Adam
9. Collegiate home of Puritanism
10. Instruction on a French I exam
11. Excessively thin
12. Avg.
16. Thursday's eponym
22. Winter Palace site
25. Sternal area
26. Penurious
27. Piquancy
31. Yoke wearers
32. Do a whitesmith's job
33. Captain with an obsession
34. Zaharias
35. Deluged
36. Loser to Lyndon: 1964
37. Rich brown pigment
39. Type of shark
40. Searched high and low
45. Ten make a grand
46. Suggestion-box contents
48. Famed publisher
49. Turkish soldier
50. Punjab prince
51. Part of a 1956 slogan
52. One of Leopold Auer's pupils
53. Pass orie's heyday
56. Whence Jack pops
57. Related to gums: Comb. form
58. "___ Daughter," Marquand book

9

**ACROSS**

1. Jumble
5. Exploits
10. Tent part
14. Helm position
15. Incipience
16. The best
17. Nebraska
20. More eager
21. Tooth layer
22. Knacks
24. Lively dance
25. Racket
28. Unit of noise
29. Greek letter
30. Unit system in physics
33. Zone
35. Nobleman
37. Rich peasant in Russia
39. Colorado
42. Little round hill
43. Wholly: Prefix
44. Dueling sword
45. Juan or Mateo
46. Female sheep
48. Leghorn's largesse
50. Fast jet
51. Enthusiastic
52. Avoid
54. Horse, herb or color
57. Garment worker
61. Illinois
65. Furthers
66. Gibson item
67. Fuel in Cork
68. Rambler
69. Loses freshness
70. Type of log

**DOWN**

1. Horse for hire
2. Liliaceous plant
3. Parched
4. Reddish-orange dye
5. Wilson's ____ Points
6. U.S.N.A. grad
7. Invite
8. Golf equipment
9. Baker or Main
10. Deadly
11. Soil type
12. Poker stake
13. Kind of rind
18. Sort of wort
19. Sly guys
23. Inclined
24. Narrates
25. Supports
26. Fight site
27. Joining peg
30. Thunder peals
31. Winner at Saratoga
32. Type of shooting
34. Expanse east of N.A.
36. Bravo or Grande
38. American Indian
40. Lucky number in dice
41. Alleviates
47. Osier
49. Pacific island
51. Come about
53. Chilling
54. Magi guide
55. Buckeye State
56. Cincinnati nine
58. Stead
59. Unwritten
60. Network, as of fibers
62. American cuckoo
63. Nothing
64. Ham's click

# 10

## ACROSS

1. Chastises
7. What Hamlet called for
13. Flower
14. Preconceives
16. Title one rank above knight
17. Earthly
18. Goddess of harvests
19. Fit for human consumption
21. Staff
22. Well versed in
24. Social event
25. Spanish whistle
26. Mortise's partner
28. Soft cattlehide leather
29. Blood ___
30. Badger's cousin
32. King's words in a musical
34. Terrible Russian
36. Eurasian range
37. Signs of spring
41. Avoid by stratagem
44. "___ mud in your eye!"
45. Vestment
47. ___ facias (legal writ)
49. Kin of Ph.D.'s
50. Night lights
52. ___ Sea, Arctic Ocean arm
53. Keats product
54. Solidify
56. Bell and Kettle
57. Cotton cloth
59. Large snail
61. Praises
62. Extra helping
63. Hosiery
64. Stair parts

## DOWN

1. Red fish
2. ___ non grata
3. I love: Lat.
4. Zero
5. Work dough
6. Long seat
7. Any faraway place
8. Mature
9. Nota ___
10. Stripling
11. Open-mesh fabric
12. Capitol fellow
13. Approximately
15. Spanish spouse
20. Competent
23. Announcements
25. Kind of supper
27. Birthmark
29. Apportions
31. ___ Vegas
33. Flesh: Comb. form
35. Spick-and-span state
37. Pyramid builder
38. Hewlett Johnson's epithet
39. Hospital worker
40. Lava
42. Strawberry's milieu
43. Income source for Junior
46. Turkey portion
48. Alleviates
50. Razor clam
51. Fencing sword
54. Roman statesman
55. Chantilly
58. ___ -de-sac
60. Mauna ___

11

## ACROSS

1. Mud daubers
6. Isinglass
10. "I Should ___," 1944 song
14. White poplar
15. Sacred picture
16. Dash
17. Create a bureaucracy
20. Click beetles
21. Broom of twigs or rushes
22. Bullfrog genus
23. Tart or napoleon
24. Resort
26. The ultimate state
28. Fling
29. Cordage fiber
31. Cut
33. Egyptian goddess
37. Numerals
38. Barton or Bow
39. Best grade
40. Spreads to dry, as hay
41. Diminutive suffixes
42. Stringed instrument
43. Former coin of Pakistan
45. Taste
47. Indication of origin in German names
48. Adjective applying to 59 Across
51. Vetch
53. Old-womanish
54. Hissing quality
59. One objective of fund management
61. Silver standard: Abbr.
62. Arm bone
63. Hill, in Honduras
64. Trireme propellants
65. Site of ancient Olympic Games
66. Ford boo-boo

## DOWN

1. Walk in water
2. Victim of Cain
3. Moved apart
4. "Oro y ___," Montana motto
5. Balmy
6. "La Bohème" heroine
7. Glacé
8. Slammer occupants
9. Pangolin's morsel
10. Divine
11. Heeling
12. Implement for Figaro
13. Napoleon, to Wellington
18. Exceed
19. Down with: Fr.
23. Sponging
24. What "X" marks
25. Lodgepole ___
27. Fourth-brightest star of a constellation
28. Daughter of Saturn
30. Pack on the attack
32. Large container
34. "Among My ___," 1927 hit song
35. Division word
36. Viewed
44. "Two of one trade ___ love": Dekker
46. Alcazar, for one
48. Norwegian seaport
49. Singer O'Day
50. Arkansas or Missouri
52. Appraised
54. Horizontal timber
55. Part of Morocco since 1969
56. Slant
57. Heart
58. Organic compound
60. "Sweet" one of song

# 12

**ACROSS**

1. S.A. rodent
5. Rascal
10. Home of government
14. "One small step for ___"
15. Slip
16. Cartoonist who wrote "Man in the Shower"
17. Tweed's nemesis
18. Basket weave
19. Word with Kansas or Oklahoma
20. Relay system: 1860–61
23. Son of Gad
24. Affirmative vote
25. Indiscretion
29. Beame or Vigoda
32. Collect
36. "___ santé!" (French toast)
38. Trading center
40. Signature shortcut for Franklin
41. Load
43. Archibald of the N.B.A.
44. Study of being
46. Ostrich or emu
48. Poker ploy
49. "___ Cape Cod," Patti Page hit
51. A terminus of 56 Across
52. Transportation abbr.
54. Nark
56. Goethals's achievement
64. Imprecation
65. Adult insect
66. Where the ginkgo grows
68. Jack ___ of films
69. Runner like Ryun
70. Conceal in the hand
71. London district
72. "Stormy Weather" composer
73. B'way group

**DOWN**

1. Criticize
2. She loves: Lat.
3. Wherewithal
4. Prefix with date
5. ___ Wences, puppeteer
6. Phrenologists' interests
7. Ostentatious
8. Speck
9. Prof's boss
10. A terminus of 20 Across
11. Lake city
12. Aardvark's diet
13. Hellman's "___ in the Attic"
21. Earl or duke
22. Bosc or Bartlett
25. Cabinet post
26. Oats, in Oaxaca
27. Loren's husband
28. A terminus of 20 Across
30. One of October's birthstones
31. Character in Wallace's "The Two"
33. "To fetch ___ . . ."
34. ___ voce
35. Dutch genre painter
37. Bionomics: Comb. form
39. Maxwell Anderson's "High ___"
42. Past
45. "___ Smile Be Your Umbrella"
47. Official minutes
50. Medicated candy
53. Soul
55. Squirrel's morsel
56. Digits
57. Angel's gear
58. Greenland settlement
59. Eastern bigwig
60. Shopper's paradise
61. Wine valley
62. Wise ___ owl
63. Speak rhythmically
67. G.P.'s group

# 13

**ACROSS**

1. Of a plant pore
7. Appropriate cry for G.B.S.
12. U.S. poet who wrote "The Place for Love"
13. Marries in haste
15. Naps
18. Corkers
19. Topgallants
20. Pro ____
21. "____ long way . . ."
22. Pier
23. ____ speak
24. This: Fr.
25. Kin in a G. & S. line
26. Prepare peas
27. Circular panel
29. Dressed ____ nines
30. London bus
33. Seed covering
36. Musical pieces
39. Money in Prague
40. Slow one
41. Church V.I.P.'s
43. Danube feeder
44. Commandment word
45. Venus de ____
46. Writer Anais
47. Up
48. ____ energy
49. Naps
52. Go to bed
53. Wearer of a silver eagle
54. Campus brass
55. Accrued

**DOWN**

1. Tam-o'-____
2. Becomes habituated
3. Sills's milieu
4. Overlook
5. Sandy's sound
6. Became less severe
7. ____ fours (teacakes)
8. With craftiness
9. "____ tricks?"
10. Bee: Prefix
11. Exited
12. Phlegmatic
14. Drawing
16. Diamondback
17. Turgenev novel
22. Self-defense system
23. In arrears
25. Sadat
26. Peculate
28. Pipe up
31. Fuse
32. Ply needles
33. "What Is This ____ Called Love?"
34. Not so arduous
35. Having a diagonal direction
37. Site of the Eisenhower Center
38. Spread out
40. Disgraces
42. City on the St. Lawrence
44. Avowed
45. Word with court or pool
47. Huge land mass
48. Pacific archipelago
50. Agnes or Jeanne
51. Sweetie

# 14

**ACROSS**

1. Anent
5. Umbrella named for a Dickens character
9. Spring in Alaska
13. Has-been's place
15. Migrant of the 30's
16. Fad or frenzy
17. Nocturnal ungulate
18. Persecutor of 4 Down
20. Welty's "Why ___ at the P.O."
21. Paul Pry
22. Werner Erhard's therapy
23. Cash in
25. Muscular contraction
27. Quartet following Q
29. Tuneful
33. Secretariat at two
36. Theatrical org.
38. Significant period
39. Swears
41. Demeanor
42. Shopping ___
43. Dye again
44. Kind of tool
46. Starboard side when sailing north
47. Memorable rock 'n' roll idol
49. Mister, in Essen
51. Work on lace
52. Ransacked
56. Geometer's postscript
59. Squama
63. De Gaulle's birthplace
64. Unscrupulous clerk
66. Part of AWOL
67. "There ___ peace . . .": Isa. 48:22
68. Former lightweight champ
69. Gantry or Fudd
70. Sly glance
71. Catnap
72. First Virginia in America

**DOWN**

1. Out of bed
2. One source of oil
3. Halfhearted
4. Boy born in a workhouse
5. Lots
6. Consanguineous
7. Home of a famous statue
8. Ball or pincushion: Fr.
9. Quang ___, city in Vietnam
10. Cod's cousin
11. "I the heir of all the ___ . . .": Tennyson
12. Shrine Bowl team
14. Manumits
19. Barrel spigots
24. Transit group in N.Y.C.
26. Betsey Trotwood's nephew
28. Having but one component
29. Paludous place
30. Beloved of 26 Down
31. Desserts
32. Huntley
33. Complain
34. Finished
35. Word with star or stone
37. Aunt, in Majorca
40. Ostentatious display
45. Prefix with form or fume
48. Clearly delineated
50. Lunar depression
53. Andes ruminant
54. Young conger eel
55. Farm-machine pioneer
56. Witticism
57. Gaelic
58. Emulate an epicure
60. Aviation prefix
61. Author of "How's Your Bridge?"
62. Fleuret's relative
65. Armstrong's "All's well!"

# 15

**ACROSS**

1. Unwind
6. Scriven
9. Actress Bo
14. Overhead
15. "Then to the spicy nut-brown ____": Milton
16. Act the ham
17. Most common throw in dice
18. Heart of a certain tart
20. January, in Cádiz
21. D.A.'s
22. Gypsy gentlemen
23. Titled ones
26. Reagan et al.
30. Ice field
31. Skedaddle
35. "See ____ . . ."
36. Ward (off)
37. Greetings from Hilo
38. Locale in Twain's "Roughing It"
40. Ethan and Zeena
41. Thin pancake
42. Out of port
45. Elegant wood
46. Crew members
47. May heroines
48. Bricklayers' troughs
49. Small streams
52. This, in Taxco
55. Winged
56. Trickster
61. Lear's trio
63. Odin, Thor et al.
64. Ramada
65. Uncle, to Pablo
66. Procrastinator's word
67. Appearances
68. Manuel or Martin
69. Rubbish

**DOWN**

1. Make an incised mark
2. O'Neill character
3. It's nothing to Chris Evert
4. Protest or testify
5. Gas used in TV tubes
6. New Testament allegory
7. Euphoria
8. Settled down comfortably
9. Fledgling in society
10. Fabric used as an abrasive
11. Calhoun
12. Bien-____ (well-being): Fr.
13. Cronin's "The ____ of the Kingdom"
19. "____ Love You," Mercer hit
24. Medieval king
25. Despot
26. Home, to cattle
27. Locale for lorgnettes
28. Oscar winner: 1958
29. Garden flower
32. Amorist
33. In the lead
34. Goalies' protections
39. Lucy's TV partner
40. Lenten observance
42. Lucky pieces
43. Sun-rooms
44. "Nature" essayist
50. Brewer's aid
51. Norse bard of yore
52. Cheese market
53. Hindu wrap
54. Subway tunnel
57. Within arm's length
58. Regarding
59. Contends
60. Blunders
62. Wage units: Abbr.

# 16

**ACROSS**

1. Quick ___ wink
4. Bouquet
9. Deere's steel implement
13. Tranquil
15. Countrified
16. Critic's encomium
17. Erasure
19. Sharif
20. "One Hoss Shay" constructor
21. Walk awkwardly
23. Have ___ (live it up)
26. Lavender or lilac
27. Highway symbol
30. ___ Vegas
32. Exacting, as a teacher
35. Gypsy Rose
36. Passes a law
39. Prefix with distant or lateral
40. "But ___ on forever"
41. Feast
43. Waves' org.
44. Fishhook part
46. Three-ply yarn having loops
47. Prefix with bar or graph
48. Bullion unit
50. Jiffy
51. Gaseous element in our atmosphere
53. Sheik's headcord
55. Ovid or Cato
57. Archie's term for Edith
60. Hurt
64. Dye source
65. Reflects on
68. Get some shut-eye
69. Birchbark, e.g.
70. Outcry
71. Persons
72. Forest denizens
73. Vote for

**DOWN**

1. Scored on a serve
2. Secure
3. A for ___
4. Cockpit
5. Daiquiri base
6. Bauxite
7. Supplies a crew
8. Even if, for short
9. Play entrepreneur
10. Valance
11. Face shape
12. "Those ___ the days"
14. Port near Hong Kong
18. Certain network
22. Classifieds
24. S.A. plains
25. Glossy coating
27. Legal plea
28. A sister of Goneril
29. Shake up the staff
31. Cement-based material
33. ___-Japanese War: 1904–05
34. Sheer fabric
37. Collar
38. Orch. offering
42. Lyndon and Lady Bird
45. Astounds
49. Filing aid
52. Take pleasure in
54. Gate fastening
56. Douglas and Wallace
57. Carpentry groove
58. Hep to or hip to
59. Southeast Asian
61. Eye feature
62. Count (on)
63. Perry's creator
66. Hostelry
67. Drowse

# 17

**ACROSS**

1. Apparel
5. Ye ___ tea shoppe
9. Clammy
13. Libertine
14. The late Orient Express
15. Place for a caboose
16. British ___ of Court
17. Grant's successor
18. Guthrie
19. Prokofiev orchestral fairy tale
22. Radio role of Jay Silverheels
23. Agcy. that electrified rural America
24. Sample the library
27. Kooks
31. "C'est ___!"
32. Unsigned, for short
33. Iroquoian
35. Conspire, in a way
36. Recumbent
37. Attain justly
38. Darkroom receptacle
39. Brinker of fiction
40. Chose
41. Polliwog
43. Religious superior
44. Fitting
45. Relish
47. Two difficult alternatives
54. Keyed up
55. Callas or Tallchief
56. August, in Paris
57. He, to Hadrian
58. Biblical land, east of the Jordan
59. Svelte
60. Glance askance
61. Khyber or Donner
62. Start of an epitaph

**DOWN**

1. Stagehand
2. Topflight
3. Smallest of a litter
4. Perilous
5. Praying female figure
6. Surrender
7. Bantingize
8. Cherish as sacred
9. Sigh with relief
10. Prefix with sol or stat
11. Suburban shopping center
12. One of the prexy's staff
14. Banquo, for one
20. Kind of wine
21. "All that wealth ___ gave": Gray
24. Spill the beans
25. Moroccan capital
26. ___ Culp Hobby
28. Cosmic cycles
29. Hold forth
30. Progenitors
32. Russian sea
34. At loose ___
36. Aerial mosaic
40. One-sixth of a drachma
42. Afterthought No. 2 on a letter
43. Of doves, hawks, etc.
46. Barrio farewell
47. "___ to thee, blithe spirit!": Shelley
48. Give the once-over
49. Gremio or Grumio
50. Rumor personified
51. "Utopia" visionary
52. Glacier in Alaska
53. "Ma, He's Making Eyes ___"

**ACROSS**

1. Economize
7. Refrain syllables
13. Glass tanks
14. Emulate Cassandra
15. Word with alcohol or varnish
16. Wapiti's relative
17. Springtime on the Seine
18. Lovely spring blossom
20. ____ Lanka
21. Highway to Fairbanks
23. Fleming's 007
24. Turkey devoured by critics
25. "The Captain's ____," D. H. Lawrence story
26. Nonstop talker
27. "____, but no cigar!"
28. Views from basement windows
30. Pistil-packing part of a plant
31. Fails to seize the day
33. Place in proximity
36. Touched with tenderness
40. First of a no-no septet
41. Librarian's backbreaker
42. Conductor Ceccato
43. Coty or Pleven
44. Ribbed
45. With full force
46. "____ got a little list . . .": Gilbert
47. Playwright Rattigan
49. R-V connection
50. "____ eat cake"
52. Range needed by an eavesdropper
54. Poem by Frost
55. Sneaky shooters
56. Snack-bar give-aways
57. Places

**DOWN**

1. Condition on Tobacco Road
2. Carrel
3. Beater for mixing mortar
4. Of a part of the eye
5. Where H.H.H. lived
6. Hair styles
7. Pollster's study
8. "And may ye better reck the ____": Burns
9. Put two and two together
10. Bides time while the heat is on
11. Chaffy
12. White bass
13. Drake's conquest in 1588
14. Disposed
19. Dit-dah system
22. Thin, glossy silk for hoods
24. Beachcomber's bonanza
26. The "hot corner" is one
27. Tip for a tec
29. Kind of acre or crack
30. Driver's warning
32. One cause of ennui
33. "____ the cruelest month": Eliot
34. Obviate
35. Batting-grip aid
37. Committed a foul on the rink
38. MSS. inspectors
39. Eatery offering
41. "The Velvet Fog"
44. Staggers
45. Height for a kite
47. Spring in Alaska
48. Defeatist's word
51. Norris Dam agcy.
53. Bex or Dax

**ACROSS**

1. Circles of glory
6. "When the ____ abroad, the mice play": Florio
11. Embarrassed action at Detroit
12. Maltreated
14. Biblical weather
17. Double-reeds
18. Four: Comb. form
19. Gosh!
20. Sudden assault
21. Like Joe Miller jokes
22. Stronghold
23. City lines
24. "____ Did You Get That Girl?"
25. Toned down
26. Mexican millinery item
28. Loving touch
29. Pennies from heaven?
31. Much impressed
34. Sparkles
38. Treat's alternative
39. Harold Pinter's forte
40. Joined
41. Meander
42. Get set for a shock
43. Hereditary transmitter
44. One serve, one point
45. Groove or fold
46. "Flying Dutchman" heroine
47. Yesterday's tears, so to speak
50. Rescind
51. Nap raiser
52. Pass along
53. Hard to restrain

**DOWN**

1. Reason for awarding a D.S.C.
2. Took steps
3. Macaulay's "____ of Ancient Rome"
4. Around a long time
5. Untidy woman
6. She introduced the one-step
7. "Every hero becomes ____ at last": Emerson
8. Porous rock
9. Mideast rep.
10. Channel to salt water
11. Sergeant fish
13. Double daggers
14. Warnings on fairways
15. Annus Domini
16. Can't do without
21. Lord of the sands
22. Blast of gunfire
24. Downfall
25. Its population was decorated for bravery: 1942
27. Actor Dern
28. Region, to Keats
30. Chosen dish by dish
31. Wind indicator
32. Pointed surgical tool
33. "Rosie" of W.W. II
35. Diaskeuast
36. Landlord's income
37. Power Noah didn't have
39. Coachman
42. Soho fellow
43. Honkers
45. Exam giver
46. Mop of hair
48. Brink of an event
49. Brew in a bag

# 20

**ACROSS**

1. Anonymous Richards
5. Records
11. Modern Greek vernacular
13. "Can Do" people
15. Is direct
17. Venerable
18. Nudges
19. ___ disant
20. Author Kingsley
21. Blinding
22. Homophone for pearl
23. One of the wetlands
24. SST, e.g.
25. Corday's victim
26. Renews
28. Worries
29. Querns
31. True up
33. Monograms
37. Emporium
38. Petioles or pedicels
39. Kind of neckline
40. Stopper
41. Other, to Pierre
42. Adduce
43. Person
44. Eastern Church member
45. Abyss
46. Levels
49. Molasses, to an Englishman
50. U.S.A.F. people
51. Tonsorial offerings
52. Suffices

**DOWN**

1. Salad ingredient
2. Hebrew measures
3. Like a snap
4. Convene
5. Landward
6. Indigent
7. Snoozes
8. Cameroons tribe
9. Free time
10. Casa figures
11. Transient of a sort
12. Composer Aaron
14. Avocet's cousin
15. Banter
16. Message-sending
21. Astronaut-Senator
22. Zoroastrian
24. Eater: Comb. form
25. Soda-fountain orders
27. Goldbrick
28. Poetic region
30. Sluggishness
31. They make amends
32. Role for Channing
34. Pilots a plane
35. Admits
36. What Hamlet said he knew not
37. Hazel or Winfield
38. Musical compositions
41. Like weak female nonagenarians
42. Belfry sound
44. Acad. at New London, Conn.
45. Food fish, sometimes called pintado
47. Wool: Prefix
48. Josh

# 21

**ACROSS**

1. Health clubs
5. Skelton role
9. Painful memory
13. Savoy beat
14. Critic's kudos
15. Kind of deck
16. Veranda
17. Giant of Norse myths
18. ___ now! (immediately!)
19. TV sitcom
22. In attendance
23. Hundred yrs.
24. Numerical ending
27. Part of Mao's name
28. Grand lady
30. Two-way ___
32. White poplar
34. Not in the pink
35. TV sitcom
38. Bided one's time
39. Definitions in puzzles
40. Good looks, to a starlet
41. Flunk out
42. G.I. garb
45. Clock setting in summer
46. Gibbon
48. Oryx
51. TV sitcom
54. Population-growth number
56. Cake worker
57. French composer
58. Tel companion
59. Opp. of feminine
60. Fragrant
61. S.A. rodent
62. Tallinn man
63. Wolfe of fiction

**DOWN**

1. Homophone for stares
2. Soft cloth
3. Nanking nanas
4. Venom
5. Watch parts
6. Like Charley's horse?
7. Display
8. Ruined city on the Nile
9. Unattached male
10. Redeemed
11. G.I. address
12. Grid "zebra"
13. What Washington did "here"
20. Word of emphasis
21. Like a green banana
25. Alice or Tim
26. Go the whole ___
29. Holy city
31. Grieving word
32. You can call him Johnson
33. Bailey of comics
34. Phylactery
35. Soviet wire service
36. Adjective for Bunker Hill
37. Despot
38. Lump of tobacco
41. Brawl
42. Kind of dictum
43. "Fats"
44. Marksman's game
47. Price for a dozen?
49. Raymond Burr TV role
50. No longer fresh
52. Lou ___, boxing star of the past
53. A day ago: Abbr.
54. Strafe, in slanguage
55. Bartok

# 22

**ACROSS**

1. Companions of bacon
5. Shoe nail
9. Ignore
13. Neighbor of Galway
14. Word with check or coat
15. Manage
16. Greens of sport and song
19. Robert ____
20. Douglas ____, first president of Eire
21. A Tara O'Hara
22. Scottish "no"
24. What waiters take
25. "____ of America": Reich
31. Sensory stimuli
32. Lorne Greene's Adam on TV
33. Actor Joel
37. Dross
38. Gallico's Mrs. ____
39. Kind of review
40. Artist Greenaway
41. Where a shamrock is a trifoglio
42. Kentucky college town
43. Romaine and cos
45. Jules ____, film director
49. Yankees' Guidry
50. Kind of bucket
51. Curved molding
54. Reuner, for short
58. Greens of locale and authorship
61. Fortress feature
62. Crow
63. He played Parnell
64. March 17, ____ Domini 1979
65. "____ go marching . . ."
66. "The ____," Grace Kelly film

**DOWN**

1. Jewish month
2. Kaplan of TV
3. Rumer Godden's "The ____ Summer"
4. Indian weight
5. County Wicklow seaside resort
6. McNally partner
7. Helper
8. Nucleic acid
9. Berate
10. ____ prosequi
11. Kind of berth
12. Novelist Aphra and family
13. Guevara
17. Quaker pronoun
18. Sacred lake in Donegal
23. "The Campbells ____ coming"
24. Handy greenbacks
25. Kind of force
26. Hilo dance
27. Part of Q.E.D.
28. Flynn
29. Shearer
30. Epic poem
33. "____ the Lilacs"
34. Steak order
35. Word with tide or song
36. Opponents of nays
38. ____ Islands, in Galway Bay
42. Monastic abbr.
43. ____ Fein, Irish political movement
44. Mr. Peck, to friends
45. Teachings
46. Hank of homerun fame
47. Old Irish hunting knife
48. Sullivan vs. Kilrain
51. Currach adjuncts
52. Nibble
53. Advantage
55. Genus of frogs
56. Hale, King or Arkin
57. Pest killer
59. Arab garment
60. McMahon et al.

# 23

## ACROSS

1. Shaw's "_____ and the Man"
5. Angler's hooks
10. _____ dixit
14. Street sound
15. Mecca in a polls
16. "How _____ Is Love?" (pop song)
17. Piedmont town
18. She blossomed in Rome
19. State flower of Utah
20. Old Glory
23. Narrow aperture
24. Cobra feature
25. Tap-tap-taps
29. Co-creator of Sir Roger de Coverley
33. Jason's band
37. Cast aspersions on
38. Excessively modest
41. Burden
42. They reign without rein
43. Swinburne's forte
46. Costa Rican's cloak
47. Classical Library founder
49. Plato's "Ideas"
52. Victims of Bobby Thomson's home run
59. Diamond Head site
60. Burrels and Seckels
61. "I ___ a dream": King Jr.
62. Others, to Ovid
63. Atelier article
64. Psychedelic experience
65. Cars of the 1920's
66. Mexican tree
67. Used a transmitter

## DOWN

1. Sans-culottes' words
2. Musical symbols
3. Mercury, for one
4. Paris visitor: 1927
5. Rio's carnival, e.g.
6. Stravinsky ballet
7. Famous Omahan
8. Callow
9. World's greatest coffee port
10. Draw-poker temptations
11. Chick sound
12. Clary is one
13. Son of Aphrodite
21. Position on an issue
22. Buncombe
26. Actress Marsh of old films
27. Chrysalis
28. Finger the strings
30. Writer of essays
31. Fontanne's late spouse
32. Units of work
33. ____ to Cerberus
34. Vegas competitor
35. Stickum
36. Bristle
39. One in stir
40. Trod the boards
44. Korean G.I.
45. Emulated Asta
48. Play it _____ (improvise)
50. Hammond Innes's "Wreck of the Mary ____"
51. Sam from N.C.
52. Shoat's sire
53. Abnormal breathing sound
54. McKinley's state
55. Rocketeer's agcy.
56. Small remnant
57. Christiania's name after 1925
58. Irish clan

# 24

**ACROSS**

**1.** Makes as good as new
**9.** Noted U.S. historian: 1834–1927
**15.** Bond bonus
**16.** Pharmaceutical ointment
**17.** Loser, to Loos
**18.** Central vein of a leaf
**19.** Back talk
**20.** Plotted on a curve
**22.** Louis or Frazier
**23.** Business-school subj.
**25.** Different
**26.** Inst. like Swarthmore
**27.** Plaza de ____
**29.** Poetic word
**30.** Atoll builder
**31.** Take tea with delicacy
**33.** Propose for office
**35.** Post-Presidential role for Washington
**39.** Intimidated
**40.** Louis XIV, e.g.
**41.** Cranial nerve
**42.** Site: Abbr.
**44.** Eve of Passover
**48.** Susiana
**49.** Casting matrix for Henry Moore
**51.** Eliminate
**52.** Road hazard
**53.** Coagulate
**55.** Set afire
**56.** Caught red-handed
**58.** Freedom of choice
**60.** Mira or Lyra, to Pierre
**61.** Baseball statistics
**62.** Synonym for 37 Down
**63.** Most tranquil

**DOWN**

**1.** Breast-of-lamb cut
**2.** Caruso
**3.** Narcose condition
**4.** Coffee-break hour
**5.** Salem's state, for short
**6.** Kind of rocket
**7.** Mansion's milieu
**8.** Lincoln's pre-Presidential opponent
**9.** Painter Winslow
**10.** Stenchy
**11.** Conjunction for Cicero
**12.** Cooking herb
**13.** Enfeeble or bleach
**14.** One up in arms
**21.** Shore bird
**24.** Panacea
**26.** Actor Hans
**28.** Marner
**30.** Greetings in Genoa, to Americans
**32.** Communicant's bench
**34.** Product maker: Abbr.
**35.** Controlled
**36.** Assess
**37.** Rebuttal
**38.** Profit windfall
**43.** Split or adhere
**45.** Cloudburst
**46.** Abridges verbally
**47.** Second checkup
**49.** Prototype
**50.** Office machine
**53.** He wrote "The Hive"
**54.** Cambio coins
**57.** Twice XXVI
**59.** Whip

# 25

**ACROSS**

1. Double, e.g.
4. ____ Alonzo Stagg
8. Q-W connection
13. Quasi
15. Go on a diet
16. Season
17. Hawaii from 1900 to 1959: Abbr.
18. Comedian Johnson
19. Light shield of yore
20. Amerind
21. British boiler
23. Former gossip columnist
25. Portent
26. ____ (Che) Guevara
31. Come ____ (happen)
33. "____ of My Dreams," old song
34. Corded fabric
35. "Cogito, ____ sum": Descartes
36. One transferring property
40. "Monkey Trial" defendant
43. Fullness of divine powers and virtues
44. Desdemona's detractor
45. Seeker of admiration in conversation via associations
50. Bumpkin or lumpkin
54. Torn-down Grounds
55. Greenstreet contemporary
56. Words said with a sigh
57. On a grand scale
58. Table before a reredos
59. Rugby score
60. Danger
61. "But to see her ____ love her": Burns
62. Pelagic birds
63. He wrote "The Wall Street Gang"

**DOWN**

1. Passage between decks
2. Rhone feeder
3. All in
4. Makes ashamed
5. Leaves high and dry
6. Ready for use
7. The ____ (vast Russian grasslands)
8. "____ vincitor!" (aria for Aida)
9. Pushover
10. Paint cleaner, for short
11. Force onward
12. Shift
14. Creator of Happy Hooligan
22. N.Y.S.E. document
24. Female Japanese diver
27. Something thrilling
28. Vexed
29. Struggles
30. Siouan
31. Narrate
32. British artist: 1761–1807
34. Knock
37. Pusilanimous protagonist
38. Oahu thrush
39. Violent behavior
40. Jazz-band member
41. Enclosures for studying in a library
42. U.S. satellite
46. Greek supt. of public works
47. Visit unexpectedly
48. Beethoven's "Für ____"
49. "The Italian Stallion"
50. Unguis
51. Redford's wife
52. Scraps for Spot
53. "Darn it!"

# 26

**ACROSS**

1. Soil
6. This starts a football play
10. Imitate Elmer Fudd
14. Where oboli were spent
15. Prefix with type or cast
16. Peruvian
17. A time to cheer and a time to weep
20. Essence of good football
21. Roi's spouse
22. Stadium sound
23. Become an expatriate
26. Former Harvard football coach
29. Party workers
30. Unfamiliar
31. Nettled
32. Served up
35. Member of the mob
36. Hebrew prophet
37. Army eleven's mascot
38. Condominium: Abbr.
39. Punters' aids or hindrances
40. Whammy
41. Girl for Igor
42. Sadat's predecessor
43. Usual time for varsity football
46. Curvature
47. Seed cases
48. Cheerleaders' exhortation
53. Shrine Bowl players
56. Tease
57. Roper
58. French law body
59. South Yemen's capital
60. Stadium section
61. Smyrna fig

**DOWN**

1. Football team (see 53 Across)
2. Malarial illness
3. Clothes, to José
4. Shook
5. Weapon for Ahab
6. Colonnade
7. College football culmination
8. ___ -American
9. Foot part
10. Sea vessels
11. Setting for a Forster novel
12. Slight
13. Person named on a check
18. Use a whistle
19. Prompted
24. Equipment for announcers
25. Notion
26. Derisive sound
27. Cockeyed
28. Insurrection
31. Part of ancient Greece
32. Baum martens
33. Or follower
34. Animal resembling a chevrotain
36. Hart's mate
37. Dessert wine
39. "No ___ for the wear"
40. Endearment: Fr.
41. Saturnine
42. Part of N.F.L.
43. Spinal-column sections
44. Jack-in-the-pulpit, e.g.
45. Mark used in logic
49. Swan genus
50. Long hair
51. Metric weight
52. Bone: Comb. form
54. Grasp
55. Larry Kelly was one

# 27

**ACROSS**

1. Group of seals
4. Serves the purpose
10. Jet follower
13. Arp art
14. Sow's newborn
15. Actor Vigoda
16. Suffix with invalid or liquid
17. Group of larks
19. N.Y. town named for a hero of '76
21. Earliest computer
22. Mideast seaport
23. Geraldine, at times
24. Vessel for wine
27. Problem re some TV programs
31. Tag
32. He said, "No man is an island"
33. Abbr. before "truly"
34. Elevator man
35. Group of lions
36. Cry like a calf
37. Scotland Yard group: Abbr.
38. Gators' kin
39. Treasure ___
40. Type of desk
42. Point in horseshoe pitching
43. League including Cin., St. L., etc.
44. Cavett
45. Settle ___ (retaliate)
48. Soaped
52. Fan-tan
54. Additional
55. ". . . like Wind ___": Rubáiyát
56. Diffuse through porous partitions
57. ___ -ran (loser)
58. Feminist org.
59. One 'twixt 12 and 20
60. Group of pheasants, in England

**DOWN**

1. Crown of the head
2. Scent
3. Period during which Charlemagne lived
4. Primates
5. Female fox
6. Gelatin
7. Ailing
8. Not to mention
9. Sculpture having immobile units
10. Secular
11. ___ Ben Adhem
12. Roman clan
13. Morse code signal
18. Record
20. Baal, e.g.
23. Archeological triumphs
24. Group of sheep
25. Cicero's tongue
26. Stay
27. Sinatra, "The ___"
28. Synthetic material
29. Desire
30. Perfume ingredient
32. Amusing
35. Enzyme
36. R.R. worker
38. Vehicle in a spiritual
39. ". . . rambling wreck from Georgia ___"
41. Organic compound
42. Group of puppies
44. "___ Macabre"
45. "See ___ and pick it up"
46. Palm starch
47. Raven's cousin
48. A Spinks
49. ___ -poly
50. Gaelic
51. ___ volente
53. Mrs., French style

# 28

## ACROSS

1. "___ Do Is Dream of You," 1934 song
5. Sized up
10. "___ boy!"
14. This may cause interest
15. Ten make a gram in Greece
16. Vindictive
17. Author of "Madame Bovary"
20. Supporter
21. Be unwilling to give
22. Marmalade ingredient
23. Wrapper
24. Ultimately
27. Optician's product
28. Understood
31. ___ Selassie
32. Soft palates
33. "God's Little ___"
34. Author of "Gil Blas"
37. Harold Teen's "Leapin' ___"
38. Stage direction
39. Take off
40. Brother
41. Jack London hero
42. Obdurate
43. Insisted on redress
44. Diviner
45. Play the siren
48. Dawns
52. Author of "Bel-Ami"
54. Sothern and Sheridan
55. Showy bird
56. Lea herd
57. X-rated, maybe
58. Steel-plow man
59. Side dish

## DOWN

1. Sea lettuce
2. Booming
3. Fasten, as with ropes
4. Among other things
5. ___ Garden, London
6. Evening, in Bonn
7. Lenient
8. Kay's follower
9. Virgule
10. Permeate
11. ___ off (in a snit)
12. Famed puppeteer
13. Prior: Prefix
18. Up
19. Roma was one
23. Subleased
24. Time and ___
25. Old German coin
26. Tropical vine
27. Famed Bolshevik
28. Word with babe or crow
29. Potter's clay
30. Lachrymose
32. Irked
33. * * *
35. Liberated
36. Chemical compounds
41. Seine feeder
42. Where to see whips
43. Like washer water
44. Very large
45. Moslem titles
46. Clair de ___ (bluish porcelain)
47. Bobcat
48. Unfaltering
49. Jib or lug
50. Danish composer
51. Ragout
53. Years on earth

# 29

## ACROSS

1. Hereford enclosure
7. Refined, as ore
14. Eastern Christian
15. Daredevil's delight
16. Like some tires or coats
17. Predate
18. Antilles
19. Whomp
20. Russian village
21. Easily bruised area
22. Commemorative pillar
23. "Patterns" or "Birches"
24. Word with head or line
25. Dissect grammatically
26. Vice follower
27. Albany enactment, e.g.
29. Pablo or Pedro
30. He wrote "Song of Myself"
33. Like Marvell's mistress
34. Cold-cubes factory
37. Rathskeller vessel
40. Kefauver
41. Diplomat knighted by James I
42. Market-research tool
43. Took a sudden interest
44. Transactions
45. Pop's brother
46. Oak or elm growths
47. Pipe
48. Antimalarial drug
50. Blueblood, for short
51. Automatic
52. Health indicators
53. Negotiator
54. Kind of kick

## DOWN

1. Léger and Braque
2. Kind of color camera
3. Sudden violent wind
4. Eucharistic plate
5. Times when Nancy is warm
6. Little Edward, to some
7. Doddering
8. Arizona copse
9. Unsharpened sword
10. Ingredient in sealing wax
11. Vibration
12. Vortexes
13. Niger valley natives
15. "Portrait of My Mother" artist: 1872
19. Kind of vote or boss
22. Like corned beef
23. Punitive
25. Hairless
26. Shoe parts
28. Implicit
29. Like a rimrock
31. Metrical accent
32. Spring bloomers
35. Wrote the musical score
36. Garden club favorite
37. Charles or Mary
38. Boy Scout, at times
39. Houdini's forte
40. Taxpayer
43. Apartment
44. Pea holders
46. Noxious child
47. Swarthy, in Tours
49. Arthur
50. Mil. mail handler

# 30

**ACROSS**

1. Servicewoman
5. Where harem girls live
9. Usher's beat
13. Texas battle scene: 1836
14. Lugosi
15. Come ___ (inherit)
16. "Total Woman" types
18. ___ time (never)
19. World's third largest island
20. Kind of parlor
22. Unclose, to poets
23. Church list
25. Wild hog
26. Tranquilizers
28. Boorish male
31. Set free
34. German dollar
36. Noteworthy
37. Piece of jewelry
39. Kathleen Winsor's heroine
40. Citizens of the "Heart of Dixie"
42. Liquor-cabinet item
43. Former D.C. team
45. Raise a family
47. Truck rig
48. Wallach
51. Like "Little Rhody"
54. Lacking pep
56. Dancer's skirt
57. "Leg art"
59. Not new
60. Act studied in law school
61. ___ away from (shunned)
62. Adam of literature
63. Just average
64. Realtor's sign

**DOWN**

1. Cutter's next of kin
2. Chaplain
3. Chaplain's word
4. Phenomenon in many modern marriages
5. Geisha's sash
6. Stray
7. Guinness
8. Japanese seaport
9. Queen's headdress
10. Among other things: Lat.
11. Sicilian spewer
12. Part of a bridal suite
13. Pulpit in early Christian churches
17. One of the anniversaries
21. Frequent topic in marriage counseling
24. Plaid garment
26. Kind of curve, in math
27. Picture in the mind
29. State or Station
30. Work units
31. Darling
32. TV statuette
33. Free at last
35. Branches
38. S.A. snakes
41. Iron men
44. Builds
46. Dodge
48. French enamel
49. Popular
50. Kind of tea
51. Part of a ticket
52. Ruminate
53. Chicken chaser's word
55. Repeat
58. W.W. II theater

**ACROSS**

1. Popinjays
7. Wrangle
13. Speech loss
14. Comaneci asset
15. Extreme; rigorous
16. American wildcats
17. Recent
18. Classify
20. "Sea of troubles"
21. Give a leg up
22. Norway lobsters
24. Musical finale
25. Princess driven mad by Hera
26. Handel's birthplace
27. A founder of Impressionism
28. Four seasons
30. N.F.L. team
32. ____ around (indulged in tomfoolery)
34. De Sade's thing
35. Having shutters
37. Tasty treat in Taxco
38. Rodrigo Díaz de Bivar
39. Sail, in Salzburg
41. Thinker; brain
44. Moslem call to prayer
45. Asparagus shoots
46. Sgt. or cpl.
47. ____-pros
48. Backup men for Gladys Knight
49. Idi of Uganda
50. Interweaves
53. Coming down in buckets
56. Leaflike appendage
57. Nautical ropes
58. "____ the Truth," TV show
59. Has a phobia

**DOWN**

1. Twist, as a wrist
2. Thingumbob or thingumajig
3. Naturalness
4. Landing craft
5. Year in Claudius's reign
6. Of religious rites
7. Supports
8. O'Neill play
9. Lone Eagle's monogram
10. Mean business
11. Outer membrane of a jellyfish
12. Does an ushering job
13. Loser to Dwight
14. Hats
19. Leather-punching tools
22. Introduced in stages
23. More uncommon
24. Infant's ailment
27. General's display
29. Sam of N.C.
31. ". . . Pumpkin-____"
32. Cling; grasp for support
33. Loathe
35. Most barren
36. Recondite
40. Reacted to a surprise
42. Tops in bakeries
43. Fireplace gadget
45. Incantation
49. Scotto forte
51. Pongid or mandrill
52. ____ de sac
54. Item for a skiff
55. Suffix with press or fail

# 32

**ACROSS**

1. Gull
6. Yearbook group
11. Les Etats-Unis
12. Seaport 90 miles SSW of Key West
14. Road to 29 Across
17. Grandiloquize
18. La Chaise et al.
19. Crustacean's spawn
20. Actor Waite in "The Waltons"
21. Outcast
22. Pert girl
23. Berg's makeup
24. "It is ___ the living . . ."
25. Sleuth Philo
26. Found fault
28. Aussie of W.W. I
29. Hell or ruin
31. For a time
34. Street lamp
38. Yonkers events
39. Eyelid problems
40. To-do
41. Cuba libre juice
42. Young mayfly
43. Get one's goat
44. Years
45. Squelched
46. What the Romans' M stands for
47. Timid one
50. Soup-server
51. Lunar ___
52. Undersupplied
53. Over

**DOWN**

1. Devaluate
2. Numerical prefix
3. Seine feeder
4. "Do ___ say . . ."
5. Meddled
6. Routine housework
7. Engineer's beam
8. Rarae ___
9. Vital fluid
10. Using a springe
11. Balkan region
13. Pronto
14. Exposition heading
15. Refusal of approval
16. Spell caster
21. Filmdom heavy of yore
22. Great: Prefix
24. Provides go-power
25. Stringed instruments
27. Cattiness
28. "Galloped the dominoes"
30. Geometric figure
31. Strong man
32. Name in aviation or architecture
33. Base-clearer
35. Questioned intensively
36. Gripe
37. Aviary sound
39. Smooth and lustrous
42. Unprotected
43. ___ Oro, Africa
45. Snick and ___
46. Matter master
48. Infuriation
49. Forefront

# 33

## ACROSS

1. He likened 23 Across to 44 Across
5. Helen's launched a large fleet
9. Ovine eating place
12. Play the siren
13. Muster many or much
15. Like Jekyll's personality
16. Côte d' ___
17. Word in Shakespeare's epitaph
18. "___ each life . . ."
19. Last letter from London
20. Storage area
21. Show embarrassment
23. Crossword puzzle byproduct?
26. Part of a ream
27. Sac of a sort
28. Balderdash!
30. Quaker-to-Quaker word
31. Leaper over Luna
34. Go to one side
35. Muse morosely
37. Word with stick or dash
38. Whatever quantity
39. Duck's cousin
40. Vivien Leigh role
41. Teasdale
42. Peninsula in eastern Arabia
44. "Saturday night special," e.g.
50. Bearded
51. "If the shoe ___ . . ."
52. Kolinsky
53. ___ test
54. Have on sale
56. Akron product
57. Vidal
58. "Be Prepared," e.g.
59. Siesta
60. It nictates
61. Tweed, e.g.
62. Light bulb, symbolically

## DOWN

1. Simon's "___ Suite"
2. European blackbird
3. In bluenosed fashion
4. Eternally, poetically
5. Easy
6. Talisman
7. A charming Channing
8. Twisting area on a road
9. Monday, in Montbéliard
10. Corroded
11. One way to tag
14. Took a wrong turn
15. "She ___ Say Yes"
20. Dither
22. Highlander's old tongue
24. "How about ___!"
25. First communications satellite
28. Sch. group
29. Envy or covetousness
30. A touch of rum
31. Swept away confusion
32. It has a handle and a blade
33. Agency under F.D.R.
35. Ennui
36. Leo's lament
37. Pahlavi
39. Teller's milieu
40. Mel and a former Pirate catcher
41. Sly and nasty
42. Pacifies
43. Nine under a dome
44. Saw
45. Kind of blind
46. Like S.F. in 1906
47. "We're ___ see the Wizard"
48. Do nutricial work
49. Garbo
55. Little pocket
56. Numerical prefix

# 34

**ACROSS**

1. Rhyme scheme
5. Lulls
10. Mendicant's request
14. Hibernian
15. Mr. Heep
16. Look
17. Brecht-Weill work
20. Devilfish's cousin
21. Gregg specialist, for short
22. Actress Joanne
23. "Impossible Dream" item
24. Dumas group
32. Generous disposition
33. Skyline element
34. Forty winks
35. All ____ (listening eagerly)
36. Raymond and 40 Across
37. Do nothing
38. Suffix with Jersey and Wisconsin
39. River of Rumania
40. See 36 Across
41. Chekhov play
44. Yesterday, to Jacques
45. Whisky
46. Stress
49. Tests
54. Nine, or long cheer
56. Suffix with six, seven, etc.
57. Substance, such as benzene
58. Girl-watch
59. Inspired reverence
60. Causes to go
61. After exes

**DOWN**

1. D.C. operatives
2. Thai money
3. Air: Prefix
4. Kitchen gadgets
5. Copper
6. Environs
7. Striated
8. Staff
9. Unscrupulous lawyers
10. Electrical unit
11. Encumbrance
12. Relative of a sea bass
13. Hitch in the best-laid plans
18. Showy bird
19. Giant grass
23. Bypasses
24. Clara Bow, "____ Girl"
25. Erica
26. Kind of cheap street show
27. Shylock, e.g.
28. Binge
29. Lake of Finland
30. Tonsorial aid
31. Sir Patrick of ballad fame
36. Headgear for clergymen
37. Program for an insomniac
39. Coruscate
40. Till now
42. Omega
43. Garden bloomers
46. "____ boy!"
47. ____ the rag
48. Manitoba Indian
49. Counterfeiter catchers
50. Tear
51. Saturnalia
52. Ubangi feeder
53. Links areas
55. High dudgeon

# 35

**ACROSS**

1. High note
4. Follower of de or ipso
9. Rough crowd
12. Faux ___
13. One-way indicator
14. Porous defense
16. Time for a football finale
19. Ex-Senator Long of Hawaii
20. Tourist's stop
21. Game-show groups
22. Clear authorization
24. Surge of blockers
25. Raw material
26. Item on the East Side or West Side
30. A.F.C. or N.F.C.
34. Wife of Wang Lung
35. Pyrenees peak
36. "Mighty ___ a Rose"
37. One of the Shaws
38. Remote outpost for Peary
39. Tops, in a division
41. Pad
43. Hurry
44. Timeout blessing
45. Feasted
49. Baseball statistic
52. Diego or Francisco
53. Remote telecast
54. Pro football pinnacle
57. Scoring plays in Rugby football
58. Behind the times
59. Brew
60. Psychic initials
61. Bayard or Grani
62. Grange

**DOWN**

1. Downs or salts
2. Writer Hobson
3. Quaking tree
4. Partner of wide
5. Referee
6. Beldam
7. Canton is one
8. Temple football player
9. King Cyaxares was one
10. Race track
11. Provincial governors in the Ottoman Empire
14. Urbane
15. Locational phrase re 16 Across: 1978
17. Finish line
18. Digging tool
23. Mars: Comb. form
24. Sidney of basketball
26. Nonsense creature
27. Ski resort in Utah
28. Nonprofessional
29. Namath's weak spot
30. Normandy city
31. "___ the fray"
32. Tidy
33. "Romola" author
37. ___ in a poke
39. Hollow, as in a bone
40. On ___ (precisely)
42. Hebrew letters
45. Uplift
46. Composer Franz
47. Zola
48. Lubricated, as snowshoes
49. Put up a stake
50. Bus-to-bus tickets: Abbr.
51. Radar-screen mark
52. Quarrel
55. AWOL's bane
56. Buntline of dime-novel fame

# 36

**ACROSS**

1. Give ___ (attend)
6. Bengali V.I.P.'s
11. Trousers measurement
12. One of the Furies
14. At the propitious moment
17. Crosscut
18. Precipice
19. Bachelor-party attendees
20. Minnesota baseball player
21. Robert, David or Jack
22. Whimper
23. Swedish county
24. Wallow in water or mire
25. Brazilian port
26. Cinder remover
28. Mercy; kindness
29. Byway intersecting a highway
31. Overseas
34. Drover
38. Muddled or maudlin
39. Londoner's wig
40. Ancestor: It.
41. Ye ___ Tea Shoppe
42. Display edacity
43. Ending with pun and fun
44. Wrestler's milieu
45. Zenana
46. Institute
47. Just barely
50. Thinly scattered
51. Dialects
52. Done
53. Horner or Sprat

**DOWN**

1. Intermesh
2. Pale
3. Rex or Donna
4. Neutral shade
5. Greek letters
6. Jaunty
7. Airborne
8. Mutt's friend
9. Play a role
10. Causative agents
11. After a fashion
13. Foo yong, e.g.
14. Agave fiber
15. Squeakers
16. Ibsen's "An ___ of the People"
21. Biblical depopulator
22. Awaits decision
24. Commit a peccadillo
25. Small, round and shiny
27. Berate
28. Oscar winner for "Two Women"
30. Be like
31. Nuclear weapon
32. Fastens the rigging
33. Bureaucratic procedure
35. Corrida figure
36. Turns aside
37. Alfred ___ Whitehead: 1861–1947
39. Shook up
42. Bring up
43. Old West vehicle
45. Obdurate
46. Discharged
48. Yangtze feeder
49. Creek

37

**ACROSS**

1. Long, swinging stride
5. Author Gardner
9. Was indebted
13. "The Flowers of ___": Baudelaire
14. Daft
16. "The Prisoner of Zenda" author
17. "Light in August" author
20. White House initials
21. Nutrition regimen
22. Cargo placer
23. City near Lake Tahoe
24. Color again
25. Pyknic
27. Venus de ___
28. Monogram of "The Sage of Concord"
31. Sacred image
32. Agent: Suffix
33. "The Brave Bulls" author
34. "This Side of Paradise" author, familiarly
39. Aquatic bird
40. White-tailed flier
41. Tolkien's tree herders
42. F.D.R. measure
43. Boy from Barcelona
44. Beau Brummell
46. Eggs, to Aussies
48. Zona ___, U.S. writer
49. Brown pigment
51. Poet Teasdale
52. Inquire
55. "To Have and Have Not" author
58. Down: Prefix
59. Like Poe's tales
60. Oil power
61. Dick or Schick
62. "Death in Venice" author
63. Governess in a Brontë novel

**DOWN**

1. Lascivious
2. "Metamorphoses" author
3. Atomic reactor
4. Added wing
5. Lily maid of Astolat
6. One of the Montagues
7. Attic
8. Spanish queen
9. Gershwin musical: 1926
10. Lewis Carroll's dreamworld
11. Sword
12. Earl ___ Biggers
15. Christmas adjunct
18. Bad time for Caesar
19. Mary Shelley novel
23. Collector's item
24. Comedy team of brothers
25. Happen
26. Certain salesmen
27. San ___, Calif.
29. "Delta Wedding" author
30. St. Louis bridge
31. "God ___ Englishman": Delderfield
35. Joining pins
36. "There is no ___ like a book": Dickinson
37. Tabard and Wayside
38. Story by Chateaubriand
44. Where Keats placed Cortez
45. Author Paton
47. ___ a time (singly)
48. Urchin
49. Mennonites, e.g.
50. "Dies ___"
51. Evening, in Roma
52. Out of kilter
53. German industrial area
54. "Cappy Ricks" author
56. Edge
57. ". . . the giftie ___ us": Burns

# 38

**ACROSS**

1. "I am monarch ___ I survey"
6. Added liquor
11. Traffic tragedy
13. Historic island west of Athens
15. Inventor's dream
17. Exist
18. Washington's strategy late in '76
19. Sgt. or cpl.
20. Neon or swag
22. Temperate
23. Tavern order
24. Settled
26. Calendar abbr.
27. Up-tight
28. Happen next
30. Echoed
32. Pacino or De Niro
34. Orderly procedures
37. Elan
40. Invierno month
41. Prefix with puncture
43. Cut
45. Weathercock
46. Final words
48. Hindu mother goddess
49. Soul, to Pierre
50. Put ___ (conclude)
52. Remove
53. Escalator
56. Struts
57. Interlock
58. Nasty expression
59. Classified

**DOWN**

1. Run
2. "Smoke-eater"
3. Tyrolean peak
4. Lupine look
5. Stringed instruments
6. Truman's birthplace
7. "I'm quite illiterate, but I read ___": Salinger
8. Siamese or Persian
9. Noted
10. Bishopric
12. Don
13. Garment features
14. "Sawed wood"
15. Sidekicks
16. Treelike
21. Ant
23. Hirsute
25. Cathedral, in Firenze
27. Lachrymae
29. Edenite
31. "Harper Valley ___"
33. Cluttered
34. Do over
35. Inflames with love
36. Rousseau was one
38. Surplus
39. Amended
42. Waves, to Ovid
44. Harass persistently
46. Wrath
47. Work assignment
50. Suffix with avoid and clear
51. Bacchanalia
54. Chemical ending
55. Top

# 39

**ACROSS**

1. Emmy's cousin
5. Cape's locale
10. Arrive
14. Gudok, e.g.
15. Lunar feature
16. Son of Ruth and Boaz
17. Prewar
19. Companion of the radius
20. "So I turn the ____ of Fancy": Riley
21. Marketplace
23. Stake
25. Shrine Bowl team
26. Illegal pitch
29. Thinks highly of
32. Lacking zest
33. Checks
35. Jerboa's relative
36. Ophidians
37. Sore mouth: Brit.
38. Raspberry stem
39. Japanese statesman
40. Less lenient
43. Perched on
44. Picaresque fellows
46. Wavers on the brink
48. Canvas
49. What aquafortists do
50. Supports for Shoemaker
54. Kitchen emanations
58. Mixer's frozen asset
59. Doctor
61. Palindrome starter
62. Decay by degrees
63. Bear or Mare
64. Numerical suffix
65. ____ up (in the bag)
66. Chastity's mother

**DOWN**

1. Place for a race
2. Tendril
3. Smidgen
4. Improves spiritually
5. Reached a peak
6. Midnight fuel
7. Herr's "All gone!"
8. Warren
9. "The ____," Shakespeare's last complete play
10. Route
11. Expunge
12. Maître d'hôtel's concern
13. Cheese in a red wrapping
18. Inclination
22. Stable staple
24. Scoreboard recording
26. Word with case or well
27. Ravioli or macaroni
28. "It's ____," Perry Como hit
29. Unfruitful
30. House and land of a lord
31. Rome's Spanish ____
34. Kind of chair or rest
38. Universal in extent
40. Comely
41. Lights up
42. Made a new recording
45. Lurch
47. Light tan
50. Begone!
51. Snorkel
52. "Father of French Surgery"
53. "Strangers and Brothers" author
55. Hit film in 1970
56. Salt tree
57. Melampus was the first one
60. Fish or suffix

40

**ACROSS**

1. Lucre
5. Hoover Dam lake
9. "___ the unseen with a cheer": Browning
14. Calpurnia, to Caesar
15. Height: Prefix
16. Beloved of Sydney Carton
17. Type size
18. Joined in the chorus
19. Palette item for Turner
20. Expression for a hard job
23. Porter's "Let's ___"
24. Alas!
25. Detonator
28. Part of an astronaut's trip
30. Small flounder
33. Relative of a hogback
35. Bartender's "rocks"
36. Ann or Charles
37. Won big
41. "___ Rhythm"
42. Patriotic org.
43. Lunar vale
44. Hymenopterist's interest
45. Wind from the Libyan deserts
48. Still
49. Cherub
50. Cuckoopint
52. Backyard plot
58. Old Harry
59. Weight of India
60. Range on Swiss-French border
61. To any extent
62. Neighbor of ancient Palestine
63. Agora coin
64. Lire in Leghorn
65. Moist, as flowers
66. Word with drag and potato

**DOWN**

1. Insect stage
2. Egress
3. Crazed
4. Con job
5. Golf club
6. Card game
7. Florence's river
8. The last shift
9. Melancholy
10. Fancy trimming
11. Response to a yodeler
12. Where Tralee is
13. Driver's area
21. Like some skirts
22. Kipling's "Soldiers ___"
25. Antilles man
26. O'Hara's "___ to Live"
27. Shipment from Sri Lanka
29. Part of TNT
30. Quotidian
31. Red Northern Spy
32. Assailed
34. Holiday in Hanoi
36. Windy City, for short
38. Dimwit
39. Told
40. Part of a horse's back
45. Olid
46. Unfledged
47. Luscious
49. Nimble
51. Barbara or Hoople
52. Kill a bill
53. Conductor Whallon
54. Foretoken
55. Brass bass
56. Gator's cousin
57. Vigorous
58. Maternal quadruped

# 41

**ACROSS**

1. Golden ____ (riches)
5. Wherewithal
10. Check
14. Et ____
15. Negate
16. Table spread
17. Mountain lake
18. One of the Ionian Islands
19. Cut of meat
20. Pirates' lucre
22. Terry and Burstyn
24. Doe or Roe
25. Humane org.
26. Man who got a "message"
29. Divert attention
33. Bay window
34. Director Forman
35. Sailor
36. Danish money in Anglo-Saxon England
37. Ex-Secretary of the Treasury
38. Prefix with chute
39. River in Sweden
40. "R.L.S." pirate
41. Raises one's hackles
42. Heart contractions
44. Adam Smith's "The ____ of Nations"
45. Shakespeare's "green sickness"
46. Baseball's Speaker
47. Word with Rio or Casa
50. Bills bearing Jackson's likeness
54. Bird with a weird cry
55. Persian water wheel
57. Advantage
58. Osprey's cousin
59. Money substitute
60. Gather the fruit of labor
61. Watchful one
62. Coupling devices
63. Make one's ____ (earn money)

**DOWN**

1. Suffragist Carrie Chapman
2. Resembling a wing
3. Via Veneto money
4. Pecuniary resources
5. Moola
6. Finnish lake, to a Swede
7. Boleyn
8. Fanatic
9. Thinks it over
10. "Almighty" item
11. Lily plant
12. Lo ____
13. Nero's bridge
21. Ride in a cat
23. D-day craft
25. Fodder vats
26. Merchandise
27. Impressive show
28. Money in Iran
29. Phone-booth money
30. In any way
31. Galley symbol
32. His purse, to Iago
34. Between meeny and mo
37. Moneyed condition
38. Money in Turkey, Cyprus, etc.
40. Money substitute
41. Saddler's product
43. "Sawbuck"
44. Inflicts
46. Two times
47. Kind of club
48. Actor Calhoun
49. Top rating
50. Hard journey
51. Thinker's reward
52. All the same, in Paris
53. Fall mo.
56. Cry of surprise

# 42

**ACROSS**

1. U.S. journalist, born in Denmark
5. A length of yarn
10. One of the "three B's"
14. Stress
16. Indeed, in Ireland
17. In ___ (eventually)
19. Long time
20. Author of "America the Beautiful"
21. Mislays
22. Brassie's relative
24. Artery
25. A second self
29. Lexicographer's abbr.
31. Rudiments
34. Prevailed
35. Exceedingly
36. Wings
37. Iraqi money
38. Astringent
39. Masseur's specialty
40. Wordless
41. Astronaut Conrad
42. Poetic contraction
43. Disappear gradually
46. Foolish
48. Ropes with nooses
52. Kind of pigeon
53. She wrote "Three Lives"
56. Rainbow
57. Goes straight ahead, as a pilot
60. Arrow poison
61. Argument
62. Cats and dogs, e.g.
63. Doubleday
64. Feudal laborer

**DOWN**

1. Evaluated
2. Blood of the gods
3. Ancient British tribe
4. Like some wines
5. Painter famed for Washington portraits
6. Vonnegut or Weill
7. Bed of roses
8. Residents: Suffix
9. Avant-gardist
10. Ulan ___, Mongolian capital
11. Plato's outstanding student
12. Happen
13. Does farm work
15. Saul Bellow's prize
18. Biblical depopulator
23. Archeologist's find
24. Dyeing equipment
26. Heath
27. Spat
28. Cheer
30. "___ are born great . . .": Shakespeare
31. Swiss stream
32. Paving material
33. Coupé's relative
37. ___ Jones's locker
38. Gibbons
40. Reveals
44. Deli machine
45. Church law
47. Veins of ore
49. Delhi dresses
50. Bean or Welles
51. Flicks unit
52. "Lollipop" in a 1934 song
53. Hoity-toity one
54. State west of N.C.
55. Ferrara family
58. Goose, in Genoa
59. Western Indian

# 43

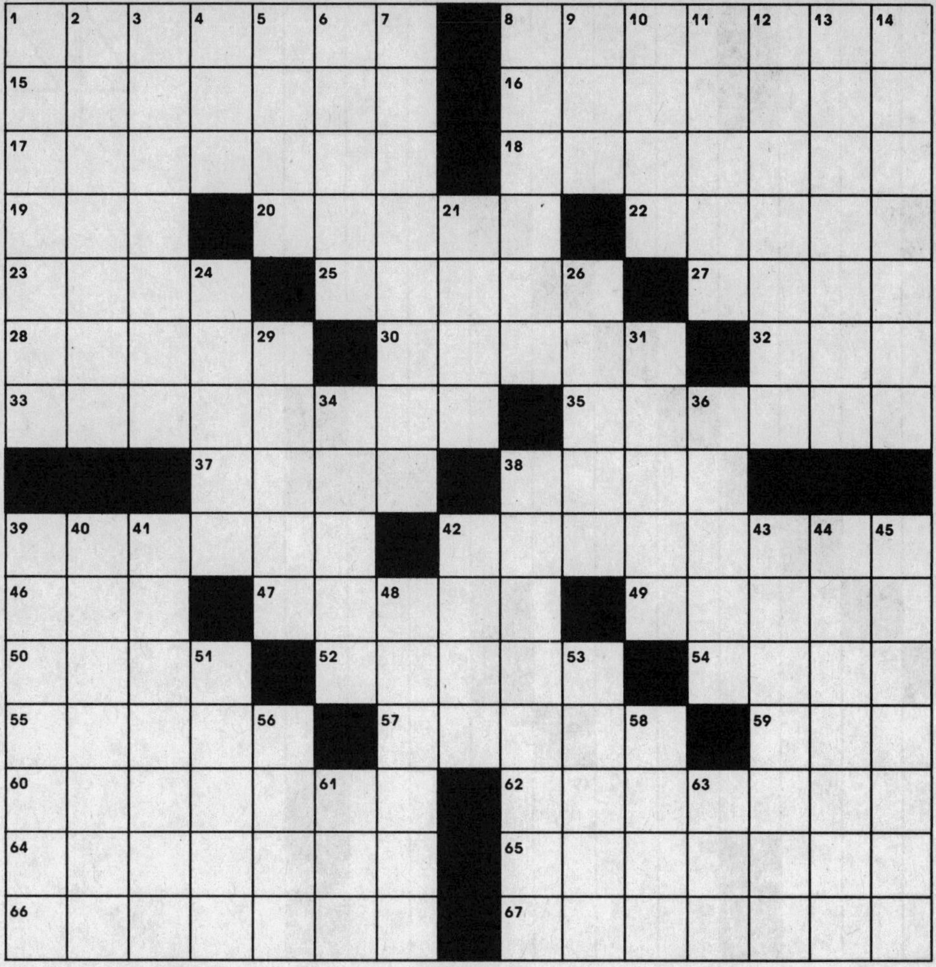

**ACROSS**

1. Monarch's crown, scepter, etc.
8. Town that lost its rats and children
15. Dodger's activity
16. Quicken
17. Actress Carmen
18. Reads aloud
19. City official: Abbr.
20. Jaded
22. Make wary
23. ___ off (used a driver)
25. Primeval abodes
27. Epochal
28. Prophet of doom
30. DNA factors
32. Supped
33. M.P.'s cry of approval
35. Mercury Theater man
37. Rigging or tackle
38. Beautiful woman
39. Concurs
42. Ritualistic suicide
46. Winged stinger
47. Put the ball on a runner again
49. Yielded, as by treaty
50. Compulsory bet
52. Missile caches
54. Beguile
55. Serene
57. "___ Moon"
59. Grassy mead
60. Accept employment
62. Unyielding
64. Prefix for type or magnet
65. Journal
66. Preordain
67. Unity

**DOWN**

1. Second try with Ali
2. Ogling hex
3. L.A. suburb
4. Political org.
5. Bit of fluff
6. Grammarian's mood: Abbr.
7. Thickening agent, from seaweed
8. Become callous
9. Donkey, in Dijon
10. Isinglass
11. M. Zola
12. Type of pass
13. Echo
14. Snuggles
21. By any chance
24. Requiem
26. Draining main
29. Hearten
31. Silken
34. Gives relief to
36. Fancied
38. Chief port of American Samoa
39. Put to shame
40. Non-Mormon, to a Mormon
41. Beds down
42. Screw pine of Hawaii
43. Fawn upon
44. Becomes contrite
45. Dreams up
48. Walk quietly or cautiously
51. Choose
53. Type of Detroit model
56. Viaud's pen name
58. Demolish
61. Vase on a pedestal
63. "All the President's ___"

# 44

**ACROSS**

1. U.S. journalist
7. Charlotte, Emily and Anne
14. Liken to
15. "Masked" creature
16. Student's dilemma
18. Hit the base-path dirt
19. ___ of eight
20. Pastoral setting
21. Kith's partner
22. Namesakes of Jacob's fourth son
23. Fine fur
24. Once ___ while
25. Leaning, as a ship
26. Cornmeal cakes
27. Fragile
29. Stops up
30. G-g-g-girl in 1918 song
31. Empty space
32. Rhone feeder
34. "Break, Break, Break" poet
38. "I ___ Be Around"
39. Defeat
40. Mao's successor
41. "___ 4 Rent"
42. Gentle heat
43. Privileges: Abbr.
44. U.S. mail center
45. Nureyev or Astaire
46. Sword part
47. Final option in 16 Across
50. Part of Ethiopia
51. Little brook
52. "Prince of the Ode"
53. Curls one's lip

**DOWN**

1. Mini-midi-maxi distinction
2. Horsey, old style
3. Jan. 1 word
4. Snitcher
5. Specify, as in a contract
6. Lukewarmness
7. Bertolt, the playwright-poet
8. "Camptown ___"
9. U.S. journalist
10. Sgt. or cpl.
11. Hard at work
12. Deposits from a geological epoch
13. Sly guys
17. Charter
18. Sideslip
22. Tropical bird, also called lily trotter
23. Ill-humored
26. Square base of a pedestal
28. Religious images
29. Impose limitations
31. Dutch painter's works
32. Winter Olympics site in Japan (1972)
33. Dvorák
34. Flambeau
35. McGovern's running mate in 1972
36. Markets for goods
37. Tweed's caricaturist
38. "Lohengrin" composer
39. Classified item
42. Cookie
45. Picasso's "___ Maar Seated"
46. Aperture
48. French connectives
49. Grain, in Grenoble

# 45

**ACROSS**

1. Quiet
5. Flip Wilson's coercer
10. River in Bavaria
14. Outfielders' name
15. ___ barrel (in trouble)
16. Foreign: Prefix
17. Amatory ploy
18. Heats up
19. Memorial Day race, for short
20. Sustained conflict
23. Fly-casting must
24. Esne and helot
27. First-anniversary gift
30. One of the Waltons
33. Neighbor of Fla.
34. Bell town of Italy
35. He suits the customer
37. Gehrig
38. Nub of the argument
41. ___ Arbor
42. Perceive, in a way
43. Pound
44. Servicewoman
45. Steinbeck migrant
46. Iron
47. First-aid contrivance
49. Smith or Bede
51. Cheapest section of a theater
58. Author of "Nana"
60. Of the line on which Earth turns
61. Former spouses
62. Hearing in court
63. Singer Lena
64. Faction
65. Automotive pioneer
66. Environs
67. Ending with pun and fun

**DOWN**

1. Dogpatch's creator
2. Jai ___
3. Kind of soul
4. Intrude by force
5. Widow's portion
6. Get away from
7. Part of speech
8. "___ la Douce"
9. Wear well
10. Political punishment
11. Fail to be specific
12. Finis
13. Scott's "Rob ___"
21. Wallace's charioteer
22. Peter and Alexander
25. Stories
26. Certain baths
27. Yellowish fruits
28. Having no key
29. Honorable
30. Fit of resentment
31. His, to Pierre
32. Profession of 43 Across
35. Light metallic sound
36. Against: Prefix
39. County in N.Y.
40. Unconditional; unending
46. Sidekick
48. Gets next to
49. Guam's capital
50. Valleys
52. Ryukyu port
53. Wife, to Caesar
54. Flag
55. Way out
56. Advice, of yore
57. River of Belgium
58. Bronx attraction
59. Popeye's Olive ___

# 46

**ACROSS**

1. "Forty buses in ___"
5. Land's end
10. D'Artagnan specialty
14. ___ Alto
15. Draw or stud
16. ___ facto
17. Scotch landscape sight
18. Kind of flu
19. Helper: Abbr.
20. Brought about
22. Confidantes, in Calais
23. Cousin of a "gee-tar"
24. ___ in the wood
25. Out of work
27. Passé
31. Fuss
32. Caused to cool down
34. Churchill's successor
36. Uses a needle
38. Sioux shelter
39. Funambulist's surface
40. Block of stamps
41. Program
43. Make a pitch for
44. Rent collector
46. Omar's product
48. Predicament
49. Suffix with super
50. Core group
52. Get the better of
57. Parisian's "Help!"
58. Merman role
59. Miffed
61. Chawbacon
62. Telephone-relay device
63. Not jaggy
64. Nick and Nora's pet
65. Decay by degrees
66. Oboist's purchase

**DOWN**

1. Police call: Abbr.
2. Cooked slightly
3. Norwegian king
4. Deplorable
5. Modern frontier
6. Talk-show person
7. Migrant farm worker
8. Use a book
9. Bald eagle's relative
10. Circle divider
11. Topsy-turvy
12. Being, Roman style
13. Quite a bit
21. Made do (with "out")
22. ___ Khan
24. Tacked on
25. Perfect
26. On skid row
27. Alpha's antithesis
28. Raised, as an ante
29. Very small
30. Bus terminal
31. Cleo's way out
33. "Thereby hangs ___"
35. Prefix for lithic or plastic
37. Lass from León
42. Molecular part
45. H.S.T. follower
47. Utensil on a pencil
49. Rhone feeder
50. Picnic ham
51. Andy's partner
52. ___ about (a certain date)
53. Disassemble
54. Deadlocked
55. Spatiate
56. Bay or bring to bay
58. Casino point
60. Tackle's neighbor

# 47

## ACROSS

1. Not care ____
5. Massenet role
10. Boxing lead
13. Pith
14. Food fish
15. Personality
16. Vibrissa
18. Operate
19. ____ patience of a saint
20. Cut
22. And others: Abbr.
24. Ending with fool or trick
25. Church features
31. Blood group
33. Historic village near Amiens
34. Weepy one
36. Grapelike fruit
38. Doubtless
41. Implement or fish
42. Dissipate
43. Dancer Gene
44. Laver maneuver
46. "____ thy narrow bed": M. Arnold
48. Nursery word
50. Stately tree
51. Lanai
55. Scads
60. One of the Gabors
61. Helmsman's course
64. Roulette color
65. Ugly
66. Juan's water
67. Bauxite or prill
68. Observes Lent
69. X-rated

## DOWN

1. C.P.A.
2. Zoo sound
3. Bohemian
4. Irritant
5. Numerical prefix
6. Retains
7. Seeks to learn
8. "The More ____ You"
9. Suffice
10. Carelessly constructed
11. Chills and fever
12. 007
14. Hones
17. "____ wish upon a star . . ."
21. Time division
23. Focus
25. Court-martial
26. Backward; inverse
27. Bonn exclamation
28. Nettle
29. "Rug" on the scalp
30. Dir. at sea
32. Molding
33. Military V.I.P.
35. Certain Alaskans
37. Word with one or how
39. U.C.L.A.'s rival
40. Sawbuck
45. Python's relative
47. Gambits
49. Cather's "____ Ours"
51. ____ Beach, Fla.
52. Eternally
53. Forerunner of surrealism
54. In statu quo
56. "____ I say, not . . ."
57. Alpine sled
58. And wife: Lat. abbr.
59. "One Hoss ____"
62. Young 'un
63. School vehicle

# 48

**ACROSS**

1. Having expectancies
7. Horatio, the author
12. Mars spacecraft
13. Part of C.C.N.Y.
16. Terrible swift sword
17. He chases rainbows
18. "____ Dick," novel by 7 Across
19. Sound from a tower
20. Lead-pipe cinch
21. Spire ornament
23. Reach or bribe
24. ____ Bay, Baltic Sea inlet
25. Cotton fabric
28. Portuguese export
29. "Two hearts that beat ____"
31. Moorehead
33. Bandleader Brown
34. Follow the bouncing ball backwards
37. Corp. officers
40. Commemorative stone
41. Like some potatoes
45. Home, in Hamburg
47. Horace, e.g.
49. Nine, in Napoli
50. Girls' names (anagram for gales)
52. High degree
53. Singer Campbell
54. Two-time movie
57. Mitigators
59. "What's ____?"
60. Dance from France
61. Eradicates
62. Pressman
63. Dental compound
64. Emulated Joseph Papp

**DOWN**

1. Cigars from Cuba
2. Spice for pizza
3. Game in which Chinese excel
4. He told Sheba to come back
5. Required
6. Angry dog sound
7. Start of a play
8. Forsaken
9. Swedish Christmas punch
10. Foils the posse
11. Add up again
12. Actress Hunt, from Chicago
14. Harsh? Hardly!
15. Banes of grains
19. Tinkling sound
22. Made a Big Ben sound
26. Swallow
27. Stag-party participants
30. Two make an em
32. A modern Caesar
35. Western Indian
36. Monotonous rhythm
37. Billy or Coogan
38. Do a brake job
39. High-low plays at bridge
42. Gigi's creator
43. Turned inside out
44. Not so sparse
46. This is very attractive
48. "Nature is ____ of God": Browne
51. Kind of board
55. Foretoken
56. Raven's haven
58. Roman's grandmother
60. Some A.M.A. members

# 49

**ACROSS**

1. Religious mendicant
6. Army bombs
10. Building sections
14. Soup dipper
15. Assert
16. Check a horse
17. "Tempest" sprite
18. Think hard
20. Little Washington
21. More watchful
23. Pronoun for a ship
24. A clash of symbols
27. Sets up a patsy
29. Guam's capital
30. Old stringsman
31. Cuddlers
35. Handle copy
36. Hawaiian island
37. Shrimp, lobster, crab, etc.
42. Hot-dish stand
44. Belief
45. Meditators
46. Voters' exams
50. Anger
51. Strong consonant
52. Oxford fellow
55. Sight "hearer"
57. Slow movement, in music
59. On the briny
60. Mailed
61. French school
62. Quid of tobacco
63. Madrileños: Abbr.
64. Fight off

**DOWN**

1. Subject of a Cohan song
2. Almost extinct
3. Colloquial
4. Pub serving
5. Loosens up
6. Revved
7. Featherbed
8. Sad procession
9. ". . . ____ apple cider"
10. Misfigure
11. Lead for a dog
12. Big colored poster
13. Derisive look
19. Wild goose
22. "____ we forget"
25. Do likewise
26. Diviner of hands
27. Scrammed
28. Less than urbane
32. Spy aurally
33. Sorry fellow
34. Takes a chair
38. In itself
39. Cheap way to see the game
40. Judge
41. Plastics ingredient
42. Treasury agents
43. Crooked cowboy
46. Delicate purple
47. Kind of lace or potato
48. Plains dwelling
49. Fruit pastries
53. Eye with pleasure
54. December song
56. Unrefined
58. Superb serve

# 50

**ACROSS**

1. Items for the blind
6. School event
10. ___ bien
14. ___ nth degree
15. "Arrivederci ___"
16. Numerical prefix
17. Pungent
18. Too severe
20. Kind of concern
21. Religious sect member
22. Military headgear
24. Fraternal organization
25. Tacks on
28. Literary collections
31. Suffixes with room, kitchen, etc.
34. "Leave no ___ unstoned" (Spoonerism)
35. Hebrew letter
36. Kind of music
37. Medley
38. Caper
40. Literary first name
41. Steals, as in a store
43. Woman's workbasket
44. "___ no more . . ."
45. Shop equipment
46. Wanes
47. Bookmaker's concern
48. Starts' companion
50. To dare: Sp.
52. Exactly alike
56. Squanders the moola
60. Hit song for Helen O'Connell
61. Own up to
62. Tropical American dog
63. State, in France
64. Western city
65. Willingly
66. Adam's third son
67. Following

**DOWN**

1. Hunter's quarry
2. In ___ parentis
3. Town in a Longfellow poem
4. Treats casually
5. Plant sometimes woven into mats
6. Distinction
7. Gad
8. Augury
9. W.W. I battle site
10. Treasure; cherish
11. Enrolled
12. Sign in a theater
13. Infamous marquis
19. Romeo and Juliet
23. Prefix with chute or graph
25. Bikini, e.g.
26. Festival of Apollo
27. Structure preventing cattle from roaming
29. Make ___ at (try)
30. Watchword or catchword
32. Fished for congers
33. Staircase
39. Lewis's Mr. Timberlane
42. Seven, in Sicilia
49. Fathers
51. Addis ___
52. Type style: Abbr.
53. Painter of melting telephones
54. Mention or quote
55. Course for a future M.D.
57. Skip
58. Knowing
59. Suffix with young or old

# 51

**ACROSS**

1. Curlewlike bird
7. Birds' migration time
11. Sportsmen's assn.
14. The Australian fig-bird is one
15. Part of the iris
16. Beater for mixing mortar
17. Birds without voice boxes
18. Birds that resemble bitterns
20. Horse's tarsal joint
21. Capital of Peru
23. Type of velvet or satin
24. Porter
25. Small finch
27. British gun
28. Snappish
30. Nordic
32. Common abbr.
33. Patellae
35. Raucous
37. Gorge
38. Meccas for children
39. Roué, at times
42. U.S. game bird
46. Farm animal
47. Taste
49. Limber
50. Eagle of many puzzles
52. Bird that impales its prey on thorns
54. Poetic contraction
55. Tinker's partner
57. King Olaf's capital
58. Custom
59. Caged mimic
61. Window in an attic
63. "____ tu," Verdi aria
64. Dresden's river
65. Resting
66. Sts.
67. Like the bills of some grebes
68. Doghouse

**DOWN**

1. Fast-flying bird of prey
2. Bunting eaten as a delicacy
3. Bishopric
4. Opus or employment
5. Sort
6. Wizard in electricity: 1856–1943
7. Blubber-loving sea birds
8. Large birdcage
9. Lunar module
10. Dweller in Nordland
11. Caxton or Zenger
12. Fish-eating sea birds
13. Item on a pupil's record
19. Dutch cupboard
22. Not qualified
25. Ages
26. Lout
29. Croquet stakes
31. Piece of pasta
34. Atmospheres
36. Spore sacs
38. African weasel
39. Bird that climbs tree trunks
40. President Bok's domain
41. Aida's rival
42. Fabric such as gabardine
43. Overstuffed footstool
44. People in Pearl Buck's "Sons"
45. European falcon
48. Crested flycatcher
51. Proposed amendment, for short
53. Eastman invention
56. Basket or beehive
58. Small songbird
60. Father of Phineas
62. Resident: Suffix

# 52

## ACROSS

**1.** Red and Black
**5.** Annapurna, e.g.
**9.** What bugbears do
**14.** Curtain color
**15.** Spike the punch
**16.** Possessive pronoun
**17.** Kitchen, e.g.
**18.** Painful
**19.** Neighbor of Bangor
**20.** Blarney
**21.** They followed that star
**23.** Calm
**25.** Enjoys a holiday
**26.** Peace offering
**28.** Necks of land
**32.** "On the ___ day of Christmas . . ."
**35.** "___ Troll," Heine poem
**37.** Glacier in Alaska
**38.** Minneapolis suburb
**39.** Rival of T.C.U.
**40.** Kind of ray
**41.** Off one's rocker
**42.** Kind of chop
**43.** Quaker in a grove
**44.** "He that is ___ anger . . .": Proverbs
**46.** Famed restaurateur
**48.** ___ acid (yellow vitamin)
**50.** Help
**54.** Stem of a Christmas plant
**58.** "Damn Yankees" temptress
**59.** "___ of snow-white horses"
**60.** Author Eliav
**61.** Indigo
**62.** Get the dice ready
**63.** French novelist
**64.** His presents come on Jan. 6
**65.** Polish city, to a German
**66.** Wang Lung's wife
**67.** Travelers' rest houses, Indian style

## DOWN

**1.** Slavish sons of the soil
**2.** Place closed at Noël
**3.** Bellowing
**4.** Plant also called star-of-Bethlehem
**5.** Earthenware
**6.** Every's partner
**7.** It begins: "Marley was dead . . ."
**8.** Attuned
**9.** Feeds the furnace
**10.** Largest atoll in the Pacific
**11.** Period like a millennium
**12.** "___ out the old"
**13.** Desire
**22.** Man of tales
**24.** "___ creature was stirring"
**27.** Make comfortable
**29.** Knoll
**30.** Jester
**31.** Where Kerman is
**32.** Planetarium in Philadelphia
**33.** Santa, to tots
**34.** Puerto ___
**36.** ___ Finklea (Cyd Charisse)
**40.** Rambles restlessly
**42.** Tennesseans, for short
**45.** Busy people in December
**47.** Strike it rich
**49.** Met basso Tajo
**51.** Chios, Samos, etc.
**52.** Move furtively
**53.** Mythical man of brass
**54.** Place for a padlock
**55.** Galba's successor
**56.** Pastoral sights
**57.** Second Mrs. Chaplin

**ACROSS**

1. Shrill bark
4. Composer Khachaturian
8. Bushed
13. Former five-franc coin
14. That, in Tours
15. Supple leather
16. ". . . the river/Is a ___" (T. S. Eliot)
19. Bailiwick
20. Hari
21. Heinous
22. Navigation system
25. News spill
29. Christened
30. Nest-egg builder
31. Win by guile
32. Points out as relevant
33. Hock swelling on a horse
34. Continuation of 16 Across
37. Announcer
38. Henry, the sculptor
39. Eared seal
40. Milton of TV
41. Face-lift target
44. Fibber's forte
45. "The Velvet Fog"
46. Like shad
47. Catch red-handed
49. Invader of 1066
51. End of quote
55. Antler part
56. Peacock of the sea
57. Elephant-toting bird
58. Anne Sedgwick novel
59. Manolete's slayer
60. Self-esteem

**DOWN**

1. Sycophants
2. On the move
3. Broadway hit in 1970
4. Complexion problem
5. Under strict controls
6. Priest's garb
7. Spoil
8. African dam site
9. Memorable stage star
10. Signature required for documents, etc.
11. "___ not choose to run"
12. Sparks or Buntline
17. Neat's-foot
18. Bradley
23. Baker's need
24. One who takes up a task again
26. Nesting area, at times
27. Jejune
28. Kesey or Venturi
30. Vacuous
31. Superfluous
32. Condensed form of printing type
33. Entry on a police blotter
34. Bristle
35. River into the Caspian
36. Standard
37. In a winning streak
40. Flee
41. Melancholy, British style
42. Parallel
43. Woman: Comb. form
45. Trace
46. Half a swimsuit
48. "It ___ a fit night . . ."
50. Roman emperor
51. Quick-witted
52. Pump primer of the 30's
53. Hogwash
54. Overseas address

# 54

**ACROSS**

1. Eden's earldom
5. Henry or Harry
10. Dutch cheese
14. Christening, e.g.
15. Daisy
16. Conrad character
17. Adjective ending
18. Manuscript book
19. Subject of "State of Blood"
20. Spine
22. A.L. player
24. Outspeed handily
25. Peeks
26. Honest person
30. Snow leopard
31. St. Paul's dean
32. Sound from 36 Across
35. Pelf in Pisa
36. Annie's pooch
38. Use a muddler
39. Finial
40. Scored on a serve
41. Trickery
42. Relative of a rat race
46. Discipline
48. What smog is called in L.A.
49. "Love . . . builds a ___ Heaven's despite": Blake
50. Veld creatures
54. Part of a cart
55. Chili con ___
57. Where the Euphrates meets the Tigris
58. Trilbies
59. Gladden
60. Favorable
61. Kin of Ph.D.'s
62. Bolivar
63. Tortoise

**DOWN**

1. Qatar native
2. Résumé
3. Of the ear
4. String of pearls
5. Witty
6. Nerve-cell processes
7. Darius the ___
8. Potato bud
9. Forte of Johnson and Masters
10. Camelot maid
11. Not snobbish
12. Old-womanish
13. Features of lions, horses, etc.
21. Source of "ear-itation"
23. Appraise
25. Aborigine of central India
26. Dover ___
27. Bon mot
28. Supreme; peerless
29. Gandhi was one
33. Brooklet
34. Openhanded
36. Arts' companion
37. Long, long time
38. Foolproof
40. Start of "Hamlet"
41. Pyramid site
43. Keys
44. Japanese religion
45. Heel over
46. Abrade by rubbing
47. Put the Indian sign on
50. Drawing: Comb form
51. "___ Here to Eternity"
52. Duck soup
53. Measure of area: Abbr.
56. Former ring king

55

**ACROSS**

1. Spellbound
5. Trig., geom., etc.
9. Musical Count
14. Business-letter phrase
15. "That's ____ learning I desire": Burns
16. Related on Mom's side
17. Kiln or oast
18. Sharp
19. Not illicit
20. S.O.S. and Mayday
23. Name meaning "the highest"
24. Song lyricist Harbach
25. N.Y.C. court tournament
26. Track event
28. Pakistani language
30. Join the Aspen set
33. "Monkey see, monkey do"
35. Inflated with air
37. Galvanizing agent
38. Secret stuff
39. Strong wind
40. Live, as cattle
42. Trial's partner
43. Anatomical duct
44. Hook for landing fish
45. Surgery reminder
46. Mariner
47. Glacier in Alaska
49. Rover's complaint
52. In the manner of a tortoise
57. Shinto temple gateway
58. ____ were (so to speak)
59. Kind of criminal trial
60. No longer together
61. 1.6093 kilometers
62. Ancient man of Iran
63. Scarlett, for one
64. Maple genus
65. Sweetened beverages

**DOWN**

1. ____ Janeiro
2. Hammering block
3. Faces on bills
4. Omar's product
5. "He ____ me to lie down . . ."
6. Atoll explosion
7. Popular film set in Austria
8. Rhode Island Reds
9. Where Waterloo is
10. As to
11. Tale of heroism
12. Romance lang.
13. Elusive ones
21. Blushing or flushing
22. Southern constellation
27. Roguish
29. Ridge of coral
30. Like one in love
31. Code word for "k"
32. Cake decorator
33. Smallest Soviet sea
34. San Juan pineapple
35. Magician's word
36. Site of the Taj Mahal
38. Not trustful
41. "Liberté, ____, fraternité"
42. Color of raw silk
45. Cassandra, to Hector
46. Pirouette
48. Useful
50. ____-France
51. Combustible heaps
52. Blind shot
53. Long, easy stride
54. Spoken
55. Bear Bryant's boys, once
56. Il Duce once ruled here

# 56

**ACROSS**

1. "___-22"
6. Moist ground
10. Phobic problem
14. Jibe
15. N.Y.S.E. rival
16. Spanish jar
17. Top or bottom round
18. Dumbbell
20. Incomplete circle
21. Pithy saying
23. Set in firmly
24. Ragamuffin
27. "Shed ___ of light Divine": Caswall
28. West Coast crustacean
30. Cut wood with the grain
33. In this place
34. From ___ Z
35. Grandson of Adam
36. Funerary items
38. Pack on board
39. From Oran to Durban: Abbr.
40. Clusters of seals
41. Toast imported from England
43. Cold-blooded creature
45. Shortly
46. Anti-establishment movement
51. Young bull: Br.
52. Pays (the bill)
53. Aggregate
54. Commager or Beard
56. Title for Macbeth
58. Stunt man's first name
59. Wheel support
60. "The ___ Sanction," Eastwood film
61. Old Persian cohort
62. Gets hitched
63. Like many a marsh

**DOWN**

1. Measure used for "a girl's best friend"
2. Athenian square
3. Plot of land
4. These: Fr.
5. Grecian courtesan
6. Ailment
7. Public face
8. Berlin hit: 1925
9. Exeter's river
10. Ant acid
11. Complex
12. Loser of friends
13. Gold region of South Africa
19. Tommyrot
22. Coupler of a sort
25. Soviet news service
26. Reconnaissance plane
29. Greets formally
30. Rise belligerently
31. Contagious
32. Swam in looping leaps
33. Males
37. Persistent notion
38. Started off
40. Fellow traveler
42. Item on a sheriff's belt
44. Terrapin
45. Scottish cakes
47. Author Dahl
48. Customary way
49. Inscribed with mystic marks
50. Abrasive polisher
51. Noah's eldest son
55. Terribly unjust
57. Waste no time

# 57

**ACROSS**

1. Money for Gaston or a Gascon
6. Elated
11. Gaffe
12. "Whiffenpoof" refrain
14. Roll of wool
15. Endure
17. Jupiter's path
18. Snide
20. Grid official
21. ____ impasse
22. Boxcars, at dice
23. Fuzz
24. But, to Ovid
25. ____ up (gauged)
26. Electron tube
27. Frameworks for bridges
29. Author of "The Prophet"
30. Campus figure
31. Mall event
32. Gems
35. Part of a pound
39. A stroke ahead, in match play
40. Newcastle's nonrequirement
41. Modernist
42. Way off
43. Soho expletive
44. Lean-to
45. Note
46. Highway sign
47. Umbrage
48. Plucky ones
50. ". . . halls with boughs ____"
52. Hawaiian garment
53. Runt
54. Impress
55. Is unsteady

**DOWN**

1. Prohibited
2. "Creation of Man" sculptor
3. "____ of all right!"
4. Sine qua ____
5. Knew
6. Maltreated
7. Family in Wolfe's novels
8. Earl's daughter
9. U.K. decoration
10. Combatant
11. Swap
13. Chair's concern
14. Freewheel
16. Repeatedly
19. Gives the gate to
22. Heat-resistant glass
23. Defamation
25. Tankard
26. Certain pickles
28. Clean thoroughly
29. Without a care
31. Small open boats
32. Crow
33. Apprise
34. Green-eyed
35. Fish dish
36. Takes a breath
37. Tease
38. Publisher of a 19th-century periodical for women
40. Popular garnish
43. "Nil nisi ____"
44. Ostentatious
46. "I Remember ____"
47. Where Met meets Met
49. Thrust out
51. Not many

**ACROSS**

1. Word with king or pint
6. Burned up the road
10. The Devil's business
14. ___ a dozen
15. Kingfish
16. Ancient queen's milieu
17. Passionate people, to Plutarch
20. U.S. group of fliers
21. Irregular
22. Less aboveboard
23. Belief system
24. Japanese sacred mountain
25. Bus station
28. Of a type of heavenly intersection
32. Cries in a corrida
33. Morning sounds
35. Drivel
37. "Love conquers all," to Augustus
40. Legendary bird
41. Polynesian language
42. Tiny particle
43. Jazzmen's jam ___
45. Intrinsically
46. Be sick
47. Was admitted
50. Hobbles
53. "Present arms!" is one
54. Camel's-hair fabric
57. From head to heel, to Horace
60. Hundred-yard ___
61. Bas mitzvah, e.g.
62. ___ spade a spade
63. Division word
64. Winglike
65. Salad days

**DOWN**

1. Droops
2. Thought
3. Brass ingredient
4. Second-largest existing bird
5. Become a permanent AWOL
6. Young codfish
7. An unwelcome guest, to Galba
8. Iroquoian
9. Period
10. As a whole
11. Number for a Henry
12. "Winnie ___ Pu"
13. Sidelong glance
18. Wrath
19. Act as an apprentice
23. "___ fan tutte"
24. Supt. or prin.
25. Way out or in
26. Saint ___ fire
27. Coin in Cardiff
29. Killer whale
30. Metal suit
31. Sacks
33. Of no ___ (useless)
34. Exec's car
36. Forbidden fruit's source
38. St. Francis's town
39. Final word
44. Poet of Lesbos
45. Kidd's specialty
48. More eccentric
49. Gumshoe
50. "When I was a ___ served . . ."
51. "___ get it for you . . ."
52. Support for a crow's-nest
53. ___ -de-boeuf (circular window)
54. Civil rights org.
55. Wallop
56. Chinese nurse
58. Word before lala
59. Buddhist people

# 59

## ACROSS

1. "____ It a Lovely Day?"
5. Irene's concern
10. Author of "The Alteration"
14. Ending with huck or trick
15. Metropolitan
16. Cyrano's outstanding feature
17. A grand duchy
19. Moslem woman's voluminous outer garment
20. Involve by necessity
21. One on the same side
23. Aspen gear
25. Small plant of the rose family
26. Activity for Dr. Quincy
29. Manages
31. Round
32. Grating
34. Comparative ending
36. Carry out, as an order
37. Half-brother of William the Conqueror
38. Relative of iso
39. ____ Percé, American Indian
40. Chef's creation
43. Obtund or obtuse
44. Place
46. Sacheverell, Osbert or Edith
48. ____ -ce pas?
49. Mme. Bovary
50. Stated
54. Just about
58. Leaf angle
59. City named for a Macedonian ruler
61. Naldi of silent films
62. Polite
63. Shoe feature
64. River of the Ukraine
65. Rag
66. Miquelon et d'Oléron

## DOWN

1. Bit of land
2. Daze
3. Upcoming
4. Fisc
5. Print
6. "____ e Leandro," Mancinelli opera
7. Touch upon
8. Solicitude
9. Employs
10. Hostile feeling
11. Maputo is its capital
12. "This ____ engaged in guessing . . .": Poe
13. Withered
18. Reporter Wallace
22. Assign by measure
24. Patsy for a comic
26. Pour ____ (intensify)
27. Swedish philanthropist
28. Luzon metropolis
29. Complain
30. "____ Never Know"
33. Fuss
35. Brooklet
38. Son of Jane Seymour
40. Tabula ____
41. Draw
42. Creamy mixture baked in a mold
45. Word with salt or wine
47. Fed
50. Fancy and Dapper
51. Stage direction
52. Author Wiesel
53. Buddhist deity
55. Of an age
56. Cuba libre juice
57. Kennel noise
60. Greek letters

# 60

**ACROSS**

1. Austrian city
5. Usher in
9. Caution light
14. Western city
15. Time ___ half
16. Let fly
17. Gowdy's place
20. Post-office worker
21. Actress Ritter
22. Also-ran
24. Scorpio's neighbor
25. Arrival
28. Sci-fi guy
33. Chalon's river
34. Adriatic port
35. Three-time champ
36. TV technician's equipment
40. Narration: Abbr.
41. Spoken
42. Speedily
43. Life jackets
46. Nurse
47. ___ de France
48. Kind of badge
50. Descendant of a son of Jacob
53. Anarchy
57. TV technicians' equipment
59. "Farewell, Pierre"
60. Dye vat
61. "Caveat emptor" sign
62. Types
63. Comply with
64. Manufactured

**DOWN**

1. Mardi ___
2. Lease
3. Diva Moffo
4. TV technician's equipment
5. Most rational
6. Plume filler
7. Cool drink
8. Caustic
9. Einstein
10. Do-re-mi
11. TV technician's equipment
12. This, in Juárez
13. Mixture of sodium salts
18. ___ sleeve (held secretly)
19. Goren partner, at times
23. Fidelity, as in art
25. Where Shillong is
26. Capital of Bangladesh
27. Tenor, for one
29. Jejune
30. ___-arms (soldier)
31. Faye or Cooper
32. Chile saltpeter
34. Enfant terrible
37. Caucasian
38. Lao-tse's doctrine
39. Against the current
44. Out of breath
45. Root and Yale
46. Monastery
49. TV host
50. Set in a groove
51. Blue dye
52. Original site of U. of Nevada
54. Sky Bear
55. "The best ___ schemes . . ."
56. Being
57. Kind of actor or radio
58. Drop bait lightly

**ACROSS**

1. N.T. book
5. Closes
10. "___ is a miniature eternity": Emerson
14. Hutch, on TV
15. Famed Yankee southpaw
16. Arena in Detroit
17. Bon voyage!
20. City near San Francisco
21. P.D.Q.
22. Lean-to
23. Turn's partner
24. Crusade
26. Ballerina Tamara ___
27. Brouhaha
30. Unit in a radar receiver
31. Top rating
32. Transport at Aspen
33. Ave atque vale
36. Devil-god
37. Fugitive from Eden
38. Gee!
39. Sound seeking silence
40. Bowie Kuhn, once
41. Grace or Gene
42. Bast fiber source
43. Paddock papa
44. Show up
47. "Man ___ not me": Hamlet
51. Au revoir
53. Ending with iron or myth
54. Macbeth, in Act I
55. "Ring" role
56. Diva Lily
57. Fete
58. Recondite

**DOWN**

1. Sinuous Nile creatures
2. Negri of silent films
3. French saint
4. Cape Cod ashtray
5. Scheduled
6. Whetted
7. Capable of
8. ___ Mahal
9. One-night stand
10. Character in "The Rivals"
11. Oxford group
12. Countenance or connive
13. It has its ups and downs
18. Sere region
19. Bear up there
23. Hour in a nursery rhyme
24. Steinbeck family
25. Dostoyevsky's "The ___"
26. Make good
27. Start of a Hersey title
28. Waste time
29. Airport across from Heathrow
30. One of the Carters
31. Large antelope
32. Relative of bipedal
34. Whence Jesus came
35. Nymph who advised Numa Pompilius
40. Raptorial feature
41. Proper condition
42. Topples
43. "___ evil"
44. Like a ballerina
45. Beak or peak: Sp.
46. Architect's rendering
47. Rusk or Martin
48. Denizen of a warren
49. Ocean phenomenon
50. Cookie
52. Electrical unit

# 62

**ACROSS**

1. Grades that don't make the grade
4. Confront
8. ___ Picchu (Incan stronghold)
13. Women's service org.
14. Moslem title
15. World supporter
16. Stunt-plane maneuver
18. Iago's forte
19. Thruway, e.g.
20. Like a persona non grata
22. Firmly implant
23. Sound reproduction, for short
24. Native of Teheran
26. Type of column
28. Arcane
32. Satan's cohort
35. Chore
37. ___ a happy smile (beamed)
38. Eager
39. Stakes
40. Lamb's pseudonym
41. Prefix for meter or liter
42. Holly
43. Member of a R.R. crew
44. Delphic priestess
46. ___ in wait (ready to ambush)
48. Pithy
50. Same old stuff, in new form
54. Promenades for Pericles
57. Dun
59. Hair ornaments
60. ". . . a ___ and hungry look"
61. Pack
62. Useful
63. "The ___ and Future King": White
64. Miner's quest
65. Inhibit
66. Suffix for prank or song
67. To-be-cont. story

**DOWN**

1. Mt. ___, Colo. peak
2. Facade
3. Little Eva's creator
4. Peregrine
5. Exchange discount
6. Fe or Au, for example
7. Nurse, at times
8. Leatherneck
9. For oxygen, 16; for carbon, 12, etc.
10. Social group
11. Abhor
12. Previously owned
17. Arrangement based on Mendeleev's law
21. Trotsky
25. Questions
27. Type of type: Abbr.
29. Parker House ___
30. "Clinton's canal"
31. Rend
32. Groove
33. At any time
34. Biotite, e.g.
36. Erotic
39. Harbor structure
43. Rare individual
45. Inferior
47. He has pressing problems
49. Midwest cylinders
51. Durant, Erskine, etc.
52. Rhoncus
53. He hacks
54. Run before a gale
55. Transport
56. Neglect
58. Gait

# 63

**ACROSS**

1. Laziness
6. Hill insect
9. Capture
12. Scruffs
13. Skulk
15. Kind of punch
16. That is: Lat.
17. "Old ___"
19. Vivacious
20. Specialty of certain "deliverymen"
21. Cole or Wood
23. Watched tots
24. Ditty
25. Hospice
30. African antelope
32. Ernie or Gomer
33. Comply
34. Road grader
36. Advertising insert
38. New cadet, for short
39. What cover girls do
41. Fry lightly
42. Bacon or Lamb
44. ". . . times that try ___ souls"
45. Egyptian god of music
46. Pulmonary cavities
49. Dr. Spock's field
53. Famed gallery
55. Stress
56. Hindu instrument
57. Provided that
58. Continuously
59. Camber
60. Foxy
61. Ames and McMahon
62. Previn

**DOWN**

1. Cut
2. Fraught
3. Secret agents
4. Newcomers in the news
5. Before D.D.E.
6. Excuse
7. Day place
8. Hambletonian
9. Complications
10. Guinness
11. Foreman
14. Israeli body
15. Carry's arrival!
18. R.B.I.'s, for one
20. "Blood and Sand" cheer
22. Blue dye
26. Other
27. Beclouded
28. Cross paths
29. "Jane ___"
30. Old wine flask
31. Kin: Abbr.
32. Experts
35. Decretal
37. Functions
40. Like cathedral window glass
43. MCMLXXIX, for one
44. Miniver or Gamp
47. Pastry workers
48. Kind of well
49. Booted feline
50. Organic compound
51. Omaha Beach time
52. Tear apart
54. River into Donegal Bay
56. R.R. depot

# 64

### ACROSS

1. More recent
6. Resort
9. Lariat
14. Divert
15. Stats re Louis, Ali et al.
16. Available
17. Trick + paths
19. Community standards
20. Inventor Whitney
21. Diamond call + court call
23. Being
24. About + halloo
26. Singer Kay
28. Honorary degree held by Betty Ford
29. Place to swim + place to dream
33. Burns and Allen Ginsberg
36. Expert + sleuth + peak
39. Shield border
40. Rent
41. Bluefin
42. Precipice + circles
44. Timid soul
45. Pelt dresser
46. Finnish novelist: 1861–1921
47. Fibrous Philippine plant
50. Demesne abodes
54. Delay
57. Mineo + a Kennedy
59. Item tossed into a ring
60. On the move
62. Norm + heir + years
64. Sifter
65. Greek letter
66. Telegrapher or electrician
67. Scraped
68. Radiation unit
69. Part of a black suit

### DOWN

1. Employee in a football plant
2. Root used as soap in Mexico
3. Hauberk
4. Superlative ending
5. Anent + drumbeats
6. Parody
7. Election Day meccas
8. While + coterie
9. Fish eggs
10. Bury + deed
11. Sportsmen: Abbr.
12. Site of Kit Carson's house
13. Choir loft
18. Old: Scot.
22. Savor
25. Change + indigenous
27. Pawnee's cousin
30. Heat units: Abbr.
31. Ages upon ages
32. Delivery cart
33. Mail
34. Killer whale
35. Zest
36. Write
37. Cheap magazine
38. Strategic org. of W.W. II
40. Money in Ankara
43. Confederate
44. Fish + howls
46. Central Iowa city
48. Antic
49. Winged
51. Author of "The Lockwood Concern"
52. Stormed
53. Cubic meter
54. Vespiary denizen
55. Huge land area
56. Roman way
58. Collier's vehicle
61. Scarlet
63. Pinch

# 65

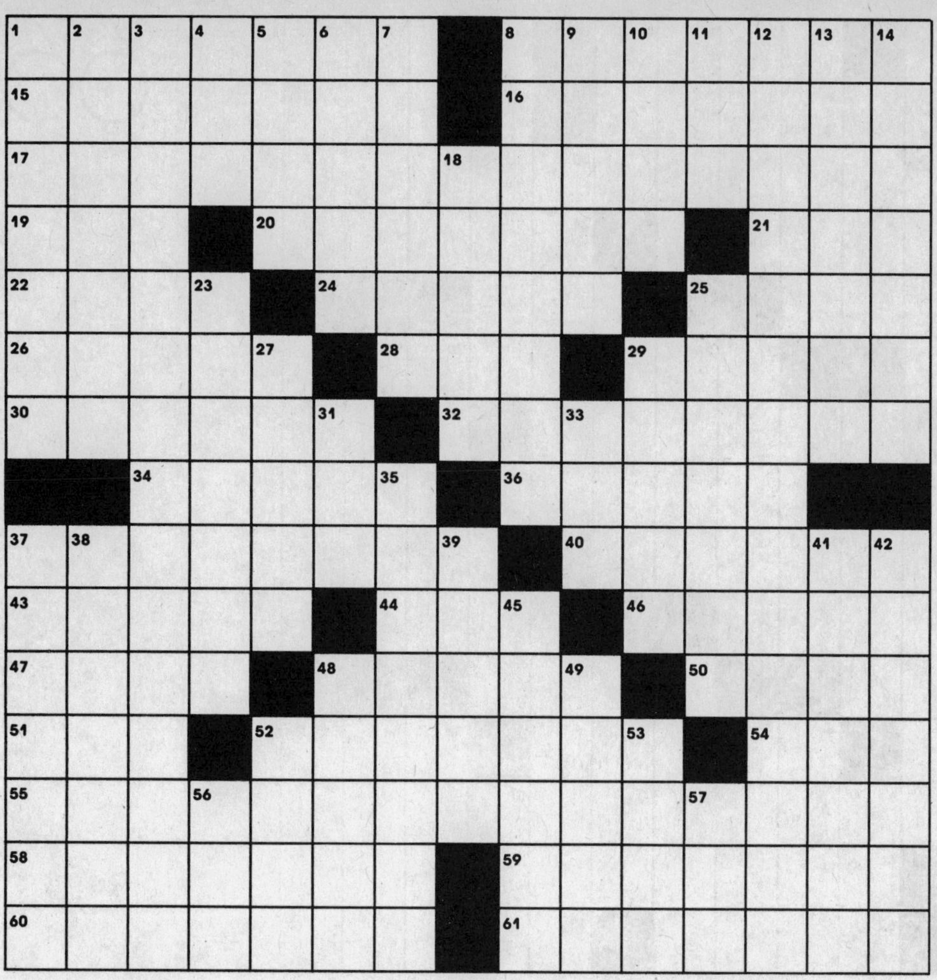

**ACROSS**

1. Wingless
8. Ecclesiast's headgear
15. Rock formation
16. Supergiant star in Scorpio
17. Philosophical doctrines
19. Coffee receptacle
20. Roman household gods
21. Born
22. Word after decree
24. Savory
25. Soc.
26. Bagnold et al.
28. Edge
29. Medieval helmet
30. Choose
32. Hit plays
34. Preminger's first major U.S. film
36. Tours toast
37. Has a speech problem
40. Cul-___ (blind alleys)
43. Cripples
44. Min. part
46. Capital of Morocco
47. Rara ___
48. French Impressionist
50. Italian monetary unit
51. Dress size
52. Expendable Mexican clay pots
54. Year in reign of Claudius I
55. Act of putting into another alphabet
58. Involves necessarily
59. Give a new name to
60. Like some eyes
61. Made a chemical analysis

**DOWN**

1. Harmonizes
2. Valerie from Galveston
3. Cause light to pass through
4. Sea eagle
5. Scrape
6. Suffixes for attend and convey
7. City on Lake Winnebago
8. Depressions and recessions
9. "You're All ___," old song
10. Election Day stats.
11. Consume
12. Potentiality for changing form
13. Family-room feature
14. Sanctions
18. Neck parts
23. Thinks
25. Awakening
27. Rabbit tails
29. River into the Weser
31. Three, in Roma
33. Terhune dog
35. Firebug
37. Flapped, as sails against yards
38. Cannes cafe
39. French legislators
41. One-horse carriage
42. Kind of glass
45. Et ___ (and so forth)
48. Thousand, to Tacitus
49. Container weights
52. Greek letters
53. Calendar abbrs.
56. Doze
57. Spanish aunt

66

**ACROSS**

1. Greece, to the Greeks
6. Europe-Asia dividing range
10. "God's Little ___"
14. Danger zone: 1962
16. Stepped on
17. Danger zone: 1944
19. Sunrise to sunset
20. Actor Eastwood
21. Frail
22. Keel part
23. Word with Antonio or Fernando
24. Counterweights
27. Renaissance humanist's interest
32. Fever
33. Twenty-one-gun ___
35. Crackpot
36. Danger zone: 1863
39. Cakes and ___
40. More prying
41. Patty ingredient
42. Grudge holder
44. Linguini, ziti, etc.
45. Force, to Fabius
46. Mend socks
48. Madison Avenueite
51. ___ Selassie
53. Sign of spring
56. Danger zone: 1775
59. Queenly name
60. Danger zone: 1945
61. Activist
62. ". . . fine women ___ crazy salad": Yeats
63. Watchful monster

**DOWN**

1. Mild expletive
2. Moon over Milano
3. Word with Susan
4. Kind of cuckoo
5. Lays in
6. Take down a derrick
7. Cloud contents
8. What Repeal was: Abbr.
9. Captain's diary
10. Foe of Sparta
11. Montana people
12. ". . . yellow brick ___"
13. Whirlpool
15. Qualified
18. Pencil part
22. Bishops' territories
23. Guest at Dionysus's orgies
24. English Channel feeder
25. Nimble
26. Impostor's forte
27. Debussy's "___ de Lune"
28. Entrap
29. Rameau's "Les ___ Galantes"
30. Music man Xavier
31. Stone memorial
33. Smudges, in a way
34. Faulkner character
37. Seventh-___ stretch
38. Terrible Russian
43. Tax cheat
44. The press: Sp.
46. Authoritative pronouncements
47. Succulent plant
48. Aldrich's "The Story of ___ Boy"
49. Ian Fleming character
50. Sapper's trap
51. Response to a pun
52. Keep ___ (persist)
53. Big Ben sound
54. Pakistani language
55. Canine examiners' degrees
57. Lamb's mother
58. Sedan

# 67

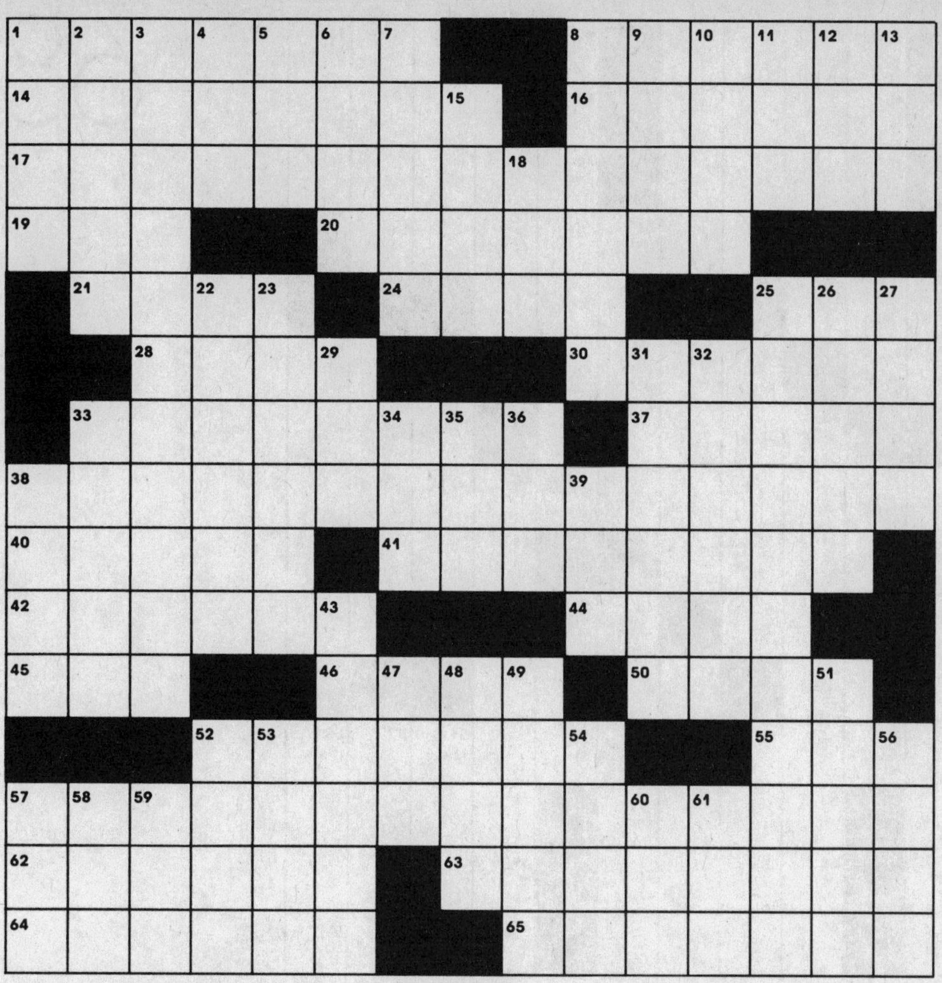

**ACROSS**

1. Native environment
8. TV actress Sanford
14. "____ Blue," 1965 film
16. Cash-register button
17. Part of Micronesia
19. Galahad's title
20. Whimpered or blathered
21. Cant
24. Sound
25. Large Italian isl.
28. Saarinen
30. He completed a leaning tower
33. Hundred-armed monster of myth
37. Large mackerel-like fish
38. Perilous expanse
40. At right angles to the keel
41. Frame
42. Playground device
44. Cather's "One of ____"
45. Mischievous wee one
46. Verb ending
50. Impudent talk
52. Parodies
55. Giant of yore
57. Marquesas, Society Islands, etc.
62. Medicine-cabinet item
63. Contrite
64. Roll or register
65. Summer fare on TV

**DOWN**

1. Muggers onstage
2. "To fetch ____ of water"
3. Great ____, in the Coral Sea
4. Certain players, as in tag
5. Mild exclamation of censure
6. Moby Dick's pursuer
7. Rings ominously
8. Part of the foot
9. Ocean flatfish
10. "Like ____ votarist in palmer's weed": Milton
11. Interdict
12. Antiquity, in poesy
13. "____ Girls"
15. Fido's tormentor
18. Author Fleming
22. Diet of Lithuania
23. Wound
25. Calm waters NE of the West Indies
26. "You can't teach ____ dog . . ."
27. Floribunda
29. Fort ____, Calif.
31. Wax-winged flier
32. Madame, in Madrid
33. August ____, German socialist
34. Corn unit
35. Actress Hagen
36. ____ Lanka
38. Headquarters
39. Workers' org.
43. Member of a flock
47. Drink delicately
48. Cut short
49. Certain fisherman
51. Be frugal
52. Pique
53. Adolescent ailment
54. Word in a New Year's song
56. Makes lacy doilies
57. Douglas ____
58. Marsupial, for short
59. Begley and Sullivan
60. Bracer
61. Summer, in Somme

# 68

**ACROSS**

1. Long-necked pear
5. Album item
9. He answered to Harry
14. Ending with buck
15. Thought: Comb. form
16. He played Queeg
17. Memorable comedian, or his biographer
18. Paltry
19. Contain
20. Song hit of 1941, with 48 Across
23. Kettle handle
24. ___ Kollo, Met tenor
25. Museum lecturer
28. Formed a single line while marching
32. 4,047 square meters
33. Makes a firm, level surface
34. French pronoun
35. Baldwin title
39. Proposal once before the states
40. Belfry sounds
41. Higher in rank
42. Agnes and Cecil
44. Queen of whodunits
46. Welshman or Irishman
47. Integument
48. See 20 Across
54. Hindu teacher
55. Craving eagerly
56. Debauchee
57. Giant, to a Dodger
58. Heavy book
59. Diminutive suffix
60. Upright
61. Dec. 24 and Dec. 31
62. Moderate

**DOWN**

1. Lesser Sunda island
2. Toward the mouth
3. Where Samuel Johnson's club met
4. Cabbage's partner
5. Knucklehead
6. Edenic
7. Connery
8. Schemes
9. "___ man's the noblest work of God": Pope
10. Set free
11. Suffering from mulligrubs
12. Word with Orange or Lyme
13. Frequent rte. of coastal storms
21. Soft shade
22. Communication service
25. Like leisure suits
26. Limonite's cousin
27. Richest part
28. Bite 'em items
29. Salad garnish
30. Angry one
31. Hot-tempered
33. Enter
36. Kennedy, in 1948
37. Dr. May
38. Like some bridges
43. Home deliverer, once
44. Disintegrates slowly
45. Author Yutang
47. "Brother, Can You Spare ___?"
48. Kind of bill or bed
49. Own
50. Ukrainian city
51. Greek letter
52. Traffic slowers
53. Shoe width
54. Sign of a long run

# 69

**ACROSS**

1. Old chest for valuables
5. Price or Sutherland
9. Reporter's quarry
14. Peau de ____
15. Land of O'Casey
16. "Wozzeck" or "Vanessa"
17. Humperdinck duo
20. Salad ingredient
21. Lake fed by the Maumee River
22. Squeak by
23. One of Mnemosyne's daughters
25. Dele or rewrite
27. Anderson's "High ____"
29. Croat's relative
31. Affected by wind or water
35. Malachite and bauxite
37. Spore
39. Speak one's mind
40. Famed soprano-director
42. Swiss river
43. Requirements
44. Mulligrubs
45. Vestige
47. Letters on a billet-doux's envelope
48. Pineapples
50. Costume for Lakme
52. Bottom acquired its head
53. Feds
55. Fable addendum
57. Words with king or carte
60. Homophone for pale
62. "The ____ Zorro"
65. Wagner's "twilight of the gods"
68. Liquor component
69. Medicinal lily
70. Smell ____ (be suspicious)
71. Lonigan of literature
72. Gelt; moola
73. Hankerings

**DOWN**

1. Court celebrity
2. Relative of a sorrel
3. Opera subject
4. Group led by Odin
5. Expunges
6. "Porgy and Bess" lyricist
7. Transportation for Tarzan
8. First name of 19 Down
9. Cutting tool on a plow
10. Gibbon or orang
11. Whale
12. Arduous journey
13. Retail consummation
18. Pogner's daughter et al.
19. Librettist for Stravinsky's "Persephone"
24. Mountain nymph
26. Hits the bottle
27. Mario's Floria
28. Conspicuous constellation
30. Chicago eleven
32. Second of a musical tetralogy
33. Willingham's "____ a Man"
34. Classroom equipment
36. First-aid contrivance
38. Elsa has one in "Lohengrin"
41. Flees
46. Metal eyelet
49. Desiccate
51. Dies ____
54. Nestlike
56. Deck out
57. Eras
58. "____ Horizon"
59. A Near Island
61. "Fiesque" was his first opera
63. ____ even keel
64. Trains with cabooses: Abbr.
66. Sorensen or Kennedy
67. Bovine sound

# 70

**ACROSS**

1. Leathernecks
8. Four-in-hand
14. "Hawkeye" on TV
16. More sprightly
17. Musician meets ex-senator
19. Regions
20. Appointment
21. Baxter and Williams
22. Brace or prop
24. Squabble
28. Gray or White
29. Tediously familiar
30. Baldness
34. Lacedaemon
35. Actor meets actor
37. Memorable journalist and family
38. They pay for rent and meals
39. Filling by a D.D.S.
40. Connors's milieu
41. Fräulein's turndown
42. City on the Saale
43. Chafing balm
47. Swedish netman
48. Kind of energy
49. Ballplayer meets doyenne
55. Parka
56. Derision
57. Mercy
58. Lincoln or Douglas

**DOWN**

1. Corday did him in
2. Point on the nose
3. Shone
4. Quechuans
5. Slangy answers
6. Musical note from Guido
7. Transmitter: Abbr.
8. Varna or Vaisya
9. Suitable for plucking
10. 100 square meters
11. Man, to Pliny
12. Ex-D.C. nuclear body
13. Essay
15. Actor meets dancer
18. Part of J.E.C.
22. Shakers and Dukhobors
23. Word with do or cut
24. Kiosk
25. Gay city
26. Kind of rail
27. Ducks
28. In high spirits
29. Show off
30. An Alan from N.Y.C.
31. Greene of TV
32. Old Greek coins
33. ____ pie
34. Catch
36. Gazelle
40. Some are sleepers
42. Truancy
43. ____ bean, used in perfumes
44. Citizen of Unalaska
45. Dipper
46. One having a bawl: Var.
47. Obnoxious child
48. Scottie's rebuff
49. O'Hara's Joey
50. Dir.
51. Great weight
52. Tussah's cousin
53. Pull someone's leg
54. Town northwest of Arnhem

# 71

**ACROSS**

1. Fly away, fly!
5. Emperor after Galba
9. Iranian coins
14. Dusting powder
15. Jogging pace
16. Follow
17. Smell ____ (be suspicious)
18. Type of salad dressing
20. Make an all-out effort
22. Three tsps.
23. No longer fashionable
24. Mexican Mrs.
27. Some M.I.T. grads.
28. Ten minus nine
29. Smidgen
32. Kind of bear or hare
34. French pronoun
35. ____ colada (cocktail)
36. Film based on Christie thriller
40. Saudi sachem
41. Subsidize
42. Languor
43. Prefix with drome and thesis
44. Stretch the budget
45. ____ Clemente
47. Start of the Three Musketeers' motto
48. Hole-in-one
49. Indigo source
51. Decalogue
58. Millipede
59. Author Vidal
60. French landscapist: 1811–1889
61. Artifice
62. Maintain
63. Orgs.
64. Square-dance groups
65. Chad or Tanganyika

**DOWN**

1. Bachelor party
2. Mata ____
3. Scandinavian monarch
4. Double quartet
5. Idle; futile
6. Cavalry, infantry, etc.
7. Bird's target
8. Indian or Western county
9. Dunkirk event: 1940
10. Waterway
11. ". . . ____ elephant's eye"
12. Fontanne's late husband
13. Latin opposite of et
19. ____ the fire (enterprise)
21. "Escales" composer
24. Undercover men
25. Commodious
26. Dog-tired
28. Parisian's O.K.
29. Moon goddess
30. Cancel
31. Sweet herb
33. Cavatina
34. Emulated the Pied Piper
35. Fasten
37. "____ to your leader"
38. Palter
39. Popular cloth on campus
44. Places for étudiants
45. Least deranged
46. Guitarist Segovia
48. Oak seed
50. Word with tender or age
51. Chits
52. Interjection for droppers and spillers
53. Baseball V.I.P.'s
54. The shakes
55. Star that brightens and fades
56. Long haul
57. Wizened
58. Lupino

# 72

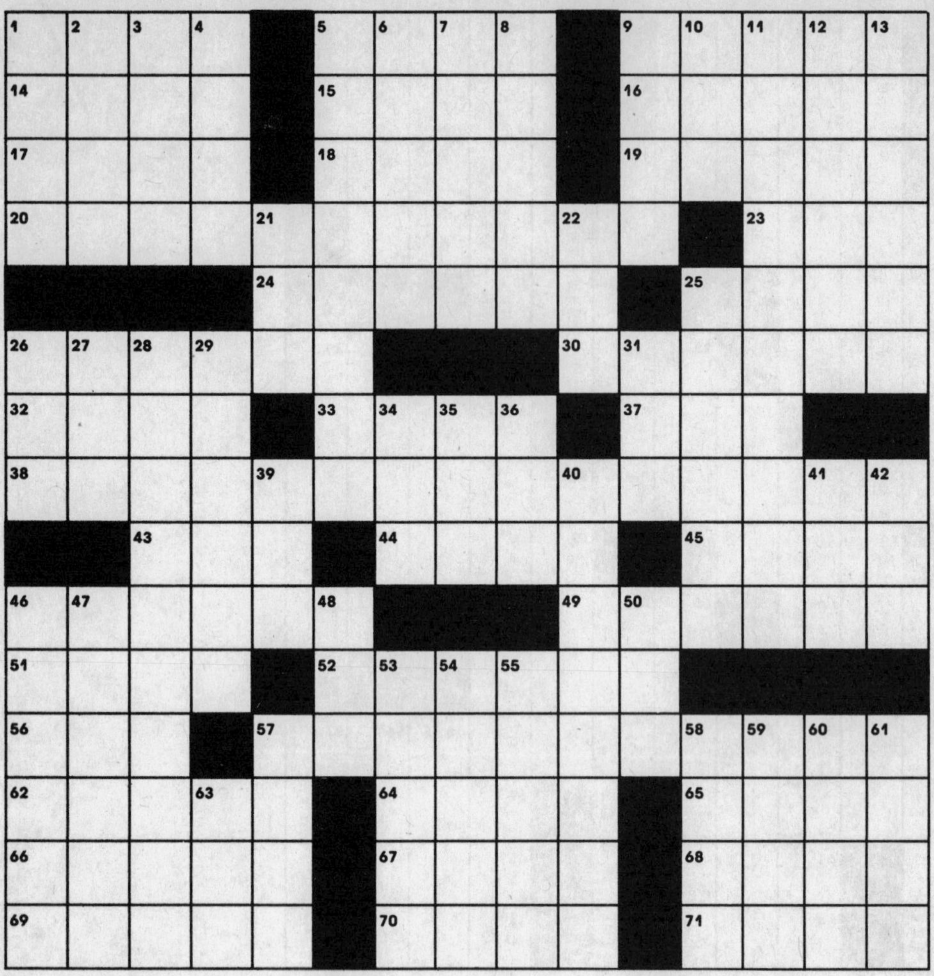


**ACROSS**

**1.** Manipulate
**5.** P.O. commemoratives
**9.** Goes hungry
**14.** Financial-page initials
**15.** Butler-O'Hara mansion
**16.** Supple
**17.** Garner
**18.** Particle
**19.** Blake of "Gunsmoke" et al.
**20.** Where did trouble reside?
**23.** Communications co.
**24.** Porch
**25.** Celestial figure, in Paris
**26.** "The ___ yet to be"
**30.** Faucet
**32.** Curved: Comb. form
**33.** Halo
**37.** Timetable abbr.
**38.** Heirloom timepiece
**43.** Suffix with class and fort
**44.** Tent part
**45.** Most excellent
**46.** Declining
**49.** H. Allen Smith's "___ Rides Again"
**51.** ___ the Terrible
**52.** Get
**56.** Ullmann
**57.** Secretly
**62.** ___ square
**64.** Opening
**65.** Solo
**66.** Horseshoe-shaped track
**67.** Give's partner
**68.** Sutter's place
**69.** Comedian Paul
**70.** Eye ___ infirmary
**71.** ___ en point

**DOWN**

**1.** Mata
**2.** "Of Mice ___"
**3.** Kind of year
**4.** Swell
**5.** Ogles
**6.** Turkic tongue
**7.** ___ cons
**8.** Dance
**9.** Spinning fiber
**10.** Point at
**11.** Part of S.R.O.
**12.** "Things ___ bump in the night"
**13.** Sonnet finale
**21.** Egg: Comb. form
**22.** Exclamations
**25.** Piece of legislation re flights
**26.** Sack
**27.** Stray
**28.** Dane or Swede
**29.** Luncheon
**31.** Felt shoe
**34.** TV band
**35.** Electrical unit
**36.** Macaw
**39.** Writer Rand
**40.** Abe, the Rail-___
**41.** Navy V.I.P.
**42.** Venturi of links fame
**46.** Stubborn
**47.** Birdhouse
**48.** Euphemistic oath
**50.** Navy's C.I.A.
**53.** Platform for outdoor concerts
**54.** Tissue layers
**55.** Asian tree
**57.** Bell, book and ___
**58.** Mention
**59.** Banshee's land
**60.** Lively air
**61.** "Whiffenpoof" locale
**63.** Clear away

# 73

**ACROSS**

1. Printing technique
7. Bistro
11. Opposite of post
14. Downcast
15. ____ Alonzo Stagg
16. U.S. cartoonist
17. Very large scales
20. Culbertson
21. Itinerary: Abbr.
22. Irish patriot: 1778–1803
23. Chair material
25. Smear
26. "____ My Heart"
27. Additionally
28. Form of government: Suffix
31. Decimal base
32. W.W. II town
34. Diminutive ending
35. Hebrew letter
37. Convention luminaries
42. "Splitsville"
43. Kind of dance or hold
44. Peking coin
45. Uris hero
47. Curved
49. Schuss
50. Flavor and body of a French wine
52. Parts of moon buggies
53. Act the accomplice
54. S.A. armadillo
56. Sky sighting?
57. Ziegfeld
58. Ecologist's concern
63. Tune
64. Roulette bet at Monte Carlo
65. Expiates
66. Essay
67. Mailed
68. Word for a slot machine

**DOWN**

1. Lady Capulet's cry: Act IV
2. Dandy
3. Compatible competition
4. Statue support
5. Glimpse
6. Yukon or Northwest: Abbr.
7. Emulates Allen at Ticonderoga: 1775
8. Very tiny organism
9. Pro
10. Town southwest of Padua
11. Aeschylean tragedy
12. Break a promise
13. Neighbor of Bethlehem, Pa.
18. Delphi denizen
19. Wee prankster
23. Amontillado container
24. Chip for the pot
25. Internist, for one
29. Nicene and Apostles'
30. Not nay
33. Singular
36. The limit, at times
38. "____ Clear Day"
39. "I have bathed in the ____ the sea": Rimbaud
40. Casanova
41. Agitated state
45. As blind ____
46. Do a mechanic's job
48. Give guiding information
51. Time interval
53. Illinois city
55. Sothern and Sheridan
57. ____ morgana (mirage)
59. College in Cedar Rapids
60. Collar
61. Defendants, in law
62. Id ____

# 74

## ACROSS

**1.** Of grandparents
**5.** Part-song
**9.** Lane
**12.** Soft leather
**13.** Ancient rival of Babylonia
**14.** It's often high
**16.** "Whiffenpoof" singers
**17.** "Mona ___"
**18.** First soprano to star in "Turandot": 1926
**19.** Potential sitter
**20.** Carol subject
**22.** Capital of Saskatchewan
**24.** Brag
**25.** Indira Gandhi's father
**27.** Boston U.'s terrier
**31.** Faux pas
**34.** Parisian's basic verb
**36.** ___ Carrée (Louvre quadrangle)
**37.** Skunk cabbage or calla lily
**38.** Compass point
**39.** "___ on earth . . ."
**40.** Author of "My Life": 1975
**41.** Night light
**42.** "Ring ___ new": Tennyson
**43.** "___ Fideles"
**45.** Home of the brave
**47.** Adjective for a fugue
**49.** Bouquets that can't be thrown
**53.** How some face a new year
**57.** Kismet
**58.** Like truth, at times
**59.** Namath & Co.
**60.** "Pretty maids all in ___"
**61.** Turkey, ham, etc.
**62.** "There ___ time like the present"
**63.** Item delivered by an actor
**64.** Roman citadel
**65.** Like ___ of bricks
**66.** Lustful look

## DOWN

**1.** Lend ___ (hearken)
**2.** Shopper's concern
**3.** Rich Little's forte
**4.** Inventory term
**5.** Syrian peasant
**6.** Et ___ (and others)
**7.** Introductions cliché
**8.** Great baritone of Caruso's day
**9.** ". . . who only stand and ___": Milton
**10.** Looped handle
**11.** "Happy New ___!"
**14.** Cue, in group singing
**15.** What Jaques called "second childishness"
**21.** Cloth of gold
**23.** Poverty
**26.** Where some are keen for keno
**28.** Put paint on
**29.** Setting for a precious stone
**30.** Yuletide cynosure
**31.** Character in "Princess Ida"
**32.** Cézanne's "Boy in ___ Vest"
**33.** Pâté de ___ gras
**35.** Movie director Clair
**39.** Atlantic City attraction
**41.** Café card
**44.** Sounds like Donne's bell
**46.** Former Mets owner
**48.** Central Roman rooms
**50.** Singer Osmond
**51.** In harmony
**52.** Ed Norton's bailiwick
**53.** Hero of a Hindu epic
**54.** Jug
**55.** Tunisian seaport
**56.** Quartet that can't sing

# 75

**ACROSS**

1. Percolate
5. Fire worshiper
10. Adjusted precisely
13. Change the name
15. Cats and dogs
17. N.K.V.D. predecessor
18. Makes worthless
19. Printer's em
20. Tennesseans, for short
21. Natives of Helsinki
22. Church feature
23. Chemical suffix
24. Twain hero
25. Celestial Ram
26. He destroys the evidence
28. Improve
29. Setting limits
31. San ____, Calif. city
32. Battery reading
34. Golden shiners
35. Where Iloilo is
36. Britain's West Point: Abbr.
38. Scraps for Spot
39. Tenement collection
40. Napoleon and Wellington, e.g.
41. Swine ____
42. Walk daintily
43. Lie hidden
44. International business process
48. Trust implicitly
49. Inclined
50. Piece of Bacon
51. Autographs

**DOWN**

1. Reasons for the casts of thousands
2. Hermia's father in "A Midsummer-Night's Dream"
3. Annapolis grad.
4. Cosset
5. Awaits decision
6. Monkshood
7. Periphery
8. Post office, to the postmaster
9. Maltreated
10. "Oh that I had wings like ____!": Psalm 55
11. African river
12. Oracle
13. Like the monsoon season
14. Kefauver
16. Gadget
21. De ____ (in reality)
22. Fight site
24. Work for F. Lee Bailey
25. Friendly relations
27. Elaborate parties
28. World's biggest holdup man
30. Environment
31. "Tamburlaine" was his first play
33. Come out
34. Removes, as clothing
35. Price of a thought
37. Queried
39. "Eleanor ____," Beatles' hit in 1966
40. Side
42. First variable star to be discovered
45. Consultants like Keynes: Abbr.
46. Dernier ____
47. Layer

# 76

**ACROSS**

1. Relief org.
5. Overcharge for tickets
10. High fliers under a cloud
14. Love, to Livy
15. He's three sheets to the wind
16. Indian of Oklahoma
17. Opening move
20. Greek letter
21. State: Abbr.
22. Small hackney coach
23. ___ of (rather than)
25. Byelorussia's capital
26. Bristly plant appendage
27. Elegance
28. Homophone for ale
31. Channel No. 1 for humans
34. Karma
35. Norse myths, collectively
36. Middle game move
39. Neighbor of Afgh.
40. Was beholden
41. Bears, to Brutus
42. Goddess of mischief
43. Tholes
44. To whom Chou seldom said no
45. Marsh birds
47. Earthquakes
50. Dark and York
52. Caution
53. Resistance unit
55. Attacking move
58. "I cannot tell ___"
59. Dull finish
60. In a bewildered state
61. Farm building
62. Dominant assumptions of a people
63. Watch over

**DOWN**

1. Ann or Elizabeth
2. Strad's cousin
3. Mountain ash
4. Fish-eating bird
5. Pilfered
6. ___ vin (chicken dish)
7. Southern constellation
8. Shelter, nautically speaking
9. Places in front
10. Stuffed seats
11. Prisons of a sort
12. Troupe's trip
13. Wizened
18. Chiang Kai-shek's haven
19. ___ days' wonder
24. Delayer's word
25. Toned down
27. Great quintet
29. Supposition
30. Dusty way
31. ___ regia (corrosive liquid)
32. Depose
33. T.V.A. facility
34. Curries favor
35. Wallaroos or kangaroos
37. Arduous
38. Picturesque
43. Ale measure
44. Unites
46. Pulitzer Prize poet: 1930
47. ___ Domingo
48. Name in telegraphy
49. Brightness
50. Bedouin
51. Ms. Montez
52. "___ liberty and justice . . ."
54. Famed U.S. anthropologist
56. Krazy ___ of comics
57. Boater, e.g.

# 77

**ACROSS**

1. Pekoe purveyors
7. "There's some ill ____ reigns": Shakespeare
13. Hangnest
14. ____ words (retract)
16. Impromptu
18. ____ over (helped to get by)
19. Barfly
20. "Cielo e ____!" (Ponchielli aria)
21. Aqua fortis
22. Pivots
23. Verbal thrust
24. Pyknic
25. Gather, in a way
26. One-on-one affairs
27. Giving substance to, with "out"
29. Spring bloomers
30. Enduring
32. Puts out
35. Espresso garnish
39. Checks
40. Kefauver
41. Relieve of
42. Fibers from candlenut trees
43. Gaul's chariot
44. Comedienne Osterwald
45. Bankbook abbr.
46. Up
47. Swedish engineer
48. Just before the deadline
51. Philip Barry play: 1928
52. Swift's flying island
53. Pardons
54. Sycophants

**DOWN**

1. Type of postage stamp
2. Steeped in lore
3. Broadcast
4. Temper; humor
5. Eleven, in Essen
6. Provoking
7. Frog or chick
8. Luxurious fabrics
9. Agent: Suffix
10. Pierre, e.g.
11. Calhoun and Van Buren
12. Logical, as a theory
15. Engineer's computation
16. Crosier
17. Timepieces
22. Climbs, in a way
23. Mentor
25. Oxfords
26. Cure, as fur skins
28. Warrens
29. Like the walls of Harvard Yard
31. With determination
32. Hebrew prophet
33. Loud speaker
34. City named for a chief
36. Encomium
37. Man of Lhasa
38. Roman official
40. Elianic works
43. Elath, to the Arabs
44. Nil nisi ____
46. Noted Italian biologist: 17th century
47. Small drinks
49. Hymn homophone
50. Daisy ____ of Dogpatch

# 78

**ACROSS**

1. Birds that ape human speech
5. Cicero's pronoun for Catiline
9. Benchley book
13. Nourishing
15. Like a weak old woman
17. Climbing shrubs with hooked tendrils
18. Natives of Gdynia
19. Icelandic letter
20. Mountain lake
21. Straw mattress
22. Hauling cart
24. Deluge
26. Atoll makeup
28. "I'd rather see than ____": G. Burgess
29. Saroyan hero
30. Canaries' cousins
31. "Scots Wha ____": Burns
34. Yellowish sweet fruits
36. Playground equipment
38. What a ques. expects
39. Destroyed
41. Start of Clement Moore's famous poem
42. Moldings
43. Where the Ginza is
44. Heat wave
48. Cartoonist Addams
49. Court decisions
50. Dies ____
52. Tool in a Markham poem
55. "____ Jacques"
56. Ticket ignorers
58. Island in the Malay Archipelago
59. Reunion sites, at times
60. Maxims
61. Chemical suffixes
62. African fox

**DOWN**

1. Redfin
2. "When I was ____ . . .": Gilbert
3. Retreats
4. N.C.O.'s
5. Tooth filling
6. Kind of sapphire
7. More brownish-yellow
8. Some railroads
9. "The ____ Sandman," 1920 song
10. "There was ____ woman . . ."
11. Author Cather
12. Freezing rain
14. Outer
16. Italian princely family
21. Played on words
23. Sloping passage
25. Causes of ear pollution
26. Toreador's cloak
27. Scene of a naval battle: July 1940
28. Lunar crater named for an astronomer
30. Metal-working tools
31. Detectives
32. Farthest from the pin
33. It, in Italy
35. Some parents
37. ____ of Eumenes, at foot of Acropolis
40. Circular tuba
43. Second-story man's crime
44. Sickle handle
45. Lace used for upholstery
46. Tropical tree genus
47. Himalayan goat antelope
48. Nightclubs
51. City in N.Y. or Ga.
53. Acknowledges
54. Existence
56. Owing the pot
57. Mauna ____

**ACROSS**

1. One of seven
7. "Papa Bear" of gridiron fame
12. Herschel's discovery
13. The ___ Cup, in yacht racing
16. Stroller
17. I.O.U. with a deadline
18. Prefix with corn or form
19. Wife of Oberon
21. Wife of Amen-Ra
22. Kind of party
24. Milne boy
25. New Orleans jazzman
26. Rock debris at base of cliff
28. Visit between whalers
29. Revolutionary patriot
30. Chilling
32. Torme
33. Penthouses
34. Tiny chorines
37. Rimsky-Korsakoff's "Le Coq ___"
38. Rudimentary root
39. Pale
42. "Ben-___," Wallace book
43. Cellini creation
45. Peruse
46. Book between Daniel and Joel
48. Davenport
49. Hindu sacred words
50. Least loose
52. Bolger
53. One of fifty
55. "And what is ___ . . . ?"
57. One of five
58. Clever escapee
59. Weird
60. Small drums

**DOWN**

1. One of twelve
2. Face of a building
3. Adverb often used with integrated
4. ___ hurry (rushing)
5. Rudely concise
6. Moving about
7. Surround
8. Space
9. Author Yutang
10. Baldness
11. Second-largest planet
13. Kettledrum
14. Jot
15. Due e cinque
20. Gowns of professionals
23. Circumspect
25. Spirals
27. Prince, e.g.
29. Coarse material
31. Comparative suffix
32. Mary Quant's style
34. Colloquial name for Lutetia
35. Where riches abound
36. Magellan was one
38. Bumpkin
39. Bouquet
40. Descendant of Noah's eldest son
41. Relative of a rhubarb
42. Dark-eyed beauty
44. Beds or bookies
46. ___ couture (high fashion)
47. Black-ink item
50. Little Antoinette
51. Indian weight
54. Patriotic org.
56. Obstruction

# 80

**ACROSS**

1. Beach houses
8. Improper
13. Seasoning mint
14. ____ land
16. Discount sources for shoppers
19. Goner's name
20. Penned, as pigs
21. Drench
22. Benefit from
23. Franks' accompaniment
24. Pandowdy
25. ____ incognita
27. One of Adam's boys
29. Ki-yi
30. Belles-lettres, perhaps
32. Soccer players
34. Monks for the commissary
36. Less prepossessing
38. Isabel Perón, e.g.
42. Remain unsettled
43. Start of a 1928 song title
45. More affronted
46. Varnish ingredient
47. Lateens and Genoas
49. Summer time: Abbr.
50. Excited
52. Twenty-four sheets of paper
53. Amin
54. Containers that create litter
58. Hon
59. Little ring
60. Unpleasant company
61. Obtainers

**DOWN**

1. Travel to and from the job
2. Stimulates
3. Wingdings
4. Wharton's "The ____ of Innocence"
5. No
6. "Plain as ____ in a man's face": Rabelais
7. As ____ silk
8. Kunta Kinte, to Haley
9. Disposition
10. Hawaiian baking pit
11. Blackjacks
12. Prying one
15. Escargots
17. A good deal
18. Beehive made of straw
23. Howled at the moon
26. Whizzed
28. Farm tools
29. Hedging on a question
31. Slithered
33. Lock of hair
35. Idle hours
36. Neptune or Poseidon
37. Called for another song
39. Pend ____ (river, peak or lake in Idaho)
40. Whitetail in summer
41. Cassatt, Chagall et al.
42. Strategy
44. Car safety device
48. Sierra ____
51. Transmission item
52. Witticism
55. Three-way: Prefix
56. Blasting material
57. Pooh!

# 81

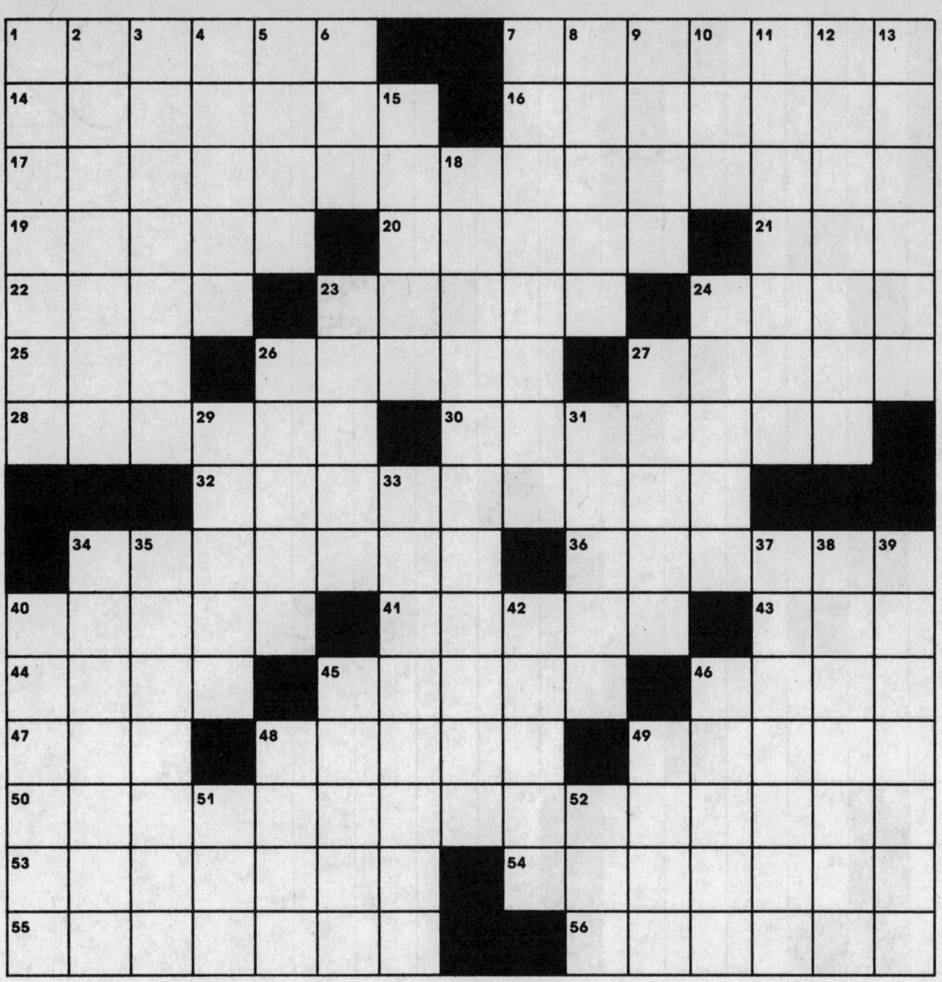


**ACROSS**

1. Misgivings
7. American and National
14. Beseech
16. Upcoming doctor
17. Aristophanes's realm of fantasy
19. Military caps
20. Calorie
21. Jan. 1 drink
22. Reclined
23. Kind of boat or iron
24. Unkind twitting
25. Eggs, to Lucullus
26. Sound of rustling leaves
27. Touchdowns
28. Classes or groups
30. Tailor's measurement
32. Literally "fat Tuesday"
34. Fastening
36. Panama and Suez
40. Examines by touch
41. Declaration signer from N.C.
43. Intention
44. Dear me!
45. Narcotic leaves
46. Hoofbeat
47. Waikiki garland
48. Tapestry
49. Piece of bologna
50. Ecstatic
53. "____ above all . . .": Keble
54. Dec. 31
55. Encumbered
56. Lays away

**DOWN**

1. Record of a voyage
2. Enjoying a furlough
3. Impossibly ideal
4. Bear
5. Spreads hay
6. Pouch
7. Eat ____ (overdo it)
8. Monstrous, old style
9. Energy source
10. Become more solid
11. Celestial
12. Uplift
13. Rough grasses
15. Conductor's "All together, now!"
18. A disembodied smile
23. Shrewd
24. Supporting timber
26. Outdoor garments
27. Mirror
29. Post or Brontë
31. Snoops
33. Disarmed a bull
34. Hell
35. Surrendered by deed
37. Halibut liver oil
38. A Tertiary epoch
39. Looms
40. Very large books
42. Wishy-____
45. Liqueur
46. Mild cigar
48. Of grandparents
49. Settee or sofa
51. The last word
52. Males

# 82

**ACROSS**

1. Famous muralist
5. Welcome ____
8. Casino items
13. Section of the Met
14. Canyon phenomenon
16. Actress Massey
17. Alan, the actor
18. Attention-getter
19. Stylish establishment
20. Pert. to divisions of mankind
22. ____ distance (stays aloof)
24. Word with hand or grand
25. Rodent hunter
26. Indeed
28. Fennec or koala
32. Confident expectation
34. Solemn promise
36. Like a chiller
37. Sourdough's quest
38. Skinflint
40. Urge
41. Game, set, ____
43. Suffix with farmer or kitchen
44. Port of Tunisia
45. Guarantee
47. Jewish song of praise
49. Crests
51. Handicaps
54. Sentimental
57. Get the better of
58. Carroll character
59. El ____, city near Cairo
61. Prefix with sol or stat
62. Of a thread
63. Word in proofreading
64. Tiring trip
65. Everybody, in Spain
66. Welcome word
67. Existence: Lat.

**DOWN**

1. Has the lead
2. Gulf of Aqaba port
3. Welcome items
4. Apprentice
5. Refection
6. Alas, to Wolfgang
7. Welcome item
8. Deal out in portions
9. Flexible
10. Pop flavor
11. Bowline
12. Capital of Yemen
15. Hebrew measure
21. Huxtable
23. Epoch
25. Skirt style
27. An ____, city in Vietnam
29. Welcome items
30. Kind of code
31. Wildcat
32. Where most feel welcome
33. Sister port of Algiers
35. ____ a pistol
38. Fraternal-society members
39. Thicken
42. Caribbean cruise stop
44. Having dividing walls
46. N.Y. summertime
48. Fighting Tigers' inst.
50. One-horse carriages
52. Parts of a car
53. Fire furnaces
54. Finn's transportation
55. Mixed bag
56. Clement
57. Fare for a hackney
60. Alphabetic finale

# 83

**ACROSS**

1. Publicity
8. Italian ice creams
14. Shoulder fringe
15. Dewey in 1948
16. Testimonial feasts, e.g.
18. Highlander
19. Hits hard
20. Flock of mallards
21. Wine cask
22. Liqueur flavoring
24. Posed
25. Parched
27. Shoot the breeze
28. Parrots
30. Ebb
32. Spectacular waterfall
34. Pugnacious person
36. Gorge
38. Eye parts
42. Fiery particle
43. Rules: Abbr.
45. Sapless
46. Dickens boy
47. Cobbler
49. Young fellow
50. Engrossed
52. Allots
54. Wagnerian heroine
55. Suffered enviously
58. Brats
59. Close of legislature
60. Worthwhile holdings
61. Worthwhile leavings

**DOWN**

1. Russian symbol
2. Food fancier
3. Orthodox
4. Fontanne partner
5. Pub serving
6. Seas: Fr.
7. Georgia river
8. Tumbler
9. Lisper's problem
10. Superman's friend
11. Alarm clock
12. Trumpet blare
13. Mosaic pieces
15. Sea anemone
17. Dracula features
23. Hard to restrain
26. Postpone
27. Coat with wax
29. Juliet's betrothed
31. Daggers
33. Monkshood
35. Like certain seals
36. Pain-killers
37. They improvise
39. Betrayal
40. Expunction
41. Calms down
42. Layers
44. An old glory
48. Hebrew measures
51. Sped madly
53. Bando and Maglie
54. Girl of comics
56. "____ by bread alone . . ."
57. Spoilage

# 84

**ACROSS**

1. Whippersnapper
11. President who weighed over 300 lbs.
15. Tantamount
16. It was once Christiania
17. Converted
18. Effort
19. Gal of song
20. Lets or sublets
21. Gala
22. Bell the cat
23. Toy on a string
24. Wire: Abbr.
27. Normand of early films
30. Football's Fighting Tigers
33. P.D.Q.
34. Bearing the name of
36. Kind of rail or plane
37. Dir. from Paris to Calais
38. Russian secret police: 1922–35
39. Drew forth
42. Man the helm
43. Anil, e.g.
44. ___ metabolism
45. Tralee's county
46. Baba au ___ (a pastry)
48. Protection
50. Between "To be" and "to be"
52. Wild; savage
54. Cut down
57. ___ Islands, SW of Samoa
58. Resemblance or semblance
60. "Too bad!"
61. Arena attraction
62. Amphibian
63. Unmerciful

**DOWN**

1. NFL team
2. Greenish blue
3. Tress
4. Relatives
5. So-so
6. Ardent "consumerist"
7. Orderly setups
8. Immured
9. Tolkien's tree creatures
10. Tale: Abbr.
11. That is ___ (in other words)
12. Horoscoper
13. Blah
14. Ale mug
21. Prefix with syllable or graph
22. Stage setting
23. Craving
24. Brought to heel
25. Modern adhesive
26. Long, thin facial feature
28. Halt in respiration
29. Desex the text
31. Part of SST
32. Loan shark's overcharge
35. Specks
40. Be next to
41. Traffic-light mechanism
42. T-bar, e.g.
47. Uplift
49. Greek physician
50. Twinkling ___ eye
51. Rub the wrong way
52. Give the sack to
53. Author Ludwig
54. Colossal
55. Anglo-Saxon letters
56. Douses
58. Watering device: Abbr.
59. E. Indian herb

# 85

**ACROSS**

1. Japanese women divers
5. "And I wore ___ red rose"
9. Twinkling
14. Explosive issue
16. Noted Spanish poet
17. At the other end of the world
18. Inner, in anatomy
19. Fun on the water
20. Brittle
22. One with a mortgage
23. Timber for the anchor
24. God's handiwork
25. Italian coin
26. Golden or Bronze
27. Like random shots
31. Harboring, as a grudge
36. Through a substitute
37. Ardent wisher
38. Engineering degree
39. Flaring star
40. Plasterers' floats; trowels
44. Duped
47. Blackbird's cousin
48. What horror films make the blood do
49. Deadly poison
51. Scent: Brit.
52. Counters acidity
54. About a quart
55. Tasty cheeses
56. Blows the game
57. Stays put
58. Greek peak

**DOWN**

1. Obsessed whaler
2. Soliloquy, e.g.
3. Successful people
4. Hurt maliciously
5. Sorry fellow
6. Tin stars
7. Call ___ day
8. It's in the bag
9. Cheap hotel
10. The strength of Samson
11. Musical Shaw
12. Milan landmark, for short
13. Brought to court
15. Think
21. Wet
24. Magical stick
28. Marshals troops
29. They go too far
30. False colors
32. Easy job
33. Steel-mill deliveries
34. Author Shute
35. Old women
40. List of court cases
41. Prehistoric people
42. Iranian money
43. Skipjack tuna
44. Sing merrily
45. TV sound section
46. Air or sea speed
50. Weather satellite
53. Chez ___ (at his house)

# 86

## ACROSS

1. Rocket parts
10. Distant
14. In working order
15. Strictness
17. Pondered at length
18. Prefix for Norman or Saxon
19. A ___ Able
20. Changed digits, as on the houses of a street
22. With confidence
23. Leg. meeting
24. Galileo's birthplace
27. Morning dunkers
29. TV's Marshal Dillon
31. Former Mideast initials
32. Anatomical pouch
35. Bench was one
37. One of Michelangelo's skills
39. Needle part
40. Compass reading
41. Haughty ones
42. One end of the Gulf of Suez
45. Ceremonial containers
46. Source, as of information
48. Smoldering coals
51. Plainly visible
53. Co. insignia
57. Reserved
58. Consigned to obscurity
60. Le ___, port city
61. Damaging parts of accusations
62. Meadows
63. Certain enzymes

## DOWN

1. Ibsen character
2. Musical work
3. Highway sight
4. Innisfail
5. Half a dance
6. Japanese seaport
7. Saltpeter
8. Settled accounts
9. Diligent
10. Saracen
11. Adjective for N.Y.C. police
12. Unprovoked attack
13. Play parts
16. Ride the ___ (hop a freight)
21. Mimicking birds
22. Decked out like an ambassador
24. Beseech
25. Insert blank pages in a book
26. "Two shakes"
28. Father of the Titans
29. Honor card
30. Became aware of
33. Formicide victims
34. Abbr. in physics
36. Come forth again
38. ___ favor (please, in Spain)
43. Miss Madigan
44. Doubleday and Yokum
46. What to do at 46 Across
47. Inner
49. Conspicuous brilliance
50. Canadian town official
52. Midmonth in Caesar's time
53. Eastern religious figure
54. "Miss ___ Regrets"
55. Heredity unit
56. Harem rooms
59. Needlefish

# 87

## ACROSS

1. Sibilate
5. Evian-les-Bains, e.g.
8. Aimless jaunt
14. Small, pointed beard
16. Untroubled by ethics
17. ___ grise (confidential agent)
18. Smallest amounts
19. Commando asset
20. Christie mystery
22. Knightly sport
23. Demeanor
24. Graffito for Belshazzar
25. Fair and fetching
26. Out of harm's way
27. Fragrant evergreen
28. Measure of area
29. Subject of a long poem by Frost
31. Nadir
33. Mass gambling
37. Ballroom dances
39. China, for instance
40. "The ___ of the Cities," book by Steffens
43. Element in Einstein's formula
44. Prized panfish
45. Pumice, in one stage
46. Moving vehicles
47. Bank deal
48. Retaliatory
50. Jack's place in the garden?
52. Scotch plaid
53. Waste away
55. It's the real thing
56. Sachet fragrance
57. Scapegrace
58. Be beholden to
59. Hypochondriac's dread

## DOWN

1. Betook oneself apace
2. Callow
3. Vivacious
4. In one's dotage
5. Grow lyrical
6. Winter overshoe
7. Menhaden or pilchard
8. Former Philippine President, ___ Magsaysay
9. "Plac'd far ___ the melancholy main": Thomson
10. Presidents on Rushmore, e.g.
11. Pickled
12. Flake
13. Filamentous plant structure
15. Dwelling cost
21. Unmindful
23. Deadeye
25. City cruiser
26. Six, at dice
27. Ailurophobes' dreads
29. Put an edge on
30. Implements for "seven maids"
32. Starry-eyed
34. Madcap adventure
35. Marriage counselor's sometime role
36. One of the Carolines
38. Citrus hybrid
40. Pioneer in U.S. cotton industry
41. Smoke
42. Forestalls
44. Shoemaker's chore
46. Record plastic
47. Full-grown pike
49. Nurse shark
50. Prepare the way
51. Candlemas or Michaelmas
54. Yawning mouth

# 88

## ACROSS

1. Carry lightly through the air
5. Nap
9. Warm-water fish
13. Cupid, in art
14. Finely ground quartz or flint
15. Garb for Lucullus
16. Part of a bureaucracy
18. Organic compound
19. Catches
20. Color for William
22. Not big, to Burns
23. Male mallard
24. Kinship
29. Kind of int.
32. "My ___," Straus song
33. Sight at Provincetown
34. Peter in re pumpkins
36. North Caucasian language
37. Denominations
39. Golconda
40. Paving stones
42. Guideway in a knitting machine
43. Mouth: Sp.
44. Ike's command in W.W. II
45. Pollution-control device
48. Raises
50. Mil. address
51. Eldest Karamazov
53. Verse that spells words vertically
58. Sumptuous
59. Large flowerpot
61. Dies ___
62. Olfactology topics
63. Bitter drug
64. Buoy attachment
65. Striplings
66. Telescope part

## DOWN

1. ___ in (attack)
2. Church "corner"
3. Toffs
4. Enrapture
5. Mint product
6. Corrida cheers
7. Mahayana movement
8. Wrest
9. Kind of knife
10. "The French ___"
11. Highly excited
12. Hill's counterpart
14. Tresses
17. Branches
21. Martha from Butte
23. Calorie counter
24. Aspect
25. Face with masonry
26. Adjective for Bryan
27. Pursuits of knights-errant
28. Cry in conceding defeat
30. Part of L.S.D.
31. Dismal, to Keats
35. Very delicious or fragrant
38. Ancient city, noted for wealth and luxury
41. European coal basin
46. Kidney bean of the Southwest
47. Second word of a fairy tale
49. Merman or Kennedy
51. Small amount
52. Bog
53. Grandson of Jacob
54. Naval officers: Abbr.
55. Distant: Prefix
56. Mangle
57. So-so grades
60. "Tobacco Road" character

# 89

**ACROSS**

1. He was "obscure"
5. Bound, in a way
10. ___ River, N.J.
14. Catchall abbr.
15. Cross as ___
16. "La donna è mobile," e.g.
17. Silent sayonara
18. TV dealer's corridor?
20. Shook
22. "___ Harold," Byron classic
23. Swiss resort
24. Touched ground
25. Crash-dieted
27. Plan or cheese
31. Pyromaniac's crime
32. Jack Frost's product
33. Have ___ at (try)
34. It's in a jamb
35. Coil of yarn
37. Dagger
38. Crossword bird
39. Nut used for flavoring
40. Games expert
41. Greeted with a ceremonial bow
43. Past and future
44. Amerind
45. South Korean premier: 1960
46. He's paid to carry, on a safari
49. Agadir and Algeciras
52. Humorist's vegetable?
54. Word with spin or light
55. Mental faculties
56. What expert typists seldom do
57. Grafted: Her.
58. Mainlanders' souvenirs
59. Some are tall
60. Put away

**DOWN**

1. Israelites
2. Its motto is "Industry"
3. Satan's purchase from Hutch?
4. Otis product
5. Cannon adjunct
6. Woodwinds
7. Pat. ___
8. ___ crow (take it all back)
9. Launder, in a way
10. Gauguin's hideaway
11. Roberts
12. Far from acrid
13. Post-Yule event
19. Bake, as eggs
21. In debt no more
24. French possessive
25. Covers, as a bet
26. A bakery has one
27. Winning
28. Actor's endowment?
29. Like good shortstops
30. They get counted
35. Maugham
36. Swiss artist
37. Implies
39. Actress Black
40. Accumulate
42. Heading on this puzzle
43. Macbeth and Banquo
45. "Hold it!"
46. Emulate Don Carter
47. Sight from Toledo
48. Italian wine area
49. Circus favorite
50. Belgrade V.I.P., once
51. Did in
53. "Unmentionable" in the Victorian era

# 90

**ACROSS**

1. Deus ex ____
8. Julius from Brooklyn
14. One of the rivers of Hades
15. Start of the eighth month
16. Kahn's book about the old Dodgers
18. Fimbriate
19. Prison burned by Wat Tyler's rebels
20. Mouth: Comb. form
21. Nefarious
23. Peddles
24. Japon, Chine, etc.
25. "There ____ old lady . . ."
27. Electrical unit
28. Jannings and Ludwig
29. Enjoyed the snow
31. Already adjusted
32. Bauble
33. He's sorry now
34. From Venezia Tridentina to Sicilia
37. Small change in Panama
41. Coattails phrase
42. Downy surface
43. Mere; meager
44. What dols measure
45. Jetties
47. Scope
48. Sea eagle
49. Daughter of Titus Andronicus
51. 106, to Scipio
52. Patrick Mann's best seller
55. Poe poem
56. Triple ____ of 1907–8
57. Pitman specialists
58. More irritable

**DOWN**

1. 1978 Cooperstown inductee
2. Straddling
3. Dress style
4. O.T. language
5. Press
6. He wrote "The Highwayman"
7. Rejoined
8. Commits a deadly sin
9. Malarial symptom
10. Pirate's quaff
11. Effortless assimilation
12. Barren
13. Most lively
15. "Pride goeth before ____"
17. Eyed amorously
22. Napoleon II's epithet
24. "The Beautiful"
26. Writer Marsh
28. ____ Yisreal (Palestine)
30. Mao's successor
31. It seldom made Cerf bored
33. He's sorry, too
34. Obstructs
35. Remove, as a page or article
36. Stimulated; thrilled
37. Where L.A. is
38. Communications pioneer
39. "One man, ____"
40. He dyes for a living
42. Stars that brighten and fade
45. "____ a pious fraud . . .": J. R. Lowell
46. Where Duccio painted
49. Gounod contemporary
50. Crafts' partner
53. Cupid
54. Knot in cotton fiber

91

## ACROSS

1. Choose
4. Discarded metal
9. Drop or fall preceder
13. Digit
14. Mongrel
15. Spruce fruit
16. ____ -a-la-Crosse, Saskatchewan
17. Establishes as law
19. Keeps company
21. Period of vigilance
22. Place one above another
23. Equest. law enforcers
25. Further review
32. Enough, to FitzGerald
33. Type of cords
34. Intimation
35. Unit of energy
36. Mystical application of words
38. Occupational suffix
39. Palindromic word
40. Ulyanov
41. French violinist: 19th c.
42. In a patronizing manner
46. Diminutive ending
47. She could change anything into wine
48. Bias
51. Like some lenses
55. Priest, at times
58. Propeller
59. ____ bellum
60. Anointed
61. Refrain word
62. Sustain the burden
63. Bete ____
64. Town in Nevada or Minnesota

## DOWN

1. Aural
2. Game played in America since 1876
3. Adolescent
4. Reproductive bodies
5. Invention
6. English arctic navigator (1800–62)
7. Behave
8. Letter on a key
9. Emulate Praxiteles
10. Symbol
11. Humdinger
12. Jerry ____, NBA Hall of Famer
17. Mint
18. Tex-Mex treat
20. Arrange in a compact mass
23. Military survey
24. Projecting rock
25. Ancient stringed instrument
26. January in Palma
27. Group of witches
28. Motherless calf
29. Topper on a tart
30. European blackbird
31. Reticulate
36. Face of an arch
37. Type of egg
41. Soon
43. More compact
44. Solve a cryptogram
45. "____ we are spoil'd": Shak.
48. Plant disease
49. Solitary
50. Square pillar
51. Denpasar's island
52. Something to cast
53. He's below a marquis
54. Roentgenogram
56. Slammer occupant
57. Azul, Negro, or Novo

# 92

## ACROSS

1. A son of Hecuba
6. Rose oil
11. Song-like on a score
12. One-celled animal
13. Its county seat is Newcastle
16. Bar and bat mitzvah
17. McKinley's birthplace in Ohio
18. Dep.
19. Singing brothers
20. Serpentine summer?
21. Knee neighbor
22. Shoot the breeze
23. Gloomy, to Keats
24. Thrift preceder
25. The principle of caring for the welfare of others
27. Boring
28. Bostonian, for one
30. Fruit on a strawberry
33. Hits the atmosphere, like a returning astronaut from space
37. Scold
38. Hexagon's sextet
39. Classic starter
40. Ethereal
41. Unser or Foyt
42. Axelrod's "The Seven Year ____"
43. MDs
44. News summary, for short
45. Native of Omsk or Tomsk
46. Aurora Australis
49. Futile
50. He played Lawrence of Arabia
51. Past or present
52. Matchmaker in "Fiddler on the Roof"

## DOWN

1. Kind of demonstration
2. Buenos ____
3. Goes to pot
4. Start for Kabibble; end for Finn
5. Most logical
6. Arabian prince
7. Rocky mountains
8. Arab's word for hill
9. Embarrassed
10. Sounds from atop a soapbox
11. Mineral and vegetable companion
12. More competent
14. Hoosier or Hawkeye
15. Fine's partner
16. Hindu music mode
20. Begin
21. Big spender
23. First Mayor of N.Y.C.
24. British military hardware
26. Tall and skinny
27. Expression of disdain
29. Move troops into new positions
30. USMA and USNA
31. Cigar smoker's choice
32. Hairy
34. Qualify one for something
35. Put jewelry in a new setting
36. Herr heir
38. Holy, at Lourdes
41. Texas A.F.B.
42. "____ an arrow into the . . .": Longfellow
44. Letters from Athens
45. Stravinsky ballet
47. Horn or type preceder
48. Jersey or Brooklyn trailer

# 93

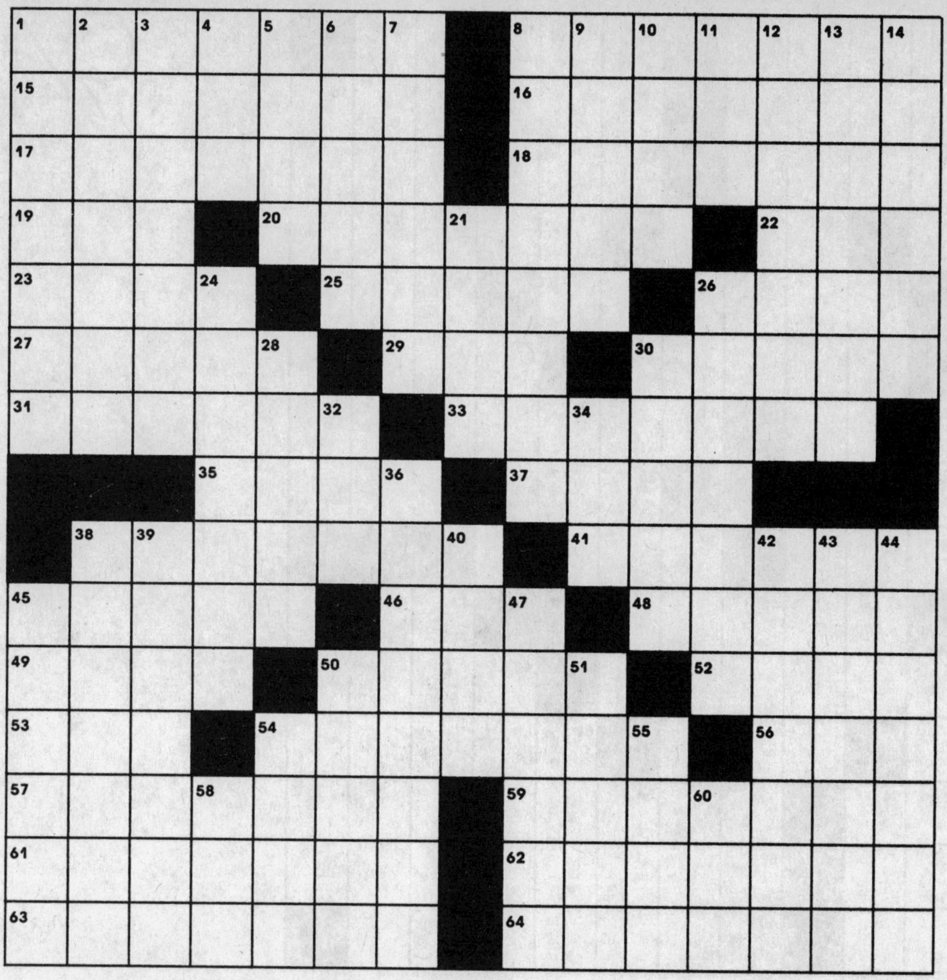

**ACROSS**

1. Sang seasonal songs
8. Malady
15. Subdue by fear or reverence
16. Sluggishness
17. Like Idlewild Airport
18. Sounds in horror films
19. Pay dirt
20. Abrupt
22. It's written on many faces
23. Annoys
25. Examine
26. Cause dander to go up
27. Writer James and ex-Met Tommie
29. Skater Babilonia
30. Amplifying device
31. Composed
33. Haunts
35. Driven obliquely, as a nail
37. Site of Pierre's chapeau
38. Baltic republic
41. Shade of blue or green
45. Relieve
46. Capek play
48. Part of a staircase
49. Still burning
50. ". . . a ____ thieves": Matthew
52. Hirsch vehicle
53. Had brunch
54. Genuine
56. Purged
57. Rush
59. Malign
61. Spring
62. Level
63. Consanguineous
64. Treacherous one

**DOWN**

1. Crowns
2. Mean
3. Backed out
4. Mouths
5. Gentle one
6. Pitchers that pour it on
7. Take it away
8. Uneasiness
9. Bring upon oneself
10. Like old flowers
11. Prior to, to Prior
12. Throwback
13. Relatives of metaphors
14. Less severe
21. Tower
24. Where to find a not-so-ancient Mariner
26. Welsh rabbit
28. Bar sight
30. Drive
32. Poetic contraction
34. Sweeter than brut
36. Emulated Peter Weir
38. Abstract
39. Respective
40. Pittypat or Polly
42. Usually
43. Gloss or concordance
44. Neptune's symbol
45. Actress Helen
47. Itineraries
50. His guide in Hades was Vergil
51. Satirical play
54. Accomplishment
55. Colleague of Bolger and Haley
58. Genetic material
60. Agt.

# 94

## ACROSS

1. Purplish red
8. Actor Biberman
13. Rogue; pirate
14. Party ____ (wet blanket)
16. Let in; insert
17. "Eat ____ . . ." (part of a proverb)
18. Uppish ones
19. Played the first card
21. Chewy roll of a kind
22. Part of MSG
23. Has it coming
25. Santa ____, CA
26. Be past-due
27. Laughing loudly
28. Part of a Latin conjugation
29. Austrian river-town
31. Turn thumbs down
33. Hit high into the air
36. Swindles
37. Washed clean
39. Many: Prefix
40. Think ahead
41. Debussy piece
43. Rebs' org. in 1860's
46. Symbol of inconsequentiality
47. Distinguished gatherings
48. Followers of upsilons
49. All that there could be
51. Memorable time
52. Buttercup's kin
53. Balkan capital
55. Like a goose
57. Ho Chi Minh City, once
58. Namely
59. City on the Aire
60. Pioneer

## DOWN

1. Bait fish
2. Autobiographical Moss Hart book
3. Portrayer of Mata Hari: 1931
4. Aphrodite's boy
5. Name for Pierre
6. Hard workers
7. Toward the front: Comb. form
8. Fitting
9. Nitwits
10. Girl in a 1916 song
11. Enticing to the opposite sex
12. One who returns after a long absence
13. ____ Beach, resort near San Luis Obispo
15. Interacts
20. Variant twosome
23. Noted So. African black activist
24. Seismic phenomena
28. Treaty partner
29. Vingt-____, gambling game
30. Snood
32. ____ -de-sac
33. Garment folds
34. Causing forgetfulness
35. Aimlessness; idleness
38. Hill's companion
39. Act of atonement
42. Swamp
43. Option
44. One in need of 39 Down
45. Up to now
47. Ecclesiastical council
48. Jeopardy
50. Spread unchecked
52. Trapper's trophy
54. Brief reply
56. Command to Rover

# 95

**ACROSS**

1. Make by hand
6. Fumeur's choice
11. Kerry's capital
12. Touch down
14. Comic kinfolk
17. Oodles
18. Haw., once
19. Seed covering
20. Tolkien's talking trees
21. Mulcts
22. Affirmative for Alphonse
23. Surface for a Bruin
24. Had the flu
25. A moon of Saturn
27. Submissive; acquiescent
29. Word with baby of flagpole
30. Touchy
32. Microwave devices
35. Dairy
39. Van Gogh milieu
40. Smokers
41. Low
42. Inlet
43. Forgo
44. Disclose, in a way
45. 10%-ers
47. Mrs. Shakespeare
48. He played Joel Cairo
49. Comic kinfolk
52. Goodies
53. Like some salads
54. End of a Churchill quartet
55. Encouraging words

**DOWN**

1. Fashions
2. Stadium features
3. "Sustineo ____," U.S.A.F. motto
4. Chemin de ____
5. Commodities category
6. Like some roads
7. Then, in Tours
8. Flinder
9. Moslem leader
10. Smoker's choice
11. On that account
13. Three in one
14. "____ Wedding Journey": Howells
15. A liqueur
16. Not so open
21. Sibelius and Nurmi
24. Radio-tube stabilizers
25. Scotto and Tebaldi
26. Inventory entry
28. Words of ken
29. Wearying period
31. Burlesque
32. French revolutionary
33. Correctly
34. Marine isopods
36. Becomes apparent
37. Reacted to a home-team touchdown
38. Joins together
40. Most lucid
43. Poznan's river
44. Undisciplined
46. Ragout
48. Forfeiture
50. "Scots, wha ____ wi' . . .": Burns
51. Shoe part

# 96

**ACROSS**

1. Columbia River youngster
5. Beetle Bailey's boss
10. Soothing stuff
14. In the Red
15. The Cow Palace, e.g.
16. Blood state: Suffix
17. Asian gulf
18. Very small employee?
20. Penniless
22. Famous missing person
23. Pickle pick
24. Supply
25. Like Lucia di Lammermoor
28. Purple writing, perhaps
29. Factory ruckus?
31. Salad of a sort
35. Cassowary's kin
36. Noun-forming suffix
37. Assayer's concern
38. Pullman strike leader
40. Seamstress does some trimming?
44. Turnpike revenue
46. Marty, offscreen
47. Feigned
50. Pre-med subj.
51. Darkling
52. Windflowers
56. Preparing to play the cello?
58. Grouse house
59. Nautically sheltered
60. Skip over
61. Disburden
62. Mamie's predecessor
63. Distance over time
64. Tied in the ring

**DOWN**

1. Heading-off spot
2. Words before were
3. Postern's locale
4. Fast time in Mecca
5. A bit of stitchery
6. A moon of Uranus
7. Tear apart
8. Serengeti sight
9. Suffer humiliation
10. Keeps out of mischief
11. Cremona artisan
12. Covered the interior
13. Sierra follower
19. Flying archer
21. Pitch provider
24. Flat on one's face
25. Cooled with cubes
26. Dog tag info
27. Slight
28. Stems
30. Triangular imperative
32. Effortless gait
33. Bellicose Olympian
34. Left on the map
39. Dens
40. Arctic transports
41. Invigorated
42. British baby buggy
43. Recited rhythmically
45. Sign of things to come
47. Make ___ at (try)
48. Oil source
49. "___ alive!"
50. Battery part
52. Rose lover
53. Cheek by jowl
54. Infinitive for Cato
55. One-pot meal
57. European high-rise

# 97

**ACROSS**

1. Place to buy a Dutch lunch
5. Shoe size
9. Sedate
14. Gaurs
15. Luck, to Louis Philippe
16. Arthur Marx
17. Eye specialist
20. Sturdy ribbed fabric
21. Puckster?
22. Chester's river
23. He searched for Franklin
24. Thumb through
25. Scorches
28. Trendy
29. Superior's Royale
33. Nimbi
34. Son of Abu Talib
35. Org. based in Mission, Kansas
36. They wait for mañana
40. Its capital is Beauvais
41. Hellenic letter
42. "You're Sixteen" singer
43. Bassoonist's purchase
44. N.T. book
45. Made a pass
46. Peruvian river
47. Mouth: Comb. form
48. ACT relative
51. A first name in fashion
52. Port of Sumatra
56. Illusionist
59. Divine love
60. Plaintiff
61. Rent
62. Yurt builder
63. Feather: Comb. form
64. Landlady in "Moon Mullins"

**DOWN**

1. Judgment Day
2. Montreal athlete
3. Annealing oven
4. Strung a racket
5. Scottish feudal lords
6. This may become spitchcock
7. Coin collector
8. Calabrese, for one
9. Tonsured
10. Touching game
11. Like a lunar sea
12. ___ dixit
13. Overlove
18. What not to take on the ice
19. Introduction
25. Flavor
26. Nobelist in 1903 and 1911
27. Cropped up
29. Overawe
30. Where Macbeth was crowned
31. Slow and solemn, to Solti
32. Quarterback Tony
37. Sheep of the mountains
38. Showed promise
39. Mount in Genesis 8:4
45. Office machine
46. Illustrious
48. Traverse
49. Ship on which Acastus sailed
50. Reds or Browns
53. It has a nucleus
54. Ex-Tiger Cash
55. "Wildfire" author
57. Kissingen, e.g.
58. In Morse, it's --.

# 98

**ACROSS**

1. Wild pig
5. Nub in yarn
9. Support
13. Vocal contingent
15. British peer
16. Storm
17. Pause
18. Timekeepers?
20. Rapunzel?
22. Rub out
23. Leghorns
24. Tennyson's "____ Arden"
25. In pieces
27. Cyclone?
30. Double
31. Dental ____
32. Artfully demure
33. Finnish poem
34. Incline
35. Feathered Arctic pirate
36. Combustion residue
37. Call up
38. Felt out of sorts
39. Cruise fare?
41. City in Utah
42. Bellini opera
43. Nautical direction
44. Old World snake
45. Tribal ruler?
49. Somnolent steer?
51. More foreboding
52. Loser to S. Grant
53. Western state: Abbr.
54. Mites
55. City on Lake Michigan
56. G-g-girl in an old song
57. Former English actor

**DOWN**

1. Hard or soft follower
2. Dairy fat substitute
3. Bus. letter abbr.
4. Teens?
5. Tractor trailers
6. Leo's lodge
7. Samovar
8. Rudolph's conservative relative?
9. Pontificate
10. Sheep tether?
11. Molding
12. Corral
14. Domain
19. Thinks, Elizabethan style
21. Formicary resident
24. Become one on the run
25. Regale
26. Kitchen aide?
27. Flaxen
28. French cathedral city
29. Pair
30. Cleopatra maid
31. Goddess of flowers
34. Rhinestone?
35. Karate move?
37. Studied attentively
38. Items of business
40. English bibliophile: 16th c.
41. Wave at Acapulco
43. Hero of a Disraeli romance
44. German hall
45. Ancient western European
46. Of wrath, to Ovid
47. Tiber tributary
48. Toothy look
49. Plead
50. Animal: Comb. form

# 99

**ACROSS**

1. Military exchange
5. Coppers: Abbr.
8. Vegetable, mineral, et al.
12. Main ingredient in menudillos
13. Prosperous
16. Tranquilize
17. Lot
18. "Dido and Aeneas," e.g.
19. Bronze: Lat.
20. Turkish measure
21. Parabolic symbol in Matthew 25
22. It's due west of Norma
23. Honorary degree held by Betty Ford
24. Public school org.
25. Danish
28. German ice
29. Pines and Man
31. Dots on a globe
33. Antiseptic
36. Unimak native
37. Orchestra section
38. Present indicative plural of "be"
39. Like certain plants or bar flies
41. Beaux ____
45. Shoot the breeze
46. Star of #1 TV sitcom, for short
47. Love, Hawaiian-style
48. Suffix with sheep or sweet
49. ____ Magnon
50. Bongo's country
51. Adjective for victim of 33 Down
55. Revise
56. Chinese revolutionary
57. "I Got Plenty o' Nuthin' " singer
58. City leveled in W.W. II
59. Certain vote
60. Superlative suffixes

**DOWN**

1. Put cash down in advance
2. NHL team
3. Something found in a trunk
4. Home state of Dale Evans
5. Group that backed R. E. Lee
6. Check
7. General for 5 Down
8. Statutes: Abbr.
9. ____ trice (quickly)
10. Floor covering
11. Saccate
12. Ponies, to a linguist
14. Found
15. Exigencies
22. Classifies
25. Wealthy ruler
26. Atmosphere: Comb. form
27. Word with barn or back
30. Sparid foot fish
32. Site of early nuclear research
33. Malnutrition in infants
34. Mahout's charge
35. Letter representing "hundred"
38. Those born on April 1
40. Small foot, commonly
42. Young or Stack
43. Leather straps
44. Puppeteer Becker
47. Platonic love
49. Piazza greeting
52. Engine part: Abbr.
53. Shoe size
54. Chromosome part

100

## ACROSS

1. Magnesium silicate
5. One striper, for short
8. Young oyster
12. Comfort, in Calabria
13. Squamous
15. Mauna Loa goddess
16. "Marty" director
17. Lazy one
18. Mediterranean port
19. One against razing historic places
22. Loop vehicles
23. Renown
24. Agile
26. Exclamation of disgust
27. Ruined
31. Shady dealer, in Soho
32. NOW's goal
33. Crescent-shaped
34. Advance actions
37. Giggle
38. Kind of hold or nail
39. Washingtons in wallets
40. Sober
41. Homophone for what oarsmen do
42. Leopold or Mischa
43. Edmonton pro
45. Some AMA members
46. In a pompous manner
53. Leah's third son
54. New Guinea's Gulf of ____
55. Toledo's lake
56. Beame and Fortas
57. Characteristic style
58. Rail
59. Pub missile
60. IBM competitor
61. Acamar or Acrab

## DOWN

1. Pack down lightly
2. Kanten
3. What a tourist may drop
4. Person like Rachel Carson
5. Pertaining to Neanderthals
6. Provide arrows with feathers
7. Alleged inventor of Russian alphabet
8. Ad lib's quality
9. Elfin being
10. "____, poor Yorick . . ."
11. Tupik, e.g.
13. Letter opener
14. A third of MCCXV
20. English isle
21. Residue of old ropes
24. Sail extender
25. Cynosure in Florence's duomo
26. Lippo Lippi, e.g.
28. Velvetlike cloth
29. Complete
30. Opera by J'Erlanger
31. N.Y.C. and S.F.
32. Behave humanly
33. Cobb or Grant of films
35. Changed the decor
36. Excessive sentimentality
41. Put cargo back aboard
42. Copy
44. Fat
45. Largest of the Marianas
46. Tall flower, for short
47. Midianite king
48. Verify
49. Status follower
50. Pony
51. Ankara coin
52. Mercury's 88 days

## 101

### ACROSS

1. Pen noises
7. "Friendship," to a Texan
12. He, she and it
14. "What ___ of work is a man!": Hamlet
16. Leave in the lurch
17. Brook
18. Hill dweller
19. Jones's prize in 1779
21. Depressed
22. Almost
24. Eldritch
25. German article
26. ___ de Lion
28. Female ruff
29. Havelock or Dock
30. Groups of nine
32. Mull over
34. Acid initials
35. Former Greek V.I.P.
36. Important Rialto activity
40. Peaked
44. ___ podridas
45. Puncture prefix
47. "Le ___ d'Arthur"
48. Grande and Bravo
49. Words of annoyance
51. Trim
52. D.C. dweller
53. Pub area
55. Iron or Golden
56. French President in F.D.R.'s day
58. Dog or hound
60. Flouts
61. Swizzle sticks
62. Threefold
63. Cuisinier's specialty

### DOWN

1. California food fish
2. Versatile Dutch musician: 1855–1932
3. Número ___
4. Entre ___
5. Pupil
6. Some sleepers
7. One of the Osmonds
8. Major work
9. Do soldering
10. Stretchable
11. Like some voyages
12. Caper
13. Gin
15. Firstborn
20. Harbor sight
23. Two Mexican provisional presidents
25. "Invisible Man" author: 1952
27. Sari wearers
29. Zimbalist
31. Rather
33. Organ for eavesdropping
36. Colors similar to sweet william
37. Food
38. Inarticulate utterance
39. Irving's "The World According to ___"
40. Paper dolls
41. Played host
42. Whatnot
43. Impedes
46. John Dickson and Vikki
49. "___ Macabre"
50. Girl's name meaning "wisdom"
53. Word with stile or table
54. Rich soil
57. Defendants: Law
59. ___ Lippo Lippi

# 102

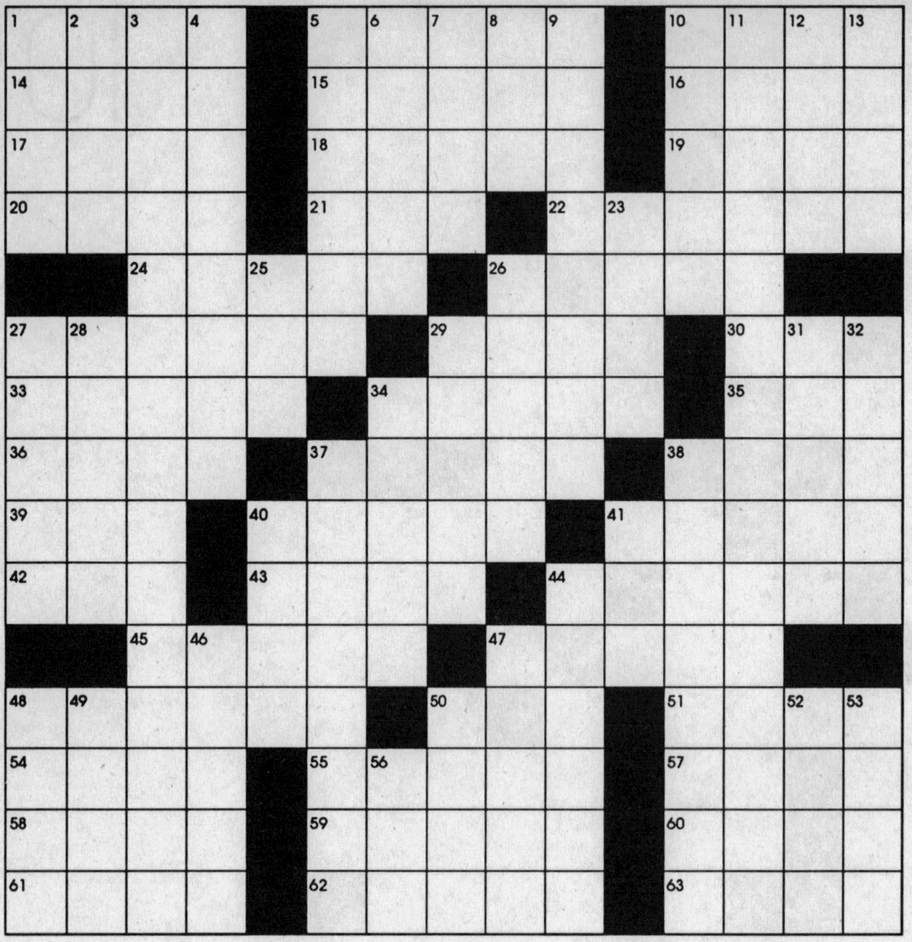

## ACROSS

1. Cry
5. Gather
10. Robeson or Dunbar
14. Largest land mass
15. African tribe
16. Grand Ole ___
17. Tiller
18. Audibly
19. Burn
20. Fire or close-out follower
21. Rather or McGrew
22. ". . . Talk ___ of Me and Thee": "Rubáiyát"
24. Filling
26. Prepare to pray
27. Typewriter roller
29. Yesterday, in Ypres
30. Sci. suffix
33. Lover
34. Stupid
35. For
36. Frosted
37. Scottish coronach
38. Support
39. Fairy queen
40. Tailless amphibians
41. Fertilizer
42. ___ Faithful
43. Ancient marauders
44. Nat ___, rebellious slave
45. Employment
47. Softened
48. Out ___ (at large)
50. Calloway
51. Opposite of yep
54. Salem ___, black Revolutionary War hero
55. A.M. buzzer
57. Fitzgerald
58. Inter ___
59. Dark brown
60. Guesswork, for short
61. Legree's weapon
62. Black-eyed or Lazy
63. Iranian ex-monarch

## DOWN

1. Exclamations of contempt
2. Out on the Coral
3. He wrote "The Souls of Black Folk": 1903
4. Wailed
5. Mideast oil-refining center
6. Archipelago or peninsula
7. Unknown auth.
8. R-V connection
9. African native
10. Pocket, in Paris
11. Memorable black labor leader
12. ___ Mountains
13. Orpheus played it
23. "The Way We ___"
25. Zodiac sign
26. M. L. Jr.'s kin
27. Boxer Carnera
28. Kind of color
29. Drives together
31. Hag
32. Deep sleep
34. Actress Keaton
37. Frederick ___, black abolitionist
38. Freedom from admixture
40. Native of Bangkok
41. Kind of feeling or issue
44. Role played by Cicely Tyson
46. Vaughan
47. "West Side Story" song
48. Gem
49. Vincent Lopez favorite
50. Headgear
52. Appeal
53. Every's partner
56. Rumanian monetary unit

# 103

**ACROSS**

1. Methodical studies
9. Photographer's gear
15. Aromatic plant
16. Undergo again
17. One of the Leagues
18. Paint
19. More urgent
20. Beaten by Fischer
22. George Gershwin's brother
23. Business abbrs.
24. Places
25. Position of control
26. Time period
27. Exert influence over
28. Chief city of Liguria
29. Word with church or play
30. Wine-cask deposit
31. Julius and others
35. Type of vacuum tube
36. Sharp
37. Alexander or John Paul II
38. Lingua franca
39. Deals with
40. Corporeal duct
43. Biblical patriarch
44. Explorer La ___
45. Swiss capital
46. Choice: Abbr.
47. Gay ___
48. Cádiz chicken
49. Explosive
51. Ploy
53. Potential
54. Synthetic-rubber ingredient
55. "___ is Eternal Delight": Blake
56. United firmly

**DOWN**

1. Nova Scotia, once
2. Decision for new parents
3. Fine arbitrarily
4. Folk histories
5. Mythical Norse giant
6. As in the original
7. Ancient neighbors of Babylonians
8. Javits, for one
9. Ashes
10. Split apart
11. Wharf-union initials
12. Olive stuffing
13. Too big a burden
14. English writer: 1873–1956
21. Downing Street number
24. Twice 21 Down
25. Mister, in Munich
27. Type size
28. Winner at Saratoga: 1777
30. Home of the brave
31. Fund-raising event by a P.T.A.
32. Unanimously
33. Bleach
34. "The ___ rim dips . . . ": Coleridge
35. "We aim ___"
37. Controversial discussion
39. Club or parlor follower
40. Relative of plush
41. Dahl or Francis
42. Nodded off noisily
44. Like a tar's speech
45. Brook or stream
47. "Turnandot" character
48. Condiment in Calabria
50. Threefold: Comb. form
52. ___ de guerre

# 104

## ACROSS

1. Soho swell
5. Broadcast seed
10. Fiery gem
14. Bireme power
15. ___ là? (Who goes there?)
16. Pianist Peter
17. Randy Matson, e.g.
19. Asgard's lord
20. Buchwald and Ade
21. Weather word in L.A.
22. Person
23. Patisserie item
24. Frantic
27. Mal de ___ (seasickness)
28. Floor supports
30. Nile denizen
32. Serial
35. Food fish
37. Soup-and-fish
38. Gadget
39. Rule from the bench
42. Philippine island or port
43. Crudely chipped flint
44. Borden weapon
46. Mat. time
47. Son of Troy's founder
48. Activate
50. Durable fabric
52. Kind of soldier
56. Choir member
57. Appears suddenly
58. Vienna, to a Berliner
59. Vertiginous
60. See to
61. Rorem and Sparks
62. Singer Helen
63. Former spouses

## DOWN

1. Twaddle
2. Honolulu's isle
3. Out of
4. Camera-lens setting
5. Ushers
6. Extend
7. Humorous
8. Arden et al.
9. ___ es Salaam
10. Of names
11. Plays the pompous precisionist
12. Neighbor of Nev.
13. Unattended
18. Nanny pushes it
21. Hurl
23. Ill-wisher
24. Isinglass
25. Withstand
26. Incoherent
28. Put next to
29. Latino dance
31. Kitchen helpers
33. Sine ___ non
34. Tactless one
36. Execration
40. Pronoun
41. To a T
45. Piccadilly Circus statue
48. Destroy documents
49. Jane Fonda's 1971 Oscar movie
50. Begin to be perceived
51. Author Wiesel
52. Remedy
53. Culmination
54. Franchot of former film fame
55. Pass catchers
57. Preclude

# 105

## ACROSS

1. "Get lost!"
6. Garment often carrying a message
12. Artist's ruler
14. Teaser
15. ". . . ___ spite": Hamlet
16. Footstool
18. Spoken
19. Simpleton
21. Was conveyed
22. Chess champion: 1960–61
23. Spuds
25. Small bird
26. Stunning stories
29. Ordinal number endings
30. Fragrant
32. Subtracted
34. World problem
35. Criterion for making a decision
37. Perfumes or their bases
40. Produce
44. Video for a price
45. Sky Altar
46. Cast constantly in related roles
47. Prince Valiant's son
48. Lawn tools
51. In medias ___
52. Each, in Ecuador
54. Combat area
55. Home for pigeons
56. Lightweight cotton
58. Put on a list for jury duty
60. Building wing
61. Cowboys, at times
62. Got the drift
63. Dehisced

## DOWN

1. Like the mean streets
2. Spiral
3. Title Selassie held
4. Verbal negative contraction
5. Interposed between those opposed
6. "High steaks"
7. Nymph chaser
8. Popular favorite
9. "Believe ___ Not": Ripley
10. Less immediate
11. Off-season baseball action
12. Blew one's horn
13. Escapade
17. Meshy
20. The ultimate
24. Shakespearean poem
27. Maestro Xavier
28. Sinuous figure
31. Suspicious
33. "___ the season . . ."
34. Berliner's article
36. Erudition
37. Without delay
38. N.Z. evergreens
39. Reformer executed for heresy in 1536
41. Clad for cooking
42. Wobble
43. Lemons on wheels
45. Seeing eye to eye
49. Poet painted by Giotto
50. Subject of a book by Margaret Mead: 1928
53. Preacher's last word
55. Job for Mason or Trent
57. Porter's "___ De-lovely"
59. Kind of corn or art

# 106

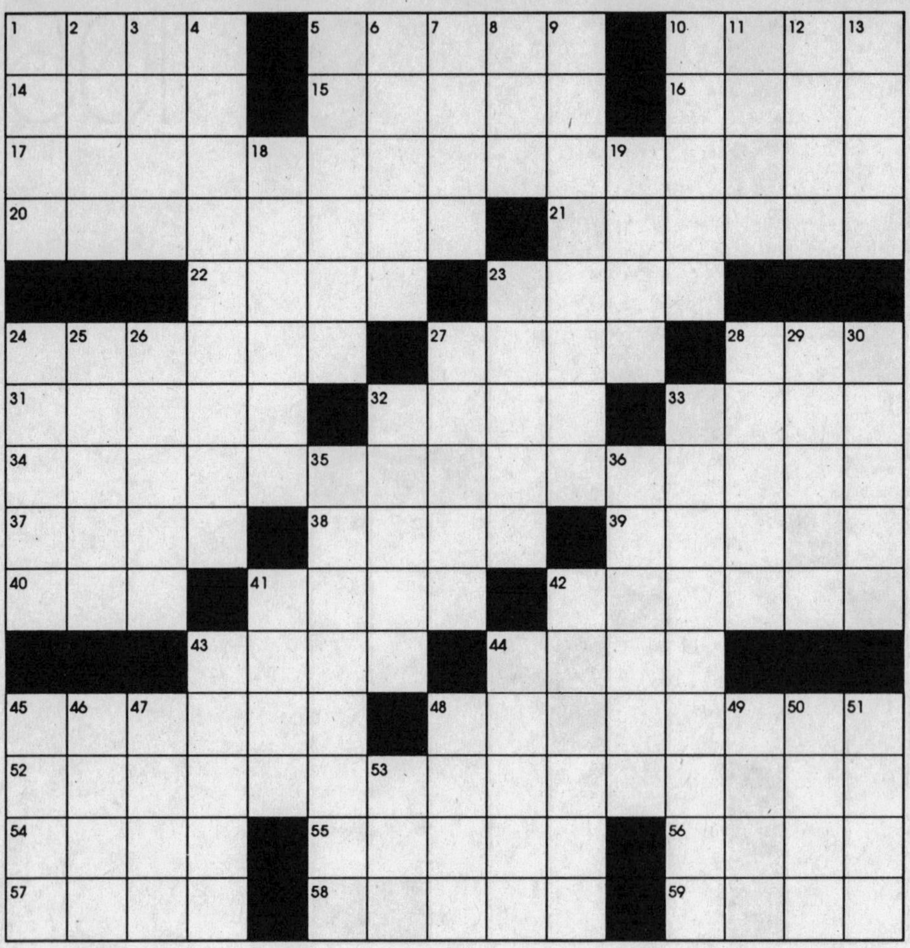

**ACROSS**

1. Play tricks
5. Test one's moral fiber
10. TV's Parker
14. Gulf of ___
15. ___-propre (self-esteem)
16. Mideastern republic since 1958: Var.
17. Italian physician and educator: 1870–1952
20. Junctions of the skull
21. Has dinner at home
22. Eight furlongs
23. Amphibians
24. Massenet opera
27. Amerind of Manitoba
28. Handle clumsily
31. ___ Domingo
32. Evening, in Paris
33. Legal offenses
34. Head of the "Flying Tigers"
37. Suffix used in names of acids
38. Geological divisions
39. Central Caucasian
40. Son of Odin
41. Narrow valley
42. Henrik and family
43. Theater section
44. Snick's partner
45. More irritable
48. Closes, as a passage
52. Author of "Has Man a Future?": 1961
54. Poet translated by FitzGerald
55. Marsh birds
56. U.S. satellite
57. Time when many "punch in"
58. Figure
59. Distort or distorted

**DOWN**

1. What a door is in
2. Month on an Israeli's calendar
3. Balzac's "Le ___ Goriot"
4. Puzzling
5. Mexican fare
6. Act like Duse
7. Freeman of the screen
8. Stock option
9. Arborescent plant
10. Ring weapons
11. Youngest of the gods
12. Draped garment
13. The depth of beauty
18. Musical key
19. Cloy
23. Canal, city and lake
24. Broad necktie
25. Mass meeting, sometimes peppy
26. "The bombs bursting ___"
27. Composer of "Over There"
28. Intermission
29. Mel or Hervey
30. Pianist André
32. Rocky debris
33. Workers in certain parlors
35. Submerged marine plant
36. Coveted annual prizes, for short
41. Church or theater following
42. Formed by stamping
43. British quart
44. Abandon a project
45. "Heaven's ___ vault . . .": Shelley
46. Kind of john
47. Pilastro or Paradiso
48. The Oder, to Czechs
49. Rolltop
50. If not
51. Side dish
53. Japanese dance-drama

# 107

**ACROSS**

1. Twitches
5. ___ myrtle (flowering shrub)
10. Replicas, for short
14. Melville novel
15. Son or brother of Osiris
16. Yearn
17. Legislative body
19. Catface
20. Part of V.I.P.
21. Pungent
22. Tuscan commune
23. River of Albania
24. The Queen's pilots
27. Thus, in Dundee
28. Amounts; portions
30. Saucers, maybe
32. Strong, spicy Irish cordial
35. Alphabetizes, e.g.
37. On the ___ vive
38. Oft heard
39. Nicknames
42. Vous ___
43. Informal alliance
44. Meth. or Pres.
46. Schedule abbr.
47. Karenina
48. Wedge-shaped piece
50. Counterfeit
52. Gave ear to
56. Leaf angle
57. Willful
58. Word on the wall
59. Prepare a cannon for firing
60. Ooze
61. M.I.T. grads
62. Prosit or skoal
63. Luge, e.g.

**DOWN**

1. Pith helmet
2. Moslem leader
3. Business abbr.
4. Strains for single singers
5. Mansion
6. Style of architecture
7. Where the action is
8. Fourth-down play
9. Atlanta's time
10. Allure
11. Stress
12. Carbonize
13. Montenegrin
18. Spring bloomer
21. Qaddafi and Sadat
23. Scheduled
24. Singer Columbo
25. "___ and his money . . ."
26. Patient under provocation
28. Relinquishment documents
29. Lace end
31. Garrotes
33. Neighbor of Ont.
34. "For ___ jolly good . . ."
36. Hasso from Stockholm
40. In the capacity of
41. Dessert
45. Libertine
48. Virtuous wife in Jonson's "Volpone"
49. Come to ___ (agree at last)
50. Kudos
51. Covered-wagon team
52. Demigod
53. Sparable, e.g.
54. Peut-___ (Parisian's) "perhaps"
55. Accomplishment
57. Cabinet section: Abbr.

# 108

**ACROSS**

1. Alamo commander
7. Proposal
12. Loner by choice
13. Valuable East Indian trees
15. Careful motorist
18. Makes patches
19. Hill's partner
20. Town of water-into-wine miracle
21. One of Jason's Argonauts
22. De Mille of film fame
23. Band date
24. Clockmaker Terry
25. Poe name
26. Column
28. Spanish wife
30. Wobbled
32. Mr. Fixit
34. Sea of the Bermuda Triangle
37. The very thing
41. Comes to heel
42. $100 bill
44. Sticky liquid
45. Foot, to Fabius
46. Flattens by hammering
47. French roast
48. Kitchen spread
50. Concerning
51. Material from flax
52. Good reason for a citation
55. Prefix for sphere
56. Golden hued
57. Lecherous man
58. Hankers

**DOWN**

1. Pedal
2. Desist
3. Closing words
4. Sauterne and Beaujolais
5. "Beauty is ___ own excuse for being"
6. Beer glass
7. Youngman gag
8. He ousted Fulgencio
9. ___-de-lance
10. Heroic
11. Despoiler
12. Small whirls
14. Like some nonagenarians
16. Groups in summer jams
17. Vented fury
22. Sounds from claques
25. Districts
26. Kind of highway
27. Halves of a score
29. Specialty of Dionysus
31. Issues
33. Steep funicular railway
34. Deep sleep
35. White poplars
36. Pares surgically
38. British schoolboy
39. Undeveloped fingerprints
40. Surrey topper
43. Sometime
46. Devoutness
47. Moon or Spoon
49. Gumbo vegetable
51. Money in Milan
53. Long. partner
54. Muse regretfully

# 109

## ACROSS

**1.** Depend on
**5.** "___, the Beloved Country"
**8.** Turned down at the corner
**12.** ___vitae (brandy)
**13.** Quaker's pronoun
**14.** Bellowing
**15.** Depressed mood
**16.** Far from apathetic
**18.** Catch off base
**19.** Playbill list
**20.** Righted a wrong
**21.** "___labor and to wait": Longfellow
**23.** Eastern visitor to the U.S. in '79
**24.** Scale notes
**25.** Autumnal sound
**27.** Sharpen
**30.** Tranquilizing agents
**34.** Sierra ___
**35.** Practice a jet pilot's art
**36.** ___ fire (electric discharge)
**38.** Poznań, to Berliners
**39.** ___ steel
**41.** Paving block
**42.** Rockefeller, in N.Y.C.
**43.** Letters at the helm
**44.** Hawkeye's home
**46.** Did some engraving
**50.** Diva Maria
**52.** Appia, Latina, etc.
**53.** The ___ Affair: 1797
**55.** Binding contract
**57.** Grain sorghum
**58.** Thread one's way
**59.** Hacks
**60.** Joie de vivre
**61.** Rubber tree
**62.** State bird of Hawaii

## DOWN

**1.** Float
**2.** Peer
**3.** Fencer's sudden thrust
**4.** Buffalo's relative
**5.** Word with cedar or hope
**6.** Touch up old masters
**7.** Slangy assent
**8.** "Divina Commedia" poet
**9.** He panicked the U.S. in '38
**10.** Book by Doris Lessing
**11.** Roof edge
**13.** Surveying instrument
**17.** Pledge at court
**19.** Native of Canea
**22.** O'Hara novel: 1949
**26.** "The law is a ___ idiot": Dickens
**28.** Methuselah's longevity rival
**29.** Dick Tracy' girlfriend
**30.** Nitwits
**31.** Cry at a Greek orgy
**32.** Moonshine man
**33.** Gilet or jerkin
**34.** Dolt in "Of Mice and Men"
**37.** Destroyers, in Navy lingo
**40.** Unimportant
**42.** Señora's domain
**45.** Engaged in, as war
**47.** Weeping stone figure
**48.** Napoleon's lot: 1814
**49.** Bob ___, singer from Hibbing, Minn.
**50.** Brought to bay
**51.** Busy as ___
**54.** Torrid or Frigid
**56.** Inst. at Fort Worth
**57.** Kingsley's "___ in White"

# 110

## ACROSS

1. Rustic
6. Coagulates
10. Kind of bean
14. Persians, today
15. Part of Q.E.D.
16. "___ the mornin' to you!"
17. Bar on a wagon
19. "___ plaisir!"
20. Name for a Lamb
21. Abruzzi cowboy
23. Saharan nomad
26. Soothe
27. Athletes at Williams
28. "Caught you!"
30. Monogram of a famous suffragette
31. W.W. II arena
32. Roman rooms
34. "But only God can make ___"
38. Barn areas for flailing
41. Principals
42. Bargains
43. Horse pest
44. Brevity is its soul
46. Part of Montana's motto
47. Portend
48. Part of C.O.D.
50. Fan
52. He puts plates on platers
54. Pub order
55. Biting
56. Sudden idea
61. Three, in Thüringen
62. Former official name of Ireland
63. Statesman
64. Valet or maid: Abbr.
65. Concordes
66. Trials

## DOWN

1. Laughter, in Lyon
2. Swiss canton of William Tell fame
3. Sprinted
4. Causes choler
5. De Gaulle's birthplace
6. "___ horse!"
7. Slip a cog
8. Toward the left: Comb. form
9. Big bargains
10. Disconnected, as notes
11. Stars that brighten and fade
12. David Frye is one
13. Somewhat, in music
18. Half of a fourth
22. Juntos
23. Rake parts
24. "___ Organization," Townsend book
25. Now, to a niño
26. "___, Harvest Moon," 1908 song
29. Waterless
32. St. Francis' town
33. Culture medium
35. Mechanical man
36. Wash away
37. A component of liquor
39. English king: 1461–83
40. Money in Haarlem
45. Pindar's home
47. Word with club or party
48. Colonial announcer
49. Root used in perfumery
51. Start
52. Crazes
53. Brazilian state
54. Crusty concoctions
57. Word with op or pop
58. Army togs, for short
59. Soak flax
60. Dalloway or Miniver

**ACROSS**

1. River of Czechoslovakia
5. "___ the Ball"
10. Island in the Aleutians
14. Give up
15. Sound loudly
16. Idle
17. Uttered
18. Farm buildings
19. Part of A.D.
20. Author of "For Colored Girls . . ."
23. Cluny product
24. Sample
25. "___ Dan," rock group
28. Like Noah's animals
31. Pooh's creator
32. Tree with fluttering leaves
35. Seine sight
36. Incite
37. Borders
38. Stinging insect
39. Latin word, often placed in brackets
40. Cobblers' equipment
41. Mountain ridge
42. Crazy Carroll character
44. Not so far away
45. County in Tennessee
47. ___ monster
48. Author of "Poem (No Name) No. 3"
52. Kind of spice
53. Town in New Mexico
54. College in New York
56. "___ for All Seasons"
57. Exult; crow
58. Founder of the Fathers of Oratory
59. Slippery ones
60. Dispatches
61. Brief look

**DOWN**

1. Military sch.
2. College administrator
3. Blue-pencil
4. Fragrant
5. Jurisdiction of a monastery chief
6. Chip off, as paint
7. Noxious weed, in the Bible
8. Painter Max
9. Forms anew
10. Jack Lemmon film: 1972
11. Varieties of mandarin oranges
12. Fork part
13. One: Sp.
21. Tony of boxing fame
22. Wise ___ owl
25. Tennis stroke
26. Shinbone
27. Kind of engineer
29. Make very happy
30. Discourage
32. Newspaper parts
33. N.C.O.
34. Part of Livy's leg
37. I.R.S. interest
38. Expressing grief or pain
40. Escape gradually
41. According to: It.
43. Subway fares
44. Hyenalike animals
46. Equal: Fr.
47. Spoil
48. "No ___ in the Street," 1972 Baldwin novel
49. "Oh, Lawd, ___ my way"
50. Coward
51. Calvary initials
52. Miss West
55. Intention

# 112

**ACROSS**

1. With ___ breath
6. Mother of Chastity
10. Peak
14. Playwright's ploy
15. Pelt
16. Way of going
17. Wallflower
20. Golfers' needs
21. Truly!
22. Single
23. Donates, à la Carnegie
25. Type of admiral or guard
27. Poet Ogden
29. More down-at-heel
32. Power unit, for short
35. Saw parts
37. Hairdo
38. Rustics ripe for ruses
42. German article
43. Helots' medieval kin
44. Grade below bee minus
45. Less zaftig
48. Gulp of gin
50. Anon
51. Role Flagstad often had
55. Ceasar's "ego," to a Berliner
57. Attaches
61. Geese, in Grenoble
62. Silly person
65. Result of a speeding ticket
66. About 2,000 feet of film
67. Cape ___ Islands
68. Form of mental discipline
69. Confessor's earful
70. Remove

**DOWN**

1. Sew loosely
2. Pale
3. "Beat"
4. Con follower
5. Phrontistery
6. Chew the rag
7. Drake's Golden ___
8. Advantage
9. Idolize
10. Past
11. Relating to heat
12. Carriage
13. Suffix with Jean or Nan
18. Mug
19. ___ fixe
24. A teakettle inspired him
26. Island of the Andreanof group
28. Novelist Georgette
29. Gives a wide berth to
30. Lightweight champ before Joe Gans
31. Multiflora, e.g.
32. "Easy ___," old radio favorite
33. Drudgery
34. Like tough jobs
36. Cookbook abbr.
39. Nautilus name
40. Sound on L.I. Sound
41. Greek letters
46. Lot's son
47. Nobelist in Medicine: 1954
49. Peanut
52. Scales in the sky
53. These outdo words
54. A Lauder
55. Doubtful
56. Sister of Euterpe
58. Teutonic trio
59. British carbine
60. Some landscapes
63. Lillie or Arthur
64. "___ Got a Secret"

# 113

**ACROSS**

1. Worthless matter
6. Deejay's stock in trade
9. Game fish
13. Spokes of a wheel
14. Khachaturian
16. Leave out
17. Words on a switch
18. Interlaced
19. Paraffinic
20. To an oyster, it's like a malady
23. Heavy weight
24. "___ my case"
25. President of Syria
29. Range player
30. Devilkin
32. Compass pt.
33. Prairie wolf
36. Ovid's "I love"
37. DXV divided by V
38. Proofreader's theme?
41. "As Maine ___ . . ."
42. Cry of amused surprise
43. Not in a state of dishabille
44. Start of the Musketeers' slogan
45. Simian
46. Yankee manager after Stengel
47. Songstress from Melbourne
49. Generally recognized
51. Have a deed
54. With 26 Down, song for French washerwomen?
57. Minnelli
60. Grazing lands
61. "When I Take My Sugar ___"
62. Ham's finale
63. Landed
64. U.S.L.T.A. star
65. Complaint
66. Article in Aragon
67. Bells the cat

**DOWN**

1. Native of Zagreb
2. Finnish port, to the Swedes
3. Embellish
4. Name for a poodle
5. Adjective for Hawaii
6. Bailey or Belli
7. Stage stuff
8. Take a shortcut
9. Rose and Orange
10. M.D.'s group
11. Milne's "Now We Are ___"
12. Farm enclosure
15. "Cry ___ River"
21. Cradle site in a nursery song
22. Discuss, mod style
26. See 54 Across
27. "And this shall be ___ unto you"
28. Believer of a kind
29. "It's a ___ life!"
31. Decimate, as an army
33. Castro's companion
34. "___ mio"
35. Road sign
36. Finnish novelist: 1861–1921
37. Chanticleer
39. "The curfew tolls ___ . . .": Gray
40. Like Alumni Day participants
45. Scottish county or port
46. Lifts
48. Happy, e.g.
50. Author Marsh
51. Aquatic fun-lover
52. A journalistic "W"
53. ___-foot oil
55. Dock org.
56. PBS series
57. Arcing shot
58. "___ Gotta Be Me," 1969 song
59. Ex, wye, ___

# 114

## ACROSS

**1.** Biographer Arthur or Barbara
**5.** Essex, Oakland, etc.
**9.** O'Neill's "___ Millions"
**14.** Frangipani, e.g.
**15.** Recipe verb
**16.** Cyrano's feeling for Roxane
**17.** Mogul capital until 1658
**18.** Impervious to attack
**20.** What satiety sans variety breeds
**22.** Operatic prince
**23.** Plumber's installation
**24.** "Golden Treasury" item
**26.** "Queen of tides"
**28.** Heroine of "The Rivals"
**33.** "Bel___," Burnford novel: 1978
**35.** Danish composer
**36.** One of Ozzie and Harriet's boys
**37.** Young or Mature
**39.** Monogram of the "Over There" man
**41.** Devoured voraciously
**42.** Peter and a Wolfe
**43.** Asymmetrical
**45.** ___ Dai, former Vietnamese emperor
**46.** Specialist in gem engraving
**50.** Slangy assent
**51.** Mewls or pules
**53.** St.-Tropez is one
**56.** Bill ___ (Jose Jimenez)
**58.** Pastry that means "flash of lightning" in French
**60.** Pertaining to pleading of lawsuits
**63.** Philippine betel
**64.** Jibe
**65.** Town near Teramo
**66.** Tallow; fat: Sp.
**67.** Bests or worsts
**68.** Site of U. of San Marcos
**69.** Wagon on tracks

## DOWN

**1.** Blame-bearer
**2.** Rims
**3.** Worship of noblemen
**4.** Intelligent
**5.** Abruptly join a confab
**6.** Virgil classic: Abbr.
**7.** Musician Shankar
**8.** Hester Prynne's "A"
**9.** Very large, as handwriting
**10.** "___ my brother's keeper?"
**11.** Post-shower garb
**12.** Choose what is choice
**13.** City on the Oka
**19.** Koestler's "Darkness at ___"
**21.** Waiters in the wings
**25.** Pungent taste
**27.** Nice night
**29.** Truman's birthplace
**30.** This gets the party going
**31.** Predatory bird
**32.** Photog's solution
**33.** Clanged
**34.** Isl. country
**38.** Apologetic word
**40.** Unguis
**44.** Tragic heroine
**47.** Mouthward
**48.** Kindly or friendly
**49.** Army poster verb
**52.** Name for a lion
**53.** Strikebreaker
**54.** Trainbearer
**55.** Breeze, to Brutus
**57.** Starter on B'way
**59.** Cat-swinger's need
**61.** Word with smart or jet
**62.** Fortify

# 115

**ACROSS**

1. Low
5. Imbricated
10. Youth changed into a bird, in a Greek myth
14. Medical suffix
15. Cat-___-tails
16. Speedy
17. Reds' place
19. Q-V connection
20. Chocolate sources
21. Slipper
23. Disinclination to act
25. Ohio university
26. Annoys
28. Soak
31. "Sharp as ___-edged sword": Proverbs
34. Hit the golf ball askew
36. Qua ___ (here and there): It.
37. Diamonds, e.g.
38. Period
39. His temple is shown in "Aïda"
40. Busy agcy. in April
41. Guides
44. Middies' inst.
45. What departing sailors weigh
47. Kind of system
49. Of stopovers for caravans
51. Member of a certain band
55. Fainting spells
58. Scene of "Beau Geste"
59. Kernel covering
60. Cistern on a street
62. Netman Nastase
63. On the market
64. Drop the QB
65. State bird of Hawaii
66. ICURYY4me is one
67. Japanese outcasts

**DOWN**

1. Lodi lawn game
2. Cambodian, e.g.
3. Because
4. Gourmet's delicacy
5. Throat parts
6. Hostelry
7. Writer O'Flaherty
8. Insect: Comb. form
9. Destruction of a god
10. House style
11. Cribs
12. Italian wine area
13. Daze
18. Jot
22. Funny fellow
24. Tree-lined walk
27. Forefathers
29. Sinatra's cohorts
30. Music to Carson's ears
31. Where SEATO once functioned
32. Pivot
33. "Forward" is its motto
35. Mosconi ploy
39. Raise by mechanical power
41. Merely O.K.
42. Vehicle for a modicum of freight
43. Spaces left by lumberjacks
46. Chipmunk
48. Swift horse
50. Rent
52. Attacks
53. Jong
54. Classes
55. Climb, in a way
56. Think Dec. 25, and you'll get it
57. Uneducated guess
61. TV actor Gulager

# 116

## ACROSS

1. Crazes
5. Hidden store
10. Confabulates
14. Blind as ___
15. "The ___," Tryon novel
16. Greeting at sea
17. Verne character
18. Sovereignty
19. "Meet ___ St. Louis"
20. Kind of flight
22. CCLI doubled
23. Doe, to stag
24. Narrator of 1,001 tales
27. Boyfriend of Tillie the Toiler
29. Ear: Comb. form
30. "Unaccustomed ___ am . . ."
31. Elderly
33. Rosy-fingered goddess
35. The Wright way to go
40. Tale told by 24 Across
44. One of the Jets' Super Bowl heroes
45. Series-ending abbr.
46. Lemon, to a horse trader
47. Côte d'Azur season
50. Chinese pagoda
52. Abstract being
53. "___ and the Jinni" (tale told by 24 Across)
58. Bond St. place
59. School org.
60. Divisions of long poems
63. Exploding star
64. Martinique peak
66. Rooftop chanticleer
67. Guinness
68. Carpenter's tool
69. Road to the Rubicon
70. Saucy
71. Abrasive cloth
72. Just in case, negatively speaking

## DOWN

1. Certain club members
2. Incite in crime
3. Inlay with gold or silver
4. Impassive
5. Clad tightly, like Lancelot
6. She comes "hot from Hell": Shak.
7. Reprove
8. Exodus
9. Pyle and Banks
10. Microgram
11. In the lead
12. Nightclub
13. "Lang" follower
21. Before sigma
25. Holler's companion
26. "___-Dee-Doo-Dah"
27. Religious service
28. Not fer
32. Two-bagger: Abbr.
34. Nominative pronoun
36. Cornet mouthpiece
37. American man of letters
38. Person, place or thing
39. Units of work
41. Hebrew A
42. Ending with cigar or wagon
43. Not quite
48. Imbibe habitually
49. High respect
51. "Oh, I ___ cook . . ."
53. Oarlock
54. Wait close by
55. Period of time, in astronomy
56. Bisect
57. Smithy's equipment
58. Ginger cookie
61. "Snake eyes," at Vegas
62. Famed muralist
65. Always, in poetry

# 117

## ACROSS

**1.** Sellers, in Spain
**6.** Safari blind
**10.** He succeeded H.C.H.
**13.** Become a member
**14.** Vizier's superior
**15.** Bumpkin or lumpkin
**17.** Airplane hazard
**18.** Chutzpah
**19.** Shells, for short
**20.** Expression involving an ultimatum
**23.** Munchausen's specialty
**24.** "___ your heart out"
**25.** Word with tag or rear
**26.** Scottish precipitation
**27.** Star of "Born Free"
**29.** Deposed
**31.** Such, in Sevilla
**32.** Grounds
**34.** Skirt accents
**36.** Lack of an alternative
**40.** Join securely
**41.** Prefix with act or form
**42.** Habit
**43.** ___ favorite
**46.** ". . . What Am I Doing in the ___?"
**50.** Middle: Abbr.
**51.** Sturgeon product
**52.** Cooking pan, Chinese style
**54.** Command to a canine
**55.** Duo in a disagreeable decision
**59.** Northern waterway
**60.** ___ animo (with evil intent)
**61.** Mystery-story ingredient
**62.** Tastes
**63.** Ratite bird
**64.** Forty follower
**65.** This, in Tours
**66.** Skillful
**67.** They have a sense re coming events

## DOWN

**1.** Mortar's sidekick
**2.** Involve necessarily
**3.** Play ducks and ___ with (squander)
**4.** Part
**5.** Dragon with Kukla and Fran
**6.** Bred
**7.** Poet translated by FitzGerald
**8.** Painter of "The Gleaners"
**9.** Hollywood Dahl
**10.** Yellow: Comb. form
**11.** Maid or cook
**12.** Ponder
**16.** Wrecks, as a car
**21.** Italian poet: 1544–95
**22.** Appends
**28.** Xavier's former spouse
**30.** What many a prin. needs
**33.** Family of the 400
**35.** Talk like some tots
**36.** Adjective for the Boston Massacre
**37.** Mushy or decadent
**38.** Leave no room for
**39.** Vietnam's capital
**40.** Blouse decorations
**44.** Fated
**45.** Malign
**47.** "What is yours ___ . . . ": Plautus
**48.** Lumberjack's cry
**49.** Good exit in a hotel fire
**53.** Chapters for hoods with hoods
**56.** Jay's home
**57.** Hebrew letter
**58.** Faure or Nadelman

# 118

**ACROSS**

1. River of Belgium
5. At right angles, asea
10. Twice DCXXV
14. ___ breve
15. Opera-box wear
16. "Hey there, sailor!"
17. Gully washers
19. Closefisted
20. At first
21. Pronouncements
22. ___ de la Frontera, city NE of Cádiz
23. Call's partner
24. Hub: Abbr.
27. Cardiologist's clue, for short
28. City's periphery
31. Letters on a perfect report card
33. It sometimes leads to a dead end
35. Black and white
37. Hush-hush agcy.
38. River flowing alongside Notre Dame
39. Horse wranglers
42. Snick and ___
43. Gosson's "___ of Abuse"
44. Police radio call: Abbr.
46. Soviet state
47. Links unit
48. Song heroine or Uncle Tom's wife
50. Colander
52. Treaties
56. Spore sacs
57. Idea
58. Small dog, for short
59. Jeweler's unit
60. Canal or railroad
61. Mtg.
62. Slag
63. Hogarth subject

**DOWN**

1. Maison figure
2. King or Alda
3. Et ___
4. His toys bring joys to girls and boys
5. Onsets
6. Of life
7. Peerage types
8. Host
9. Degrees for postgrads
10. Literally, "hand-cares"
11. Controls
12. Cover completely
13. Vega's constellation
18. Beget
21. I.O.U.'s
23. Passenger vehicle
24. Famed director
25. ___ Shevchenko, Ukrainian poet
26. Ticket stubs
28. Pacific coast flowers
29. Czech patriot
30. Man the helm
32. Antipasto garnish
34. Clangor
36. Oarlock
40. Have at the weeds
41. Basketwork material
45. Neckwear
48. Smoke for Fidel
49. Stage direction
50. Dolts
51. Words of understanding
52. Sandarac tree
53. Uncas's beloved
54. Composer Satie
55. Pintail duck
57. A-E connection

# 119

**ACROSS**

1. Nick Charles's dog
5. Slightly open
9. Wager
12. Fissure
14. Chromosome part
15. Kid
16. More domesticated
17. One acre, e.g.
18. Arm bone
19. Spoil
21. Describing wild horses
23. Baden-Baden, e.g.
24. Carved slab
25. Mail
28. "The Princess on the ___"
30. Dreary
34. Chorus section
35. Unemployed
37. Z's Greek counterpart
38. Gladly, to Shakespeare
39. Regimens
41. Particle
42. Scourges
44. Feds
45. Part of T.L.C.
46. Negates
48. Half a fly
49. Garbed
50. Jan Steen's style
52. Stat on a sports page
54. Place for a medicine cabinet
57. Mob
61. Neglect
62. Skeptical interjection
64. One of Pauline's adventures
65. Eye part
66. Anklebones
67. Polished
68. Pismire
69. Dirk of yore
70. Flower part

**DOWN**

1. Beginning of a drama
2. This may be grand or little
3. Weather forecast abbr.
4. What Hanukkah is
5. Khan
6. Its rededication is celebrated at Hanukkah
7. Concerning
8. Raised
9. Brazen
10. Feudal slave
11. Word with other or rather
13. Wanderlust appeaser
15. Hanukkah hero
20. ___ transit
22. Pelvic bone: Comb. form
25. Whitened
26. Skin color
27. She wrote "Three Lives"
29. Revise
31. Brass or lead, e.g.
32. Where oboli were spent
33. Crippled
36. Summers, in Nice
40. Scoff
43. Prophet
47. Noses
51. Type of type
53. Conversations: Slang
54. Gaucho's weapon
55. Last word
56. Slight color
58. Churlish child
59. First word of motto of N.H.
60. Type of sch.
63. Shake a leg

# 120

**ACROSS**

**1.** Sharif
**5.** Verse unit
**9.** Shades the windows
**13.** Place of a historic signing: Sept. 17, 1978
**16.** Writer Harte
**17.** Prestigious award
**19.** N. Eng. campus
**20.** Big ___, Calif.
**21.** Going on
**22.** Gruntlings
**24.** Caesar's tongue
**27.** Ending for count or shepherd
**28.** Vociferous
**31.** Birds ___ feather
**33.** Heavyset
**34.** Yeah's opposite
**35.** Co-winner of 17 Across: 1978
**39.** Good buddy
**40.** Like molasses
**41.** Map letters
**42.** Blown up
**44.** Day, in Durango
**46.** ___ Janeiro
**47.** New Jersey tea
**51.** Young otter or fox
**54.** Ending for Brooklyn or Bengal
**55.** Número ___
**56.** Candidate for 17 Across
**60.** On ___ with
**61.** Co-winner of 17 Across: 1978
**62.** Wilder or Hackman
**63.** Catch sight of
**64.** Tiny particle

**DOWN**

**1.** Confess
**2.** New Zealand native
**3.** ___ as life
**4.** Reciprocal of poise
**5.** Supplies a computer with data
**6.** Ripeners
**7.** N.E.A. offshoot in the Pine Tree State
**8.** ___ Raton, Fla.
**9.** Overseas
**10.** Not normally cast, as votes
**11.** ___ Percé Indians
**12.** Agnès or Agathe
**14.** Namesakes of pianist von Alpenheim
**15.** Ship-shaped clock
**18.** Courteous
**23.** Spare
**25.** Foolish
**26.** Utmost
**28.** Crusader's horse
**29.** "___ valentine"
**30.** ___ elbows (mingle)
**31.** Muscat native
**32.** Kindred soul
**33.** Tire part
**36.** Concurs
**37.** Tooth
**38.** Spot for 37 Down
**39.** Through
**43.** Hold fast
**44.** Come to see
**45.** Inklings
**47.** Pass another racer twice
**48.** Overcome
**49.** ___ a time
**50.** Rich cake
**52.** Where cows browse
**53.** Window or counter follower
**56.** Spree
**57.** Mimic
**58.** Certain hockey players: Abbr.
**59.** Crash into

# 121

## ACROSS

1. Pervert
5. Urchin
9. Fanatic
14. Winglike
15. Wine town
16. Col. Tibbets's mother
17. Venetian fishing boat
18. Fragrant flowers
20. Nuclear meltdown in a recent film
22. Wore
23. Glacial ridges
25. Lying beneath
29. All things considered
31. Dyer's color
35. Ile de la Cité's river
36. Ending for Hallow
37. "___ Call You Sweetheart"
39. Tulle
40. Rock bottom
43. Crockery
46. Salty minerals
48. Mouthlike part
49. Represent
51. Sheikdom of songdom
55. Harte's Ah Sin
59. ___ tree (bushy shrub)
61. Pound or Stone
62. Composer Jakob: 1550–91
63. Hyson and oolong
64. Dregs
65. Gather
66. Hebrew letter
67. Drives aslant, as nails

## DOWN

1. Oversee
2. Don Ho's hello
3. "___ Robert" (Bob Feller)
4. You or me
5. G.I. Janes
6. Pale
7. "Put ___ writing!"
8. Discoveries
9. Announces
10. Liven
11. Fine porcelain
12. Type
13. Prosecutors, for short
19. District
21. Held or Sten
24. More sensible
26. Two-base stat.
27. Power: Abbr.
28. Hussey and Roman
30. Marcel's pate
31. Coin
32. ". . . ___ little song": Goethe
33. Burma, Thailand, etc.
34. Radiate
38. Wine: Comb. form
41. Means
42. Novelist Sabatini et al.
44. Peking nana
45. Most cautious
47. Topers
50. Mitchell's Butler
52. W.W. II beachhead
53. Uncle Miltie
54. Irish playwright-poet
56. Fencing sword
57. In order
58. Ready money
59. Part of a dance's name
60. Part of a Western

# 122

**ACROSS**

**1.** Kind of bunt or race
**5.** Their motto is "Semper Paratus"
**10.** Hedge plant
**12.** Oriental staple
**14.** Former Barbary State
**15.** Victor Hugo hero
**16.** Refuge
**17.** Mother-in-law of Ruth
**19.** Kin af aves.
**20.** Gulf of the Arabian Sea
**21.** Rich tapestry
**22.** "___ yourself"
**23.** Finished first
**24.** Damage
**25.** English poet-clergyman
**26.** One of the Cyclades
**27.** Whalebone
**28.** Euphoric
**32.** Elegant carriage
**33.** Tanker tender
**34.** Kept a secret watch on
**35.** Titan who wasn't 28 Across
**36.** Disorderly crowd
**39.** Loser to Taylor in 1848
**40.** Nonsensical
**41.** Pharmacist's word for wax
**42.** Diminutive suffix
**43.** Midshipman
**44.** Of muscular power
**45.** Be a donee
**47.** Manage or run
**49.** Concerns of a probate court
**50.** Elysée, e.g.
**51.** ___ Park, Colo.
**52.** Thurber's "The ___ Animal"

**DOWN**

**1.** Pushed; forced
**2.** Mature
**3.** English river
**4.** Colloid
**5.** Appears
**6.** Equal: Prefix
**7.** Grain beard
**8.** Newscaster Harry
**9.** Guard
**10.** Madrid museum
**11.** "Cat on a Hot ___"
**12.** Sand bar
**13.** Swell
**14.** Melt
**18.** Tutor of Alexander the Great
**21.** Part of a stage
**22.** Sorrow
**24.** Palatable
**25.** U.S. Vice President: 1925–29
**26.** Natives of Lublin
**27.** Relative of "Avast!"
**28.** Ambiguous
**29.** Natives of Katmandu
**30.** Divides into three equal parts
**31.** Follow the hunt on foot
**35.** Coadjutors
**36.** Threaten
**37.** Declaim
**38.** Bundle
**40.** Redeems
**41.** Lithophyte, for one
**43.** Quote
**44.** Seaport in Honduras
**46.** Take tiffin in London
**48.** Jack of clubs

# 123

**ACROSS**

1. Stria
7. Sudden, violent activity or feeling
12. Honeycomb component
13. Something done in a hurry
15. Unimportant
17. Dingles
18. Wholly
19. "___ Love You," 1934 song
20. Buffalo's lake
21. Opera features
22. Physical body
23. Fancy or Dapper follower
24. Sky Ram
25. Hacienda units
26. Word with little or big
28. Shoe parts
29. Rapid series of notes
31. Popular N. Eng. fish dish
33. State policeman
36. Nag
37. Besom, e.g.
38. Euclidean abbr.
40. Factual
41. Man of Adak
42. Fiji's capital
43. Ending with aster
44. Show-biz awards
45. Novelist Robbe-Grillet
46. Beyond reproach
49. Madrid money
50. Irks
51. Rel. of an Amati
52. Homophone for grade

**DOWN**

1. Army V.I.P.
2. Lie
3. "___ mio"
4. Has
5. Anatomical duct
6. Funeral rites
7. Hard fats
8. Loblolly
9. Do something
10. Aspen gear
11. Noxious effluvia
12. Tarried
13. Even
14. Disney's middle name
16. Place for failures
21. Ancient Celtic priest
22. Shrewsbury's county
24. Radiant
25. ___ and Gomorrah
27. Concur
28. Treat with disdain
30. Alarm clock's function
31. Reliquaries
32. Most inexpert
34. Uniform
35. Scolded
36. Tankard
37. Radarscope phenomena
39. Margrethe and Dinesen
41. Draw ___ on
42. Having a dull blue color
44. Numerical prefix
45. Pier, to an architect
47. Dry: Prefix
48. "___ the ramparts . . ."

# 124

**ACROSS**

1. Han Solo's element
6. ___ Liberty
10. Pass over
14. Highway maneuver
15. Hawkeye's state
16. ___ mecum (handbook)
17. Brought to light
18. Spoke like Porky Pig
20. Father of Hannibal
22. St. Agnes's or St. John's
23. Bell and Kettle
24. Container for a roll of film
29. Formality
34. Emulate Socrates
35. Samovars
37. Grenoble's river
38. Father of Alexander the Great
42. Grant absolution
43. Ngo Dinh ___
44. Mister, in Madrid
45. Haberdashery measurement
47. State embracing part of the Bad Lands
50. Hayfield
52. Scull
53. Father of Charlemagne
60. Zealous
61. Remorseful ones
63. Bookie's concern
64. Moll's milieu
65. N.Y.C. hotel of yesteryear
66. Painter of "The Duchess of Alba"
67. Highlands vernacular
68. Preliminaries at a track meet

**DOWN**

1. Stand-in
2. Egyptian deity
3. Nimbus
4. Thickish liqueurs
5. Salad plant
6. Catchall wd.
7. Tittle
8. Horde from the hive
9. Brazilian dances
10. Between mind and matter
11. Wine-press residue
12. Product of reflection
13. Do a haymaker's job
19. Adhesive material
21. Surcease
24. Site of the Blue Grotto
25. Blanched
26. Hydroplanes
27. Crushed; oppressed
28. In conclusion: Fr.
30. Peer Gynt's mother
31. Spawning grounds for trout or salmon
32. Bo-peep's staff
33. Lucy Ricardo's rinse
36. Hook's sidekick
39. Twisted tale
40. Slanting type
41. Early lecterns
46. Household
48. Ardently collegiate
49. Play the firebrand
51. Rose oil, e.g.
53. Word form with meter or motor
54. Swirl
55. City NNE of Corsica
56. Certain brooders
57. Rim
58. Actress Shaw of B'way fame
59. Student's pony
60. Kind of leg or ear
62. Group in h.s.

# 125

## ACROSS

1. Droplet
5. Port of Spain
10. Top-notchers
14. Too
15. Off
16. Patsy
17. "March King"
20. Vague quantity
21. San'a money
22. Have-not
23. Baneful thing
24. Trapper's item
25. Comic-opera composer
33. Unclothed
34. Radioactivity unit
35. Nigerian people
36. ___ impasse
37. Engraving tool
38. Splotch
39. Part of R.S.V.P.
40. Certain containers
41. Work out
42. "Rockin' Chair" composer-lyricist
45. G.I. addresses
46. Big ___
47. Stoker's prop
50. Afrikaans
52. SHAEF sector
55. "The Music Man" composer
58. U.S.S.R. river
59. ___ Hills (HUD head for G.R.F.)
60. Can cope with
61. Colloids
62. Flounder through water
63. Henna user

## DOWN

1. ___ California
2. N.C. college
3. Pallid
4. Quiet flower
5. Pages for binding
6. Where the Ob flows
7. Deli pickle
8. Mar. 15, in Italia
9. Airship
10. Grizzled fur color
11. Achievement
12. Comfort
13. Be featured
18. Exultant
19. Château unit
23. "___ You're Smiling . . . ," 1928 song
24. Rigid insistence on nicety
25. Discomfort
26. Two-to-one, e.g.
27. Refrain syllables
28. Diving apparatuses
29. More reliable
30. Rural estate
31. Superior
32. Dynamite man
37. Eclogues
38. Physics Nobelist: 1922
40. Like many manuscripts
41. Certain oar
43. Judges' rappers
44. Book of the Bible
47. Complacent
48. Now's partner
49. Nuncupative
50. "Comin' ___ the Rye"
51. Cobbling tools
52. Make out
53. Kind of bag
54. ___ about
56. ___ qual (just as they come)
57. Legendary English king

# 126

### ACROSS

1. Ostentation
5. Word before Judgment or Supper
9. D.S.O. designee
13. Satan's delight
14. ___-frutti
15. Effluvium
16. "Look alive!"
18. Heap
19. Fernando, Alfonso et al.
20. Certain fertilizers
22. Grub St. denizen
24. Ring: Comb. form
25. Diamond dealer
29. Pertaining to a skin ailment
32. Put up with
33. Leak out slowly
35. Young Madrilenian
36. Ahab's or Lear's emotion
37. Llamas' milieu
38. Plant violently
39. Area east of the Urals
40. ___-do-well
41. Philippine timber trees
42. Trumpeter's stage signal
44. Adjective for an untouchable
46. Bob Hope sparkler
48. Rests
49. On deck
52. Painter compared with Bruegel
55. It has a double-reed mouthpiece
56. Valued too highly
59. Campaign verb in the 50's
60. Chief Justice after Marshall
61. Squirrel's nest
62. Vichyssoise ingredient
63. Within: Comb. form
64. Shade of blue

### DOWN

1. Fix prices
2. Word with time or throw
3. Particle
4. Practice a form of deception
5. Schisgal drama: 1964
6. Solar disk
7. Stiff-upper-lip chap
8. Photos of yesteryear
9. William Boyd role
10. Forte of William Allen White
11. Part
12. Bauxite and stibnite
14. Mario's beloved
17. General at Gettysburg
21. British medical org.
23. Money in Copenhagen
25. "___ Theme," movie song
26. Humble
27. Blind purchase
28. Alpine sound
30. Atlas section
31. Thicket
34. Kamikaze planes
37. Counteractive remedy
41. Olivier, for one
43. Samuel's teacher
45. Popeye's hungry pal
47. Aneurin of England: 1897–1960
49. Turnpike payment
50. Drama award
51. Transported
53. Pound or Stone
54. Pinniped
57. Erskine contemporary
58. Red 1 or Blue 5

# 127

## ACROSS

1. Certain exams, for short
6. Cleopatra's killer
9. Subordinate's response
14. Sluggish
15. Definite article
16. Wide-awake
17. Robert Nagy is one
18. Mexican matzohs
20. TV program once hosted by Groucho
22. Atmosphere: Comb. form
23. Chemical suffix
24. Wonderland's mad one
27. Dove's call
28. Numbers man: Abbr.
31. Hindu garb
32. Where fodder ferments.
34. Merchandise
36. Groucho the doctor
39. Reconcile
40. Layer
41. Astronaut Slayton
42. Dominique, e.g.
43. Agcy. once run by Ickes
45. Soundness
47. "___ Na Na," TV program
48. The John Birch org., for one
49. Movie of 1937 (see 36 Across)
57. Flight having risers
58. Floor: Fr.
59. Trattoria meat dish
60. Blemish
61. Bulgarian capital
62. In ___ (tousled)
63. Con's opposite
64. Scalp lock

## DOWN

1. Gary or Eugene
2. ___'clock (dandelion)
3. Bill of fare
4. Testing period
5. Wall or Fleet
6. ___ Gen.
7. Scat!
8. City on the Wabash
9. Settle definitely
10. Dragon of TV fame
11. Narcissist's love
12. Dies ___
13. Certain punches: Abbr.
19. The Bee Gees, e.g.
21. Tom ___, former Yankee
24. Terre ___
25. Inert gas
26. Lariat
27. Fountain drinks
28. Vinegar bottle
29. Troublesome
30. Racketer Arthur
31. Pahlevi
33. Omaha Beach vessel
35. Edward VIII in 1936
37. Greek god of the west wind
38. Cancel
44. British servicewoman
46. "Desire hath ___": Burton
47. Flying jibs
49. Monad
50. Evans from Uvalde, Tex.
51. Drive down lightly
52. Romanov title
53. Paragon
54. ___ au lait
55. Auspices
56. Proverbial septet
57. Karlovy Vary is one

# 128

**ACROSS**

1. Innkeeper, in Imola
5. Montana group
9. ___ fide
13. Debatable
14. ___ d'oeuvre
15. Shankar's instrument
16. "Cruel seas," e.g.
19. Have, in Inverness
20. Mars' Greek counterpart
21. Basket fodder
22. Loser at sea in 1588
24. Part of H.M.S.
25. "Mozart was a child progeny," etc.
32. River under the Ponte Sisto
35. Grand-___ home run
36. Hawaiian neckwear
37. Pothers
38. "Ain't it a ___!"
39. German basin
40. Skid follower
41. ___-bêche (philatelist's prize)
42. Restaurant feature
43. "Peter Piper picked . . . ," e.g.
47. Dancing sound
48. ___ quo ante
52. Pronouncements
54. Teasdale
56. Cytoplasm component
57. Relative of 16 Across
60. Spotlight color
61. Steak order
62. Laze
63. Garden starter
64. Organic compound
65. Look, in a way

**DOWN**

1. D-day beach
2. Submarine finder
3. Revered symbol, to some
4. Old English letter
5. Church song
6. Do ranch work
7. Love god
8. Parapsychologist's subj.
9. North Indian language
10. Early U.S. statesman: 1725–83
11. Car of the 40's
12. Humerus limb
15. Well-known coccus, for short
17. "M*A*S*H" role
18. Not out
23. Iowa city
26. Hebrew tribe
27. Rio de la ___
28. Part of a clone
29. Butter slice
30. Word with square or corn
31. Begetter
32. Scarlett O'Hara address
33. "The Fallen ___": Graham Greene
34. Try for a strike
38. One ___ a time
39. An Arabian capital
42. Destroy a car
44. Yearned
45. Spud
46. Begin's land
49. Swap
50. Surrender word
51. Suffix for sooth or gain
52. Kind of school
53. "Let ___," Beatles hit
54. Survey
55. Hairdo
57. ___ de deux
58. Anger
59. Leo the ___ (Durocher)

**ACROSS**

1. Poker holding
5. ___-deucy
9. Help request
12. "___ Solemnis"
13. Pug or Roman
14. Former Eastern ruler
15. Polyphonic composition
16. Refrain syllables
17. Josip Broz
18. Forever
20. In a different way
21. Kirghiz range
22. Lunchroom
24. Cereal flour
28. Known: Fr.
30. Chicago district
31. "Two of one trade ___ love": Dekker
33. Orange or Indian
37. Alfresco
39. Sumptuous feast
41. Merman
42. Grate
44. Site of Bryce Canyon
45. Lure
47. Animal tracks
49. Church district
52. Nice seasons
54. Haley
55. How degrees are sometimes awarded
61. ___ prius (kind of court)
62. Rochester name of fame
63. Salute
64. State of pique
65. Tied
66. Right of possession
67. Itch
68. Zaire's Mobutu ___ Seko
69. "Voi lo sapete," for one

**DOWN**

1. Nuclear particle
2. Terrier of films
3. Words of understanding
4. Wickerwork material
5. Sinuses or Roman halls
6. Entablature feature
7. Son-in-law of Elon
8. Toadies
9. Stand out in a crowd
10. Western flick
11. Ostentatious
12. Date still to come
14. Existing condition
19. Antelope having short, twisted horns
23. Soon
24. Arctic sight
25. Juillet follower
26. Lillian or Philip
27. Dogmatic assertion
29. Globes
32. A first name in architecture
34. Detroit product
35. Equipment
36. Biblical verb endings
38. Seine sights
40. Basilica projections
43. Lemurs
46. Announces the hour
48. Flatfish genus
49. Garden plant
50. Straighten
51. Plant exudation
53. Steak type
56. Main part of a church
57. Roulette bet
58. Actor Jacques
59. Majorca, for one
60. Broke bread

# 130

## ACROSS

1. Relative of a windsock
5. Impressionism originator
10. Bijoux
14. Kind of type: Abbr.
15. Cinched
16. Corn lily
17. Accordion
19. Numerical prefix
20. Surpass
21. Restrain
23. Go back to square one
24. Seven, to Pablo
25. N.Y.S.E. initials
26. Parley
29. Pierre's dream
31. Cash
32. Número ___
33. De ___ (posh)
34. ORT is one
35. "Meet ___ St. Louis"
36. Title of courtesy, for short
37. Military armor
39. Snippy
40. Professor's captive audience
42. Famed N.H.L. retiree
43. Wroth
44. Followed
48. Commune ESE of Perugia
50. Like an anchorite
51. Hairdo
52. Impractically idealistic
54. Dillon of "Gun Smoke"
55. Open, in a way
56. "I never ___ man I. . ."
57. ___ out (just manages)
58. Anthony and Barbara
59. Cap or jacket

## DOWN

1. Kepi feature
2. "Ave ___ vale!"
3. Endings with cosmo and astro
4. Curriculum choice
5. "Magic Flute" composer
6. "___ of robins . . ."
7. His ___, the boss
8. Environmental prefix
9. Woven cloth
10. His frescoes can be seen at 48 Across
11. Treasury
12. Smidgen
13. Moselle feeder
18. Inspirit
22. Wriggling
24. Chansons
26. Vintner's purchase
27. Carat or dram
28. Thither
29. Oxidize
30. Decorator's adjective
31. ___ Carlo
33. Bandleader Brown
35. Canada's ___ Provinces
37. Hyson and bohea
38. Treasured relic
39. Lineament
41. Is rudderless
42. Ship decks
44. Botulin, e.g.
45. Of a kind of braid
46. Lady with a lyre
47. Poet Thomas
48. Pinnacle
49. Barfly
50. S, M or L
53. Sturm ___ Drang

**ACROSS**

1. Socialite, for short
4. Shopper's consideration
8. Bethlehem product
13. Change for a five
15. Discordant
16. Bisect
17. Viva voce
18. Dover ___
19. Peregrine
20. Rationale for cooperation
23. Vikings or Giants
24. Taboo word
25. ___ polloi
27. Man-made fabric
32. Slander
36. "___ fan tutte"
39. Tradition
40. Attempt at cooperation: 1920–46
43. Other, in Ponce
44. Prefix for toxin
45. Great Lakes acronym
46. Sawbuck
48. N.F.L. man
50. Portico
53. Lure
58. Biblical directive for cooperation
63. Withstand
64. Form of John
65. Prefix for space or gram
66. Dorian Gray's creator
67. Slope
68. Angered
69. Something to get up
70. Word with dog or bob
71. Half a fly

**DOWN**

1. Surname in a Blackmore novel
2. Register
3. N.Y.C.'s former mayor
4. Gambling house
5. What a señorita flashes
6. Chicken or egg follower
7. Roma-Firenze vehicle
8. Kind of daisy
9. ___ in the saddle
10. Lamb
11. Tied
12. Afford temporarily
14. Central European
21. Hindu statesman
22. Country of 21 Down
26. Object of worship
28. Muse of history
29. "___ at the Top": Braine
30. French river or department
31. Cape
32. Track of a deer
33. Homophone for meat
34. Deserve
35. Contest, Greek style
37. Frequently, in poesy
38. Pert one
41. Kind of worm or work
42. Strip of leather
47. Value
49. Checked by pulling
51. Certain courts
52. Hammer's partner
54. Siamese
55. Jacques ___, French composer
56. Centers
57. Eat away
58. Enactments
59. Necrology
60. Disgusting
61. Work attributed to Snorri Sturluson
62. Facility

# 132

**ACROSS**

1. Adjective for 1980
5. Gambling game
9. Contemptuous biblical exclamation
13. "The King ___"
14. Up's companion
16. "___ se habla español"
17. ___ Schary
18. Come up to expectations
20. Careless
22. Done over
23. Mine find
24. Streeter's "___ Mable"
25. Predicament
28. Naval officer's ornamentation
32. Man in the van of a clan
33. Smetana's "The Bartered ___"
34. Famous Czech play
35. "___ Misbehavin'"
36. Vehicles in "M*A*S*H"
37. Membrane of a bird's beak
38. Name of "Follies" fame
39. Czech statesman
40. Parsonage
41. Identified in a lineup
43. Lean sideways
44. Sholem Asch's "___ River"
45. Billiard table rim
46. Telephone part
49. Sign on a movie marquee
53. Villainous act
55. Theatrical award
56. Canal started in 1817
57. Signification
58. Actress Louise
59. Actor Parker
60. Belgian river
61. Arabian Sea gulf

**DOWN**

1. Callow fellows
2. Chemical compound
3. Seaport in southern Spain
4. Rhubarb, country style
5. Front
6. Maltreat
7. Hayward role in "I'll Cry Tomorrow"
8. Word with go or grow
9. Drove into
10. Bluish-green
11. Boiled or baked dessert
12. One of 25 Down
15. Duds
19. Eldritch
21. Advance info
24. Insipid ones
25. Assisting group
26. It sounds cold but it's hot
27. Continued
28. Sheltie or Saluki
29. Actress Dunne
30. Nightingale, e.g.
31. Tributary to the Colorado
33. Pulitzer Prize winner: 1944
36. Shirts for Franco Harris
37. Girl in a T. A. Daly poem
39. End-all's partner
40. Annina, in "La Traviata"
42. Barbara Bel ___
43. Sculptor featured at Kennedy Airport
45. Singer Della
46. Alphabetical quartet
47. Remarkably fine
48. "___ Born"
49. Cock's coterie
50. Annul
51. Nine: Prefix
52. Nolan of baseball
54. Former Tunisian ruler

# 133

**ACROSS**

**1.** What Queen Mab waves
**5.** Pro ___ (proportionally)
**9.** "The ___ Man," Sammy Davis Jr. hit song
**14.** Song for Leontyne Price
**15.** Components of psyches
**16.** Cognizant
**17.** Loser to Joe Louis in 1946
**18.** Blacks, in Bologna
**19.** Hayworth and Coolidge
**20.** The Black Muslims
**23.** Chisholm Trail town
**24.** Brioches
**25.** Before: Prefix
**28.** Part of a new car purchase, often
**31.** Fisherman for congers
**33.** Morns
**34.** Black, e.g.
**38.** Black Muslims' leader
**42.** Goren's clean sweep
**43.** Second person
**44.** Form of somniloquy
**45.** Formative
**48.** Brooke was one: Abbr.
**49.** Shakespearean character
**52.** Cupid
**54.** Black Muslim leader slain in 1965
**59.** Ancient region of Asia Minor
**60.** Paintings by Cassatt
**61.** Tip-top
**63.** Grinder's instrument
**64.** "It's a Sin to Tell ___"
**65.** African tribesmen
**66.** Requirements
**67.** Small marks
**68.** Settle in cozily

**DOWN**

**1.** Army woman
**2.** Steinbeck character
**3.** Actress Foch
**4.** Alighieri
**5.** Impressionist painter
**6.** Program
**7.** Tauromachy figure, in Madrid
**8.** Quasi
**9.** Johnny or Kit
**10.** "Where there's ___ . . ."
**11.** Of birth
**12.** Small amounts
**13.** Truckler's automatic response
**21.** Prefix with mural
**22.** Modern Celts
**25.** Church parts
**26.** Former Spanish coin
**27.** Fitzgerald or Logan
**29.** Sirs' mates
**30.** Australian bird
**32.** Popular street name
**34.** Successor to L.B.J.
**35.** Otis of baseball fame
**36.** "If I Didn't ___," 1939 song
**37.** Anthony of England
**39.** Relative of a violin
**40.** Actress Le Gallienne
**41.** Race track in Berkshire, Eng.
**45.** Pie ingredients
**46.** Baldwin's "Go ___ on the Mountain"
**47.** Rainbows
**49.** Love, to Carlo and Sophia
**50.** Kitchen appliance
**51.** Homeric work
**53.** Spoil
**55.** Cargo
**56.** Heller's Minderbinder
**57.** Part of the ear
**58.** Son of Seth
**59.** Charged atom
**62.** Sum, es, ___

# 134

**ACROSS**

1. Bivouac
5. Hackney
8. Pony
12. Medicinal lily
13. Certain squabs
15. Hick
16. La. Purchase acres
17. ". . . man is a mere insect, ___": F. P. Church
18. Presently
19. Assumes
22. Transients from Canada
23. Hinny's relative
24. J. F. Cooper heroine
26. "Fragile: Handle ___"
31. Duchesse, e.g.
32. Lima is its capital
33. Macedonian and Mohammedan
34. Cause light to pass through
37. Chief resource in scholardom
38. Palm fibers
39. More fantastic
40. Suburb of Scranton
42. Kind of beer or miss
43. Legal principle
44. "___ the stilly night . . .": T. Moore
47. Harlequin, Pantaloon et al.
54. Pay close attention
55. Enveloping glows
56. "Un bel di" is one
57. Cacholong
58. Writer William Gilmore ___: 1806–70
59. Actress Virna
60. Strike out
61. Suffix with Bengal or Tyrol
62. Kind of oyster or pearl

**DOWN**

1. Famed suffragette
2. Temple of Athena ___, at Tegea
3. Mindy's TV friend
4. Smollett hero
5. Words bleeped by TV censors
6. Vehicle for Gary Cooper: 1932
7. Toughs having a turf
8. Abstract doctrines
9. Peewee
10. ___ d'amore
11. Conduce
13. Diamond decision
14. Layer
20. Johns, in Ireland
21. Volcanic debris
24. Burnett or Channing
25. Eared seal
27. Beggar in the "Odyssey"
28. Plowed land
29. Assessor
30. Danish weights
31. Battle site: 1944
32. Marshall ___
35. Lake, county and state park in Minn.
36. Column style
41. Philippine guerrilla in W.W. II
45. Kegler's "inning"
46. U.S.S.R. press agency
47. Booted
48. Cassette
49. Opposite of written
50. Creator of Mamie Stover
51. Part of HOMES
52. Piece of high ground
53. Reputed to be

# 135

**ACROSS**

1. Cabinet category: Abbr.
5. Estate units
10. Rotating gear
13. Mesopotamian city in biblical days
14. Nova Scotian town
15. Pindar's products
17. Solver's present position
20. Facial photos
21. Dole's state
22. Strop
23. Beak part
24. Bolster the brakes
27. Military matériel
31. Kind of prof. or pres.
32. ___-cake (children's game)
33. Conjunctions
34. Components of this puzzle
39. Shoe width
40. Seine tributary
41. Peruvian Indian
42. Quaked
44. Strong man
46. Benjamite of I Chron. 8:15
47. Leisurely life
48. Spread out a scroll
51. Enter and exit, e.g.
55. This puzzle's proportions
57. Auto pioneer
58. Protester's ploy
59. Diminutive or distaff suffix
60. Compass point
61. Expressionless
62. React to reveille

**DOWN**

1. Studio spinner
2. Daredevil's first name
3. Peacock constellation
4. Hobbits' habitat
5. Make melodious
6. Crinkly fabric
7. Reims roads
8. Beautician Westmore
9. ___ the skin (drenched)
10. Eye part
11. Bustles
12. Sight in N.M.
16. Draft initials
18. Element having atomic number 10
19. French region noted for stone monuments
23. Crow's crop
24. Adjust
25. Baghdad bigwig
26. River embankment
27. Made up one's mind
28. Proper and common words
29. Set of beliefs
30. City on the Ruhr
35. Improvise on a clarinet
36. Ever energetic
37. North Sea feeder
38. Woes wailer
43. ___-tung
44. Lustrous
45. ___ now (presently)
47. Finally, to Félicité
48. Alien's aircraft?
49. Ramses' river
50. Certain postal addresses
51. Have an ___ grind
52. Abominable Snowman
53. Queens nine
54. Snick and ___
56. Kind of picker or wit

# 136

**ACROSS**

1. Ella of Conn.
7. Convince
13. A Kennedy or a Stevenson
14. Feeders of fires on freighters
16. Siege Perilous site
17. Overseer
18. Mo from Ariz.
19. ___ branch
21. Botanist Gray
22. U.S. social reformer: 1849–1914
23. Struck
24. Flaccid
25. Hostelry
26. Scrutinize
27. Barracks decoration
28. Ice ___
29. Quality
30. Stylish
31. Brush material
33. Vocalist Vic
36. Gaelic nobleman
37. Science deg.
40. Pistil part
41. Happy
42. Butt
43. Procures
44. Slapping sound
46. Father
47. Prefix with sect
48. Kanone, e.g.
49. Abuser of Oliver
50. Storehouse
52. John or Jill of films
54. Develop an idea
55. Diatribe
56. More profound
57. Over there

**DOWN**

1. Road builder's task
2. Variety of lettuce
3. Walter and I. W.
4. Promote successfully
5. Angel's favorite sign
6. Armless sofas
7. ___ as a fiddle
8. Heater
9. Angered
10. Hawaiian guitar, for short
11. Stays
12. Dutch scholar: 1466–1536
15. Brisk
16. Roman senate
20. "Lindy"
23. Get home
24. Fabricator
26. Rigid
27. Wielded
30. Unit of weight
31. ___ d'oeuvre
32. Mirth
33. Military ID
34. Affirmed
35. Leader among Fauvist painters
37. Bucket or fire follower
38. Seaman
39. Edit
44. Glide over
45. He makes heaps
46. Hodgepodge
48. Catch
49. Flowerless plant
51. Summer, on the Riviera
53. ___ de la Plata

# 137

**ACROSS**

1. Inquires
5. Spring time in Spain
10. Plant disease
14. Stylish
15. German statesman slain in 1919
16. Game originated in Persia
17. Hawaiian hand-waver
19. Balanced
20. Shoulder wrap
21. Cutting tool
22. Ryan's girl in "Love Story"
23. Item waved by a fan dancer
25. Rose and Seeger
27. Ethiopian prince
30. Faced with a predicament
32. Sine ___ non
34. Eden's man
36. They waved from outer space
38. Seek funds
40. Hand-waving Frenchman
41. Spanish handshaking official
43. Nothing but
44. Affirmative
45. Most weird
47. Composer Rorem
48. Be freehanded
50. Autumn blossom
52. U.N. labor unit
53. An N.C.O.
54. Like Eric the Red
58. Tail-wagger on film
60. Braking devices on railroads
62. Faith order
63. Lena or Marilyn
64. Arabian gulf
65. Tennis-elbow symptom
66. Orange or Indian
67. Like a nonesuch

**DOWN**

1. Exclamations in Berlin
2. Close
3. Kind of gram or meter
4. Sell tickets illegally
5. Villain's cry
6. Parade or concert hand-waver
7. Most spicy
8. Seer's phrase
9. Celtic Neptune
10. Type of wheat
11. Hollywood hand-waver
12. Rubber tree
13. Heavy weight
18. Where to buy pastrami
22. Vulcan's home
24. On one's own
25. Having the least
26. Medical stitching
27. Grating
28. Worships
29. A hand-waving come-on
31. Demonstrators' activity
33. ___ as a beet
35. Prefix with handle
37. Upper air: Abbr.
39. Mire, in Mexico
42. Place for some hand-holders
46. Honor cards
49. Make joyful
51. Helicopter part
53. Abbrs. outside some dramatizations
55. Eternal City, to Italians
56. Boom or gaff
57. Medieval drudge
58. As mad ___ wet hen
59. Big Board's Big Brother: Abbr.
60. However, for short
61. Designating a maiden name

# 138

**ACROSS**

1. Word with tight or still
4. Elementary
9. Agile
13. Bow
15. Broadway musical
16. Canadian Indian
17. Bigfoot's Asian cousin
18. Passover dinner
19. Certain paintings
20. Motto of a 1775 flag
23. Chimney powder
24. Awkward
25. Uncultivated
28. Remuneration
30. As bald as ___
31. Relative of the hula
32. Holder of an LL.B.
35. Old Glory
39. Suffix with Annam
40. Void's partner
41. Lariat
42. Squander, possibly
44. Dais
45. Fall flower
47. Voyage
48. Feature of the 1777 flag
53. Word with flat or angle
54. Bayou
55. Drudge
57. Soil
58. Loser to Dwight
59. Shopper stopper
60. Chooses
61. "Thanks ___"
62. Holiday drink

**DOWN**

1. Triple agent
2. Angered
3. In ___ (entirely)
4. Give
5. Prevent
6. Word with step or stroke
7. Virginia willow
8. Sweater named for a general
9. Treats at tea
10. Groom
11. Sublease
12. Sycophant's favorite word
14. Homer the artist
21. Molar, e.g.
22. ". . . ___ nation under God"
25. The high cost of leaving
26. Winners of five dogfights
27. Ore deposit
28. Brandish
29. Of grandparents
31. Astound
32. Turkestan range
33. Ballet skirt
34. Jets, Mets or Nets
36. Opposing change
37. "Dieu et mon ___"
38. States of chaos
42. Tasks
43. Part of m.p.h.
44. "The ___ a bucket of ashes": Sandburg
45. Anchor position
46. Out of funds
47. Slammer on the links
49. Conductor Akiro ___
50. Ending with citron
51. Horse color
52. Storage bin
53. Words at the altar
56. Part of a journey

# 139

**ACROSS**

1. Silly fool, in Soho
5. Van Druten's "I Remember ___"
9. Words of praise on a book jacket
14. Madcap
15. "___ and Civilization": Marcuse
16. Logrolling tournament
17. He wrote: "A bit of talcum/Is always walcum"
19. Author Cobb
20. Dickens
21. He wrote "Fables in Slang"
23. Great amount
25. Ermine
26. Erect
28. Involve necessarily
32. She wrote "Gentlemen Prefer Blondes"
37. Reel, e.g.
38. One of Ghent's rivers
39. Tom Lea's brave bulls
41. Snood
42. Chick chatter
45. "Nize Baby" creator
48. Flank and New York
50. Lamb who wrote about a pig
51. Files
54 Sequence
57. He wrote about a jumping frog
61. Palls
63. ". . . nothing like ___"
64. Creator of Ah Sin
66. Indian lute
67. Let out surreptitiously
68. Hammett heroine
69. Carbines
70. ". . . ___ the fray"
71. Turkey follower

**DOWN**

1. Walked
2. Stake
3. ". . . tribute to whom tribute ___": Romans
4. It's sometimes put before the horse
5. Kingsley's "___ in White"
6. Part of a Kipling line
7. Asch book
8. ___ as a pistol
9. Robin Hood, e.g.
10. Swit of TV
11. Nicaraguan group
12. Publisher Whitelaw ___ (1837–1912)
13. Costa or scapula
18 Hercules-vs.-lion site
22. Caviar
24. Book by Herbert Gold
27. Woolf's "A ___ of One's Own"
29. ___ Domini
30. Desserts
31. Some tennis plays
32. Site of the Jungfrau
33. Muscovite's refusal
34. Listener's phrase
35. Mouth: Comb. form
36. Dover ___
40. Capital of Manche
43. He wrote "Montcalm and Wolfe"
44. Fratianne and Babilonia
46. Band for holding a saddle
47. Glowing
49. Compass pt.
52. Casals
53. Temptress
55. Lapse
56. Backward: Prefix
57. Mozart's "Coronation ___"
58. Mine access
59. Birth or death follower
60. Without admixture
62. Install in office
65. Ref's decision

# 140

## ACROSS

1. Wearing brogans
5. "Eye in the sky"
10. Niacin, e.g.
14. Twining plant
15. City in Utah
16. Poem by Victor Hugo
17. Latvian city
18. Leporidae
19. "How now! ___?": Hamlet
20. Inclusive abbr.
21. ___ effort
22. Grimalkin
23. Solstices
26. Rent
27. Word with fish or lock
28. Deloul or hageen
32. Liqueur
37. End of a Stein line re pigeons
38. Simulated
40. Sheepskin used in bookbinding
41. Bodily
43. "I intended ___": Dobson
44. Month: Abbr.
45. Writers' changes: Abbr.
47. Equinox times
56. Having a long, narrow muzzle
57. Pas-de-Calais town
58. Antithesis of apteral
59. Affront
60. Chile-to-England shipment
61. Precise
62. Former name of a European republic
63. Brakes
64. ___ du Nord, Parisian depot
65. Aldebaran is one
66. Plant of the mustard family
67. Priestley's "___ End"

## DOWN

1. Broadcast
2. Part of Hispaniola
3. Wind instrument
4. Distributed
5. Globe
6. P.L.O. leader
7. Andalusian city
8. Charred, as chateaubriand
9. Sparks's plea
10. Startle
11. Mosconi ploy
12. Vacant
13. Arrest
22. Some are in pounds
24. House extension
25. Reputed to be
28. Coif
29. Welsh rabbit ingredient, often
30. Disserve
31. Lisper's nemesis
32. Expanse east of N.A.
33. Relative of a fulmar
34. Also
35. Pulitzer Prize playwright Mosel
36. Direction letters
38. Prolific author, for short
39. Supercilious
42. "Gentle ___ Mind," 1967 hit
43. Deadly creature
45. Purfles
46. Evaluate
47. Kiangs
48. Like a region during an outage
49. Diadem of a sort
50. Shoe part
51. ___ Dame
52. Scope
53. Homeric work
54. Mother-of-pearl
55. Immature
60. Org. for Cowboys, Giants et al.

# 141

**ACROSS**

1. ``Krakatit'' author
6. Forum language
11. Feral
12. Cancels
14. Ready to fight
16. Bovine waif
17. Dinero
18. Bask
20. City on the Oka
21. Discourage
22. Hence
23. But, to Ovid
24. Thermoplastic
25. Pensive poem
26. ___ Sea, off NW Australia
27. Essayist who called himself Nestor Ironside
28. Any imminent danger
32. Sore
33. ___-garde
34. Madison Ave. types
35. ``Took ___ . . . and broke his leg'': J. Buchan
36. Old freighter
39. Dressed
40. Hair: Prefix
41. Cable
42. ___-Tiki
43. Pacific islands
44. Scope
45. Like le Carré's fiction
48. ``Who ___ Cock Robin?''
49. Blackbirds
50. ``Oft have I ___ timely-parted ghost'': Shak.
51. Rundown

**DOWN**

1. Sponged
2. Use
3. Summon by intercom
4. ``Hen fruit''
5. ``___ the Keys'': E. D. Biggers
6. Let up
7. Elan
8. Salts
9. ``Rose ___ rose . . .''
10. Media vehicle
11. Put by
13. Get comfy
14. Dust-ups
15. Slowness in progress
19. Poet who sounds unmusical
21. Runyon
22. Vote in
24. Neighbor of Tyre
25. A jacket and a collar
26. Attempted
27. Big hit
28. Not busy or active
29. Marriage
30. Turks
31. Alligator pears
35. Fleet
36. Stimulating
37. Exhorts
38. Tavern order
40. Occupied
41. Carried on
43. Word with white or fire
44. Bring down the house
46. Cheer for El Cordobés
47. Payable

# 142

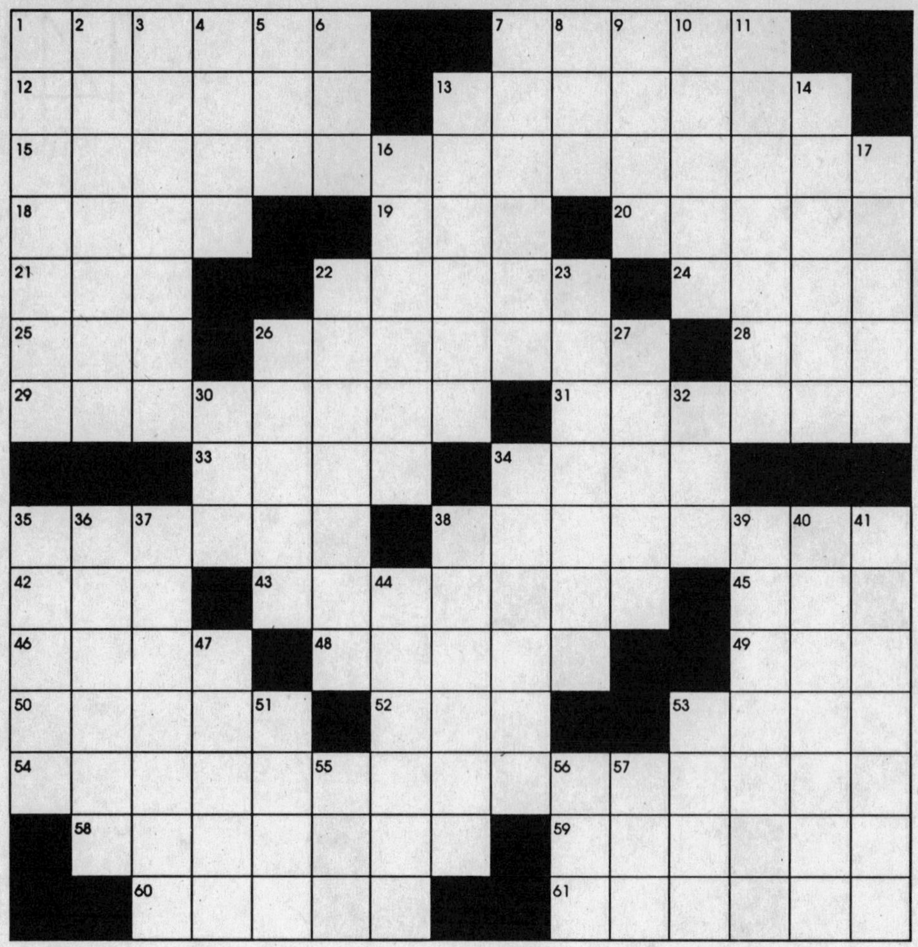

## ACROSS

1. Calling
7. Muddle
12. In danger of
13. U.S. college member
15. Incessantly, in a way
18. Renaissance family
19. Saturn's wife
20. ___ limit (draws the line)
21. Dep.
22. Circular
24. Prescribed custom
25. Miller's "___ My Sons"
26. Western ranges
28. Architectural wing
29. Legal precedent procedure
31. Headgear for Anglican bishops
33. Rainbow forms
34. Dumas ___: 1802–70
35. Share the lead
38. Unsupported
42. Rudiments
43. ___ out (failed)
45. N.L. player
46. Absolute
48. Marsh birds
49. Cote cry
50. Historic village near Verdun
52. T-man or G-man
53. Butter portions
54. Incessantly, in a way
58. Gives the lie to
59. Sound of little bells
60. Motherless calf
61. Argued with impudence

## DOWN

1. Assaults
2. Peter or James
3. Certain ad offerings
4. Being, in Barcelona
5. Biblical verb ending
6. Monarch, in Marseille
7. More compact
8. Female lobster
9. N.T. book
10. Word with wise
11. More fuliginous
13. Conqueror's goal
14. Steal the steer
16. Exactly as stated
17. Asian units of weight
22. Hackney coaches
23. Kingly name in Egypt
26. ___ iron
27. Engendered
30. Use a hand shuttle
32. Arab word for hill
34. Victory celebration
35. Pool ploy
36. Titania's spouse
37. Analyzed poetry
38. Left Bank headwear
39. Builds levees
40. Puget Sound seaport
41. Kept in a cache
44. Chewy confection
47. Released
51. Tobacco variety
53. Lily of operatic fame
55. Panay group
56. Grid linemen
57. Farrow

# 143

## ACROSS

1. Domain
7. Future replacements
13. They've got the goods
15. Kind of battery
16. From La Spezia, Italy, to Hyères, France
17. Fire and fury
18. Dill herb of the Bible
19. State of deep despair
21. Sentry post: Abbr.
22. Thespian Hagen
23. ___ up (adjust)
24. Sampler beginning
25. Conventicle group
27. Spinal component
28. Kind of step or neck
29. Passive
31. Van's place in an army
32. Nary a soul
33. Box up
34. Slyly malicious
35. Most relaxed
37. Doctor the drink
38. Chinese dynasty
39. Nigerian group
41. Valley of the vines
42. Refreshers of a sort
43. Picnic pest
44. Birth month of D.D.E.
45. Silents star Love
47. "___ the wild blue yonder"
48. Largest of the Ryukyu Islands
50. Star's sub
52. City near Bucharest
53. Earthly
54. "And steep my ___ in forgetfulness?": Shak.
55. Marked with lines or grooves

## DOWN

1. Comic opera's Oscar
2. Kind of matter
3. Hit the ceiling
4. Emulate Robert Giroux
5. Arikara
6. Earns a demerit
7. Drew's milieu
8. Like London's Savoy
9. ___ poetica
10. Cause to hit the ceiling
11. He has "I" trouble
12. Where Kerry met Kerrey
14. Cracker
15. Wood or fungus that smolders when lit
20. Give the gate
24. Baby wear
26. Moscow vehicle
27. Great ___
28. Fat, in France
30. Rhythmical scheme
31. Coat fastener
33. Be formed (of)
34. Patch plasterwork
35. Items to be puckered
36. Survivor-takes-all insurance
37. Busybodies
38. Some of the Kenyans
40. Blotto
42. Salamanders
45. Diamond point
46. Seine summers
47. Japanese receptacle
49. Readings on vanes
51. Curve segment

# 144

**ACROSS**

1. Warsaw ___
5. Fingerprint
10. Ovid was one
14. Winged
15. Old hat
16. Moro
17. Rani's garb
18. Fools
19. Small dam
20. Doctor for barflies?
23. Shoe width
24. Yang's partner
25. Doctor for film stars?
33. Goes on the lam
34. Off Broadway award
35. Haggard opus
36. Suffix for velvet
37. Third man's namesakes
38. Above, to Key
39. Break bread
40. Beget a foal
41. More competent
43. Doctor for elitist mothers?
47. Suffix for Brooklyn or Jacob
48. Kin of aves.
49. Doctor for old gamblers?
57. China or dynasty
58. Where the Ganges flows
59. "Do ___ others . . ."
60. Feudal slave
61. Rural structure
62. Venerated object
63. Norman of TV fame
64. Highway oasis
65. Crack the whip

**DOWN**

1. Historian's forte
2. Kirghiz range
3. Fish dish
4. Cut into three parts
5. Typewriter part
6. TV offering
7. They, in Palermo
8. On the briny
9. Fashions anew
10. Lout's amorous advance
11. Bullring cries
12. Work on copy
13. Craggy hill
21. Congressional votes
22. ___ Grande
25. Milieu of some tramps
26. ___ Domingo
27. ___ man, mine blaster
28. "Angélique" composer
29. Edmonton hockey pro
30. Capri or Ischia
31. Actor Martin
32. Hawaii before statehood: Abbr.
33 Understands
37. Constellation
41. Play part
42. High tea offering
44. "The ___ they come . . ."
45. Jeanne d'Arc, e.g.
46. Neighbor of Lebanon
49. Solomonic
50. King of Siam's friend
51. Divider's word
52. Mine entrance
53. Roof component
54. Quechuan Indian
55. Kind of smasher
56. ". . . and then there were ___"
57. Brooks or Ott

# 145

## ACROSS

1. Hall of Fame pitcher
6. Nervous, excited condition
10. Like an envelope at the P.O.
13. Tediously wordy
14. Figure: Comb. form
15. Roman 102
16. Painting by Van Gogh
18. Marsh elder
19. Whit
20. Painter of "Maids of Honor"
22. Not jaggy
23. Trig terms
24. Swiss canton
25. "___ Tag," play by Barrie
26. Actor Keach
27. Small river islands
29. A la ___, cookery term
30. Grape seed
32. Plea
35. Orchid tubers
36. Given to traveling
37. Stage curtains
39. Pollution factor
40. Recumbent
41. ___ passim (so everywhere)
44. Home-school org.
45. Unfinished
46. "Strange Interlude" heroine
47. Baseball: Slang
49. Cry of distress
50. O.A.S. member
51. "Man at the Crossroads" muralist
54. ___ Léman, Genève
55. Faulkner character
56. Father of the Titans
57. Word on a stop sign in Rome
58. Sacks for packing coffee or sugar
59. Waistcoat

## DOWN

1. Furrow or hollow
2. He screams for teams he esteems
3. Kern's "___ River"
4. Routing word
5. Second phone: Abbr.
6. Playwright Rattigan
7. N.H. peak that inspired a Hawthorne tale
8. "I Get ___," 1951 song
9. Prepare a salad
10. Pertaining to squirrels
11. Hedonist's advice
12. President when Pancho Villa revolted
13. Used a lever
17. Of birds
21. Migratory game birds
23. Marsh bird
26. Ballet star Lavery
28. Draft initials
29. Rancheros' ropes
30. ". . . I stand ___ upon a rock": Shak.
31. Sontag
32. He lost to D.D.E.
33. Offer
34. Lengthen in time
37. Rat-race participants
38. Copland composition
40. Member of the sacerdocy
41. Bon ___ (tea rose)
42. Doing the same thing daily
43. Residences for Miró or Dali
45. Potter's field
46. Kind of engagement
47. Hoop or skirt predecessor
48. Gouda's relative
52. Toupee, in slanguage
53. South Korean city

# 146

**ACROSS**

**1.** Ingredient in some dyes
**5.** Geladas of Ethiopia
**9.** Propitious
**13.** Bullfrog genus
**14.** Site of Jesus' first miracle
**15.** Knot again
**16.** One concern of a personnel chief
**18.** Leaves out
**19.** Lack of an alternative
**21.** Basic verb in Versailles
**22.** Makes picots
**23.** Twists of paper for lighting candles
**26.** Dweller alongside the Oder
**30.** Twin crystal
**31.** Ducking-stool victim
**32.** Cruise port
**33.** Noted N.F.L. linebacker
**34.** Dilutes
**35.** Numerical prefix
**36.** Author Deighton
**37.** Aegean gulf
**38.** Cahn-Styne creations
**39.** Rude dwelling
**41.** Nostrum
**42.** Sen. McGovern's birthplace in S.D.
**43.** Lance once raised high by Carter
**44.** In any way whatever
**49.** Knack
**50.** Counterfeit
**52.** Sharp rise on Wall Street
**53** Double negative
**54.** Friend in a fray
**55.** Killer of Eric IV
**56.** Kennedy figure
**57.** Wildcat

**DOWN**

**1.** Altar on high
**2.** Thin wood strip
**3.** "I appeal ___ Caesar": Acts 25:11
**4.** Spanish resort on the Mediterranean
**5.** Equity members
**6.** "Common Sense" author
**7.** Son of Seth
**8.** Countenances
**9.** Derelict
**10.** Auricular
**11.** Locale
**12.** Start of a reply to Virginia
**15.** Poked around, as in search
**17.** Agave fiber
**20.** Aulae and odea
**23.** Subject of the science of osmics
**24.** Old: Comb. form
**25.** The cake may take this
**26.** Descendant
**27.** Goddess of peace
**28.** Pointed toward
**29.** Like a charivari
**31.** ___ violet
**34.** Prohibition
**35.** Gist
**37.** Piquant
**38.** ___ alba (kaolin)
**40.** Artificial fly
**41.** Clergyman or schoolman
**43.** Salt solution
**44.** Reveal indiscreetly
**45.** Where Albie Booth once starred
**46.** Novel title meaning "a rover"
**47.** Oleaginous
**48.** German name for Cologne
**49.** Monastic title
**51.** Greek personification of night

# 147

**ACROSS**

1. Savory jelly
6. Knight's backup
10. Attend Choate or Andover
14. City ESE of Bombay
15. Site of the Pearl Mosque
16. Iranian coin
17. Exercise an option
18. Word with tide or time
19. "Three Sisters" character
20. With exuberance
23. River nymph
24. Stands
25. Fastens
28. Kind of trust
30. ___ lazuli
31. Lunar terrain
35. "That Certain Feeling" author
36. Heart line
37. Cross or Duke
38. Pleistocene mammals
40. Section of a long poem
41. Mug
42. Civilian cousins of batmen
43. Decalogue defier
46. Skirt of the 60's
47. Scarlett's form of escapism
53. Shankar
54. Grin broadly
55. Burn the ends
56. Curare
57. Flow along
58. Part of Aquinas's credo
59. East Indian herbs
60. Actress Markey
61. Pompous ones

**DOWN**

1. Copied
2. Matchless
3. Rondel, e.g.
4. Self-contradictions
5. Dozes lightly
6. Locale of Sam's lengthy error
7. Pet bat in "The Munsters"
8. Pacific sailing vessel
9. Hot, dry wind of southern Calif.
10. Unsophisticated, narrow-minded traits
11. All het up
12. U.S. $10 coin, until 1933
13. Pinter products
21. Sonny's sibling
22. Okefenokee denizen
25. Goeduck or gweduc
26. User of a prayer wheel
27. Sacred bull
28. Carried
29. Molders
31. Purely academic
32. Princess changed into a magpie
33. Printing-paper size
34. Father of Cainan
36. Charming
39. Period starting on the second day of Passover
40. Variation of rummy
42. ___ blanc
43. Diagonal support for a sail
44. Dweller in Qum
45. Drabble offering
46. Emulated Marceau
48. O'Casey
49. Rikki-tikki-___
50. London's ___ of Court
51. Gula
52. Clears

**ACROSS**

1. The Cosmos' game
7. Hampshire's quarters
10. Tourist center on the Jumna
14. Channel swimmer Gertrude: 1926
15. Sundial letters
16. Land bordering the Persian Gulf
17. Sit down with an old favorite book
18. Strength of a certain current
20. He kayoed "Two-Ton Tony": 1939
22. Deviation
23. Acolyte or credenza
24. Morning hrs.
26. O'Hara's Joey
29. Back comb
30. Litigious one
32. Singer from Boston
34. Adam's ___ (water)
35. Cynosures at cotillions
37. Like some glasses
39. Heavy overcoats
40. Consecrate
41. Zoo inhabitant
42. "___ a Kick Out of You"
43. United
44. Fills to repletion
46. What "she didn't say"
47. ___-Magnon
48. Leontyne and Vincent
50. Implement for a quadrireme
52. Adjective for the bald eagle
57. Forte of the Vienna Riding School
59. Ask
60. Discoverer of the Cape of Good Hope
61. M. Anderson's lofty place
62. Irish goblins
63. "The ___ to you!"
64. Relatives of aves.
65. Certain clouds

**DOWN**

1. Gavrilo Princip, e.g.
2. River with a fragrant sound
3. Game fish
4. Homophone for cruise
5. Kite
6. Robin, for one
7. Twins or cats
8. Tone color
9. Kennel sound
10. Bruit
11. Poem probably written at Stoke Poges churchyard
12. Music adopted by the Beatles
13. Afresh
19. Cleans the slate
21. Many tubs and palettes
25. Prefix with millionaire
26. Coin of Yugoslavia
27. ___ acids
28. Kind of sherbet
31. Cattail of India
33. Less open
35. Valuable assets
36. Speedy crossers of the Atlantic
38. Provides a dotation
39. Set free
41. Fasteners for stockings
44. Tap
45. "Eyes have they, but they ___": Psalm 115
49. Relish
50. Concern of Jimmy the Greek
51. Song for Domingo
53. Bowlers
54. Wild mango
55. Ohio or Utah, to René
56. Ricky Ricardo, on TV
58. Dir. of San Diego from Reno

# 149

**ACROSS**

1. Oriental park
9. Floors in a maison
15. Gastropod mollusks
16. Noted soprano
17. ___ Mountains (Calif. range)
18. Begrudged
19. Chi.-to-D.C. direction
20. "On Your ___"
22. Cotton machines
23. Reduces a sail
26. Adapts machinery for new uses
28. French-Belgian river
30. Fits of angry temper
31. Sighting
34. "Haste ___"
38. Auld lang ___
39. Relative of the turkey trot
40. Soften; disarm
42. Cecropia
43. Outlets for low-priced items
45. Myrmecologist's interest
46. Ten: Comb. form
47. Slippery critter
48. Egress
51. Union general
55. Composer Khachaturian
56. Baccalaureate deg.
58. Yugoslav city
59. Vivacity
61. Gleams faintly
64. Block
65. Underground activity
66. Rotary ___
67. Bags

**DOWN**

1. Kind of tiger or wasp
2. Humiliate
3. Indian noblewoman
4. In the manner of
5. Comic actor DeLuise
6. Part of some sigs.
7. Head of la casa
8. Respects
9. ___ out (supplement)
10. "La Cumparsita" and "Blue"
11. "___ Chorus"
12. One who denies
13. Lambs' mas
14. Elegiac
21. Phidian creation
24. "___ and Fantasy," 1943 film
25. Solar or circulatory follower: Abbr.
27. Danish city
29. Sverige
32. Arrow poison
33. Tormé and Brooks
34. N.Y.C. gallery
35. Most prolific auth.
36. Medical college in Ohio
37. Of the summit
38. Mink item
41. Check
44. Contemporary of Mondrian
46. Noted missionary on Molokai
49. Tuesday, in Paris
50. Zeena's spouse in a Wharton book
52. Close by: Poetic
53. Threnody
54. Curves
55. ". . . hear ___ drop"
57. Lobster-meal items
59. Pronoun for a ship
60. Three, in Milano
62. "___ Oncle," Tati film
63. N.Y.C. transit agency

# 150

## ACROSS

**1.** Norm
**4.** Part of an oriel
**8.** Cry of a flushed snipe
**13.** Rash or insolent
**15.** Pole used in Scottish games
**16.** Old, unpleasant woman
**17.** Relative of Franco
**18.** Emulate Pele or Orr
**19.** These never shake love, says Shakespeare
**21.** Cuprum-stannum alloy
**22.** Wire job
**24.** Evening, in Evian
**25.** Kind of palm or pepper
**27.** Uses a divining rod
**31.** Speed up
**35.** Swiss river
**36.** Royce's fellow traveler
**37.** Namibia, formerly: Abbr.
**38.** Purify
**39.** Russian river
**40.** "The ___," Hellinger opus: 1934
**42.** Conceal or blush
**44.** Certain trucks
**45.** Dutch portrait painter
**47.** Thus
**48.** Jungfrau is one
**51.** Connect, as with links
**55.** Drum signal
**57.** Source of hemp fiber
**58.** Frameworks in clay modeling
**60.** King of Naples: 1808–15
**61.** Playfully coy
**62.** Gujarat, in India, is one
**63.** Palindromic Latin infinitive
**64.** This might give you a laugh

## DOWN

**1.** Thick soup
**2.** Stulms
**3.** Branches
**4.** Crested, as a woodpecker
**5.** Perfect, to Armstrong
**6.** This follows 24 Across
**7.** Anglo-Saxon underdogs
**8.** General who defeated Hannibal
**9.** Screeches
**10.** He mocked Demeter and became a lizard
**11.** Skin
**12.** Cupid, to Clytemnestra
**13.** Site of the Taj Mahal
**14.** Mergers
**20.** Manner
**23.** Intrinsically
**25.** Dare
**26.** Sheer cotton fabrics
**28.** What Indira said to her dresser
**29.** Cogito follower
**30.** Viewed
**31.** Calla lily, e.g.
**32.** Beloved of Uncas
**33.** Roderick Dhu's group
**34.** Makes the wild mild
**38.** Folded or pleated
**40.** Honduran port
**41.** Ape or parrot
**43.** Woolly
**46.** Pale
**48.** Open courts
**49.** Type of soil
**50.** Luxurious
**51.** Machine parts
**52.** Adjoin
**53.** Place named for a mythical Irish queen
**54.** Strife was her shtick
**56.** ___ oil, used in varnish
**59.** Map abbrs.

# 151

**ACROSS**

**1.** Mandible
**4.** Explosive sound
**8.** Hypothetical particle, in physics
**13.** Site of the William Tell legend
**14.** Hawaiian dance
**15.** Peace Prize Nobelist: 1950
**16.** Numismatists' interests
**18.** Pasch
**19.** Argues illogically
**21.** Greek peak
**22.** Loosen
**23.** Butted
**27.** Squalid
**31.** Nautical direction
**34.** Whispers sweet nothings
**35.** Norm or printed form, in Firenze
**36.** Curt
**38.** Brightly colored beetle
**39.** Small sailing ship
**40.** Sport on horseback
**41.** Word with man or dog
**42.** Boredom
**43.** Attorney, e.g.
**45.** Perfume oil
**47.** Basilica area
**51.** Parlor game
**57.** Less giving
**58.** Crustaceans called mantis shrimp
**59.** Money, in Toledo
**60.** ___ lang syne
**61.** "You ___ My Lucky Star," 1935 song
**62.** Endings with mob and gang
**63.** Similar
**64.** Harrison or Ingram

**DOWN**

**1.** Huge
**2.** Zodiac sign
**3.** Paul McCartney's singing group
**4.** "How's that again?"
**5.** Herbert or Downs
**6.** Opposite of aweather
**7.** Costume balls
**8.** Low Sundays
**9.** Tipsy
**10.** Play opening
**11.** Beginning for stat or meter
**12.** Who wrote "Who?"?
**15.** Vegetable
**17.** Russian leader of yore
**20.** German connective
**24.** Judges or juries, sometimes
**25.** Pout
**26.** A Stooge
**28.** Gists
**29.** Adhesive
**30.** System of exercises
**31.** Religious superior
**32.** ___ Allison, colleague of puppeteer Tillstrom
**33.** Redirect
**35.** African nation bordered by Mauritania
**37.** Waste
**38.** Part of a cord
**40.** Examination
**43.** Shellac is one: Abbr.
**44.** Kind of light or gate
**46.** Beginner
**48.** Pivotal
**49.** Springe
**50.** English county
**51.** Rel. degrees
**52.** Delay
**53.** Relative of a fulmar
**54.** Word form with poise or distant
**55.** Grump
**56.** Ocean movement

# 152

## ACROSS

1. Bistro
5. Emperor after Nero
10. Soprano Moser of the Met
14. Leaf-stem angle
15. ___ a time
16. Part of Q.E.D.
17. Capp's ___ the Hyena
18. Rock bottom
19. "Render therefore ___ Caesar . . ."
20. Beasts with taking ways
23. Roosted or rested
24. Surety bond
25. He spied with Igal et al.
28. In favor of
30. Hairy
34. Room for Scheherazade
35. Extremely minute
38. ". . . ___ clock scholar"
39. Beasts with imagined ailments
42. Auditory; auricular
43. Writ involving debts
44. Monogram of Tusitala
45. Nickname
47. Dir. from Boston to Brockton
48. Blends
50. Actor Clunes
52. Concha or pinna
53. Beasts with delusions of grandeur
60. Neighbor of Malta
61. Secretary of Defense: 1969–73
62. Decem et tres
63. Make salt, in a way
64. Give ___ (try)
65. Best of films
66. Honshu pariahs
67. Flight: Fr.
68. Appear

## DOWN

1. Part of a horseshoe
2. Babilonia feat
3. Dandy's partner
4. Pass, as time
5. ". . . ___ forth": Matt. 24:26
6. Resinous Philippine tree
7. "___ and the Swan," Yeats poem
8. Commander of the Constitution (War of 1812)
9. Heart chambers
10. Feminists' quest
11. Abdul-Jabbar's ___ shot
12. Polka followers
13. Foofaraw
21. Parisian's smoke
22. Kennel sound
25. Silver salmons
26. Private chambers
27. Rabbit fur
28. Goldfinches
29. Exeunt ___
31. Discover
32. Locale of the talus
33. Word before goose, gull or seal
36. Article written every day
37. Dernier ___
40. Stop signs
41. One of David's generals
46. Home of Sen. Heflin
49. Kin of kudus
51. ___ May, in "Tobacco Road"
52. Where Saul saw a seeress
53. Castle defense
54. Actor Stone, who played Henry Aldrich
55. Farrow and Slavenska
56. Ship on which Hercules sailed
57. Ike, to Mac in the 30's
58. Pastoral group, in poesy
59. Land overrun by Burmese: 15th–16th centuries
60. Double this for a nag

# 153

**ACROSS**

1. Mona ___
5. Tackles
10. "Valse ___"
12. Unpaid bill
14. Hangover time
17. Links unit
18. Inner: Prefix
19. Standoff
20. Enraged
21. In the thick of
22. Corn bread
23. U.S. caricaturist
24. Media member
25. Billed and ___
26. City in Georgia
28. Tumult
30. "On a ___," 1902 song
35. Wipe out
36. Stria
37. Marsh birds
40. Corp. officer
42. Writer Wallace
43. Wallach and Whitney
44. Of space
45. Eroded
46. ___ Ch'ang, Chinese god of literature
47. Nessen and Ziegler
48. Hill dwellers
49. Continually, in a way
54. Arrow poison
55. Ancient Chinese philosopher
56. Of prisons
57. N.Y.C. and Balto.

**DOWN**

1. Sweetened the soil
2. Equi-
3. Cargo carrier: Abbr.
4. Virgil's epic
5. Doles
6. Idiom
7. Casa Mrs.
8. W.W. I outfit
9. Dermic artwork
10. "Walden" author
11. Master again
13. Catherine de Médicis was one
14. Certain tones on a scale
15. Uncaring
16. Nothing to lean on
21. "There's ___ slip . . ."
22. Smut, for short
24. Erects
25. Journalists: Abbr.
27. "I Get ___," 1951 song
29. Princely
31. Spenser's starwort
32. Certain teas
33. "___ Rainbow," 1939 song
34. Most recent
37. Overcast
38. Of oil
39. Telephone
41. Atelier items
44. Macaw
45. Tarries
50. Charlemagne's dom.
51. Neutral shade
52. Criticism
53. Forget-me-___

# 154

## ACROSS

1. Eisenhower, Carter et al.
7. Thimblerig object
10. Kind of scientist in cartoons
13. He played Lawrence of Arabia
14. Grows pale
15. Arab robe
16. Candy
17. Germanic language of yore
19. Begets
21. Life principle; soul
22. In fact
23. Van Doren from S.D.
24. Coin
27. Airport in Israel
28. Metal for cans
29. Hebrew letters
31. "___ bin ein Berliner": J.F.K.
33. Tooth
35. On the level
36. Pronoun for a doe
37. Legal plea
38. Wrong
39. River once called Obringa
40. "___ means!"
41. Sign of nervousness
42. Business deg.
44. Spot for a pad
45. Power
47. Ancient rival of Athens
49. Colder
50. OPEC
54. Operatic text
56. Crane fly
57. N.Z. or Ire.
58. Kind of light
59. Like some twists of fate
60. Sensibility, in Sens
61. Top chess player: 1960–61
62. ___emptor

## DOWN

1. Uvula
2. Take ___ the lam
3. Sound from Big Ben
4. Best U.S. chess player at 15
5. Without help
6. Medieval silk
7. ___-walsy
8. What a checkmate causes
9. NE corner of India
10. Emperor of Mexico: 1864–67
11. Loathsome
12. Mother of Perseus
14. Title held by 61 Across, 4 Down and 18 Down
18. Top player: 1975–85
20. Pope's "___ to Abelard"
24. Young whale
25. Zeno's philosophy
26. Insignificant
30. Sault ___ Marie
32. Book on plants
33. Fairy queen governing men's dreams
34. Cause one to get steamed up
43. Bitter cold
45. Small skin lumps
46. Council of ___: 1545–63
47. Liquor made in northern Mexico
48. Weasel's tropical cousin
51. Rodgers product
52. Lamb
53. Milk: Comb. form
55. "___ and Sympathy"

# 155

**ACROSS**

1. Cousin of "Ciao!"
5. Adjective for some stores
10. Crack is one
14. Stirred up
15. How the Frosts treated the Snows?
16. An alternative to medium
17. Israeli song?
20. Swift works
21. Bribes
22. Sale condition
23. Name on a D.C. hospital
25. Trouble on the set
28. Locus of power
29. Where to shed care
32. Ellery's rival
33. "Meanwhile, back at the ___ . . ."
34. Set the pace in a race
35. Locale of a certain hog?
39. Colleague of Monty
40. He wasn't afraid of Virginia Woolf
41. Latin start for Hamlet's soliloquy
42. Jr.'s elder
43. North Sea feeder
44. Toxophilite
46. Tribulations
47. Like Wayne's grit
48. Boite belle: 1915–63
50. Likely to succeed, as a starlet
53. What divers in pools do?
57. Number of Worthies
58. Jackson Sec. of War
59. Salver familiar to solvers
60. SALT participant
61. Square one
62. Disseminates

**DOWN**

1. What sports pick up
2. Jaques's heptad
3. Cato's covering
4. In a stew
5. Kind of acid or oxide
6. Companion of pains
7. Tries for a prize
8. Amice's relative
9. Solution used in ablutions
10. Stonehenge priest
11. Spot for #1 horse at a derby
12. Garden planters
13. Command to Dobbin
18. ___ prius court
19. Auhor of "Egmont"
23. Nice income
24. "___ to his choice . . .": Kipling
25. Coin of ancient Rome
26. Three-wheeler
27. Mayflower passenger
28. Media man Morley
29. Tramp in a bog
30. Kind of British pudding
31. Crawler or summer
33. Pierre's apparel?
36. What Macduff didn't do
37. Word in a threat
38. The take
44. Like Romeo or a Dromio
45. Unwrought or uncouth
46. A symbol of thinness
47. English dynasty or choreographer
48. Nantes vegetable
49. Physicists' concerns
50. Bright star
51. Fiddler in a fire
52. Chew on
53. Kokoon
54. French possessive
55. Type of trick for a Ranger
56. Prefix for function

# 156

**ACROSS**

1. Flattened a flat
6. ___-ski
11. Pay up
12. Bit of candy
14. Home of Sen. Danforth
17. Leaning
18. Makes less unruly
19. Hari ___, river in Afghanistan
20. German article
21. Shankar plays it
22. Spring follower
23. Quick to learn
24. Wall unit
25. Shipment to a paper mill
26. Turncoat
28. Small electronic organ
30. Lukewarm
32. Historic Anne
35. Menu phrase
39. Oil cartel
40. Signal light
41. Cries of surprise
42. Mil. unit
43. Ecstasy
44. Mad. and Lex.
45. Alfonso's queen
46. Rigid framework
47. List of candidates
48. Home of Sen. Levin
51. Strip
52. Has a yen for
53. "Up to here"
54. Put down seed

**DOWN**

1. Softens
2. Reconciled
3. Kind of poker
4. Yalie
5. Fated
6. "___ Crackers"
7. Enigma
8. Singer Columbo
9. Psyche component
10. Lizard
11. Old Glory item
13. Hike wearily
14. Lieu
15. Preoccupation with possessions
16. That is, to Tacitus
21. Squelched
22. Vitro di ___, Venetian glassware
24. Entreat
27. Vote in
28. Cauterizes
29. Stride
31. Enduring works
32. "Underwhelmed"
33. Unzipped
34. Emissaries
36. Despoiled
37. Greek letters
38. Site of the Krupp works
40. Like some columns
43. June V.I.P.
44. Breathing
46. Aqueduct pest
47. Artie or Irwin
49. Genetic key
50. ___-Magnon man

# 157

## ACROSS

1. Org. for Welby
4. Pound division
9. One of a loving Latin trio
13. Nice pronoun
15. Lend ___ (listen)
16. Carter
17. Carters
20. Art work
21. Offspring
22. Missiles, when dried
23. Sound of surf
25. Expedite
28. Pinball disaster
29. Queen killer
32. Show name
33. Club for the trap
34. U.S. overseas radio agcy.
35. Carters
39. Peer Gynt's mother
40. Organ supplier
41. Word in a Coleridge title
42. Title in D.C.
43. Anatomical canal
44. Creator of Sergius O'Shaugnessy
46. Decision mechanism
47. Montenegrin, e.g.
48. Theatrical locale for toys
51. Esculent
54. Carters
58. Positional word for seamen
59. Chaucerian tale-teller
60. ___ est percipi
61. Sunder
62. Patroon's property
63. Greek goddess

## DOWN

1. Helmut's "Alas!"
2. Catty comment's rejoinder
3. Actor Ray
4. High-kicking exhibition
5. A lord in "Macbeth"
6. Adjective at the bar
7. Thrash
8. Mil. hardware
9. Liqueur base
10. Wire measures
11. Rights org.
12. Scottish island
14. Textbook selector
18. Left Bank notion
19. Attacked, as by the love bug
23. Jockey
24. Character in "Three Sisters"
25. Barriers having trenches or ditches
26. Calumniate
27. Singer seeking sailors
28. Drift
29. Efficacy
30. Abbeville's river
31. Liquidator
33. Sinks
36. Anoesia
37. Barracks items
38. What certain guards do well
44. Vocation
45. Sea fed by the Syr Darya
46. Clocked
47. Quibbling evasion
48. Door position
49. Favus
50. Treasury investigators
51. Earl of Avon
52. "David and ___," 1962 film
53. Packy ___ (Hope as a boxer)
55. Estuary
56. Govt. aid to opera, etc.
57. Rosalynn Carter, ___ Smith

# 158

**ACROSS**

1. Auction action
4. Lee of films
8. Abet
12. Mind
14. ___ up (got hep)
15. Cruising
16. Mall event
17. She takes a bow at a luau
19. Simferopol's locale
21. "Thy hand is but ___ to my fist": Shak.
22. Lizards' look-alikes
24. "It ___ laugh": Pinero
25. Rice's "Street ___"
27. Neutral shade
29. Work ___
33. Committee V.I.P.
36. Educ. group
37. Feed-bag helping
38. Stood well
39. Sch. groups
40. Full of: Suffix
41. "Dickie Dare" and "Dixie Dugan"
43. Ride a bike
45. Collection
46. "Steppenwolf" author
47. Obi
49. Tonsorial service
51. Film directed by Joshua Logan: 1956
54. Conforms
57. How a turkey is greeted
59. Pour ___ (accelerate)
60. Without
61. The cats
62. Vacation spot for a doge
63. Winkle out
64. Absquatulate
65. Overawe

**DOWN**

1. Variety of pear
2. Construction member
3. Limned
4. The Blackbirds' inst.
5. Spanish land area
6. Certain orthoptera
7. ___ Ababa
8. Get the ___ (master)
9. Suffix for inchoative verbs
10. Give the eye like a bad guy
11. Sports standard
13. People of Sana
14. Reporter's question
18. Author Myrer ("The Last Convertible")
20. Pitcher that wouldn't last long in Shea
23. Earth mover
25. Reporter's triumph
26. Thriller episode
28. Book by Ade: 1896
30. Scrupulously clean
31. Harvests
32. Steel splint, in armor
34. Instructor at Pebble Beach
35. G.I. wear
39. Carry the day
41. Rank
42. Senator Cochran of Miss.
44. Basketball statistic
48. Unbending
50. Cuts and cures grass
51. One of Hollywood's Bridges
52. Jardinieres
53. Soccer great
55. Foofaraw
56. Fluff stuff, in CB lingo
57. Mil. award
58. Taradiddle

# 159

**ACROSS**

1. Haymarket attraction
8. Preserved
14. Taller and thinner
15. Traveling players
17. Experience
18. Kind of horse or camel
19. Zsa Zsa said it several times
20. Gourmand
22. About 39 inches in England
23. Classify
25. Tellers of twisted tales
27. Sub ___ (secretly)
28. Meredith Wilson's "The ___ Man"
30. "___ and Whispers," Bergman film
32. Cartoonist who created Ferd'nand
33. Hardens
35. Castanets
37. Engrossed
39. Stamp stuff
40. Tool for a tailor
44. Sounds of derision
48. Calloway
49. Pens
51. Genuflect
52. Kayo blow
54. Ejects
56. River on the Broads
57. Gypsy's card
59. Rove furtively
61. Most West Pointers
62. Gourmet
64. Part of a car
66. Atom splitter
67. Fer-___, pit viper
68. Muzzles
69. Max in "Hart to Hart"

**DOWN**

1. Platitudes
2. "Dime" of song, e.g.
3. Support
4. Jack Benny's secret
5. Tucker out
6. Queenly
7. Amatory
8. Movie-credit word
9. Dep.'s opposite
10. Rich soil
11. Oca or yam
12. Representative example
13. Letter opener
16. Untrustworthy people
21. Dumbo's "wings"
24. Wedding-cake parts
26. Otaries
29. Kind of room or mate
31. True grit
34. Signs of rubeola
36. Showy flower
38. Mechanisms for switches
40. Sea duck
41. Tidbits
42. Native of a European peninsula
43. Calchas, for one
45. Change anew
46. Playwright Rattigan
47. Having little force or validity
50. Swashbucklers' needs
53. "___ and His Brothers," 1960 film
55. Nectarous
58. Garb for "Swan Lake"
60. Tra trailers
63. Rubbish!
65. Smuggled

# 160

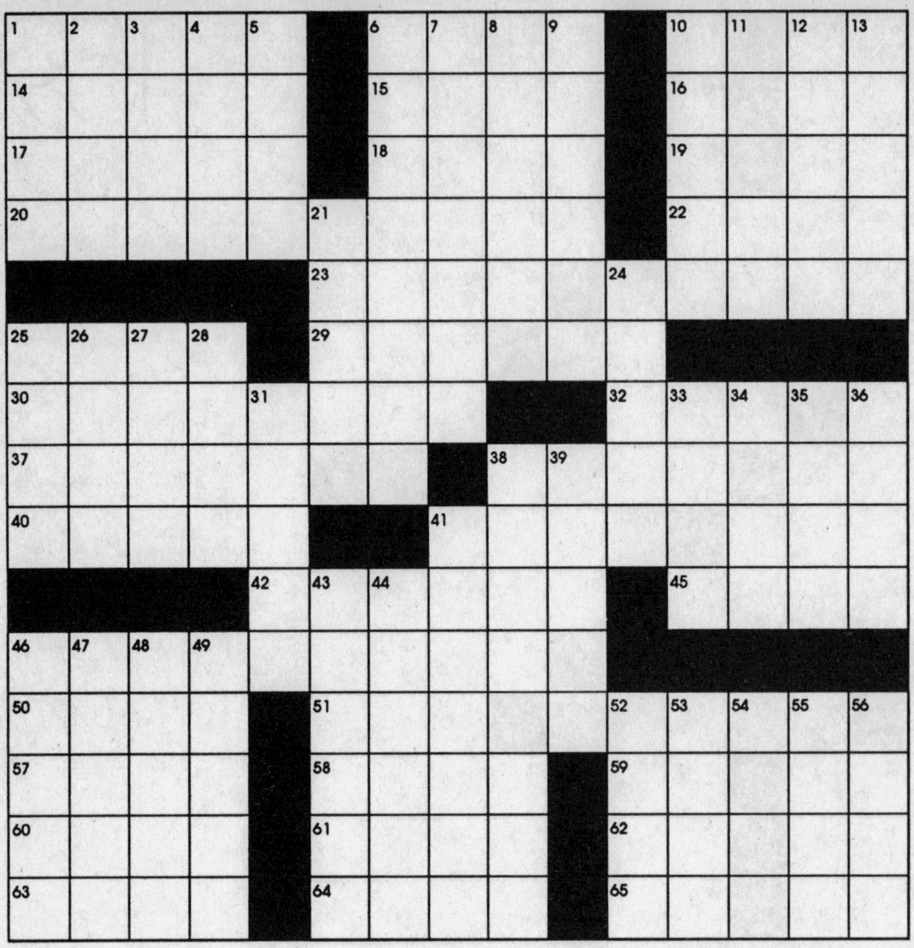


**ACROSS**

**1.** Lassoed
**6.** Rub clean
**10.** Edicts
**14.** President ousted by Amin in 1971
**15.** Solar disk
**16.** Like a 1913 Liberty Head nickel
**17.** Marine skeleton
**18.** Tiber tributary
**19.** Seaport in Algeria
**20.** Informal party with light refreshments
**22.** Clips
**23.** Moderate
**25.** Yoke
**29.** Route 1 is one
**30.** One receiving a share
**32.** Rabbit fur
**37.** Repellent in a closet
**38.** Bent
**40.** Japanese word meaning "first generation"
**41.** Ripples or rustles
**42.** Halo; nimbus
**45.** Kind of wave
**46.** Disjointed
**50.** Reverberation
**51.** Prophetic disclosure
**57.** Encompassed by
**58.** One place to see an ibis
**59.** Merits
**60.** Subdued
**61.** Word between speak and mind
**62.** Country youth
**63.** Utopian spot
**64.** Famed T-man
**65.** Narrow passage in an English cathedral

**DOWN**

**1.** What Sisyphus pushed
**2.** Joseph Robinson plays it
**3.** Algeciras is one
**4.** Berliner's budget
**5.** Secluded valley
**6.** Aeneas was one
**7.** Battologize
**8** Examine
**9.** Charm
**10.** It rises from a rose
**11.** Kin of a honey locust
**12.** Fishing net
**13.** What gibberish doesn't make
**21.** Mother of Azan
**24.** Versatile material
**25.** "Shut up!" in Siena
**26.** Greek W.W. II military org.
**27.** What eleemosynars give
**28.** Brood or dawdle
**31.** Region of the femur
**33.** Egyptian cross symbolizing life
**34.** "___ Moon," 1920 song
**35.** Sweet spire
**36.** Set of boxes
**38.** Ida or Ino
**39.** Lariat
**41.** Some Mardi Gras celebrants
**43.** "___ Me," Bill Withers hit song
**44.** Plant also called "live-forever"
**46.** Enraged
**47.** Tuareg, e.g.
**48.** Region, to Ruskin
**49.** Ancient
**52.** Minus
**53.** Small boat
**54.** Preacher's advice
**55.** Shred
**56.** Anglo-Saxon laborer

# 161

**ACROSS**

**1.** Athenian archer
**5.** Postpone
**10.** This has a "grate" sound
**14.** Type of beetle
**15.** Tagliavini's tunes
**16.** Former lightweight champ
**17.** Aliform
**18.** Wine seller, for one
**20.** Air one's wares
**22.** Bet on both teams
**23.** Half of many a course
**24.** Black who was really white
**26.** Kind of solution
**29.** Video V.I.P.'s
**33.** Jalopy
**34.** One of Luna's appearances
**35.** Kind of duct
**36.** Ethereal
**37.** Blow + spurt = ___
**38.** Burden for a Bedouin's camel
**39.** Spot for an ad
**40.** Intended
**41.** Pithy
**42.** What admen push
**44.** Departed from the party
**45.** Actress Dana's opposite?
**46.** Abbe who is definitely not a cleric
**47.** Conjecture (about a tree?)
**50.** He puts on many an act
**54.** Where plugs are manufactured
**57.** Heroine captivated by a captain
**58.** Arithmetic for young G.W.
**59.** Ceremonies that sound correct
**60.** Old rhyme for hit
**61.** Like some TV "People"
**62.** Distort a report
**63.** X, X, X

**DOWN**

**1.** Quod ___ faciendum
**2.** Mork or Mindy
**3.** Place for a race
**4.** Person of honor
**5.** Playwright now found in Wis.
**6.** Chop-worn
**7.** Marcel Marceau, e.g.
**8.** "I think, therefore ___"
**9.** Part of a fly
**10.** R & R for Junior
**11.** Far from fecund
**12.** Angler's tangle
**13.** Athlete who once got his kicks
**19.** Alpine riser
**21.** Virginia creeper (not Dare!)
**24.** No longer linked
**25.** Simba's share, at least
**26.** Scaramouch
**27.** To the back
**28.** Key follower
**29.** Refrains from
**30.** Out in the open
**31.** "Hair-dew"
**32.** Up to here
**34.** Home at Shea
**37.** Call's partner
**38.** Air show
**40.** Fancy footwear
**41.** His debut came in '32
**43.** Peter's three-time utterance
**44.** Least furnished
**46.** Give some dash to a bash
**47.** Bongo of Gabon
**48.** Do a kitchen-police job
**49.** Germ for a TV pitch
**50.** Kind of bank
**51.** Prime ___
**52.** Monocular deity
**53.** Cry of a backward star?
**55.** Certain connections
**56.** Nada

# 162

## ACROSS

**1.** "M*A*S*H" actor
**5.** Has dinner
**9.** Vibrant
**14.** Faustian commodity
**15.** Father Flye's famous correspondent
**16.** Composer of "Pavane for a Dead Princess"
**17.** November choices
**20.** Highway maneuver
**21.** Tyrrhenian and Timor
**22.** Weather satellite
**23.** Leader of the Afrika Korps
**25.** Gerrymander, perhaps
**27.** Coating for iron
**29.** Jazz dances
**33.** Name of 12 popes
**37.** Othello, for one
**39.** Lachrymal
**40.** Victor over H.M.S. Guerrière
**43.** Emulates a Lippizaner
**44.** Apply a mordant
**45.** Hack and rip followers
**46.** Certain barge cargo
**48.** River to Cairo
**50.** County north of San Francisco
**52.** Flash lamp
**57.** Gad
**60.** Slalom obstacle
**62.** Ready for broadcasting
**63.** Big Eight 11
**66.** Alamo ordeal
**67.** Bar to equity
**68.** Early Montanan
**69.** Trucklers' responses
**70.** Swing around
**71.** Mend

## DOWN

**1.** Supreme national god of Assyria
**2.** Keno's relative
**3.** Wheat variety
**4.** Yegg's undoing
**5.** Time for bears
**6.** Sounds of aversion
**7.** Hopper in an Eastertime tune
**8.** Bristles
**9.** Rainbow
**10.** Wordsworth, Coleridge and Southey
**11.** Famous name in lithography
**12.** V.F.W. members
**13.** Maxwell of columns, films and parties
**18.** Don Juan's mother
**19.** Philosophies, perhaps
**24.** Sketch
**26.** Westernmost point of the Aleutians
**28.** Bozo's beezer
**30.** Eldest of the Pleiades
**31.** Place for a figurehead
**32.** Roget's wds.
**33.** Run smoothly, as an engine
**34.** Words of understanding
**35.** TSgt's branch
**36.** Rugby play
**38.** In clover
**41.** Greek peak
**42.** "Upon ___ rock . . ."
**47.** Word after a minor premise
**49.** Holy Roman emperor
**51.** Feet of common measure
**53.** Estancia
**54.** ___ citato, footnote words
**55.** Kentucky college
**56.** Son of Henry
**57.** Cheerful
**58.** Tom Joad, for instance
**59.** Porters
**61.** Son of Rebekah
**64.** Males
**65.** Suffix with verb

# 163

## ACROSS

1. Set right
6. History student's concern
11. Join
12. Meaning the contrary of what is expressed
14. Simmer down
15. Do some rum-running
17. Burstyn or Terry
18. Irish hero
20. Aye neutralizer
21. Crucifix
22. Word with cast or side
23. Fright, in France
24. Raggedy one
25. Singer-songwriter Simon
26. Pouch between bone and tendon
27. Paul Dresser song: 1905
29. Devil's paternoster
30. Comers in the frog pond
32. Tried mightily
35. Boned the fish
39. Princess Anne, to Margaret
40. Dorian Gray's creator
41. ___ of nerves
42. Facts, briefly
43. Pares pears
44. ___-majesté
45. Retainer
46. Emerson's middle name
47. Religious art work
48. Where ginkgoes and ginsengs grow
50. Gabble
52. Carriage house
53. Yon's partner
54. Noted 18th-century mathematician
55. Clear sky

## DOWN

1. "The letter is ___ by half a mile": Shak.
2. Held sway
3. Versed in
4. One of the little people
5. Postponement
6. Appall
7. Ready for combat
8. Track man
9. One of the Siamese twins
10. Fifty-six in '76
11. Hong Kong is one
13. This may be subordinate
14. One of the Spice Islands
16. Wildcats
19. Appeased
22. Birthplace of 54 Across (older spelling)
23. Iago's "trash"
25. Garlic segment
26. Blow reveille
28. Gradually: Mus. dir.
29. Respiratory infections
31. ___-wisp
32. Enjoy the fragrance
33. Lack of discernment re music
34. Caller on the court
36. Small loudspeaker
37. Festival named for a dawn goddess
38. Gloomy, to Keats
40. Confusion; turmoil
43. Like yesterday's fad
44. Adjective for a slender bender
46. What banshees do
47. Substance
49. Big bird
51. Mark Russell's forte

164

**ACROSS**

1. Scottish caps
5. Man for whom the REO was named
9. A few
13. Jai ___
14. Léonie's laughter
15. Examine
16. Rope fiber
17. Water, in Palermo
18. Initials since 1922
19. Irish whisky
21. Singer James
22. Incumbent upon
23. "___ mio"
25. "___ Haw," TV show
27. Completed
29. Silenced, in a way
33. Where Shah Jahan built a mausoleum
35. Goddess who caused much ado
37. Marie Thérèse, for one
38. Native of Mosul
40. Prefix meaning "the same"
41. Bigwigs on campus
42. Sick of the rat race
43. Another prefix meaning "the same"
45. In a ___ (upset)
46. Parade-ground command
48. Cubitus
50. Monogram of a great poet
51. Half of a 60's comedy team
53. Arrow poison
55. Je ne sais ___
58. Adjective for "Tom Jones"
62. Dipper milieu
63. Tarsus
64. Nomadic Moslem
65. Tennis score, for short
66. Refusals
67. Agree
68. Crooner Columbo: 1908–34
69. Wig style
70. Arabian gulf

**DOWN**

1. Freud's "Totem und ___"
2. "___! poor Yorick"
3. Pretense
4. Basic exercise unit
5. Killer whale
6. Ogden Nash statement vis-à-vis candy
7. Amphetamines
8. Porpoise
9. Window washers tools
10. Winkle out
11. Hazard for a helmsman
12. Biblical scribe
17. More than
20. WW II setting
24. Contents of a tub
25. Israeli port
26. Kind of monkey
28. Canal of song
30. The largest invertebrate
31. Bandleader Skinnay
32. Villa ___, in Tivoli
34. Lincoln, F.D.R. et al.
36. Miedaner's "The ___ of Anna Klane": 1977
39. ___ facto
44. Habituate
47. Home for Juan
49. Orangutan, e.g.
52. "The ___ Madelon Claudet," 1932 film
54. Icelandic volcano
55. A fraction, fractionally
56. Variant of Hindi
57. Medical suffix
59. ". . . believe ___ in me": John 14:1
60. Barcelona or Madrid
61. Shangri-La of a sort

# 165

**ACROSS**

1. Insurgent
6. Secateurs
12. Full of spirit
14. Unfriendly
16. Abridgement
17. "Necktie party" figure
18. Mrs. Sundance in a film
19. Kudos
21. Small ape
22. ENE or WSW
23. Creeper
24. Counterclockwise
25. Genethliacons, e.g.
27. Stow cargo
28. Climbing plant of Asia
29. This is smaller than 36 Across
31. Kind of jaw or eye
32. Apple variety
33. First name of Amahl's creator
34. Pule
36. Daily occurrence at the shore
40. Jiggers
41. Curlicues in writing
42. Wireless word
43. Buster Brown's dog
44. Wang ___, Pearl Buck hero
45. Domesday Book money
46. Name of fame in a national game
47. Ignite
49. "Trinity" author
50. Salary
52. Hit song in 1953
54. Ruddy duck
55. Less jumpy
56. ___ Abbey, U.S. painter
57. What Genuine Risk ran for in May

**DOWN**

1. Destructive vortex
2. Asmara's province
3. Elementary particle
4. Tokyo's former name
5. Small mass
6. The Alamo, e.g.
7. Not necessarily a home
8. Actual being
9. Siamese coin
10. Small streams
11. Separates into filaments
12. "___ her damask cheek": Shak.
13. Diffuse widely
15. Actor Leon ___: 1881–1951
20. Coadjutor
24. Shed
26. Ariel, for one
27. Thorny tree
28. Hokum
30. Lots and lots
31. Musicians' stints
33. Titters nervously
34. "___ While You Work," woodcarver's song
35. Made helpless
36. Something to lend
37. Substance resembling dentin
38. Ridicules
39. Hit man
40. German sculptor-painter: 1440?–1533
41. Reindeer's feeding grounds
44. Napery
47. Civil War cap
48. Legendary Irish king
49. Allies of Kit Carson
51. "Treasure Island" character
53. Fam. member

**ACROSS**

1. Habre's land
5. City transport
8. Furnish
14. Milos Forman film: 1979
15. Qua ___ (here and there): It.
16. Grosse ___, Mich.
17. Shakespeare title: Abbr.
18. Counterpart of the Pac.
19. "Can-Can" composer
20. Miner's quest
21. Je ne sais quoi
22. She was born free
23. Effete
25. Server's edge, for short
27. Not counterfeit
30. Half a quote from Samuel Butler
33. Copper
34. Carry on
35. New-car odometer reading
36. Basin adjunct
38. Birthright barterer
40. Fret or chafe
43. Concerning
45. Electronic device
49. End of quote, after "but"
52. Dreyfus ally
53. Neighbor of Belg.
54. Funnyman John
55. Codlike fish
57. Rikki-tikki-___
59. Terminal: Abbr.
60. "... as ___ resting-place ...": Lincoln
62. Zoological suffix
63. Christie thriller
64. Zephyr
65. Sml., med., ___
66. Russian range
67. Famed TV cat
68. Source of an archer's bow
69. Cassidy was his role

**DOWN**

1. In a jumble
2. Fun on the farm
3. Plane-wing part
4. Bacheller's Darius
5. Steady date
6. Blue hue
7. Foe of Richard I
8. Add
9. Brooklyn Bridge buyer
10. Betty Rollin book: 1976
11. Easternmost of HOMES
12. Hwy.
13. Word with Alte or Bingle
21. Commotion
24. Joplin opus of 1902, with "The"
26. Switch
28. Número ___
29. I trouble
31. Due follower
32. Mauna ___
37. Ex successor
39. Fraction of a min.
40. "The ___," B'way play of 1975
41. Cry of amused surprise
42. Pregame cheerleader
44. How actress Wood dressed?
46. "Star Wars" captain
47. Where to find some cubes
48. Monument of Giza
50. English, to Juan
51. Pompey's "In what place?"
56. Indiana Jones foe
58. Top-of-the-Mark treat
60. Defense device: Abbr.
61. Back
63. Collar

# 167

**ACROSS**

1. Not of the clergy
5. ___ out (parachutes)
10. Works on samplers
14. Pet bat in TV's "The Munsters"
15. Shoelace tip
16. Red-cased cheese
17. Second in a Greek series
18. Climbing plant
19. Cover the bathroom wall
20. Golfer/football player
23. David and Goliath, e.g.
24. "Light-Horse Harry"
25. Inclining at sea
27. Over six million Egyptians
32. Insensitive
33. Org. for a G.I.
34. Like a draft animal
35. With end of 20 Across, rock 'n' roll singer/actor
40. Snack
41. Whitney or Wallach
42. Blithen
43. Abstruse
46. Redeyes of European waters
47. U.N. labor agency
48. On one's rocker, perhaps
49. With end of 35 Across, patriot/president
56. Couple
57. Comedian Nye
58. Skirt style
60. Teenager's trouble
61. Upper crust
62. Rarae ___
63. Rathskeller quaff
64. Passé
65. Set of similar objects

**DOWN**

1. Women's ___
2. Antiquing device
3. Whit
4. Lobster's kin
5. Nureyev vehicle
6. Exchange fees
7. "Now ___ me down . . ."
8. ___ an ear (hearken)
9. Mature male zebra
10. Sofa of a sort
11. Emulate Robert Giroux
12. Street in Manhattan
13. Duck
21. Body cavity
22. Comparative suffix
25. Former president of Panama
26. Milk: Comb. form
27. Kind of foot
28. Chemical suffix
29. Bedouin or gypsy
30. Egresses
31. Word in a New Year's song
32. Algonquian tribe
36. Cast the dice again
37. XXIX x XIX
38. ___ fille
39. City official
44. Repair clumsily
45. Lodge member
46. Reached on the wireless
48. Kind of fence
49. Reason to exercise
50. Fenway Park slugger
51. Last Stuart ruler
52. City in Kansas
53. Symphonic poem by Varèse: 1965
54. Spelunker's study
55. Zsa Zsa has several
59. Suffix with real or social

# 168

## ACROSS

1. Enervates
5. Had at the weeds
9. Emergency currency
14. Orchestra member
15. Isolated
16. Verify
17. Mother Goose character
20. Blows up
21. Fresh
22. Alleged sky sight
23. Be anxious; fret
24. Must
26. Destiny
27. Univ. degree
30. ``Flick''
31. Meditate steadily
32. Vault
33. These bear portraits of Cleveland
36. Gyre
37. Inducement
38. Call up, as memories
39. Ukr., for one
40. Kill a bill
41. Like caramel
42. Flag
43. Wield an ax
44. Hi-fi must
47. Discusses in detail
52. Mrs. Thatcher's residence
54. Motor
55. Sea dog
56. Give off
57. Log in
58. Homophone for use
59. Aria, e.g.

## DOWN

1. Peau de ___
2. Jack-in-___ (E. Indian tree)
3. Kind of deck
4. Solitude
5. Bringer of bad luck
6. Susann's ``___ Is Not Enough''
7. Part of B.P.O.E.
8. Impaired: Prefix
9. Domain
10. Ceramic piece
11. Actor's concern
12. Muscovite
13. Vivacious
18. Sent skyward
19. Lunar feature
23. Jeweler's unit
24. Wickets
25. Parisian's property
26. Large book
27. Subordinate to
28. Like a cantankerous critter
29. Church feature
30. ___ Liberty
31. Photoengraving
32. Active, alert persons
34. Opera by Weber
35. Order
40. TV fan
41. Storage boxes
42. Valuable find
44. Word with slip or swipe
45. Actor Rip
46. Change the text
47. What marmots do
48. Flirt visually
49. Verne hero
50. Linden
51. Bismarck
53. Honshu bay

# 169

**ACROSS**

**1.** Move imperceptibly
**5.** Proverbs
**9.** Machete's cousin
**13.** Org. head
**14.** Man of Adak
**16.** Inter ___
**17.** Lawman Wyatt
**18.** Eremite
**19.** Neighbor of Mont.
**20.** Clandestine
**23.** Gimlet flavoring
**24.** Modernist
**25.** Duvalier's country
**27.** Hold back
**32.** Cole Porter song: 1929
**33.** Of flight: Prefix
**34.** Neighbor of Eng.
**35.** Any imminent danger
**39.** Belief
**40.** Revile
**41.** City in a Browning poem
**42.** Coastal area
**45.** Move effortlessly
**46.** Raggedy doll
**47.** Certain S. African
**48.** Ready to fight
**55.** Eager
**56.** Dissipate
**57.** Nobelist in Chemistry: 1934
**58.** Hackman or Wilder
**59.** Ashlar, for one
**60.** Spotless
**61.** Frankfurt an der ___
**62.** Lab substance
**63.** Dele not

**DOWN**

**1.** Energy cartel
**2.** Certain exam
**3.** Kamikaze's plane
**4.** Trellis for shrubs
**5.** Deli item
**6.** Unassisted
**7.** Make one's way
**8.** Took to court
**9.** City on the Penobscot
**10.** Ye ___ Tea Shoppe
**11.** Perjurer
**12.** Mighty tree
**15.** Lintel
**21.** Tampered with a check
**22.** Procure
**25.** Part of a ship's bow
**26.** Bouquet
**27.** Drafted again
**28.** Of an age
**29.** Felt malaise
**30.** Drama by S. Johnson
**31.** ___-ce pas?
**32.** Greek letters
**33.** Churchill's "___ Country"
**36.** Bergamots
**37.** Eyed amorously
**38.** Sounds in a sylvan setting
**43.** Oshkosh native
**44.** "Ode ___ Grecian Urn": Keats
**45.** Infallible truth
**47.** Conductor Walter
**48.** Rest-home occupants
**49.** Color of a photographic image
**50.** Boxing promoter's concern
**51.** Choirboy's collar
**52.** In ___ (bogged down)
**53.** "The Way We ___"
**54.** Word heard at the U.N.
**55.** Bygone

# 170

## ACROSS

**1.** Chicken farmers, e.g.
**9.** Kilimanjaro topper
**15.** Short lyrical poem
**16.** Baritone role in Verdi's "I Lombardi"
**17.** Gotham highway
**18.** Beautifies
**19.** "Without further ___"
**20.** Circumference
**22.** Use a shuttle
**23.** Dress-shirt item
**25.** Cassettes
**26.** "I ___ to bury Caesar . . ."
**27.** Decorated metals
**29.** Opp. of pos.
**30.** Smith
**31.** Handle clumsily
**33.** Exempt
**35.** Cozzens best seller: 1957
**39.** Checked one's mount
**40.** Ho Chi Minh City festival
**41.** Fossil resin
**42.** Diminutive endings
**44.** Storehouse
**48.** Interviews
**49.** Had flu symptoms
**51.** Calhoun of movies or boxing
**52.** Univ. figure
**53.** Look upon with disdain
**55.** Kind of dancer
**56.** Opening or gap
**58.** Produce
**60.** Garb
**61.** Echidna or pangolin
**62.** Oscillate unsteadily
**63.** Legumes

## DOWN

**1.** "Seat of consciousness"
**2.** "___ Singapore," 1940 film
**3.** Imbue with high-mindedness
**4.** N.Y. summer time
**5.** Offspring: Abbr.
**6.** "Adam Bede" author
**7.** Writer whose pen name was Jeremy Lord
**8.** Drove faster
**9.** Bridge player's unhappy declaration
**10.** Scurrilous fellows
**11.** Relative of the id
**12.** Tad products
**13.** Dominant group in Vietnam
**14.** Put bills on walls
**21.** Sponsorship
**24.** Testifies in court
**26.** First name of 21st U.S. President
**28.** Thrifty one
**30.** Unser's "thing"
**32.** United
**34.** Kennedy transient
**35.** V.I.P.
**36.** Aden native
**37.** Set free
**38.** Chess man
**43.** Unruffled
**45.** Maine product
**46.** Emulated Pitt
**47.** Office workers
**49.** Goose genus
**50.** "La Vita Nuova" author
**53.** Certain
**54.** ___ off (angry)
**57.** Coalmouse
**59.** Strike smartly

# 171

**ACROSS**

1. "___ girl!"
5. Waned
10. Govt. cost-of-living barometer
13. ". . . the loveliest woman___": Yeats
14. Put forth effort
15. Voiceless consonant
16. Stertorous
17. Honeybunch
19. "Love Is___": Irving Stone
21. Grub
22. Pastures
23. Long-stemmed drinking glasses
26. Dagger's partner
28. Branching
29. B'way hit by Schisgal: 1964
30. Inflame with love
32. "___Harrington," Meredith novel
36. Expert
37. Bother
39. Japanese woman diver
40. Southwest sight
42. Bogyman
43. Court stroke
44. Bluegills
46. Employers
48. Sometimes they're polished
51. Arabian spirits
52. Current movie maker
53. Dickens character
56. Lover
60. Cookbook verb
61. These may be wild
62. Activate
63. Organic compound
64. Dir. from Reno to Niagara Falls
65. Gather
66. Split

**DOWN**

1. Habile
2. Binge
3. Sweethearts
4. Painter ___ del Sarto
5. Lanchester and Maxwell
6. Weep and wail
7. Lucky draw in a tournament
8. Busy time on the Riviera
9. Telegraph message part
10. Copper: Comb. form
11. Secret
12. New slants
15. Naval engineer
18. Troubles
20. Like Goya's "Maja"
23. Gongs
24. Love affairs
25. Actor Peter: 1904–64
26. Word with shell or bake
27. She wrote "Kiss the Boys Goodbye"
28. Picaresque character
31. Japanese-American
33. Sweetheart
34. Cupid
35. Collars
38. Bear
41. Doubleday and Dean
45. Rave's partner
47. Talk-show host
48. Honeymooners' lake in the West
49. New York city
50. Fill with joy
51. Agrees
53. Word with pot or up
54. Object of devotion
55. Become tender or gentle
57. Singing syllable
58. Emoter
59. Brook's cousin

# 172

## ACROSS

1. Proceeds
4. Author of "The Immigrants"
8. Start of a nursery rhyme
14. Fighting temper
15. Construction item
16. Fictional sleuth ___ Lupin
17. River in China
18. Irresolute
20. Put out
22. Hindu ascetic
23. Difficult age
24. Capone, Jolson et al.
25. Italian wine
29. Antiknocks, e.g.
31. Map addendum
32. Flower receptacles
33. Consecrate
34. Current measures
37. Miami's hiemal boast
38. Babe Ruth's first name
39. Native of Shiraz
40. Ingredient of ouzo
41. Containers for colorful mixtures
45. Varnish ingredient
46. Police-call letters
47. Author Alex
48. ___ Haute
50. Fruity desserts, for short
51. Islands north of New Guinea
55. Op or Pop
56. "___ emptor"
57. Hindustani
58. Compass dir.
59. Isolate
60. Flay
61. Prefix with pathetic

## DOWN

1. Khrushchev
2. Expunged
3. Tightened
4. Pentagon V.I.P.
5. Aldrich's "Story of ___ Boy"
6. Algonquian
7. Toys
8. Pitching error
9. Lorraine Hansberry hit: 1959
10. High, as inflationary prices
11. "___ Mir Bist . . ."
12. ___ Arbor
13. Arm of the Medit.
19. Young maiden
21. Meccas for scholars
24. Rosary beads
26. Europe's neighbor
27. Release, as anger
28. Suffix with major or cigar
30. Phrase of understanding
33. Bates or Arkin
34. Laboratory medium
35. Part of the writing on the wall
36. Petits ___
37. Bassinet
39. Satellite of Saturn
41. Eng. legislative assembly
42. St. ___, city NNW of London
43. At hand
44. Solar follower
49. Estimate
50. Middle: Prefix
51. King's superior
52. Cupid
53. DIII doubled
54. Annoy

# 173

**ACROSS**

1. Longfellow's "mighty man"
6. End of an O'Neill title
10. Super Bowl team: 1980
14. Fields
15. Discontinue
16. Russian city on the Ussuri
17. Fashion designer Simpson
18. Eighth note
19. Part of a skirt
20. Inheritance of the firstborn
22. Dance of the Islands
23. Eyots
24. Preface: Abbr.
26. "___ to Heaven," 1928 song
30. Arena attraction
31. Novel of 1847
32. Little ring
36. Insult
40. Impute
41. Waste bit by bit
42. Inert element
43. Some Plymouth Rocks
44. Tumblers
47. Author of "A Sentimental Journey"
50. Epochs upon epochs
51. Astragali
52. Ell feature
58. Cassini
59. Hebrew month
60. Dieter's no-no, for short
61. Like Croesus
62. Anderson of "WKRP in Cincinnati"
63. Destroy
64. Dillon of "Gunsmoke"
65. Scoria
66. Rialtos

**DOWN**

1. Try
2. ___ operandi (procedures)
3. Road for Remus
4. Pitch
5. Country show on TV
6. Fairness
7. Gear for divers
8. Great Lake State: Abbr.
9. ___ of the Cross
10. These are made when Dobbin gees
11. Cyrano's feeling toward Roxane
12. Phil Donahue's wife
13. P.G.A. Hall of Fame name
21. Burnford's "Bel ___": 1978
25. ___ dimittis (permission to leave)
26. Unguis
27. Russian bay
28. Louis Viaud's pen name
29. Direct
30. Pastoral plaint
33. Double talk, at times
34. Oil-yielding tree
35. Some folding money
37. Egyptian symbol
38. Their aides constantly see stars
39. Bitter vetch
44. "Iron Man" of Ruth's day
45. Father of Gawain and Gareth
46. Garland
47. Williwaw
48. Sylvester's beloved in "Rocky"
49. Superior group
50. Capital of Guam
53. Teraph
54. Kaye of ballet fame
55. Growl
56. "___ for Life": Irving Stone
57. Hot saisons in Savoie

# 174

**ACROSS**

1. Prefix with chapel
5. Nativity-play accessory
9. Become more friendly
13. Opposite of bust
14. Overleaps
16. Unit of loudness
17. First of nine in "Strange Interlude"
18. Skewbald's relative
19. Dane who composed the opera "Lamia"
20. Actor's supreme delight
23. Awl, for one
24. Quartet in "No, No, Nanette"
25. Doe or Roe
28. Goddess of the moon
32. Pen pals' go-betweens
35. Welcoming garland
36. Simple sugar
37. Land unit
38. Belli or Bailey: Abbr.
39. Cue part
40. "The Foggy, Foggy ___"
41. "___ Clear Day"
42. Prefix with foil or pan
43. What some losers suffer
45. Man on a certain path
47. ___-Aryan
48. Force for followers of a John Paul: Abbr.
49. What Horace called "a short madness"
53. Comedian's delight
60. ". . . ___ for my steps": Psalm 57
61. Molière's Harpagon, for one
62. Essence
63. Catchall words
64. Winter period in Barcelona
65. Baltic feeder
66. Took part in the Grand National
67. Ibn-___
68. Noted Danish novelist: 1869–1954

**DOWN**

1. Confuse
2. Night: Comb. form
3. Destroy, as a car
4. Outstanding
5. Shoshonean Arizonan
6. Cole Porter's "I ___ Love"
7. Heather
8. Conductor Klemperer
9. Disease-carrying insect
10. "___ soit qui . . ."
11. ___ Domini
12. Break of a habit
15. Former British coin
21. Wycherley was one
22. Opposed
26. Tapper for a tyro at the piano
27. Script order
28. Range topped by Belukha
29. ___ operandi
30. Words of the enlightened
31. Machines seams
32. Clear snow
33. Chaplin's widow
34. Mira or Rigel
44. Many-sided figure
46. Make susurrous sounds
50. Cicerone
51. Character in "Elizabeth the Queen"
52. Small rocket, for short
53. Heavyweight champion: 1934–35
54. "Not ___ us the praise . . .": Kipling
55. Make use of a library
56. Flippers
57. Cruising
58. Tacna's country
59. Urge

# 175

**ACROSS**

**1.** Humerus is one
**5.** Asexual: Comb. form
**9.** More sincere
**14.** Sermon word
**15.** Quintet less duet
**16.** Like pancake batter
**17.** Be facetious
**18.** Emulate a devil chaser
**19.** Stage device
**20.** Opener at a trattoria
**23.** Tie or money follower
**24.** Inventor-clockmaker Terry
**25.** Monkeylike
**28.** Pluperfect starter
**30.** Ventilated
**34.** In re
**35.** Olive for Ovid
**37.** Aegean island, also called Ios
**38.** Trattoria course
**42.** Energy source
**43.** Compete for the America's Cup
**44.** Chorus member
**45.** Von Bismarck
**47.** Lab item for Dr. Carver
**48.** Acronymic beams
**49.** Literary monogram
**51.** Serve, with "on"
**52.** Trattoria main dish
**59.** Belief
**60.** Painting, to Picasso
**61.** Meteorological prognostication
**62.** Coin for Begin
**63.** Glacé
**64.** Raison d' ___
**65.** Shakespeare's "are you able?"
**66.** Elephant's-ear
**67.** Cimino's "The ___ Hunter"

**DOWN**

**1.** ___ California, Mexico
**2.** Straw in the wind
**3.** Brooding place
**4.** Sirenic
**5.** "Take the ___," Strayhorn song
**6.** Get the point
**7.** Solecistic contraction
**8.** Marquand sleuth
**9.** Ho Chi Minh is one
**10.** Gogol's land
**11.** One
**12.** Inside: Comb. form
**13.** Gypsy gentleman
**21.** Writer Sylvia's family
**22.** Jason's helper
**25.** Gran ___ d'Italia, Apennine group
**26.** Current supplied for a circuit
**27.** Intended
**28.** ". . . this chase is ___ follow'd": Shak.
**29.** Holmes called him "The Oldest"
**31.** Like an ament's comments
**32.** Martinet's imposition
**33.** Letter ending
**36.** Alpha Aquilae (star)
**39.** Tripod for Georgia O'Keeffe
**40.** Pedro's uncle
**41.** Fixed an antique
**46.** Zoo denizens
**48.** Site of Fort McIntosh
**50.** Attack
**51.** Din's burden
**52.** Lope de ___, Spanish dramatist
**53.** Hip to
**54.** Milk, in Champagne
**55.** Killer whale
**56.** Please a gourmand
**57.** Place for a tread
**58.** Humdinger
**59.** Between tic and toe

# 176

**ACROSS**

1. Married man's septennial problem
5. Exterminates
9. This may figure in an hourglass figure
13. Snooks, to Brice
14. Staten Island or Dobbs
15. Beyond the ___
16. Kanten
17. Subject of many a Truffaut film
18. News item
19. First line of an equinoctial verse
22. Little island
23. Jackie Onassis, ___ Bouvier
24. Foulard spoiler
27. Incarcerate
29. Golf org.
32. Second line of verse
35. Dumbbell
36. Org. in "Odd Man Out"
37. These may be wild
38. Third line of verse
43. Disconsolate
44. Cainan was his son
45. Bury
46. You can have a blast with this
47. Department at D.C.
48. End of verse
56. Brilliant stroke
57. Metal mold
58. Let out, as in sewing
59. Prompt
60. Petioles
61. "Song of India," e.g.
62. Textile worker
63. Where she had bells
64. "___ we forget"

**DOWN**

1. Adversary of Iraq
2. Neighbor of Ghana
3. Tooth's partner
4. Towel marking
5. Moderate
6. Press
7. Stupefy
8. Otologist's device
9. Fine porcelain
10. Freud's "Totem und ___"
11. "I cannot tell ___"
12. Still
14. Breakfast cereal
20. French bread
21. Understands
24. Roman woman's garb
25. Like some showers
26. Nick Charles's dog
27. Panaceas
28. Lake bordering Uzbekistan
29. Carlton Fisk guards it
30. U. of Florida athlete
31. Suburb of Liège
33. Late Yugoslav leader
34. A size of paper
35. Emigrés, e.g.
39. Dispatched
40. Tangle
41. Traffic signals
42. Concerning
46. Thin candle
47. Basic units of matter
48. Whig's opponent
49. Enormous
50. Within: Comb. form
51. U.S. author: 1909–55
52. Genuine
53. Filly's mother
54. Sale words
55. Straight from the bottle
56. Something chewed on a pasture

# 177

**ACROSS**

1. Brace
5. Belled the cat
10. Lose effectiveness
14. Behold, to Brutus
15. Cat-___-tails
16. Diva's solo
17. Shaw play: 1898
20. Musical piece
21. Kind of scholar
22. Breakwater
23. Gyrated
24. Furious
26. Kind of dive
27. Statute
30. Most likely dice throw
31. Look
32. Soho blackjack
33. Shaw play: 1917
36. Advice, in Arles
37. Bombast
38. Sheeplike
39. Colloid
40. Car salesman's car
41. Frock
42. Seeds rich in protein
43. Barrow
44. Move swiftly
47. Menu phrase
51. Shaw play: 1932
53. Code word for A
54. Nose about stealthily
55. Mme. Bovary
56. Lager, e.g.
57. Rouen's river
58. Appear

**DOWN**

1. Favorites
2. Hurt
3. Wine bucket
4. ". . . nature yet ___": Wordsworth
5. One of Walt's creations
6. Battery terminal
7. Prevalent
8. Windup
9. Mailer work with "The"
10. S. African writer
11. Like the Sinai Peninsula
12. Merchandise available
13. Minstrel's repertory
18. Consecrate
19. Eschew
23. Middle of Byron's famous trio
24. Can. municipal official
25. Serve to clarify a situation
26. "___ evil . . ."
27. An Armstrong
28. Orgs.
29. Sound of glee
30. Chase fungoes
31. Baby buggies
32. Insurance options
34. Disintegrations
35. Roman who wrote: "Persian luxury, boy, I hate"
40. Letter opener
41. Not beyond one's capability
42. King whom Tito deposed
43. Word with glass or oil
44. Use a dirk
45. Bride-___
46. Heavy, for one
47. Thine, in Lyon
48. Where Sinclair Lewis died
49. Not light reading
50. Fine cheese
52. Poetic word

# 178

**ACROSS**

1. Oriental weight
5. Twilight of the ___
9. Singer Janet Baker et al.
14. Hawkeye in a TV series
15. Film roll
16. Growing out
17. Alertness
19. Hit hard
20. Sib
21. Let in
23. "The boast of ___ . . .": Gray
26. Discomfort
27. An oc.
28. French spirit
29. Bixin and oleate
31. Pronoun for a hind
32. ___ emptor
34. Tease
36. "___ generally shammin' . . .": Kipling
38. Sixth ___
39. At a distance
40. This is served at Sing Sing
41. Pub
43. Theater sign
44. Strike out
46. News agcy.
47. Recent: Prefix
48. Aldebaran, e.g.
49. Hot-tempered person
51. City celebrated by William Carlos Williams
54. Gardner first name
55. Idiot
56. Between earls and barons
60. She changed men into swine
61. ___ fixe
62. The Iberian Madonna is one
63. Detroit lemon
64. Wets with drops
65. Refuse

**DOWN**

1. Hebrew letter
2. He won in Zaire: 1974
3. "Spoon River" poet
4. Space dog
5. Expert chess players
6. Wine: Comb. form
7. Caries
8. Follower of bob or dog
9. Show graphically
10. Ecclesiastical ban
11. University degree
12. Diminutive suffix
13. Something for the birds
18. Color or flower
22. Acclaimed creations
23. Attacks
24. Member of a minority group
25. Disclose
29. Abate
30. One who frightens
33. P.O. item
35. Danish or Norwegian monetary unit
37. Judge's pronouncement
42. Part of TNT
45. OPEC is one
49. Derogatory, in a sly way
50. Shifting
51. Tempo
52. During
53. Roman poet
57. Emulate Betsy Ross
58. Fashion
59. Upward bend in timber

# 179

## ACROSS

1. What a deceiver weaves
4. Quench
9. County in N.C.
13. ___ follicle
15. Electrician, at times
16. Police team
17. Work, hobbies, social events, etc.
19. Quinine byproduct
20. "Go to Hades!"
22. U.S. Olympic diver Louganis
23. Hold back
24. Salad of a sort
28. Safari sights
32. ___ yellow, an acid dye
33. These rolled in Robespierre's day
35. Guanaco's cousin
36. Christie novel
38. Demons, in Glasgow
40. Arthurian lady
41. Quarterback ___, gridiron play
43. Squirrels' nests
45. Time period
46. In which King was once the queen
48. Least shapely
50. Atahualpa was one
52. Role for a Zimbalist
53. Relative of "Well, look who's here!"
60. Powder
61. Adulator's forte
62. Earthenware jug
63. Englishman's stunning defeat
64. Proceeds
65. Common follower
66. This may be tall or short
67. Belgian-French river

## DOWN

1. "How's that again?"
2. "To ___ his own"
3. Snack
4. Turned
5. Pressed a suit
6. A spore is at its core
7. Young guinea fowls that sound poetic
8. Not genuine
9. Construct
10. What a ruler holds
11. Lucifer lost this
12. "___, Brute?"
14. Raised strip
18. Former Russian distance
21. Backbone of a ship
24. "Thou ___ not then be false . . ."
25. Fresh air
26. Oscar winner for "Two Women"
27. Like events on Walpurgis Night
29. Indian V.I.P.'s wife
30. Arabian V.I.P.'s
31. Former Egyptian V.I.P.
34. Member of "The Gashouse Gang"
37. Demonic
39. Crossword-puzzle pattern's characteristic
42. Eccentricity
44. Black-suit item
47. Flouts
49. Exanimate
51. Key for Elgar
53. Lade
54. Picket
55. O'Neill's mother
56. Tijuana tidbit
57. Container for a nostrum
58. ___ cap (mushroom)
59. Shirt sizes: Abbr.

# 180

**ACROSS**

1. Units of angular measurement
8. Sites of some venditions
13. Tale told by an oldster
15. Prepares for action
17. Tale of woe
18. Battologize
19. Nice friend
20. Kind of door or scale
22. Japanese woman diver
23. Edna Best's hometown
25. Monkey wrench
26. Take ___ view of
27. Weasel
29. Epithet used by H.S.T.
31. Part of the handwriting on the wall
32. Ancient ascetic
35. Islamic month
37. Press
38. Port on the Firth of Lorne
39. Type of butterfly
42. Certain bulbs
45. Golf scores
46. ___ de plume
48. Siouan Indians
50. Part of a monogram: Abbr.
51. A Scandinavian
54. Chief
55. Trippet
56. Shoots from stems of plants
59. Refrain syllable
60. Marbles
62. Made to order
64. Devastating
65. Tailless
66. Inventor of farm machines
67. Surrounded

**DOWN**

1. Indian rulers
2. Windflower
3. Infers
4. Ferber's "___ Palace"
5. U.S.N. officers
6. Fibers combed from wool
7. Blot
8. Weaver's purchase
9. Shake ___ (hie)
10. Corded fabric
11. Feared
12. Miler's sine qua non
14. Icelandic literary works
16. Long part of a spider plant
21. Luzon native
24. ". . . those move ___ who have learn'd to dance": Pope
26. Deadly fungus
28. Dramatist or drama critic
30. Hindu gentleman
33. High point
34. Place on a list
36. Saint-___, French port
39. Heroic
40. Emulated John McGraw
41. Archbishop
43. Depict
44. Conceal
47. Mediterranean island
49. Like Unter den Linden
52. What "shalom" means
53. Father of Troilus
56. Something to shed
57. Cay
58. Slightly twisted wool
61. Brew in Brest
63. Harem room

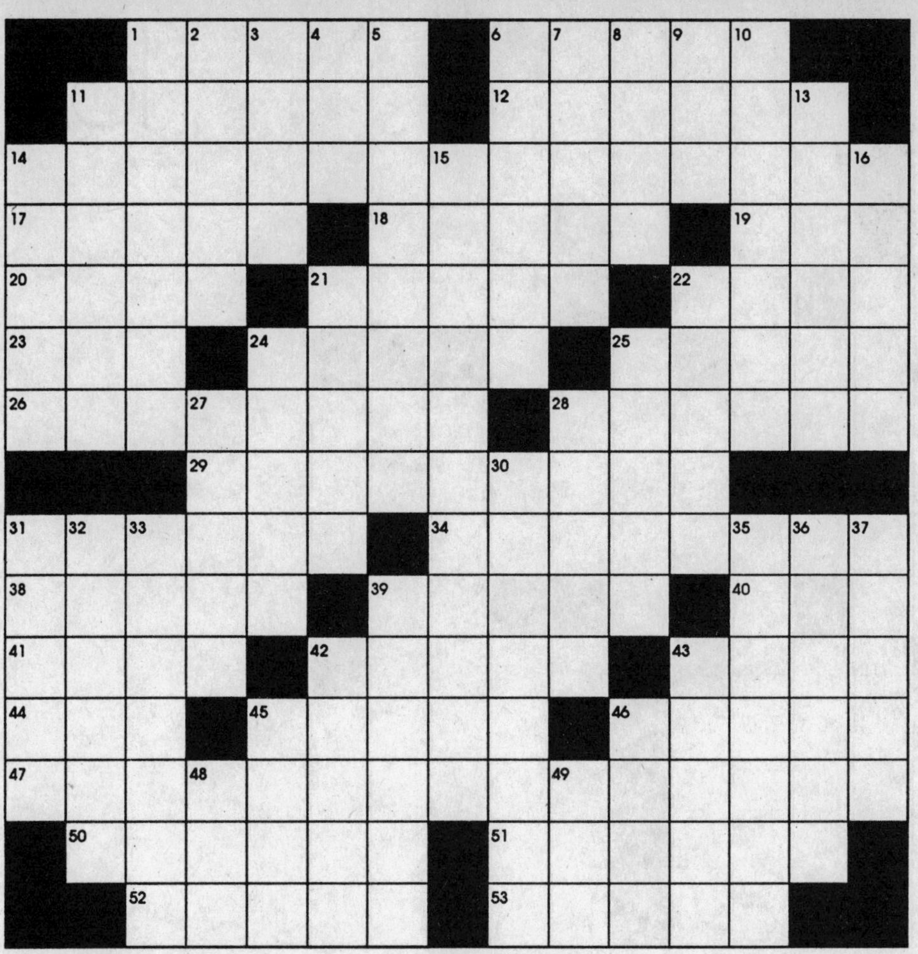

**ACROSS**

1. Spats
6. "___, the heavy day . . .": Richard II
11. Sword of Damocles
12. "Whether 'tis ___ . . .": Hamlet
14. U.S. writer: 1871–1945
17. Admonishes
18. Permission to leave a diocese
19. U.S. power complex
20. Faulkner's "As ___ Dying"
21. Chief hellion
22. Glass-making material
23. Embouchure
24. Macho types
25. Alla ___
26. Secular group
28. Contributed to a common stock
29. Sour
31. Ear prominence
34. Walter Pater was one
38. Book-jacket blurbs
39. Hordeola
40. U.K. party
41. Reputation
42. Attraction at Chichen Itza
43. Food fish
44. Pres. Smeal's org.
45. Nigeria's capital
46. Old court dance
47. "An ___," novel by 14 Across
50. Office item
51. Ionesco
52. Umbrageous
53. Orchestra section

**DOWN**

1. Remedial treatment
2. Literary device
3. G-men
4. U.N. outfit
5. Moved steadily or swiftly
6. Like certain Indians or wolves
7. Tracking system
8. Further
9. Year in the reign of Antonius Pius
10. Small falcon
11. Wearer of a comic mask
13. Freshen
14. Gabardine, e.g.
15. Partial excuse
16. Chid
21. Truck rigs
22. Would-be sophs
24. Deceive
25. Engagements for Mike Tyson
27. Quinella, e.g.
28. Propounds
30. Dublin's province
31. A sodium carbonate
32. Radar antenna housing
33. They declare openly
35. Field hockey teams
36. Immoderate speech
37. Hard wood
39. Honeyed
42. Sprinted
43. Pent up
45. ___ Halaby (Queen Noor of Jordan)
46. Capitol Hill aide
48. Cheerleader's yell
49. Wish undone

# 182

## ACROSS

1. Former president of Panama
6. Place below the Acropolis
11. Letter addenda
14. Budlike outgrowth
15. Adjective for some evening gowns
17. Shock
18. Peopled
19. Hawaii, e.g.
20. Light meals, in London
21. Pungent odor
22. Celtic
24. Q-U connection
25. Ultimatum word
26. Landon
27. Feminist's concern, for short
29. Golf term
31. Italian poet: 1798–1837
38. Pennsylvania, in New York
39. Individual renderings of roles, scores, etc.
40. Cigar residue
41. Acquire
42. Gangster's rod
43. Slightly open
46. A Gershwin
48. Works ___ (museum pieces)
51. Dishevel
52. Praise
54. ". . . all seem pendulous ___": Poe
56. Resistant to melting, as certain metals
58. Kind of salami
59. Unlike a juggernaut
60. "I ___ Anyone 'Til You," 1938 song
61. Patriotic org.
62. Steel, in Sedan
63. Lock

## DOWN

1. Moslem titles of respect
2. Mean
3. French tense
4. Famous violinmaker
5. Auctions
6. Stulm
7. French W.W. II hero
8. Turkish weights
9. Sauerbraten accompaniment
10. Priestly vestment
11. Corolla part
12. British guns
13. Coarse grass
16. Those well read
23. Alexis, son of Nicholas II, was one
26. Field: Prefix
28. Bellow
30. Pit-___
32. Explains
33. "The Pearl of ___ Island," Stowe novel
34. Villa d'___ at Tivoli
35. Border stream
36. Gifts
37. N.Y.U. or L.I.U.
43. Off the mark
44. Political faction
45. In regard to
47. Teacher, of sorts
49. Altercation
50. Lend ___ (heed)
53. Caribou or pudu
55. Phooey!
57. Watering place

# 183

**ACROSS**

1. Not temp.
5. Kind of tool
9. See
13. Music halls
14. Lamb
15. Stuffed ___, delicacy
16. Dutch cheese
17. May celebration
19. Late pop singer
21. Person's characteristic disposition
22. Nice wood
23. Chaucer's "The House of ___"
24. A.T.& T., familiarly
27. Female gangster
31. Tapestry
32. Precipitation
33. Lehar work: 1911
34. Energetic one
35. Ilk
36. Pith
37. Landlady, in León
38. Otherwise
39. Dramatist who wrote "An Ideal Husband"
40. Marjorie Main role
43. Plunkett's "bombs"
44. Leader who fought Mikhailovitch
45. Something to hold
46. Font of knowledge
49. Kind of inheritance
53. Rich vein of ore
55. Loosen or lessen
56. Fencing swords
57. So be it
58. Laundry cycle
59. Requirement
60. Attention-getting sound
61. McCullough's "The Path Between the ___"

**DOWN**

1. Anne Sexton creation
2. Icelandic epic
3. Quantity of paper
4. Fairy-tale character
5. Send again
6. At ___ (perplexed)
7. Relieves parents
8. Exclamation of disgust
9. Maddox or Pearson
10. Turkish army corps
11. General Bradley
12. Actor Stubby
15. Hellman's "The Children's Hour," e.g.
18. Make effective
20. Mil. officers
23. Laissez-___
24. Title similar to Mrs.
25. Bouquet
26. Short recess
27. Clergyman's residence
28. Parts of ships
29. Dodge
30. Grades
32. "___, Ma Baby"
35. Go-___ (lively one)
36. Woman who heads a household
39. Word with glass or enamel
41. Imprinted with acid
42. Playing pieces
43. Strong
45. Dims
46. Augury
47. Lasso
48. To ___ (perfectly)
49. ___ apple pie
50. Nucha
51. Its northernmost point is Cape Chelyuskin
52. Contact ___
54. Circuit

# 184

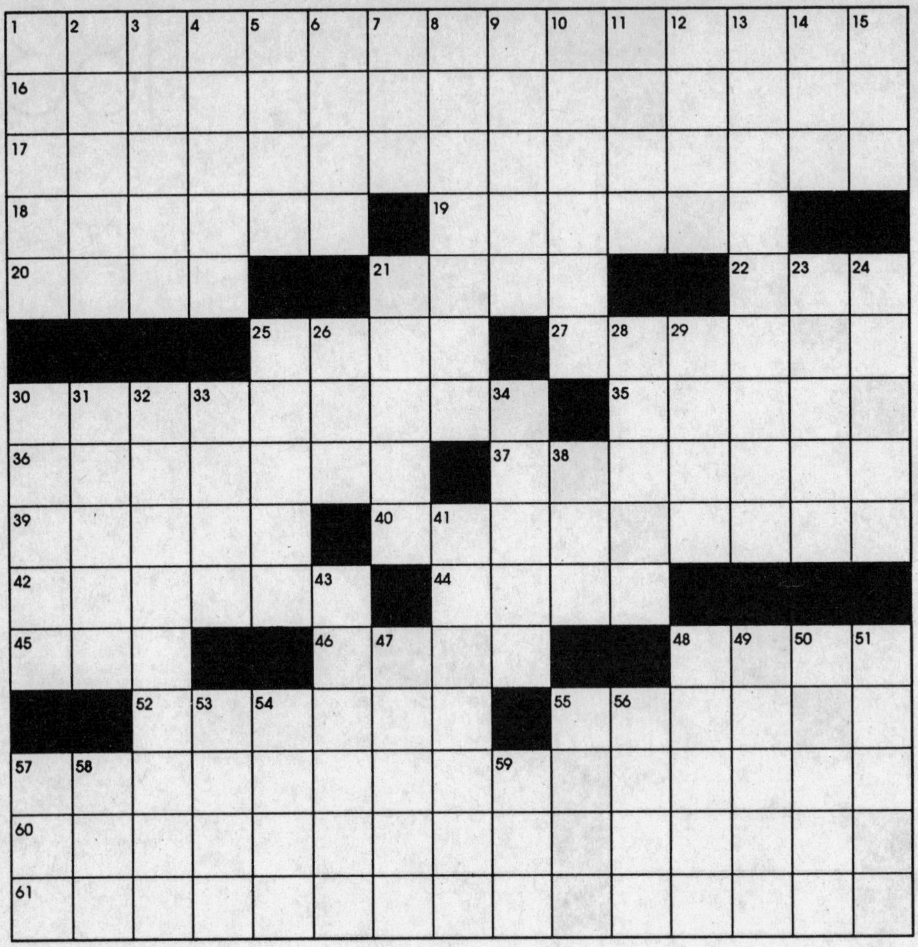

## ACROSS

1. An Oscar winner in 1977
16. La Guardia was one
17. Milton tragic work
18. Liquid part of fat
19. Ear inflammation
20. Incise
21. This requires an ans.
22. Yerkes or Lick, for short
25. Neither masc. nor fem.
27. Scolding
30. One resigned to reverses
35. British bishop's headdress
36. Player like Mantle, Mays or Musial
37. Attained
39. Twist, in Taxco
40. Sultry spring winds in Egypt
42. Reflexive pronoun
44. Calpurnia's needle
45. Book of the Bible: Abbr.
46. Sea eagle
48. Mosel tributary
52. An English poet and a U.S. actor
55. Dessert specialty
57. Famed protégé of Lorenzo the Magnificent
60. Oxygenating of venous blood
61. Breakfast offering

## DOWN

1. Part of a casquette
2. Chateaubriand creation
3. Contents of an onomasticon
4. "___ Venner," O. W. Holmes novel
5. Capital of Valais, Switzerland
6. Rational
7. Literary collection
8. Certain stews
9. Indulge in cabotinage
10. Actress Darcel
11. "True ___"
12. ___ e bisi, Venetian dish
13. ___ Apostles
14. Cicero's "Alas!"
15. Nav. officer
21. Eccentricity
23. End of a Presidential name
24. Pungs
25. Pertaining to birth
26. Greek letter
28. Collect
29. Translation for 12 Down
30. His first hit was "Splish Splash"
31. Wash out
32. Places catering to licentious tastes
33. Suffix with inchoative verbs
34. Vestige
38. Nandu's look-alike
41. "Star Wars" role
43. Demon wolf of Norse mythology
47. Fortification
48. Instrumental composition
49. In ___ (peeved)
50. British track
51. Catherine de Médicis was one
53. Writer Claude ___
54. River on The Broads
55. Labyrinth
56. Place for a race
57. Scientific principle
58. Poetic "before"
59. Unclear

# 185

## ACROSS

1. President, actor or actress
6. President, comedian or actress
12. Footstool
14. May and Stritch
16. Toxic liquid
17. Ancestry
18. Nol of Cambodia
19. Item cast at a casino
20. Stripling
21. ". . . for me and my ___"
22. Wou-wous
24. ". . . faces in the ___": Pound
26. Honor
27. Pithy
29. "No seats" sign
30. Philosopher Kierkegaard
31. Ancient ascetic
33. Co-writer of "What Kind of Fool Am I?"
35. Study group
37. Mousse au ___
41. Sister of Moses
46. Nongregarious one
47. Lynx or cougar
49. Barry or Robert of film fame
50. Fit to ___
51. Derived from apples
53. Prepare a salad
54. Japanese statesman
55. Ethylene, e.g.
56. Fabled bird
58. She wrote "The House of Incest": 1949
59. Leaseholders
61. Worship
63. Soviet republic
64. Those imposing retribution
65. President, actor or actress
66. President, actor or actress

## DOWN

1. Expiators
2. Monastic title
3. Surrounded by
4. ___-depressive
5. Shows scorn
6. Commonplace
7. Epic about a siege
8. Alight
9. They, in Thüringen
10. Wild asses or catapults
11. Invalidates
12. Flattened at the poles
13. Figures of speech
15. Moon goddess
23. Dir.
25. Like a satellite's path
26. Crazy, in Crécy
28. Belgian Surrealist: 1860–1949
30. Sheer cloth used for curtains
32. Conger
34. "___ a Camera"
36. Indonesian port or hair oil
37. Chennault of Air Force fame
38. Most peppery
39. New York city
40. Third letter
42. Putrefy
43. Socrates, at times
44. Judicial inquiry
45. Certain feudal lords
48. Somewhat weary
51. Lanza or Cavaradossi
52. Cryptographer
55. Mil. rank of 37 Down
57. Book by Robin Cook
60. Bandalore, e.g.
62. Deighton or Dawson

# 186

**ACROSS**

1. Manhandles
5. Prefix with phone or cycle
9. Root of a plant
14. Position of a copy editor
15. Stettin's river
16. Subject to ablation
17. Together: Mus. dir.
18. Bashful
20. Self-sufficient people
22. The blowing of a whale
23. Golden plover
25. Sra.'s counterpart
28. Dir. from Boston to Buzzards Bay
29. A memorable West
30. Larger than life
32. Punches out material on a machine
36. Role for Clifton Webb: 1952
37. Nevada city on the Humboldt
39. Grannies, e.g.
41. Check
42. Anita, Monica or Clara
44. Drivel
46. Dress style
48. Attention
49. Exactly
52. Palindromic word
53. Unsparingly
57. Member of an Alaskan group
58. Actress Trish Van ___
59. Item bitten by an onychophagist
63. Bakery employee
64. In the wind
65. Pianist Von Alpenheim
66. Manhattan's Jaspers, e.g.
67. Basking ___, N.J.
68. Joker, e.g.
69. Concerning

**DOWN**

1. O.T. book
2. One of the Huxleys
3. Locale in a Dee Brown title
4. Lee's Traveller
5. Old fogy
6. Old English letter
7. Simpletons
8. Texan's pancake
9. Disproves
10. Smell ___
11. Haiti's Baby ___ Duvalier
12. Chemical suffix
13. Marked, as a ballot
19. Elegant, as the Claridge
21. Surface of water, to a tar
24. Meet with fellow grads
25. Official spokesmen
26. Appear
27. Operation in "The Sting"
31. Antarctic sea
33. Smidgen
34. Trifle
35. Dutch master
37. "___ Quam Videri," motto of N.C.
38. He was the Cowardly Lion
40. Enveloped securely
43. Olympics participant
45. "Vissi d'___," Tosca's great aria
47. Sacred: Comb. form
50. "There's ___ text in Galatians": Browning
51. Prefix with dynamics or nuclear
54. ___ Wars of ancient times
55. Chateaubriand novel
56. Icelandic river
57. Excited
59. Very much
60. "___ Loved You," 1945 song
61. Place east of Eden
62. Begin's land: Abbr.

# 187

## ACROSS

1. Make the copy right
5. "What, fifty of my fellows at ___!": King Lear
10. Bid-closing word
14. Mother of Clytemnestra
15. Do a seamstress's job
16. Freshwater mussel
17. Bunyan's bog
20. "___ the Way," 1957 song
21. Debauchee
22. Hi-fi relative
23. Bern's river
24. Former TV host
25. Dwarfish boy in Scott's "Kenilworth"
33. ___ Tages (one day): Ger.
34. Edmonton hockey player
35. Wonderment
36. Claudius, for one
37. Marcius Porcius and family
38. A gun for Tommy Atkins
39. Balzac's "___ Fille d'Eve"
40. States of nonexistence
41. Uses a parachute, with "out"
42. Smollett hero
45. Dundee turndowns
46. Atramentous fluid
47. French port on Strait of Dover
50. Casey's spot, once
52. Grapple's milieu
55. Legendary English outlaw
58. Mackerel's relative
59. Fanon
60. Words of ken
61. Swerve
62. Thruway exits
63. County in Fla.

## DOWN

1. Joy Adamson heroine
2. Dingle
3. Valentino or Gable, once
4. Kind of cross
5. Landward
6. ___ En-lai
7. "That's ___," Sinatra hit
8. Suffix with cow or drunk
9. Warns, as a clairvoyant
10. Adjective in a rave
11. ___ about
12. Masher's spiel
13. Bygone bird
18. Up for ___
19. Where to find a riser
23. Busy as ___
24. Furry or hairy
25. Disgusted
26. Jungle climber
27. Word with circle or tube
28. "The ___ smooth . . .": Hesiod
29. Giant
30. Dyeing process
31. Tom ___, "Seven Year Itch" co-star
32. Past or future, e.g.
37. Likes or loves
38. George Baker's "Sad" one
40. Mystery writer Marsh
41. Twofold
43. Charm
44. Flinders
47. Half of DCX
48. Shipboard direction
49. Erato's prop
50. Hoax
51. Hired hands
52. "The Forty Days of ___ Dagh": Werfel
53. Like Enos
54. "How do I love ___ . . ."
56. Refrain syllable
57. Resembling: Suffix

# 188

**ACROSS**

1. Labyrinth
5. Spongy cake
9. Resource
14. Take ___ view of
15. Israel's former U.N. representative
16. Release from bonds
17. Indian princess
18. Eustis or Jay
19. Movable personal property
20. Mary ___, late black educator
23. Common French verb
24. Paravane
25. Matelot's milieu
28. Prynne et al.
31. Kind of accent
33. Madison Ave. output
34. Study hard and late
38. First black woman elected to Congress
42. Broadway's Oscar
43. Muumuu accessory
44. Waste maker
45. Word with bed or brain
48. Sparks's desperate call
49. Driving force
52. Quaff for Quintilius
54. "The Moses of her people"
59. Fong of Hawaii
60. Pro ___
61. Unwraps, poetically
63. Ragged
64. Promote peccancy
65. Parade ___
66. European yard
67. Word with handed or footed
68. Gaelic

**DOWN**

1. Botch
2. First of the first pair
3. Metallic element
4. Rousseau classic
5. Caption in a diet-pill ad
6. Casas, maisons, etc.
7. Stinging remark
8. Join a poker game
9. Zeros
10. Miss Piggy's prominence
11. Item for Danny Fisher
12. Duck down
13. Thy, in Tours
21. Late blues singer Waters
22. Trunks
25. Galleon part
26. Ham's call word for E
27. Acropolis sight
29. Still
30. Th, in Anglo-Saxon days
32. Essay
34. Slangy suffix with hot or got
35. Singer-actress Diana
36. Choir voice
37. Fr. titles
39. Tropical resin
40. Apt anagram for aye
41. Landscaping item
45. Former CORE director
46. Carroll's crazy character
47. Treat as identical
49. Stallone's co-star in "Rocky"
50. Mystical card
51. Clear the board
53. Subject of some Italian songs
55. Historic periods
56. Verboten
57. Little is one
58. Gangsters' former nemesis
59. Fimbriate
62. Jeanne d'Arc, e.g.: Abbr.

# 189

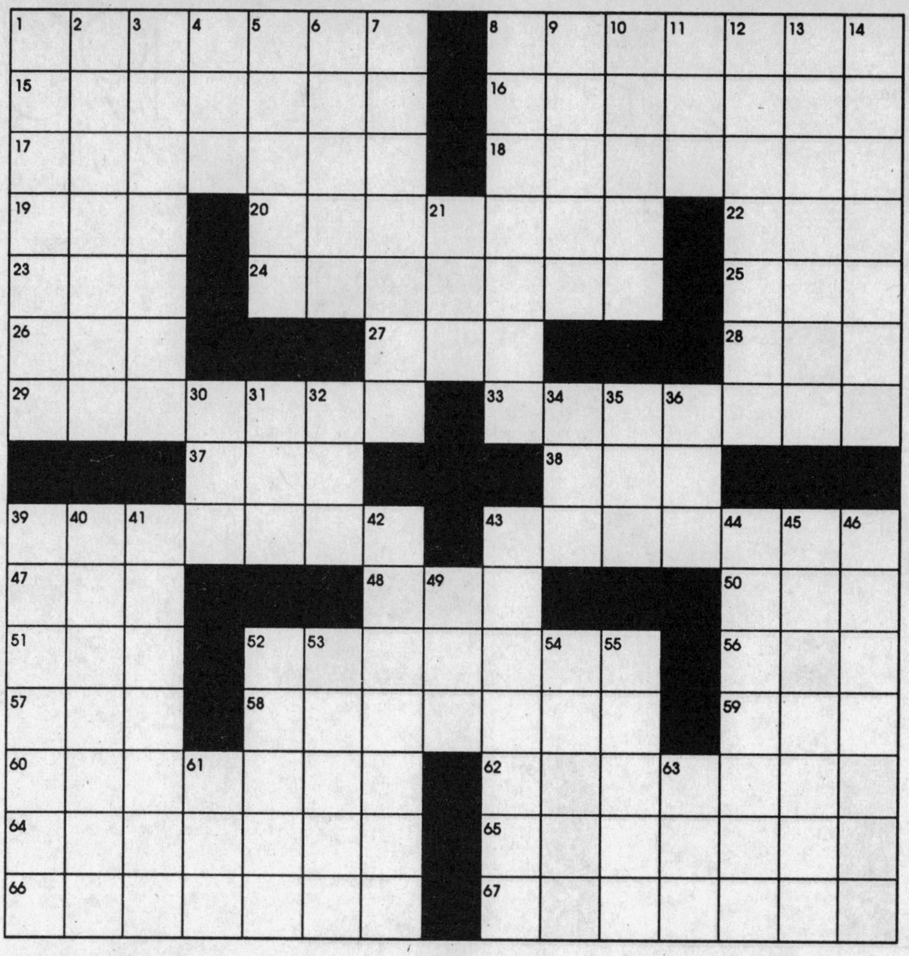

**ACROSS**

1. Calumniator
8. Soil
15. ___ Islands, in the Indian Ocean
16. Passes, as time
17. Dance introduced by the Castles
18. Certain muscles
19. Insulate a steam boiler
20. Mischievous menace to moppets in Munich
22. One of Tom Watson's concerns
23. Year in the papacy of Gregory I
24. Marks of disgrace
25. Sothern or Landers
26. Qua ___ (here and there): It.
27. Vane letters
28. Heel's companion
29. Some headmasters
33. Lake ___, N.Y.
37. Outcome of severe annoyance
38. Parseghian
39. Cut down with a scimitar
43. Pestle, for one
47. A.F.L. partner
48. Suffix with auction
50. English Channel feeder
51. Pharmacist's "in equal quantities"
52. Talk-talk-talk gathering
56. Army man, for short
57. Grid positions
58. Jackleg
59. Friend of David
60. Goddess of the moon
62. Stretches tight, as sails
64. Shortest distance between two points
65. Hillary's conquest
66. Protein derivatives, such as gelatin
67. Pokes fun at

**DOWN**

1. Seethe
2. Handcuff
3. Plaintive, as a poem
4. Sales stimulators, for short
5. Formal procedures
6. Chris of tennis
7. Correspondence items
8. Early
9. Oates heroine
10. Some are in chains
11. Chef's creations: Abbr.
12. Send to Coventry
13. Suppliers of wool
14. Ascetics of the second century B.C.
21. Bk. of the Bible
30. Draw
31. Governor of Indiana
32. Female ruff
34. Mideastern initials: 1958–71
35. Dernier ___
36. Preserve fruit
39. Sacred insects of Egypt
40. Site of the Grand National
41. One blowing his own horn
42. Cheapens
43. Met the new arrivals
44. Ordained
45. Kind of account
46. Draws up a new catalogue
49. Triton
52. Urchin
53. Ammonia compound
54. Oily
55. More authentic
61. Actor Wallach
63. Quang ___, city in Vietnam

**ACROSS**

1. Barter
5. Member of a pastor's flock
9. New growth
14. Opus that opened at a hall in Memphis
15. Betel palm
16. "___ diem!"
17. Burl in wood
18. 15.4324 grains troy
19. City east of Jamestown, N.Y.
20. Rodgers-Hart musical: 1937
23. More dignified
24. First ___
25. Oil-yielding tree
26. Inhabitants of Haifa
31. Houston pro
34. Kind of acid
35. Tavern order
36. Rodgers-Hammerstein musical: 1959
40. Musician Brown
41. Profit from sowing
42. Not mounted, as stones
43. Female hormone
46. Suppositions
47. Costal byproduct
48. "___ shame about Mame?"
52. Rodgers-Hart musical: 1940
57. Canadian physician
58. S-shaped molding
59. ___ about (snoop)
60. Beseech
61. Close
62. N.C. college
63. Tend
64. She, in Vichy
65. Agr. is one

**DOWN**

1. H. H. Munro
2. Proverbial foursome
3. Antarctic cape
4. July 4 celebrants
5. ___-love (paramour)
6. Up ___ (cornered)
7. Rodgers-Hart musical: 1938
8. Tonsorial item
9. Smelting refuse
10. Binary compound
11. Neighbor of Wash.
12. Colorful fish
13. Yurt, e.g.
21. Proscription
22. "The ___ jealousy heareth all things"
27. Sign at a crossing
28. Highland Mary, e.g.
29. Opponent for Bjorn or Vitas
30. Their ism causes a schism
31. Salt tree
32. "___ only a bird in . . ."
33. Stanford-Binet or Schick
34. It's above the shank
37. Pressing person
38. Off-duty attire
39. Like Anon's output
44. Put back in the oven
45. Exaggerate
46. Belong
49. Just about perfect
50. Oar pin
51. Legendary storyteller
52. Dances
53. ___ Royale
54. Mirth
55. First-class
56. Budget item

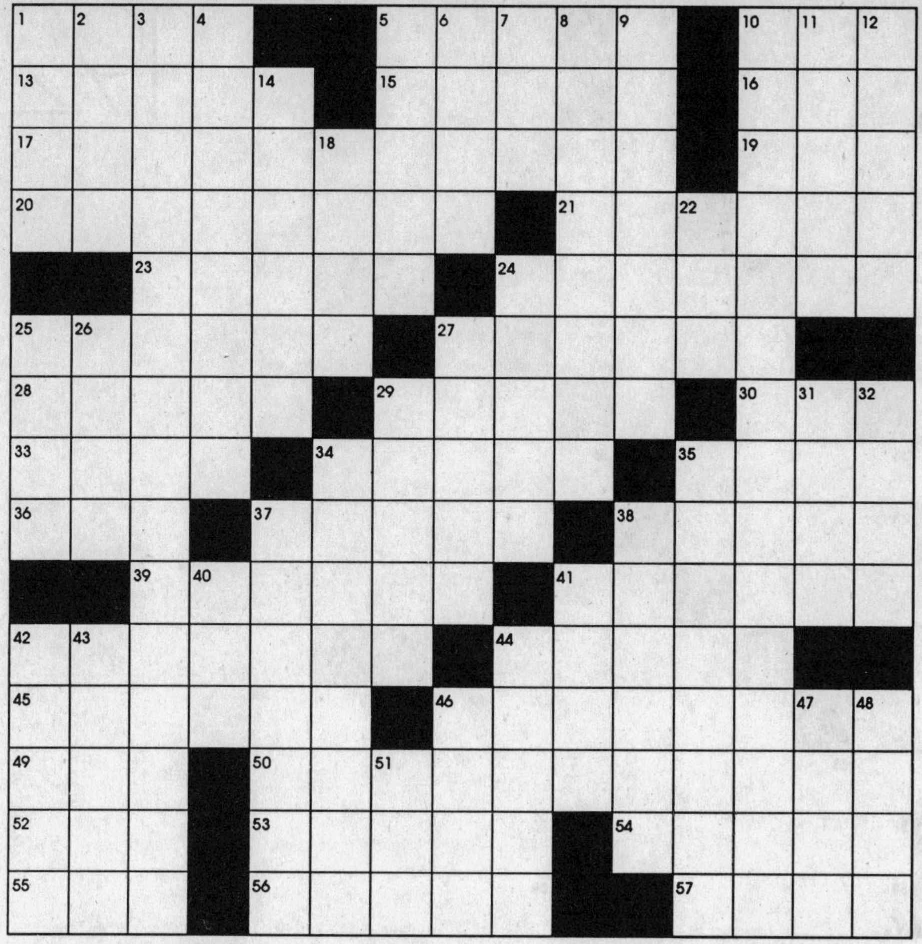

# 191

**ACROSS**

1. Riga native
5. Liberty Bell flaw
10. Vast amount
13. Had flu symptoms
15. Bellow's March
16. Shooter
17. With 50 Across, a Lincolnian phrase
19. Eastern V.I.P.
20. Lover
21. Horn
23. Unpleasant
24. Eating aid, for some
25. Person holding goods in trust
27. Cherry red
28. "Wait ___ Dark"
29. Mark's counterpart
30. "___ the ramparts . . ."
33. ___ trap, in a marksman's game
34. Trap and French followers
35. Beehive's cousin
36. One of the Lincolns
37. Abounding with bracken
38. Ice-cold
39. Continuous band of hull planking
41. Of the nostrils
42. Particulars
44. Pod used for fodder
45. Some primates, familiarly
46. Most svelte
49. Touch of approval
50. See 17 Across
52. Dir. or suffix
53. Changes course
54. Learner
55. Word of encouragement
56. "Lust for Life" author
57. Do office work

**DOWN**

1. Map coordinates: Abbr.
2. Reverberation
3. Subject of Lincoln's phrase
4. "I cannot ___"
5. Given to malicious gossip
6. Hayseed
7. Ready whisky for market
8. Rain collectors
9. Of a chemical compound
10. Physical symbol of Lincoln's philosophy
11. Gung-ho
12. Well informed
14. Girl, to a poet
18. Cloy
22. Military inst.
24. Hon
25. Washout
26. Singer-composer Paul
27. Harridan
29. Place-setting pieces
31. Innisfail
32. Emulated Revere or Sheridan
34. Metes
35. Balloon operator
37. Sudden scares
38. F.D.R.'s birthstone
40. Beach acquisition
41. Ingenuous one
42. Famed dwarf
43. Obliterate
44. Picked
46. Site of Pres. Jackson's grave
47. Kind of son or daughter
48. Penn pronoun
51. ___ patria

# 192

**ACROSS**

1. Touch upon
5. Discard
10. Mine access
14. Bonheur or Raisa
15. Unwrite
16. Dust-up
17. "Tobacco Road" author
20. ". . . the sweet ___ of books": Longfellow
21. Let
22. Oxford
23. Bitter, in Bordeaux
24. Hood's roscoe
27. Decamped
28. Small drink
31. Gaffe
32. Ponder
33. ___ contendere
34. "Bellefleur" author
37. Andreanof island
38. Trumpeter Al
39. ___ Oro, in NW Africa
40. Buddhist sect
41. Forswear
42. Vexed
43. Center of activity
44. Topers
45. Emerge
48. Shone
52. "Jane Eyre" author
54. Broz
55. Nary a soul
56. Opposite of addict
57. Luge or cutter
58. Flavor
59. Okinawa port

**DOWN**

1. Metric land units
2. Buttonholer
3. U.N. power
4. Conduct an inventory
5. Doyen
6. Candia's isle
7. Risqué
8. ___ rule
9. Headlong
10. Embattled
11. "___ eat oats . . ."
12. Shiftless
13. Blabbed
18. Belong
19. Exploit
23. Mete
24. Mecca's region
25. Undercut
26. Indo-Iranian
27. Like some animals
28. Yuccalike plant
29. ___ France (former name of Mauritius)
30. Watched the birdie
32. Where Mt. Katahdin towers
33. Fastens firmly
35. Noncom's pride
36. Spellbinder
41. Adjust the radio
42. Peanut
43. He imprisoned St. Peter
44. Exec's employee
45. Quintet in Gounod's "Faust"
46. Comedian Silvers
47. Canapé topping
48. Suppress
49. Draft status
50. What Deseret became
51. Shoe size
53. ___ man (unanimously)

# 193

## ACROSS

1. As tight as ___
6. Blemish
10. Orchestra led by John Williams
14. Sierra ___
15. Aureole
16. Central American tree
17. Hitchcock put-down re thespians
20. Kanga's kin
21. Another Sierra
22. Sea lion's cows
23. She played Nora Charles
25. Read through
26. A Goldwynism, with 45 Across
28. Le Mas d'___, near Toulouse
31. "The new gas"
32. Actress Claire
35. Crammed for exams
39. Backwatered, in a scull
41. Romaine
42. Widow of Ernie K.
44. Carl of movies and TV
45. See 26 Across
50. Einstein, e.g.
52. Pandect
56. Crow
57. Chase originating in N.Y.C.
58. Flange
59. "___, Mr. De Mille" (famous tag line)
62. Spouse
63. Kind of mail
64. Sheer
65. Swelter
66. Has to pay
67. Itsy-bitsy

## DOWN

1. Clock-radio device
2. Lure
3. Part of a dynamo
4. Número ___
5. An Annie of 1946 and 1966
6. Omniscient radio character
7. Wage
8. Away from the gales
9. Bird of legend
10. Firecracker
11. Kibitzing
12. Chopin's people
13. Part of a Mae West line
18. Problem for Bush
19. Brian from Worcestershire
24. African river
25. Milne's ___ Corner
27. Unseld of N.B.A. fame
28. Cosell's milieu
29. Where to view a gnu
30. Imply
33. Court divider
34. Cutting tool
36. Chester Proudfoot of "Gunsmoke"
37. Edible Japanese herbs
38. Greek letters
40. To coach a thief?
43. Beauty lover
46. Humidity problem
47. Rich and Worth
48. Girls, girls, girls
49. Floor plan
50. Microbes
51. Permission to leave Oxford
53. Hopping mad
54. Bewitcher
55. Abrasive
57. Tobacco cud
60. The ___, rock group
61. Chief John Duncan was one

# 194

## ACROSS

1. Airport arr. estimates
5. Asiatic palm
9. Not straight
14. Seduce
15. Singer Ed
16. Pat or Debbie
17. Melville title
18. Urban aeries
20. Meter unit
22. Mezzo-soprano Obraztsova
23. Air: Comb. form
24. Author Tarbell
27. Urged (on)
30. It's common or proper
32. Gibson girl's shape
38. One of the Siamese twins
39. Old World cont.
40. Goal
41. Get benched
42. Tropes
46. Drudge
47. Composed type
48. Dissenting voice
49. Perez stat.
51. Double this for a perfume-yielding tree
55. William Safire, once
59. Resin source
62. Bone: Comb. form
63. Zodiacal sign
64. "Mean ___," 1929 song
65. Henri's head
66. Plaster used as a surface
67. Oklahoma city
68. Kind of master

## DOWN

1. Summon
2. Dravidian tongue
3. Soap plant
4. Inadvertent creator of phrases like "well-boiled icicle"
5. Valley of the grapes
6. "___ a man with . . . "
7. Five-year periods
8. "Just ___ twig is bent . . . ": Pope
9. "___ Ben Adhem"
10. Turning to vinegar
11. Hagler stats.
12. Wind dir.
13. Jazz guitarist Montgomery
19. Mount where Aaron died
21. Word with tail or tongue
25. Drench
26. Of gold
28. Stick on
29. What "the walls have"
31. One of the Low Countries: Abbr.
32. Clout
33. Kind of soup
34. Boredom, to Sophia
35. Unthreatened
36. Printing sign
37. Damage
43. Joyce book
44. Fraternity letter
45. Gould or Nugent
49. Ad ___ (pertinent)
50. Midler
52. Confused
53. Hideaways
54. Irene Papas, e.g.
56. Mexican's "Give way!"
57. Half: Prefix
58. Tobacco, informally
59. Valise
60. Land measure
61. Fleur-de-___

# 195

**ACROSS**

**1.** Pen
**6.** Simulacrum
**11.** Not random
**12.** Harmful
**14.** Famed lexicographer
**17.** Famed cowboy singer
**18.** Loud
**19.** Taradiddle
**20.** Actor Douglas
**21.** Wed
**22.** High wind
**23.** Enzyme
**24.** Spree
**25.** Macadamized
**26.** Trust
**28.** Uniform
**29.** TV recording medium
**31.** Farmer's concern
**34.** Recidivist
**38.** Certain moldings
**39.** Conform
**40.** Wish one hadn't
**41.** Pops
**42.** Addicts
**43.** Insipid
**44.** Adherent: Suffix
**45.** Lead-in, for short
**46.** Portage craft
**47.** Lexicographer, to 14 Across
**50.** Star in Aquila
**51.** Without bias
**52.** Bivouac units
**53.** Dos y cinco

**DOWN**

**1.** Spendthrift
**2.** He wrote "Poor No More": 1959
**3.** "The Lord ___ shepherd . . ."
**4.** Greek letter
**5.** Polish
**6.** Do harm
**7.** Temperamental
**8.** Caught in the grip of la grippe
**9.** Brig. or Lt. follower
**10.** Subjugate
**11.** Junket at sea
**13.** Workman
**14.** Senegal's capital
**15.** Difficult tasks
**16.** Hard up
**21.** "Mork and ___"
**22.** ___ darn (cared)
**24.** Uses a come-on
**25.** Lab glassware
**27.** Climbers on campus, perhaps
**28.** Reindeer herdsmen
**30.** Flowers named for their scent
**31.** Spots for Mehta and Ozawa
**32.** Christie
**33.** Provided another hand
**35.** Move on wheels
**36.** Panegyric
**37.** Book by D. S. Freeman
**39.** Garden bloomers
**42.** Dark
**43.** Cow
**45.** "___ Old Cowhand"
**46.** American Indian
**48.** Hwy.
**49.** Twice CCLIII

# 196

**ACROSS**

1. Thalia, Aglaia and Euphrosyne
7. Believer in God
13. Home of violinmaker Guarneri
14. Rodent-catching canine
15. Boxing Day in England, for one
16. Meantime
18. Dodges
19. Native of Bornholm
20. Kind of jacket
21. Camus work
22. Undulating dance
23. Better than better
24. Item stored in a buttery
25. Japanese currency
26. Symphony by Liszt
27. Made a stab at
30. This could bog down a jogger
32. What a hobo hits
33. Grammatical no-no
34. Los Angeles boulevard
37. Roman palace, now a museum
41. "Take ___ of sparkling eyes": W. S. Gilbert
42. Couturier's line
43. Three-faced one
44. Maman's man
45. Courted a ticket
47. Rosary beads
48. "The voice that breath'd ___ Eden": Keble
49. Organ adjunct
50. Delitescent
52. Places for acting and transacting
54. Branch off
55. Original publisher of The Tatler
56. Applied a bandage
57. Less relaxed
58. More acidulous

**DOWN**

1. Acts like a toady
2. Has some connection
3. Chemical compound
4. Body of national laws
5. Namesakes of a Spanish queen
6. Follower of hear
7. Something to be endured
8. Politician Marcus Alonzo: 1837–1904
9. Diminutive suffix
10. Ending meaning "native of"
11. Ranger in Paradise
12. Gulf of the Adriatic
13. Crab's claws
17. Harrow student's parent
19. Push for payment
22. Hopper of Hollywood
23. Deal with a roast
25. Twelve moons
26. Effort
28. Lana's first husband
29. "This Is ___ Life"
30. Did a harvest job
31. William, in Dublin
34. Steam
35. Dueler of a sort
36. Spin a yarn
38. Opposite
39. Erinys, for one
40. Settled down snugly
42. Drill sergeant's call
45. Clergyman's scarf
46. Challenging puzzle
47. Event at Alamogordo: 1945
49. Canonized women of Fr.
50. Coin of Ankara
51. Declare decisively
53. Dawson of football fame
54. Banned insecticide

# 197

**ACROSS**

1. Male raccoons
6. Westernmost of the Aleutians
10. Glass-making material
14. Circuit
15. Author of "Battle Cry"
16. Reckless
17. Senseless talk
19. Nonworking
20. Indefinite amount
21. Some floral creations
22. Not so challenging
24. Empty talk
26. Helices
29. Pourboire
30. Coccagee
31. Twaddle
36. De novo
37. Adhered
39. Wampus
40. Silverware item
42. Goof
43. Actress Sothern
44. Fat
46. Foul, vulgar, abusive talk
51. Hangnest
52. Segment
53. Backward or upward: Prefix
56. Command to go
57. Nonstop talker
60. Joint
61. Large convex molding
62. Overseer of a manor
63. Urges
64. Bishoprics
65. South African province

**DOWN**

1. Rum cake
2. Sultanate in the Mideast
3. In a competent manner
4. Disencumber
5. Excellent
6. C.P.A.'s products
7. Rubbish
8. "___ folly to be wise": Gray
9. Early activity of Gregory Peck
10. Gambol
11. Spokes
12. Key or cay
13. Soothing word
18. "Camino ___," Williams play
23. Vipers
24. Begins to form
25. District on the Thames
26. Begone!
27. Loblolly
28. Fancy
31. A deaness is one
32. Run away à la Jessica
33. Double negative
34. Takes to court
35. Raison d'___
37. Hits the pitch
38. Word with bow or hand
41. Dinner ___
42. Bird sometimes called a stake driver
44. Certain marbles
45. Dress detail
46. Sylvan
47. Goddess of peace
48. Flax product
49. Ore veins
50. Show mercy
53. Assist a yegg
54. Loser to Joe Louis: 1941
55. Figure skater's spinning leap
58. Garden tool
59. T.V.A. relative

# 198

## ACROSS

1. "___ is that music . . .": Keats
5. Arrangement
10. One of the Oceanides
14. Like Emerson's bridge
15. Red snapper
16. All by herself on stage
17. Othello's words as he stabs himself
20. Kind of double for Goren
21. Got up
22. Sight from Bern
23. First word of "The Aeneid"
25. Transfer pictures
29. Basis of all, to Lucretius
30. O'Neill one-act play
33. Slithering
34. Plato dialogue
35. "O! swear ___ by the moon": Juliet
36. Macbeth's last words
40. Actor Torn
41. Sioux dwelling
42. Iroquoian group
43. Last word of "Ulysses"
44. "___, Lice and History," Zinsser book
45. Something unpaid but due
47. Certain ephemera
48. Botanist Gray: 1810–88
49. Broadcast
52. Gutenberg was one
56. Cleopatra's last words
60. First-rate
61. Path, in Paris
62. "God's Little ___"
63. Play by Topor
64. Our salad days
65. Mother of Zeus

## DOWN

1. Lippo Lippi
2. Milwaukee's gift to the theater
3. Icelandic collection
4. Kind of job or set
5. Thread holders
6. Consume avidly
7. Waste allowance
8. Sound of disgust
9. Dish at a luau
10. Stars seen by Servius
11. Where Dryden lived
12. Founder of Troy
13. Old Gynt's widow
18. Fast breaker
19. Milton's "least erected spirit"
23. ". . . ___ in the affairs of men"
24. Sound of surf
25. Speak out against strongly
26. Eldritch
27. Samples of films
28. Nautical affirmative
29. Medieval kingdom
30. Habituate
31. Religious maxims
32. Upper regions of space
34. Egypt's native Christians
37. Grasping at ___
38. The obverse of a coin
39. "___ the ramparts . . ."
45. Remarks to the audience
46. Hindu princess
47. Honors with a party
48. Author of "The Green Hat"
49. Role for Pavlova
50. "___ Swell," Rodgers-Hart song
51. Bombast
52. Whimper
53. Absolute ruler
54. Do aquatints
55. "O ___ Ben Jonson!"
57. Bowler or sailor
58. Violinist Bull
59. Biblical affirmative

# 199

## ACROSS

1. Party popper
5. Flit
9. Nervy
11. Becomes different
13. Steeplejack, at times
14. Data for the I.R.S.
16. Swinburne's "___ Atque Vale"
17. Enthusiasts
19. With 8 Down, for now
20. To some extent: Prefix
22. Klein creation
23. Spiral
24. Dido
26. Silkworm
27. Ten ___ (stop transmitting)
28. Obvious derision
30. Contestants
32. Borrower's interest re interest
34. Juncture
35. Winter wear
38. Sour
41. Former Barbary state
42. Flash often accompanying a dash
44. Cornered
46. ___ muchacha (this girl): Sp.
47. One-eighth of a peck
49. Wan
50. Golfer's concern
51. Grotesque
53. Free electron
54. Home of the collegiate Cowboys
56. Bedeck with small stars
58. Circumscribes
59. Motion support
60. Tetranychid
61. Cincinnati nine

## DOWN

1. Alley Oop, for one
2. Prospector's prospect
3. Swiss owner of a posh hotel
4. These are bent in orisons
5. Subject of a Giotto painting
6. Parts of ellipses
7. Brazilian coffee
8. See 19 Across
9. Several
10. Fireplace
11. Some possessions of Itzhak Perlman
12. Baseball-season climax
13. File
15. Fish
18. "Toute la ___," Hugo work
21. Sluggard's problem
23. Impossible dream
25. Subject of Shelley's "Adonais"
27. Pamphlet
29. Beat for a P.O. man
31. Export from Calcutta
33. Bears
35. Cardinal Cardinal in the 40's and 50's
36. Provisional, as a council
37. Emulate the eagle
39. Quits before becoming superannuated
40. Partner of lo
41. Fabled archer
43. Long lock
45. The force is with it
47. Completely
48. Acuminate
51. Clobbered, in days of yore
52. Needlepoint, for one
55. "Mon ___ Pierrot"
57. Silent agreement

200

## ACROSS

1. Incited, with "on"
6. Extort
11. City lying almost on the equator
12. Dawns
15. One needing three more wins to become champ
18. Western Indian
19. Whence many an icicle hangs
20. In spite of, for short
21. Claire and Balin
22. Has more than half a loaf
23. Unwitting accomplice
24. Mythical bird
25. Double agent
26. Saki
27. Foreign trait of behavior
30. Summer ___, Canyon's bride
31. A memorable Josip
32. Time beyond measure
34. Resort lake (193 sq. mi.)
37. Like some jet fighter seats
42. Bushbuck's cousin
43. Approve informally
44. Mother's command
45. "Leave all ___ to the gods": Horace
46. Pug's fists
48. Put ___ writing
49. These score six pts.
50. Expressways
51. Thirteen tarts, at times
52. Lack of enthusiasm
55. Grommets
56. Hagiographist's subject
57. Seek a well site
58. Indian attendants

## DOWN

1. March or September event
2. Camellike creature of S.A.
3. Measures the circumference
4. This makes Henri a girl
5. Bucks fawn over her
6. Postpone
7. Poems, in poesy
8. Periods for geologists
9. Energy source
10. Large sea snails
13. Like a superannuated salt
14. Plant offshoot
15. Quantity for Richard Hoe
16. Attain
17. Daunts
22. Bonkers
23. Arkansas River city
25. Bogged down
26. ___ Python
28. Choice entree
29. Most likely to inherit the earth
33. Edible tubers
34. Develop a bite
35. From dawn to dusk
36. Bugged
38. Hidden difficulty
39. $C_6H_6$
40. Avant-garde styles
41. Jackets or collars
46. Famines after feasts, in a way
47. Edict
48. Architectural style
50. Sigh of relief
51. European invasion date
53. Ziegfeld
54. Switchback's relative

# 201

## ACROSS

1. Small swamp
4. Wife of King Latinus
9. Varnish resin
14. J.F.K. word
15. St. Peter's original name
16. Chicago airport
17. Agnes Copperfield, ___ Wickfield
18. Nozzle
19. Astro Ryan
20. Lithuanian-born sculptor
23. Repute, on Fleet Street
24. River in Lower Saxony
25. Letters of a certain class
28. Secret
33. Phad is one
36. ___-ran
38. Poison
39. Netherlands-born painter
42. Type of mosquito
43. Pier
44. Mikhail Fyodorovich was one
45. Comprehends
47. Sicilian volcano
49. Stew, in Sorrento
51. F.D.R. Cabinet member
55. American-born painter
61. Astir
62. Kind of roof gutter
63. Kind of trip
64. Diamond's center
65. Football's Greasy ___
66. ___ Year's Day
67. Twilled cloth
68. ___ Bell (Anne Brontë)
69. Suffix with arch

## DOWN

1. Type of clock
2. Mountain nymph
3. Cretan-born painter El ___
4. Remove all doubt
5. Abundant supply
6. Gosden role
7. French-born painter
8. Opponents
9. Musical composition
10. Expression of mild surprise
11. Ancient Indic language
12. Smell ___
13. Memorable bridge expert
21. 17th-century poet Francis ___
22. School org.
26. "O! ___ Fortune's fool": Shak.
27. Auto pioneer
29. Connection
30. Plant stem
31. Singer Simone
32. Employee on a RR
33. Stolen goods
34. Rank of organ pipes
35. Actor Robert
37. 1930's migrant
40. ___ corps
41. Decide upon
46. Black Hawk, e.g.
48. Kind of hut
50. Where Accra is
52. N.H. city
53. Peak in the Bernese Alps
54. White; spotless
55. Western eleven
56. Woodwind
57. "This Is ___ Life"
58. Vital organ
59. Part of Q.E.D.
60. Cairo's river to Carlo or Carlos

# 202

**ACROSS**

1. Seafood item
5. Nest robber
10. Flop
14. Golfer's target
15. Valor, virtue, etc., in sum
16. Not quite closed
17. Typeface: Abbr.
18. Shankar's strings
19. Palermo pooches
20. Potluck at a comic's table?
23. New Year's Eve word
24. "___ to worry"
25. Ladd classic
28. Fri. follower
31. Brown shade
35. Kind of book
36. Fellini film, with "La"
38. School org.
39. See 20 Across
42. OPEC concern
43. Pyle and Kovacs
44. Membership
45. Steel-plow pioneer
47. Printers' measures
48. Panache
49. Old English letter
51. Stadium feature
53. See 20 Across
61. Pulitzer Prize author: 1958
62. ". . . to fetch ___ of water"
63. A bowl of cherries?
64. "Rosebud," e.g.
65. Street show
66. Spare
67. Famed Scottish philosopher
68. Word with rehearsal or parade
69. Siberian tent

**DOWN**

1. Smart
2. Portnoy's creator
3. "Merry" in a game name
4. Operatic singing style
5. Artist's need
6. Place for a nose
7. "___ horse!"
8. Etc.'s relative
9. Showed an oldie
10. "___ the drawing board"
11. City in Calif.
12. Nobel Prize author: 1929
13. Shipboard jail
21. Ar predecessor
22. Madrid memos
25. Bore
26. Memorable Sonja
27. Of a straight line
29. "In ___ that's romantic": Gilbert
30. Museum offerings
32. Marquand hero
33. Underpriced item
34. Enologist's interest
36. S.U. unit
37. Prefix with function
40. "___ body cry?": Burns
41. In an exalted way
46. Ebb
48. French possessive
50. Granted
52. Skye and Wight
53. Obi
54. Eskimo abode
55. Think
56. Train in the ring
57. Thun's river
58. Place
59. In the distance
60. Scar on a car

# 203

**ACROSS**

1. Kind of opera or box
5. Last of a claro
9. Salt, to a pharmacist
12. Sphere's leader
13. Egyptian sun god
15. "Cogito, ___ sum"
16. Make a call
17. "___ and Sane Fourth": Masson
18. Pusher's nemesis
19. Mecca for embarrassed Buckeyes?
22. At no time, to Tennyson
23. Samoan seaport
24. To-go, e.g.
26. Frankish king's SW hideout?
30. Thin wedges
31. Then, in Tours
32. "Come weal, come ___ . . ."
33. Wash
34. Cather's "___ Lady"
35. Director Clair
36. ___ pro nobis
37. Harvest fly
38. King of filmdom
39. Where Arnie holed out?
41. Gets by
42. W. Indian shrub
43. Ball or strike
44. Dapple's digs?
50. Something often killed
51. Author of "A Lonely Rage"
52. "___ Cheatin' Heart"
54. Deucy's mate
55. Letter-shaped fasteners
56. Escutcheon band
57. McGrew of balladry
58. Librarians' degrees
59. Dickens's "'umble person"

**DOWN**

1. Disconsolate
2. Auricular
3. Oriental nurse
4. Where Solidarity struck in N.E.?
5. One with a quota
6. "___ with Love"
7. Iguana's cousin
8. Bluffer's seat near Pierre?
9. Mmes. of Mexico
10. Kind of biology
11. Nessie's nest?
14. Venice or Singapore
15. Chou ___
20. Makes a right turn
21. Ullmann and others
24. Novelist John or Mary
25. Competitor
26. Dagger's companion
27. Scandinavian
28. Taboos
29. Sea: Ger.
30. Spill over
31. Sonoran mayor's place up north?
34. Most ethereal
35. Incredible Midwest village?
37. Copper
38. Tenn. men
40. Brighton buddy
41. Fondle
43. Indianapolis team
44. African native village
45. Type size
46. Portend
47. What teamsters do
48. Deteriorated
49. Mickey Rooney, né ___
53. Kind of theater, for short

# 204

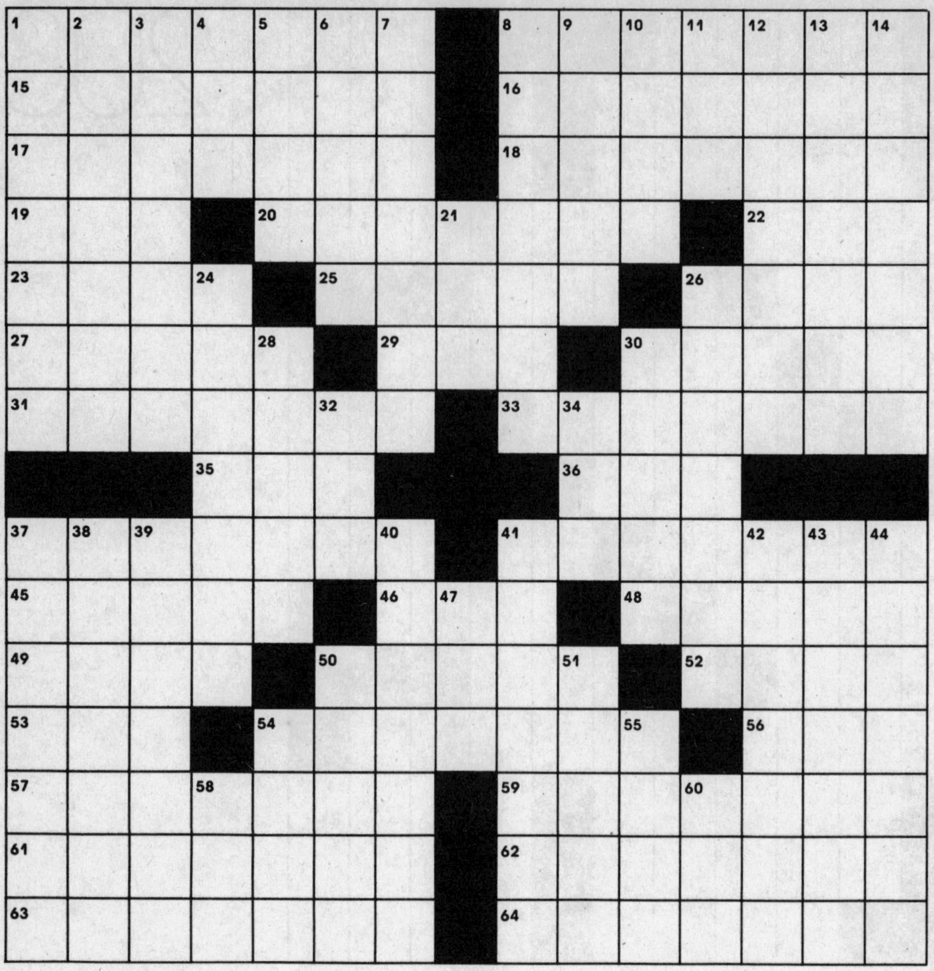

**ACROSS**

1. Advanced study group
8. Kind of glaze or mosaic
15. Shutdown
16. State since Dec. 14, 1819
17. Nimrod's activity
18. Cloudy
19. Feminine suffix
20. Gallery
22. "The Gilded ___," 1873 novel
23. Glove Gehrig wore
25. Smallest amount
26. English actor-manager: 1853–1917
27. Turn inside out
29. Brother of Osiris
30. Shrill, trilling sound
31. Examines anew
33. Routes for the jet set
35. Dir. from Dayton to Daytona
36. ___ culpa
37. Carpenter's horse
41. Sanction
45. Sidewalk spectacle
46. Grow drowsy
48. Alcohol-heated receptacles
49. Ancient calendar date
50. Composer Copland
52. Pungent wit
53. Snap
54. Mail man
56. Hyson or Assam
57. Kind of work
59. Caustic
61. Immutable
62. Daily grind
63. Calms
64. Looked high and low

**DOWN**

1. Intrigant
2. Baffling
3. Griffin, e.g.
4. Ending for novel or journal
5. Darkness, in Dijon
6. Synthetic fiber
7. Backslide
8. Rummy variation
9. Choose
10. Broadway playwright
11. ___-Bekr, Mohammed's successor
12. Tropical affliction
13. Poetic technique
14. Goes at full speed
21. Scottish explorer
24. Locks
26. Frustrates
28. Discrimination
30. French delicacy
32. N.J. neighbor
34. Devil's offspring
37. Three-baggers
38. Project, as joy
39. Built
40. Outer tooth layers
41. Magi, e.g.
42. Painting the town red
43. Capital of Drôme
44. Like the landed gentry
47. Gold, in Granada
50. Old chests for valuables
51. Town SE of Bordeaux
54. "___ Misbehavin'"
55. Newspaper section, for short
58. ___-la-la
60. Actress Joanne

# 205

**ACROSS**

1. Subject
6. Candle bracket
12. Vegetable
14. Vegetable
16. O.T. prophet
17. Greek letter
18. Elect
19. Actor Selleck
20. Regret
21. Heat meas.
22. Film critic
24. Harvests
26. Roulette bet
27. Eagle's nest
29. H.S. study
30. Touch, e.g.
31. Voiced harshly
33. Competitions
35. Part of ancient Greece
37. Gambling mecca
41. Vegetable
46. Marine mammal
47. Brit. business abbr.
49. Vegetables
50. IOU
51. Loses 55 Across
53. Plenty of horn
54. Every
55. Sitter's creation
56. Hwy.
58. Hurok
59. Vegetable
61. Kind of exam
63. More obese
64. Cleveland team
65. Matriculates
66. Rage

**DOWN**

1. Spotted sandpipers
2. "____ Clear Day"
3. NATO's basis
4. Life fluid for Zeus
5. Peals
6. Stinger of the Southwest
7. "L'Etranger" author
8. Theater award
9. Network initials
10. Paper copies, familiarly
11. Vain one
12. Informal male gathering
13. Tropical fruit
15. Acclimates
23. Sass
25. Greets abruptly
26. Bess Truman, ____ Wallace
28. Certain fisherman
30. "Le Grand Orange" of baseball
32. Hammarskjöld
34. Kind of picker
36. Measuring instrument
37. Subway slowpokes
38. Jenner, for one
39. Crumbly cheese
40. Doggie doc
42. Soak flax
43. Ad ____ (to an extreme)
44. Native
45. Sacred songs
48. Skin layer
51. Snake or car
52. Limited term of duty
55. Old stringed instrument
57. Taro root
60. Young Pharaoh
62. Shooting match: Fr.

# 206

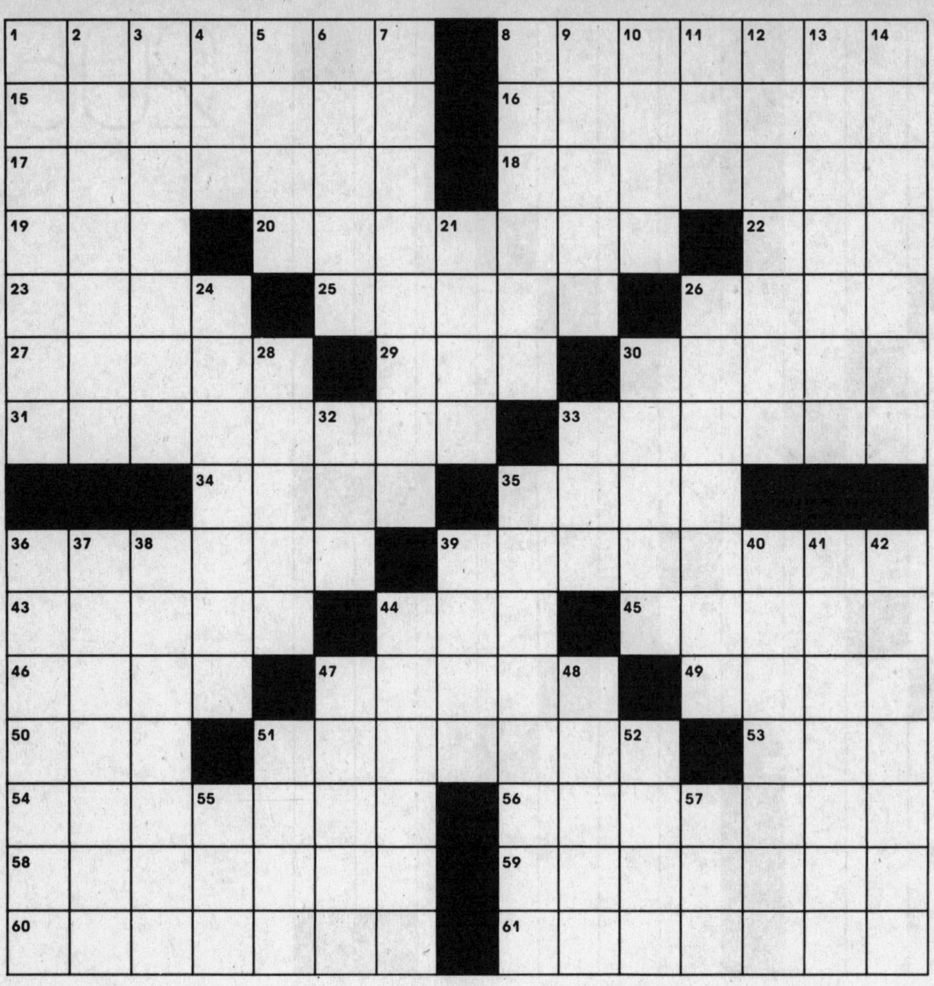

**ACROSS**

1. ". . . ____ like the pard": Shak.
8. Grates
15. Hercules, 12 times
16. Writer who was fond of a pond
17. Forte of Isocrates
18. Parachutist's need
19. Antique
20. Fishy
22. Dir. from Tampa to Ocala
23. Bird with a bird brain
25. Merits
26. What you eat
27. Hard wood
29. Carry
30. Quinks, e.g.
31. They take care of caries
33. Most of Noah's passengers
34. Soaks flax
35. Rod
36. Syracuse is here
39. Tanks for rain water
43. "Don't ____ on Me"
44. Spice of life: Abbr.
45. Beezer
46. Drummer's feat
47. Goddess of agriculture
49. Andrews of films
50. Suffix with Paul or Joseph
51. Chandler's products
53. Brazil or hazel
54. Stance
56. Fence in
58. Muse whose name means "to delight well"
59. Pool game
60. He purposely kills time
61. They work on boards

**DOWN**

1. Pedigreed
2. Piercing place
3. Biblical nether world
4. Decay
5. Showdown edge
6. Scary
7. Cures meat in a certain way
8. Kind of bean
9. Unwanted twosome
10. Rodeo item
11. Rainbow
12. Showy flowers
13. End of a Wilde title
14. Czech range
21. Shank
24. Being judged
26. Kingsley play: 1935
28. Give
30. Restroom sign
32. Swine's confines
33. ____-relief
35. Telly's predecessor
36. Stars' followers
37. Eliminate
38. Small keyboard instrument
39. Kind of queen
40. Colony site: 1585–87
41. Addict's antithesis
42. Old Greek coins
44. Form of fakery
47. "____ diem!"
48. Pea's relative
51. Undulate
52. Tug's tow
55. ____ Aviv
57. She played Nora Charles

# 207

**ACROSS**

1. Quack's remedy
8. Vulgar
13. Ants that enslave other ants
14. Substance used by watchmakers
16. Foolish
17. Token
18. Slip a cog
19. Scion of Esau
21. Tobacco chewer's wad
22. Hang around
24. Dept. Haig quit
25. Gershwin's "Our Love Is ___ to Stay"
26. Cords and Mercers
28. Org. involved in withheld taxes
29. Gets bogged down
30. Relative of a trawl
32. Most exorbitant
34. Rec-room sites
36. Jim Thorpe's alma mater
39. One of the Bowls
42. Rather tipsy
43. Conductor de Waart
45. Molokai denizen
47. Fr. titles
48. Smug smile
50. Use a steel ball
51. Incomprehensible time span
52. Flophouse
54. Sweet's partner
55. Bobolink
57. Silly
59. Downstairs person
60. Secured, in a way
61. Faulkner's "As I Lay ___"
62. Unlucky

**DOWN**

1. Richardson heroine
2. In love
3. Do a voice-over
4. Type of dye
5. Loblolly product
6. Namesakes of Geraint's wife
7. Festive neckwear
8. Ida's island
9. Winter coat
10. What a lemon might lead to
11. Unfeigned
12. These leave 'em in stitches
14. Put on a Little act
15. Not given to bravado
20. McLuhan subject
23. Wee weaknesses
25. Jazz devotee
27. Slow mover
29. Cerium or cesium
31. Tee forerunner
33. Part of G.B.
35. Argon or neon
36. Small but juicy roles
37. Well protected
38. Part of an astronaut's flight
40. Milky glass
41. Enacts a new building ordinance
44. Jerry of Broadway
46. Ends a divorced state
48. Shoptalk
49. Cracked buckwheat
52. Custard dish
53. Victor at Dien Bien Phu
56. Word form with form
58. Contraction of nihil

# 208

**ACROSS**

1. Indian prince
6. Currier's partner
10. Cigar ending
14. Solus
15. Force
16. Temple
17. Michelangelo work
18. 1960 TV PATSY winner
19. It's full of baloney
20. Like cooking apples
22. What Gleason's Reginald puts on
24. Panama
25. Humbug's partner
27. Jackie Gleason
30. Parisian preposition
32. Sheltered at sea
33. "Elmer's ____"
34. Pisgah's summit
35. "This Nearly ____ Mine"
36. Combustible heap
37. Busman Ralph
39. "Move it!"
42. "Amos Moses" singer
43. Wallace's Ben
44. Austen novel
45. Astonish
46. Snub-nosed dogs
47. The best
48. Bumbler created by J.G.
51. Alan Ladd film: 1946
52. One-tenth of a sen
53. "Animal House" house
54. Produce interest
56. Verdi's Ethiopian slave
58. Flimflam
60. ____ de résistance
63. Mulligan's meal?
64. Words of perception
65. What kind of fool am I?
66. Hither
67. Salty swallow
68. Full of gusto

**DOWN**

1. Shoot the breeze
2. MacGraw
3. Crazy Guggenheim's chum
4. Pilaster
5. Greene's "The ____ of the Matter"
6. A protector of baby Zeus
7. Faces
8. Complete
9. Hypnosis inducer
10. Apoc. book
11. Classic sitcom
12. New Orleans's Green Wave
13. Superior
21. Unfroze
23. Bacchus aide
25. "The ____ Dick," 1940 film
26. Assert
28. Verve
29. Castle tower
31. Start of a West line
36. Strive for
38. ____ iniquity
39. Quasimodo's creator
40. Diamond group
41. Annie Oakley
43. Opponent for Minnesota Fats
45. Iranian Moslem
46. Extol
48. Rubbish
49. Do what Glenn did
50. A Bolivian capital
55. Ready for reaping
57. Fear of God
59. Berry or Murray
61. Op. ____
62. Tarzan actor on TV

# 209

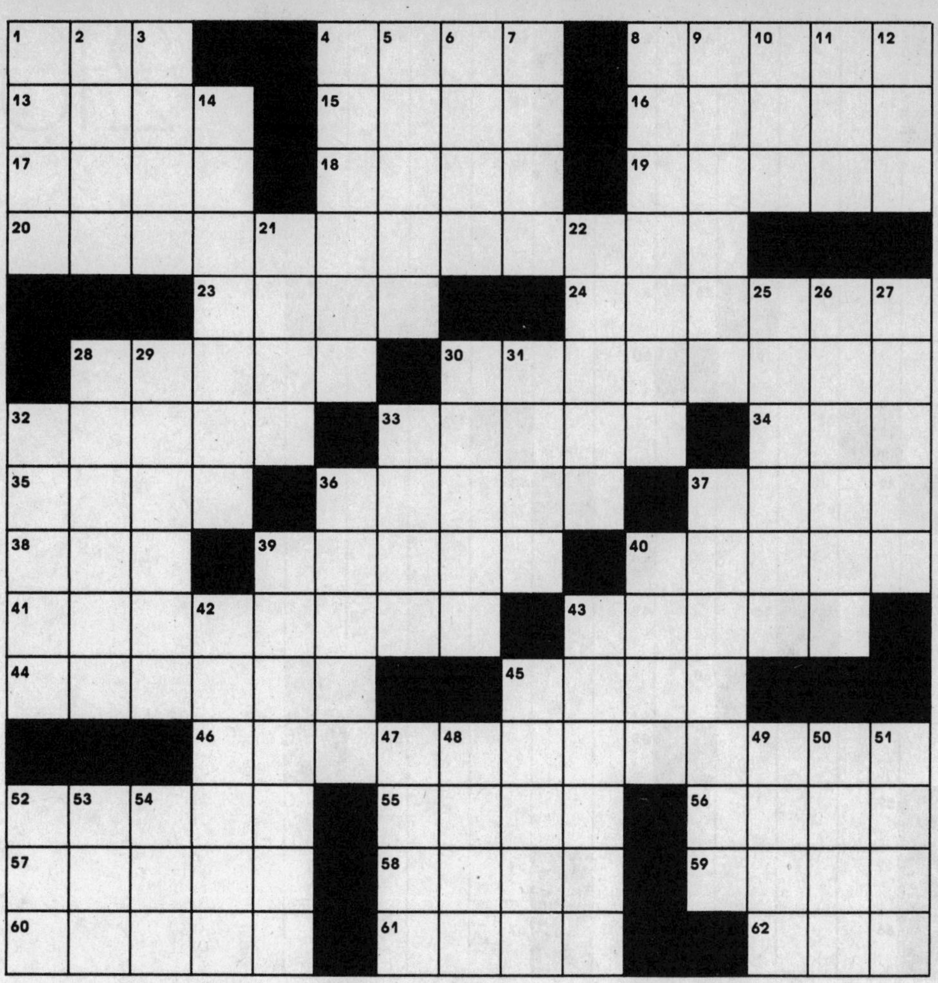

**ACROSS**

1. Composer ___ Dittersdorf
4. Simplon is one
8. Flash flood
13. A Waugh
15. Dash
16. Yucatec
17. Tea, in Tewkesbury
18. Kind of bank
19. ___ la Cité
20. Mexico's "smoking mountain"
23. Safe's partner
24. Ecclesiastical vestments
28. Burst of energy
30. Thin; insipid
32. Cache
33. Alarm
34. Siouan
35. Gaelic name for Ireland
36. Companions of heels
37. French tire
38. Jackie's second mate
39. Footwear for Jiggs
40. Bad news for motorists
41. Energy producers
43. Domain
44. Actor in "True Confessions"
45. Certain missiles
46. Montezuma's capital
52. Something paid by a friend
55. ___-Bah, in "The Mikado"
56. Facilitate
57. Inhabitant of 46 Across
58. Weight deduction
59. ___ of passage
60. Set of three hounds
61. Brit. money
62. Land east of Eden

**DOWN**

1. Nita or Theda
2. Spread for a spread
3. ___ tide
4. Certain stickler
5. Like the Victory of Samothrace
6. Surfeit
7. Cinch
8. Infatuated
9. Lack of color
10. Ever, in poesy
11. Bit
12. Chemical ending
14. Finish
21. Wag
22. Met bass-baritone Simon ___
25. Stander or Barrymore
26. Regard
27. Conclamation
28. Social gathering
29. Designating a fine, white marble
30. Droops
31. A son of Hera
32. Got the oral message
33. Emulate a hawk
36. Fishing lure
37. Sculptor's material, at times
39. Seventh-inning ritual
40. Trailer, for short
42. "Thine alabaster ___ gleam": Bates
43. Cronkite's successor
45. Kind of dinner
47. Chooses
48. Prince Albert, e.g.
49. "Upon whose bosom snow has ___": Kilmer
50. Concerning
51. Want
52. Type of French lace
53. Verb-forming suffix
54. Part of a RR system

# 210

**ACROSS**

1. Italian river
5. More shameful
10. Valley
14. Garner
15. Have effect
16. Opposite of aloft
17. Least of the least?
19. Irritate
20. Town south of Lille
21. Curved sword
23. Oriental bird
25. Suit to ___
26. Greedy coloratura?
30. Hindu religious writing
34. Walks through water
35. ___ Barkley, V.P.
37. Toupee, colloquially
38. Struggle
39. Wept
40. Arrived
41. Operate
42. La Croce ___ (The Red Cross, in Roma)
43. Room for entertaining
44. Roundabout way
46. Where streetcars are sold?
48. Ready for the reaper
50. Lackluster
51. Stratford's new star?
55. "___ Jimmy Valentine"
58. Nyoro peasants
59. Purple brew?
62. Quod ___ demonstrandum
63. C'est ___ (That's a laugh!)
64. S. Pacific food plant
65. Cob or drake
66. Ben and Sue of films
67. Thomas Hood's "Eugene ___"

**DOWN**

1. Branch
2. Whitelaw ___, journalist
3. One-billionth: Comb. form
4. Poppy parlor
5. Reputed "Fountain of Youth" site
6. Cuckoo
7. Phoenix five
8. Low-branched evergreen shrub
9. Paid up
10. Conn. town
11. Landed
12. "Damn Yankees" role
13. Water pitcher
18. "The ___," Genet play
22. Middle point
24. People of Pannonia
26. Edgar, e.g.
27. Indefinite
28. "___ Care," 1905 song
29. Tilted, as a ship
31. Singing syllables
32. Hearsay
33. Representative
36. James ___, gourmet chef
39. Army fourth-grader
40. Nonharmonic note
42. Spoil completely
43. Like Hop-o'-My-Thumb
45. Elaborately decorated
47. An order of herbaceous plants
49. Each one
51. Throat-clearing sound
52. Miles from Okla.
53. Like Sabin's vaccine
54. Exchange premium
56. Chinese gelatin
57. Lab substances
60. Prince Valiant's son
61. Gypsy gentleman

## ACROSS

1. File sect.
5. David Copperfield's forte
10. Culloden Moor fighter
14. Gazetteer datum
15. Cockatoo's cousin
16. Job for Mason
17. Colleagues of March 19 patron
19. General locale of Nazareth
20. Doesn't become superannuated
21. Smooth, easy pace
23. License plate
24. Certain ships
26. March 19, to some
30. Papal cape
31. Grow toward evening
32. Cannoneer's plug
35. Loupe
36. Jung and Sagan
37. Famed dweller in Nazareth
38. Spud bud
39. Health, to Henri
40. Strass
41. Role of March 19 patron
43. Accented
46. Bit of land
47. Jonah
48. A preceder of spring
52. Within: Comb. form
53. Swallows' March 19 mecca
56. Suffix with origin
57. Swedish dollar
58. Arabian bigwig
59. Tribunals
60. Line of chatter
61. Soprano Clamma ___

## DOWN

1. Large: Comb. form
2. Of wrath: Lat.
3. Noted muralist
4. Temple of Jupiter and its hill
5. Riding academy
6. Some are fine
7. Proceed, in Dundee
8. Kind of vb.
9. Mt. Rainier's range
10. Parsimonious
11. Kshatriya, e.g.
12. Withy
13. Cause of Alice's pool
18. Fix a typo
22. Wise ___ owl
24. Made a cartograph
25. Stableboy in "The Highwayman"
26. Part of a pump
27. Deuce topper
28. Burroughs heroine
29. Goalie who popularized masks
32. Wear's partner
33. A Johnson
34. Batik expert
36. Clergymen
37. Was of consequence
39. Middling
40. Emulate Raphael
41. Opera by Giordano
42. King of Iraq: 1921–33
43. Bundle exported to Russia
44. John Todd's radio role
45. Helicopter part
48. Golconda
49. Nicaraguan native
50. Anagram for nail
51. Erudition
54. Famed Dadaist
55. Next: Mus. dir.

# 212

**ACROSS**

1. Snug as ___ . . .
5. Vestments
9. N.Y.C. airport
12. Diners' cartes
14. Compass point, in Cancun
16. Rubber tree
17. Web-footed choristers?
19. Pay or hey follower
20. Book backs
21. Small portions
23. Mephitis
25. Year in reign of Gregory I
26. Comrade of d'Artagnan
28. Cudgels or cleats
32. Elgar subject
35. This precedes Obadiah
37. Displaced turf on a course
38. Et ___ (plus, in a way)
39. Honeydew, e.g.
41. Mother of Castor and Pollux
42. Places for kayos
44. Aggravate
45. Songbird
46. Cowboy meets
48. Andrea ___
50. Tryggvesson
52. Brahman precepts
55. Prior to birth
59. Used a powder puff
61. Suffix with baron
62. Daffy Duck?
64. Wood: Comb. form
65. Director Lubitsch
66. "___ pray"
67. Reply to Virginia
68. Cyclone centers
69. Dream states

**DOWN**

1. A.C. amounts
2. Horn signals
3. Not fired
4. Test-tube turbit?
5. Actress Sothern
6. Draw ___ (decide)
7. Mope
8. Held a job action
9. Martial art
10. Tart
11. Ivories
13. Get wind of
15. Detected
18. He tutored Queen Elizabeth I
22. Extinct Dixie redstart?
24. Slugger's quest
27. Unanimous
29. Word with green or glade
30. Mine mother
31. Ollie's pal
32. Samlet
33. Hodgepodge
34. Matter's master
36. Goes it alone
40. Chilean Nobelist: 1971
43. Relief
47. Trenchant wit
49. "The Thrill of ___," Doris Day film
51. Marcel Pagnol comedy
53. Let up
54. Whey of milk
55. Fairy
56. Martha from Butte
57. Lowell has three
58. ___-majesté
60. Drillers' degs.
63. Rocky elevs.

# 213

**ACROSS**

1. Tasse qualifier
5. Batter's locale
10. Behaves like a tout
14. "____ Get It for You Wholesale"
15. Fiddler's need
16. Old weapon
17. "That's how you spell Chicago!": Part I
20. Ages and ages
21. On the briny
22. Turn on an axis
23. Spud
25. Lip
26. He made a mint in mines
28. Carlton Fisk's colleagues
32. Deplaned
33. Lean and hungry look, e.g.
34. "Diamonds ____ Forever"
35. Car pts.
36. French-door components
37. Chinese city
38. Inconclusive conclusion
39. First-grade subj.
40. Dividing word
41. Chicago Museum of Science and ____
44. Put weight on
46. Simpatico
47. "The mouse ____ the clock"
48. Antonym for 44 Across
51. Sentry's word
52. Dawn goddess
55. See 17 Across: Part II
58. Mete out
59. De Mille ballet
60. Prefix for plane or space
61. Tennyson heroine
62. Ache, emotionally
63. Gun type

**DOWN**

1. Las Vegas lure
2. Narcissus spurned her
3. Asserted
4. Business abbr.
5. Like a programmed computer
6. Hermit
7. Shortest continent, in a way
8. British can
9. Catches the Metroliner
10. Dreaded fly
11. Peruvian indigene
12. Bog contents
13. Very dry
18. African teas
19. Multitude
24. Martial ____
25. Gloss
26. Papa Doc's milieu
27. City northwest of Chicago
28. Chicago weather forecast
29. Martyr at Rome: A.D. 64?
30. Wax rhetorical
31. Inert gas
33. "The Treasure of the Sierra ____"
36. Clumsy repairing
37. In ____ (in position)
42. Conjoint
43. New thin ice
44. Peregrine
45. Theater org.
47. Less prevalent
48. Cover a bet
49. Unsigned, for short
50. Year in the reign of Edward VI
51. "Mary ____ little lamb . . ."
53. Karloff portrayal
54. Part of a.s.a.p.
56. Great miler
57. Bag

# 214

**ACROSS**

1. Happen
6. Molecule component
10. ____ California
14. "____, ma prima . . .": Verdi aria
15. Machete's kin
16. Certain stadium
17. As compared with
18. Chemical compound
20. Fresh
21. Sky mysteries
23. Sojourns
24. Strange
26. Potter's must
27. What a prof proffers
29. Hanky décor
33. Rara ____
34. Intensify
36. TV's Vigoda
37. Rice dish
39. Noshed
40. Eyewitness
42. Large photo: Abbr.
43. Word of serendipity
46. Slavic ruler
47. Felt indignation
49. Wobble
51. On the rocks
52. Role for Valerie Harper
53. Worsted
56. Prospect
57. Marbles game
60. Utter engrossment
62. Fine violin
64. Nary a soul
65. Author Murdoch
66. Beard eraser
67. Enter
68. Take on cargo
69. Cooperstown's Vance

**DOWN**

1. Arabian sultanate
2. "I ____ to bury Caesar . . ."
3. Artists' pens
4. Samovar
5. Reprobates
6. Execrate
7. Trifles
8. Timeworn
9. Glacial deposit
10. ____ Day, post-Christmas holiday in England
11. Grasping
12. Nephrite, e.g.
13. City NW of Nîmes
19. Elliptical
22. Browse
25. Sky Bear
26. Ivan's coin
27. Frolic
28. Sheeplike
29. Allotted
30. Hoopla
31. Nautical term
32. Blithe
35. Like the otary
38. Epeeist
41. Biting
44. Dicer or ricer
45. Wimbledon great
48. "My Sister ____"
50. Henry VIII's fifth
52. Washer cycle
53. Ell
54. Melville novel
55. Atlanta arena
56. Invalid
58. Gamut of a sort
59. Lean, tough and strong
61. Retirement plan, for short
63. Lea sound

# 215

**ACROSS**

1. Amicus ___ (friend of the court)
7. Cartels
13. Immediately
14. Marin subject
16. What two-year-olds do
17. Squawk box
18. More appropriate
19. Carpenter or fire follower
20. Monad
21. Property claim
22. Incipient nestlings
23. "Mother ___," old song
24. Theater section
26. Gravy enhancer
27. Articles
28. Trevi number
29. Bingo officials
30. Loafer, e.g.
31. ". . . add ___ unto a fault . . .": Shak.
32. Trifle ingredient
35. Seine site or sight
36. ___-fi
39. Bruckner and Chekhov
40. English offshoot
42. Gear for Krupa
43. What rulers hold
44. Wrongful act
45. Cornmeal
46. Basis for some soldiers
47. Elbow
48. Brings into play
51. Press component
52. Wife of Odysseus
53. Meadowlands competitors
54. Wall panels
55. Scanty

**DOWN**

1. Tree with beanlike pods
2. Visionary
3. Cads
4. Purpose
5. Box-elder genus
6. Ending for racket or profit
7. Yurts
8. "Brother ___," 1938 film
9. Function
10. What mobile QB's do
11. Tangible
12. Clergyman famous for slips of the tongue
14. Barbershop offering
15. Irish patriot's family
19. Saw eye to eye
22. Ball-park statistics
23. More unctuous
25. Allen and Frome
26. Ship's kitchen
29. Crocodile's relative
30. Plugged
32. Counter item in a diner
33. Not classified
34. Staying power
36. Phil Rizzuto's nickname
37. Thanksgiving-dinner V.I.P.'s
38. Burning
40. "I heard ___ man say": Housman
41. Cayuga Lake city
43. Hitchcock's "The Thirty-Nine ___"
47. Insult
49. Half a Philippine city's name
50. Actress Caldwell
51. Letters after letters

# 216

**ACROSS**

1. Ullmann
4. "___ delights not me": Shak.
7. Tongue-lash
12. Mineral used in insulation
13. Fictional captain
15. Quay on a river
16. Yemeni seaport
17. Philippine fort
18. "Golden Boy" playwright
19. Producer who discovered Judy Garland
22. Name of three canals
23. Whopper
24. Adherents
25. Cancel
28. Feast in the open
30. Tibetan monk
31. Angelico, e.g.
32. School of American art
36. Warren Beatty's sister
39. ___ as a pin
40. Pub offering
41. Skin
42. Nog and negus
44. Parting word, in León
45. Dross
48. Lure for Bobby Shaftoe
49. Church facility
50. Creator of Abie the Agent
56. Halos
57. An amino acid
58. Whodunit item
59. Stand of trees
60. Montand
61. Weight unit
62. Carpenter, at times
63. Veneration
64. ___ de vie

**DOWN**

1. Fashionable beach resort
2. Desserts
3. "Julia" Oscar winner: 1977
4. Like a he-man
5. ___, skip and a jump
6. Russian ballerina who defected to the U.S.
7. Liquor flavoring
8. Actor knighted in 1934
9. Patisserie's need
10. "___ c'est moi"
11. Pigeonholes' loci
12. Salvation Army off.
14. Irreducible
20. "The Bells" poet
21. Ace and queen, e.g., in a bridge hand
25. A Lanchester
26. Cheers
27. Cole Porter's "I ___ Love"
28. Peep
29. Atlas abbr.
31. Object believed to have magical powers
33. Half of CCVI
34. ___ Hegirae
35. Rorem et al.
37. Roman household god
38. Smith and Capone
43. Poor
44. W.W. I initials
45. Chases flies
46. Lady in Petrarch's sonnets
47. Highway-sign feature
49. Stage
51. North Sea feeder
52. Eject
53. Pen name of fame
54. Honey
55. ___ volente

# 217

**ACROSS**

1. Persona ____
6. Suffix with system
10. What a priest says
14. Called
15. Safari blind
16. Claudia ____ Taylor Johnson
17. "West Side Story" girl
18. Famed basketball coach
19. Creator of "the sack"
20. Marriage counselor, at times
22. Flag designer: 1818
23. "St. Jerome" painter
25. Kin of yellow fever
26. Macrogametes
27. Stat. for George Foster
30. Rarae ____
31. ____ knot (marry)
34. "Dante jet Virgile" painter
37. Wildcats
38. This gives ade
39. Antique car
40. Colombian people
41. Store event
42. "Descent from the Cross" painter
50. Greek resistance org.
51. Adjective for masterworks
52. Umbrella supports
53. Complain
54. Arctic abode
55. Sec. of Transportation under Reagan
56. Island off Brazil
57. Ali, thrice
58. Pueblos' erstwhile foes
59. Rev. Moon's group, e.g.
60. Phrygian Adonis

**DOWN**

1. Tree knot
2. Indian princess
3. Gina's friend
4. Wyoming range
5. City or province in Turkey
6. Like pocket dictionaries
7. "Le Promenoir" painter
8. Hinder
9. "Lost Horizon" director
10. Ohio stream
11. Opposite of 20 Across
12. Man of iron
13. Natives of Cagliari
21. Desires
24. Echo lost all but this
27. Electrical unit
28. Purchase
29. Far from fireproof
30. Close, poetically
31. Circus performers
32. Hurry
33. Outside: Prefix
35. Overages
36. Country visited by Gulliver
41. Mexican shawl
42. Hidden
43. He wrote "The Rock": 1934
44. S.A. rodents
45. City on the Mohawk
46. Rope loop
47. Brilliance
48. Biblical mother-in-law
49. Spills

# 218

**ACROSS**

1. Agreement
5. Indifferent
9. "The Admirable Doctor"
14. Tree ____ (quiver tree)
15. Of an epoch
16. Shad
17. Pivot
18. Preakness winner: 1963
20. Yurt
21. Explosive initials
22. Passageways
23. Place a horse in a race
25. Zigzags on a cat
27. Sudermann's "____ Sorge"
29. "Cherry Orchard" quartet
30. Quatrain scheme
34. Hole puncher
36. ____ ear and . . .
38. Island off Venezuela
39. Gulf Stream stakes race
42. Suggestive looks
43. British weight unit
44. Methane, for one
45. Division preposition
46. Region in SW India
47. Until
49. Practices telegraphy
51. Synecdoche, e.g.
54. Spinner of sorts
58. Kennedy abbr.
60. Cognate
61. Triple Crown winner: 1937
63. The Swedish Nightingale
64. The Summit, at Houston
65. Dugout
66. Grafted, in heraldry
67. Jewish month
68. No, in Minsk
69. Curser's euphemism

**DOWN**

1. Sticky stuff
2. Singer-pianist Peter
3. Kentucky Derby winner: 1943
4. Seesaw
5. Jacob Ammann's followers, e.g.
6. Praying figure
7. California stakes race
8. ____ Rosebud, 1914 Kentucky Derby winner
9. Fundamental principle
10. Castor and Pollux
11. Composed
12. Bone: Comb. form
13. Famed crime fighter
19. "Mirth-quakes"
24. Marsh birds
26. Belief formula
28. One, in Apulia
30. 100 square meters
31. Kentucky Derby winner: 1932
32. Swedish rock group
33. Horses or trees
34. Gudrun's victim
35. "Say ____"
37. Funny Bean
38. Skilled
40. To's companion
41. Babylonian sky god
46. Bud
48. Irish seaport
49. Jampan
50. Gaze at steadily
52. 15th-century ship
53. Over
54. Ballet bird
55. Prefix with mutuel
56. Incenses
57. Actress Wynter
59. Completed a hurdle
62. Hunter or Fleming

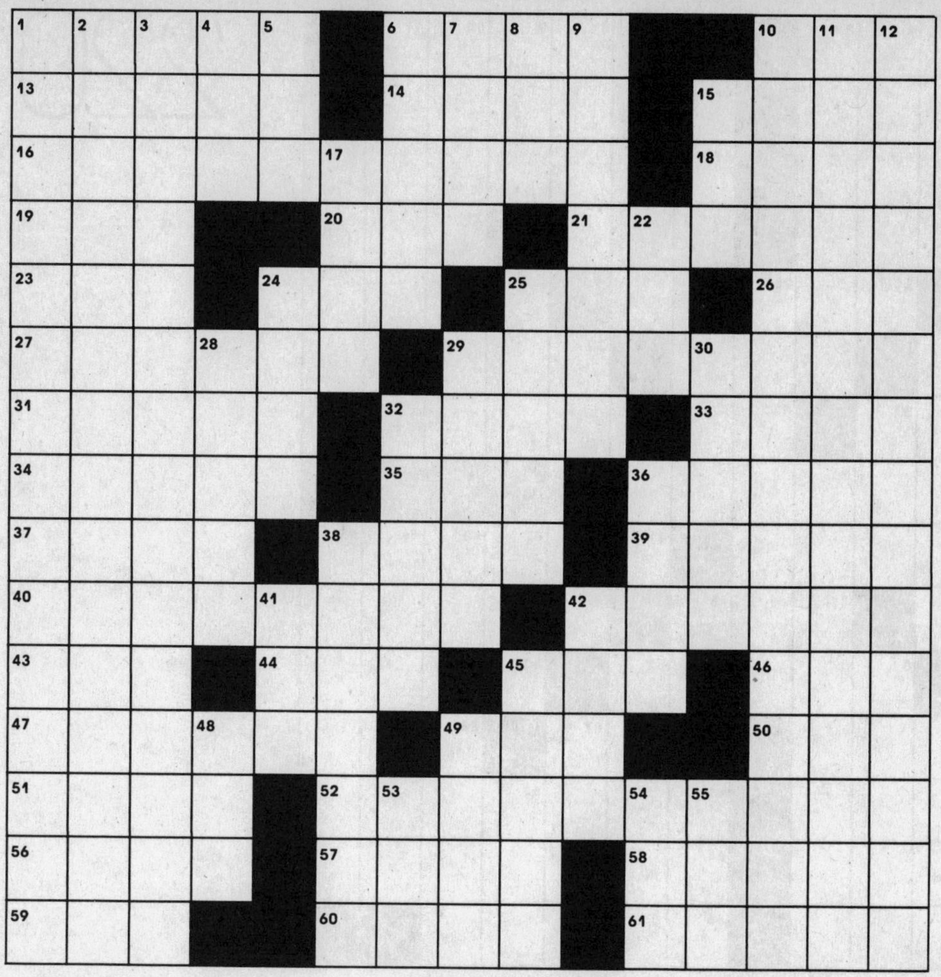

**ACROSS**

1. Coarse cotton cloth
6. N.Y. mayor
10. Chance, formerly
13. Verso's opposite
14. Matty, Felipe or Jesus
15. A Marx
16. Supporters of mob rule
18. "Thou ___ lady": King Lear
19. Hindu title
20. Klutz
21. Mountains between Tibet and China
23. Companion of poivre
24. Behave
25. Gain
26. Poetic palindrome
27. Solidarity leader
29. Kurosawa film: 1951
31. The Moor, to a madrileño
32. Inquiry: Abbr.
33. Pro ___ (proportionately)
34. "I see a bad moon ___"
35. Actress Hagen
36. Spanish gentleman
37. "How ___ the little busy bee . . ."
38. Grove on a prairie
39. Walsy's partner
40. Air: Comb. form
42. Military docs
43. Keats subject
44. Somewhat: Suffix
45. Mandible
46. Horse "somebody bet on"
47. Wheel of fortune?
49. Anger
50. Hosp. group
51. Where to get views of gnus
52. Ambushes
56. K-P connection
57. Redact
58. Met's Marilyn
59. Sidewinder shape
60. Pearl Buck novel
61. Other nations, to Israelites

**DOWN**

1. Popular diversion
2. Dens
3. Football trainers' concerns
4. One N.L. team's insignia
5. Cry of triumph
6. Jeweler's unit
7. Norwegian king
8. Small bed
9. Malamutes
10. Part of the British Museum
11. Parma's gift to music
12. Part of the harmony of the universe
15. Mo. neighbor
17. Caesar's erstwhile partner
22. Prefix with corn or verse
24. ". . . unto us ___ is given"
25. A source of bran
28. One of Job's visitors
29. Entire: Mus.
30. Fear
32. "___ the raven . . ."
36. Eject forcibly
38. Steel plates used in 13th-century armor
41. Farrow
42. Dress style
45. Wisecracks
48. Equal: Prefix
49. Miner's discovery
53. Wedding words
54. Modern Teutonic tongue: Abbr.
55. Court

# 220

**ACROSS**

1. Pine Tree (or 23d)
6. Sunflower (or 34th)
12. Having a stiff upper lip
14. Eggs on
16. He was the 35th
17. Geological epoch
18. Avena sativa item
19. Polite address
20. Prefix with function
21. W.W. II craft
22. Tropical trees
24. Ransack; plunder
26. "So long!" in Sorrento
27. Howard Hughes became one
29. Three-time champ
30. Jarrell and Ciardi
31. Fixed machine part
33. Painting the town red
35. Peach (or 4th)
37. John III ___, King of Poland: 17th century
41. London insurer
46. Ward off
47. Nav. bigwig
49. Poet Marianne
50. Editor's mark
51. Polar globe-trotter
53. Kermit of "The Muppets"
54. Onassis nickname
55. Marsupial, for short
56. Wd. ending
58. Grape, for one
59. P.G.A. champ: 1974
61. Diameter of a gun bore
63. Feral fellows
64. Incarnate deities
65. Silver (or 36th)
66. Lone Star (or 28th)

**DOWN**

1. Treasure (or 41st)
2. Rhone feeder
3. Puts in reserve
4. Zenith's opposite
5. N Ohio city
6. Firewood
7. Part of a biblical trade-off
8. Sgts., e.g.
9. "___ 'em, Cerberus!"
10. Artist's studio
11. Having feeling
12. Scandinavian toasts
13. Sine qua non at an afternoon affair
15. Bristly
23. Tennis unit
25. Sunshine (or 27th)
26. O. Henry's "The ___ and the Anthem"
28. Synonyms man
30. Sacred song
32. In medias ___
34. Be under the weather
36. County in 25 Down
37. Post-Nasser First Family
38. Invaded; ravaged
39. Give credence to
40. Wrath
42. Word of discomfort
43. Guinean coast group
44. He might give you a bum steer
45. Smokes, in Dogpatch
48. Capital of Oman
51. Wound textile yarn
52. Urbane
55. Latvian port
57. Fiber for making linen
60. Hebrew letter
62. Call ___ day

# 221

**ACROSS**

1. Peels
6. Funeral orations
12. Llama's cousin
13. Witty saying
14. Ton of bricks at Fort Knox?
16. Freshwater fish
17. To love, in Paris
18. Guido's high note
19. Sussex river
20. Lots of land
21. Hebrew lyre
22. Columbus campus initials
23. Winter precipitation
24. Orb
25. Apply
27. Fumed
29. Seine tributary
30. Der ____ (Adenauer)
31. Filling with sediment
34. Short solo
37. Tires, in Tours
38. Sped
40. Peruke
41. Sales term
42. Ancient Chinese
43. "____ creature was stirring . . ."
44. Greek letters
45. Kind of fish or mint
46. Agave fiber
47. Fasteners that may pop?
50. Lassos
51. "Babes ____"
52. Builds
53. Light craft

**DOWN**

1. Time off for enjoyment?
2. Rapidly
3. Foolhardy
4. Old French coin
5. Crusader's adversary
6. Fencing weapons
7. Prevaricator
8. Curved moldings
9. Medusa's sisters?
10. Place for a ringlet
11. Daubed
12. Waken
13. Ants
14. Scout unit
15. One of Ireland's names
20. Foreign
21. Winged
23. Indian dresses
24. Cold
26. Ballet skirts
28. Biblical weeds
31. Shiny ornament
32. Provincial
33. Links features
34. Tart
35. Giants
36. Bedouin head cords
39. Macaws
42. Espies
43. An explosive, for short
45. Phidias creation: Abbr.
46. Musial
48. Twitch
49. "Faerie Queene" lady

# 222

**ACROSS**

1. Dick, Tom or Sam
6. Rosary components
10. Vegetables?
14. Similar
15. Carpenter's groovy creation
16. Freedom from discomfort?
17. Actor Bruce
18. Name before Arthur
19. Soft touches
20. Affable Arizona Indian?
23. Pig follower
24. Where to put your dough
25. Detroit ten
27. Buttercup part
31. Like Elroy Hirsch's legs
33. Jezebel's deity
34. Before the mast
36. Get up
40. Dislodge a jockey
42. Blow from Aaron's rod
44. Canadian peninsula
45. This never meets West
47. Sud's opposite: Fr.
48. Beast akin to a wildebeest
50. What expiators make
52. Wretched
55. Go overboard
57. Watches?
58. Funny girls
64. ___ Fitzgerald
66. Bombay bigwig
67. Nick-name
68. Change course
69. Spirited self-assurance
70. Heating devices
71. Gaelic
72. Manche's seat
73. What gibberish doesn't make

**DOWN**

1. Reverberated
2. Hodgepodge
3. Spanish port
4. Stretched out
5. Trust
6. Nothin' is like this gal
7. Curtain-rod hider
8. Dutch cheese
9. Beethoven's "Moonlight ___"
10. Cheerleader's asset
11. G.W. was this man's sitter
12. Famous fisherman
13. Mosquitoes, fleas, etc.
21. Layers of irises
22. Turkish soldier
26. Marine
27. ". . . ___ in a rug"
28. Miracle site
29. Cries of surprise
30. Became one while on the run
32. Sounds of fans
35. Viewed
37. Press
38. Voiceless sound, in phonetics
39. Terminates
41. Souvenir
43. Copper town in Namibia
46. Stimulating ire or vim
49. Idolizes
51. Family close to the Reagans
52. Wholly holey utensil
53. Edmonton athlete
54. Gets one's goat
56. Hersey town
59. Vassar purchase
60. Archibald of the Celtics
61. Printers' measures?
62. Greek letters
63. Correspondence courtesy, for short
65. One hundred square meters

# 223

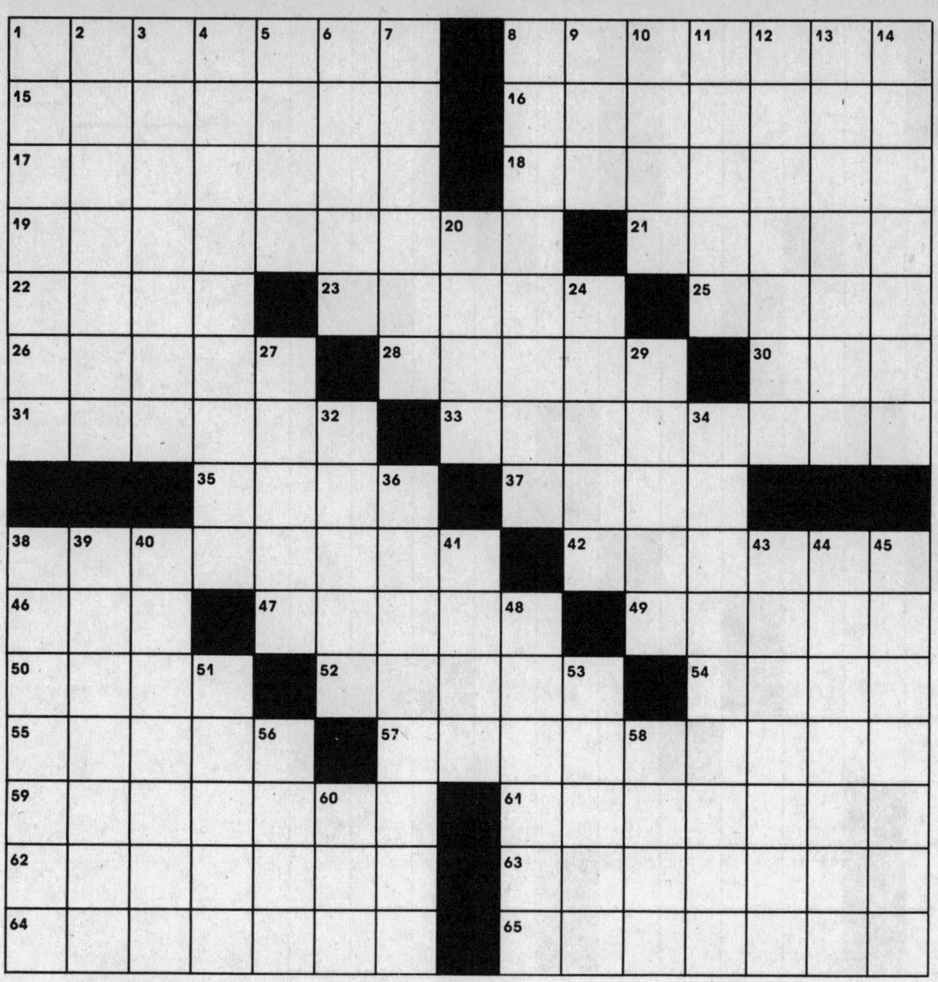

**ACROSS**

1. Certain speech sounds
8. Covered passageways
15. Military ornament
16. Supply
17. Semiautomatic weapon
18. Issue
19. Cloth for a G.I.
21. Shylock's friend
22. "The ____ of Spring"
23. Star of "M"
25. A Peace Nobelist: 1946
26. Deprive of weapons
28. Hideaways
30. Niihau neckpiece
31. Pertaining to the chin
33. Prude
35. Hibernia
37. Light brown
38. Fiery particle
42. European flatfish
46. Former nuclear org.
47. Redheaded Met
49. Dame Nellie
50. Roman racing column
52. Broadcast
54. Simpleton
55. ____ facie
57. Humperdinck
59. Wool fat
61. Exultant
62. Part of a French motto
63. Spanning
64. Effaced
65. Exercised suzerainty

**DOWN**

1. Dignified propriety
2. Milkily iridescent
3. N.J. river or town
4. Underminer of principles
5. "I cannot tell ____"
6. Court star
7. Unsaturated alcohol
8. Not feverish
9. Type of runner
10. Partisan: Comb. form
11. Per ____
12. Devil: Comb. form
13. Sights at Newport, R.I.
14. Scottish pony or dog
20. Aba wearer
24. Issue violently, as a volcano
27. Visible impressions
29. Whey of milk
32. Rhythmic cadences
34. Famous trial city
36. Set in order
38. Had a taste
39. Noble body
40. Oral
41. Curdle
43. Large tuna
44. Thrust forward
45. Squealed
48. Impoverish
51. Soap substitute
53. Catfish, in Cottbus
56. Got off
58. Indonesian island group
60. Doctrinal suffix

# 224

**ACROSS**

1. "___ a man with . . ."
5. One more time
9. Developers' concerns
14. Went like sixty
15. Handle a problem
16. "___ Love Has Gone," 1964 song
17. Lyricist born June 18, 1913 (all pop songs herein are his)
19. Golfer with an army
20. Verboten
21. Galley word
23. Retreat
24. Lake Albert group
26. "Playing ___," Hochman book
28. Furnishes
31. Infested
34. Panache
35. Photographer James Wong ___
37. Vapor: Comb. form
38. Couperin's "Le Tic-___-choc"
39. Musical finales
40. Hudson rival
41. Prill and mispickel
43. Is contrite
44. Reads meter
46. Dicer's seven
48. Sashay
50. Erect
51. Produce interest
52. Gridiron "zebra"
54. Gumshoes
56. Loses color
59. Instrument for Stern
61. Hit song of 1957 (Academy Award)
64. Kitchen device
65. NASCAR event
66. Custer's last major
67. Coeur d'___, Idaho
68. Bedouin chief
69. "Let It ___ . . . ," 1945 song

**DOWN**

1. "___ Magic," 1948 song
2. Castle protection
3. Writer Bombeck
4. Earthquake
5. Harmony
6. Ship that picked up Glenn
7. Williams team
8. "All That Love ___," 1972 song
9. Enclose
10. Her, in Hamburg
11. Hit song of 1955, with "The"
12. Jay Gould's railroad: 1867–72
13. Witnessed
18. "Because ___ Mine," 1951 song
22. Sidewall protections
25. Hit song of 1944
27. Domesday Book money
28. River celebrated by Burns
29. Plant life
30. Song from a 1953 film
32. Ratifies
33. Springe part
36. Serenata
39. Bustard's kin
42. Realm of Helios
44. Miles or Vaughan
45. Ella of comics
47. Call it a day
49. Ceiling beam
52. ___ avis
53. Conductor Cooper
55. Goren coup
57. Gershwin biographer
58. ". . . in corpore ___"
60. Hamilton bill
62. W.W. II boat
63. "Whoopee!"

# 225

**ACROSS**

1. Mescal is one
7. "Oh, my," in Mainz
10. Immovable
14. Maltreat
15. Scarf
16. "Deep calleth ___ deep . . .": Psalm 42:7
17. "___ Mater," well-known hymn
18. Photographer's gear
20. Swill
21. Guides of a sort
22. Mine vehicle
25. Boat part
26. A summer baby
27. ___ Sunday
29. Remnants
30. Chump
31. Condiments
33. Uses up
34. Plantations
41. Rhythm instruments
43. Suffix with poet or hero
46. Ireland's ___ Islands
48. Spirit away
49. Crop
50. Goof, for Guidry
51. Petition
52. ". . . the forest ___": Longfellow
54. City on the Mohawk
57. Fitting
58. Expiator
60. F.F.V. group
61. Frost's "The Road ___ Taken"
62. Altercations
63. Says further
64. Forage plant
65. Grass type

**DOWN**

1. Ancient Roman receptacle
2. ___ sax
3. Showy and cheap
4. Mexican flower
5. NATO member
6. Determined
7. "Bring me ___ of wine": Aristophanes
8. Makes more compact
9. Shared equally
10. Point Barrow apparel
11. Neighbor of Zambia
12. Cordwood measures
13. Unfinished works of art
19. Troubles
23. Name of three English rivers
24. Patch
27. Ottawa-N.Y.C. dir.
28. Jinx
32. Kind of clause
35. PBS members
36. Proscribed
37. Firedogs
38. German
39. To Grecophiles, this is KTL
40. Fleet flier
42. Short socks
43. Simba's prey
44. Did some nagging
45. Pinched
46. Burrows et al.
47. Hollow
53. Caribou's food
55. Preprandial reading
56. Gaelic
58. Line from "Annie"
59. Tiu's day: Abbr.

# 226

**ACROSS**

1. Alg. or trig.
5. N.Y.C. social club
10. Positively charged particle
12. Fly
14. Plunger's phrase
17. Of one of the senses
18. Between the lines, in a way
19. Crony
20. Weight allowance
21. Like some lions
22. British Open winner: 1964
23. Ethnic ending
24. Certain Egyptians
25. Boo-boo
26. Vedette
28. Scribble aimlessly
29. Solo
31. N.H.L. team
34. Costs
38. Moslem V.I.P.'s
39. No-see'ums
40. Ending with pay
41. Strong trend
42. Profs' posers, at times
43. Neighbor of Mex.
44. Montague ____, Sayers sleuth
45. Slow down
46. Canyon of comics
47. Grammatical taboos
50. Damascene
51. Dishonors
52. Arenose
53. Teen follower

**DOWN**

1. Stapleton or O'Hara
2. Box-score entry
3. Place for money
4. Straddler
5. Jousters' needs
6. Sidestep
7. Diamond glove
8. Scrooge word
9. Allowance
10. Row of bricks
11. Store sign
13. Pottery finish
14. Postmark info
15. Massasauga, e.g.
16. Hard look
21. See 47 Across, e.g.
22. Daft ones
24. Nice movies
25. Stadiums
27. "The Velvet Fog"
28. Lamebrains
30. Landlubber's lack
31. Placed
32. Puebla pals
33. Villains in oaters
35. Beatles' "Strawberry Fields ____"
36. Antipasto items
37. Bulldozes
39. Type of knot
42. Attendant on Artemis
43. ". . . ____ to heal"
45. Thin, rolled pancake
46. Forest creature
48. Undergarment
49. Sound of discovery

# 227

**ACROSS**

1. Mineral resistant to electricity
5. "Lucky Jim" author
9. Place for a feather
12. Nigerian capital
13. Hersey town
14. Cape Horn native
15. Neuron components
16. R.A.F. and Luftwaffe
18. Rhetorical evasions
20. Guidry stat.
21. Lusitania's last gasp
22. Garden swinger
23. She has her pride
27. Biblical suffix
29. Raison d'____
30. Due
33. Central patios
37. Stargazing by mariners
40. Set firmly
41. Stand
42. One of the Marianas
43. Romaine lettuce
45. City E of Monterey Bay
47. Both: Prefix
50. Part of i.e.
53. U.S. press org.
54. 2007 for Jamestown
60. Ancient Semites
61. Flirted optically
62. Gamble
63. A wine from SW France
64. Open pies
65. Enzyme
66. Part of A.A.A.
67. Song or gab follower

**DOWN**

1. Long coat
2. Pet bat in "The Munsters"
3. Pond ripples display this
4. Guarantee
5. Opposite of "Saludos!"
6. Polo
7. Steep the tea leaves
8. Carbon particles
9. Shipment from 12 Across
10. Concerning
11. Outmoded
12. Ingredient of japan
13. Indian mulberry
17. Pythagorean proposition figure
19. James or Marsha
23. Capriole
24. ". . . but thinking makes ____": Hamlet
25. These are often wild
26. Gob
28. Chinese pagoda
31. Grandmother of Enos
32. "Buenos ____"
34. Black Sea feeder
35. Smidgen
36. Duck genus
38. Siouan
39. President called "American Caesar"
44. October classic
46. Keep away, at sea
47. Middle Eastern gulf
48. Clio and Thalia, e.g.
49. Scold harshly
51. Abundance
52. Mortise partner
55. Writer Bombeck
56. D.C. advisory group
57. "____! poor Yorick"
58. Lease
59. Football dists.

# 228

**ACROSS**

1. Lyra
5. Scene of "Tosca"
9. Flag
12. Kandahar chief
13. Cousins of elites
14. They may bless the I.R.S.
16. Prominent positions
18. Elects
19. Tenant
20. Abandons
22. Dior creation
24. First editor of "The Overland Monthly"
25. Provisions provider
28. Old Faithful, e.g.
31. Ornament
32. Runs in neutral
35. 100 square meters
36. Boston ___ Orchestra
37. Callao coin
38. Kind of coat or table
39. "That mighty ___ of song": Wordsworth
40. Linguine, e.g.
42. Ornamental loop
43. Tar
45. Decays
47. Persons, places or things
49. "Merry" in a game name
50. Decorations on Gen. Grant's shoulders
53. Bantingized
57. City on the Rhine
58. June 6, 1944, in Ike's final plans
60. Army ___
61. Cronus was one
62. Double preposition
63. Switchback's kin
64. Julian and Sidonian
65. Indites

**DOWN**

1. Albert or Carnegie
2. Nice girlfriend
3. Tire mounts
4. Manglers
5. Control dishonestly
6. Renowned publisher
7. Mate
8. Allay
9. "Star Trek" character
10. Nonsense
11. Wicket, e.g.
13. Tune
15. Conscription agcy.
17. Ascertain
21. Exceedingly, in music
23. Santa
25. Devices on guitars
26. Idolize
27. Star performers
29. Gaffe
30. Lets
33. What "i" and "j" have in common
34. Andean quadruped
38. Made neat
40. Pope ___ VI: 1963–78
41. Funicello of film fame
42. Braid
44. Rainier and Vernon
46. Ancient
48. Step
50. Recede
51. Small opening
52. Miss, in Madrid: Abbr.
54. Record of a sort
55. Word with blue or fives
56. Retreats
59. Farrell's "___ House McGinty"

# 229

**ACROSS**

1. Chaise
5. Guesswork, for short
9. Butts
13. Arouse
14. Trunk
15. Issue
16. Much-used vegetable oil
17. National antonym
18. Sped
19. Person from Bonn?
21. Enervate
23. Part of the Polish-E. German border
24. Asian desert
25. Disgraces
28. Administer or conduct?
32. Ponderous works
33. Sacred book of Islam
34. "Summer ____," Hassam painting
35. Parthenon, e.g.
36. Amplify
37. Some canonized persons: Abbr.
38. Panza's Dapple
39. Is excessively fond
40. "____ Body?": Sayers book
41. Sycophants?
43. Oft-traded pieces of paper
44. Mild expletive
45. Gush
46. Overthrown
49. Strong person?
53. Very much
54. Criminal
56. Caused
57. Amount, to an R.N.
58. Topple
59. Once again
60. Daniel or Isaiah
61. Bail
62. Monster-infested loch

**DOWN**

1. Some air pollution
2. Part of a stud-poker hand
3. Affirm
4. British small landholders?
5. Word with system or cycle
6. Sch. authority
7. Compass pt.
8. Swindler?
9. Hire in advance
10. Frenzied
11. Bog
12. British weapon
14. Softens
20. Epinicia
22. Abba
24. Pierces
25. Err
26. Theater audience
27. Faulty
28. Germanic god
29. Former B'way hotel
30. Embdens, e.g.
31. Abates
33. Soared
36. Brave or resolute?
37. Amerind medicine person?
39. Genoese magistrate
40. Sound of relief
42. Turmoil
43. Disburse
45. Was eminent
46. Crazes
47. Tropical plant
48. Mislay
49. Rosebud, e.g.
50. Hippie's hairdo
51. Lemon and lime followers
52. Word
55. Org. headed by W. D. Ruckelshaus

# 230

**ACROSS**

1. Star with a tail
5. End of a Stein line
10. Pest for 1 Across
14. "____ End": Christie
17. Christie mystery
18. Ayres
19. "It might have ____"
20. Berliner's budget
21. Spanish and Vulgar
23. Slayer of Castor
25. Some of the upper classes
29. Manumits
33. Mollify; alleviate
35. ____-jongg
36. Christie mystery
41. "____, Two, Buckle My Shoe": Christie
42. To the letter
43. Brillat-____, gastronomist
46. He sang with James
50. More's opposite
51. "____ Russia with Love"
52. Antonia Fraser's "Quiet as ____"
54. What Miss Marple works on
58. Here, to Poirot
59. Christie mystery
63. "Cat ____": Christie
64. Napoleon won here: 1806
65. Mixers
66. Galley word

**DOWN**

1. Hugo's wife and daughter
2. Stern
3. Taipei's land
4. Part of NATO
5. Skin problem
6. Teased
7. Augury
8. U.S.A.F., for one
9. Id attachment
10. Fly in Uganda
11. "____ boy!"
12. Poirot's "Hush!"
13. Barbie's boyfriend
15. Center of activity
16. In advance
22. "For sure!" in Sevilla
23. Castle and Rich
24. Tree: Comb. form
26. A friend of Pooh
27. "That which is ____ reasonable": Hegel
28. Inserts
30. Flightless bird
31. Moms
32. "Murder, ____ Said": Christie
34. Asian holiday
36. Not neg.
37. Queen of Spain before Sofia
38. Gun a motor
39. Solo in "Star Wars"
40. Norwegian king
44. One of the ex-Yalies
45. Revoke: Var.
47. Ribbed cloth for dresses
48. Famed coach, born in Norway
49. Surrounded by
52. Alas!
53. Kind of sign
54. Open to both sexes
55. Italian harp
56. Arts' partner: Abbr.
57. Unit of work
59. ____ Mahal
60. Football positions: Abbr.
61. Greek letter
62. Roman bronze

# 231

**ACROSS**

1. Compact
5. D.A.V. member
8. Corrida attraction
14. Singer Anita
15. "___ declare!"
16. Barely sufficient
17. A Louis victim: 1937
18. Short snort
19. Sopwith's W.W. I fliers
20. Chennault, for one
23. Rhyme royal
24. Like Idlewild, e.g.
29. Faeros whirlwinds
30. Boss of the pvts.
32. Chiton's relative
33. Try ale, gingerly
35. Red Baron's foe
38. Home of Phillips U.
39. A-one
41. Kid's shooter
42. Henri follower
43. Platoon, for one
44. Swift's flying island
46. What she didn't say, in Kern's song
47. Tenner minus one?
49. Las ___ (two o'clock in Taxco)
50. Seat for Snerd
52. Former Italian prime minister
54. Opposite of Rocky Rd.?
57. Movie flier in 1939
60. Mystery flier
64. Singer Rawls
65. Norse hammer thrower
66. Synthetic gem
67. Steno's abbr.
68. ___ 1 (long odds)
69. Companions for Artemis
70. Tonkin chaser
71. Parvenu

**DOWN**

1. Dorchester dudes
2. Allan-___
3. Movie flier in 1964
4. Source of sulfuric acid
5. ___-et-un (Riviera blackjack)
6. Polish, in a way
7. African antelope
8. Telethon V.I.P.
9. Gets some lore
10. Banff bonnet
11. Haitian hero
12. Electrical unit
13. Hosp. locales
21. Hopeful or hopeless ending
22. Architectural innovator
25. To ___ (precisely)
26. Aerial-circus proprietor
27. Type size
28. Playpen comments
30. Peregrine
31. Sand-cement mortar
33. Gulled
34. Mich. county
36. Zero, in soccer
37. Notwithstanding
40. Dance
45. What there ought to be
48. Bond anew
51. Such being the case
53. Laughs, in Le Havre
54. Arrive at
55. Caledonian: Comb. form
56. Palpitate
58. Swiss Abstractionist
59. Times immeasurable
60. Hit sign
61. Ear: Comb. form
62. Versatile truck, for short
63. Hush-hush org.

# 232

**ACROSS**

1. Musical symbol
5. Emulated Plummer
10. British baby's "wheels"
14. Radiant disk
15. Potlatch
16. Shankar specialty
17. U.N. agency
18. Angry
19. "___ and out"
20. Gotham address
23. High roller's town
24. Paris chef's need
25. Wintry fallout
28. Before juin
31. Lauder who makes scents
35. Snake sound
36. Forty winks
38. Six-legged warrior
39. See 20 Across
42. WSW's opposite
43. Pavarotti, e.g.
44. Painter of "Dog Barking at the Moon"
45. Like stickum
47. Explorer Johnson
48. Chevets
49. Japanese woman diver
51. CCXV x X
53. See 20 Across
61. Yours, in Tours
62. Mariner's direction
63. Teutonic trio
64. Clique
65. Bristles
66. Ceorl's cousin
67. Crystal sound
68. Greenwings
69. Rather and Rowan

**DOWN**

1. Stylish
2. "Arsenic and Old ___"
3. Dash
4. Ottoman
5. Of bees
6. Charlemagne, to Calabrians
7. "The Tender ___"
8. Julia ___ (Judy Canova)
9. Users of Red 2
10. Roams stealthily
11. Great review
12. Stores fine wine
13. Mecca for shoppers
21. Macerate
22. Donjons
25. Hampshire Downs
26. Tarzan's "rope"
27. Hazards on high roads
29. Dumas follower of Louis XIII
30. Kind of contest
32. Broadway horde
33. ___ nous
34. Belief system
36. French co.
37. Popeye's affirmative
40. Original meanings
41. Burst inward
46. Attractive
48. Chemists' org.
50. Nautical command
52. Doles
53. Locarno ___: 1925
54. Gudrun's husband
55. Racing-form word
56. Fencer's arm
57. Part of N.B.
58. ___ Major
59. Vols' home
60. Doesn't tarry

# 233

**ACROSS**

1. Indy entrant
6. Cheapen
12. Contribute
13. Word form with magnet
15. Vehicles in a Cross-Cory song: 1962
17. Efficacy
18. Fish-eating mammal
19. Seamen's chat
20. Flinders
21. Neil or Carly
22. Quickly, to Caesar
23. Song from "A Chorus Line"
24. Sorrow, to Ovid
25. ". . . swears that ____ made of truth"
26. Burgundy and Chianti
28. "Devil's Dictionary" author
29. Small printing device
31. Not long ago
34. Gunfighters' wear
38. Brainstorms
39. Molder
40. Teachers' org.
41. Fraction
42. High jinks
43. Spoken
44. Wooden core
45. Font feature
46. "Marmion" author
47. Golden Gate milieu
50. Goa, formerly
51. Brinker's argent prizes
52. Fuller's thistle
53. Took on

**DOWN**

1. Took turns
2. The opposition
3. Poker verb
4. Soissons season
5. Shrank from
6. Bill collector's quarry
7. Drew or Terry
8. Pilsener, e.g.
9. Gram. case
10. More theatrical
11. Undependable
12. Clergyman
14. Cause to seep through
15. Shultz post under Nixon
16. Airy
21. Actor Tufts
22. Thorax
24. Christie's "The Seven ____ Mystery"
25. Pantywaist
27. T. H. Benton's "Threshing ____"
28. Bartók and Lugosi
30. Striped bass
31. Enzyme aiding digestion
32. Obdurate
33. Roman playwright
35. Beclad
36. Leading mules, in Málaga
37. Brackish
39. Rye grass
42. Exit
43. Mexican pine
45. Casa women: Abbr.
46. Catface
48. Neighbor of Ala.
49. Schuss

# 234

**ACROSS**

1. Kind of sandwich
5. Corroded
8. Like some arches
14. Level a Londoner's lodgings
15. Endeavor
16. Cal Ripken is one
17. Galosh
19. Ornament
20. Mary Tyler and Dudley?
22. Medieval helmet
23. S.A.T., for one
24. Icelandic literary work
26. Madame de ___
29. Helios and Hurok?
33. Taper
35. City in Paraguay
36. Early auto
37. Equip
38. Jonquil shades
41. Telpher
42. Ripen
43. F.F.V. name
44. Lunt, to Fontanne
46. Sandy and Snoopy?
49. Winkles out
50. Where Pizarro landed: 1532
51. Scoter
53. Swindled
56. Sibelius and Saarinen?
61. Muppet musician
63. Napoleon, for one
64. Tomorrow, in Toledo
65. Lobster coral
66. Sun helmet
67. "Horn" contents
68. Outcome
69. Kind of dragon

**DOWN**

1. Cut short
2. "___, Come Back to Me" (Mauna Loa's song?)
3. Addict
4. Roundly rebuked
5. Greek mountain
6. Dolly Varden, e.g.
7. One employing binoculars
8. Front de Boeuf, to Ivanhoe
9. Pride of Philip II
10. "Balanced" people?
11. This has heddles
12. In addition
13. Nutcracker's suite
18. Malodorous
21. Former treaty org.
25. Sketches
26. Spat
27. Boreal forest
28. Osborne's "Look Back in ___"
29. Naps
30. Roman underworld
31. Smallest
32. Blisters
34. Sniggler for wrigglers
39. Abatement
40. Parodies
45. Ensembles
47. Pithecanthropus
48. Narrow-minded teacher
51. Sing like Bing
52. Rowed
53. Humid
54. Single
55. Kind of needle
57. Land measure
58. Image
59. Calif. city
60. Small piece
62. Ballad

# 235

**ACROSS**

1. Bric-a-____
5. Headquartered
10. Ineffectual person
14. Carty of baseball
15. ____ Berliner, microphone inventor
16. "____ that Shakespeherian Rag": T. S. Eliot
17. Robards movie: 1965
20. Profundity
21. Treat with an antiseptic
22. Lambs' dams
23. Poisonous snakes
24. Theater backdrop
26. Bird, to Brutus
27. Dan Beard's org.
30. Reference work
31. Aroint thee!
32. Part of P.O.W.
33. Hit song of 1928
36. Enjoy Lucullan fare
37. Particle streams
38. Air a view
39. Synagogue enclosure
40. Scenery
41. A.L. team
42. Rosinante, e.g.
43. City on the Oka
44. Make safe
47. Tanker pollution
51. Sondheim hit: 1973
53. Male do
54. Kinshasa was its capital
55. U.K. trolley
56. Finish line
57. Sten and Held
58. Brontë heroine

**DOWN**

1. Thin nail
2. Baptism, e.g.
3. Yearning
4. Where to buy kegs
5. Be suitable to
6. Stockpile
7. Transgressions
8. Yore
9. Determination
10. Sylvan area
11. Peach Bowl winner: 1982
12. Une alpe
13. Watch the birdie
18. Withdraw a request
19. Truncates
23. Acknowledges
24. Step
25. Dull sound
26. Nautical cries
27. U.C.L.A. player
28. Inks
29. Wimbledon great
30. "M*A*S*H" star
31. The candidates
32. Fish wrapper
34. Sideboard
35. He wrote "The Bigelow Papers"
40. Delhi dress
41. Secs
42. Justice
43. H. Parker's "Fairyland" is one
44. Dep.
45. Madrileño's mushroom
46. Child's play
47. Crural area
48. Off course
49. Kennel sound
50. Salinger lass
52. Leatherize hides

# 236

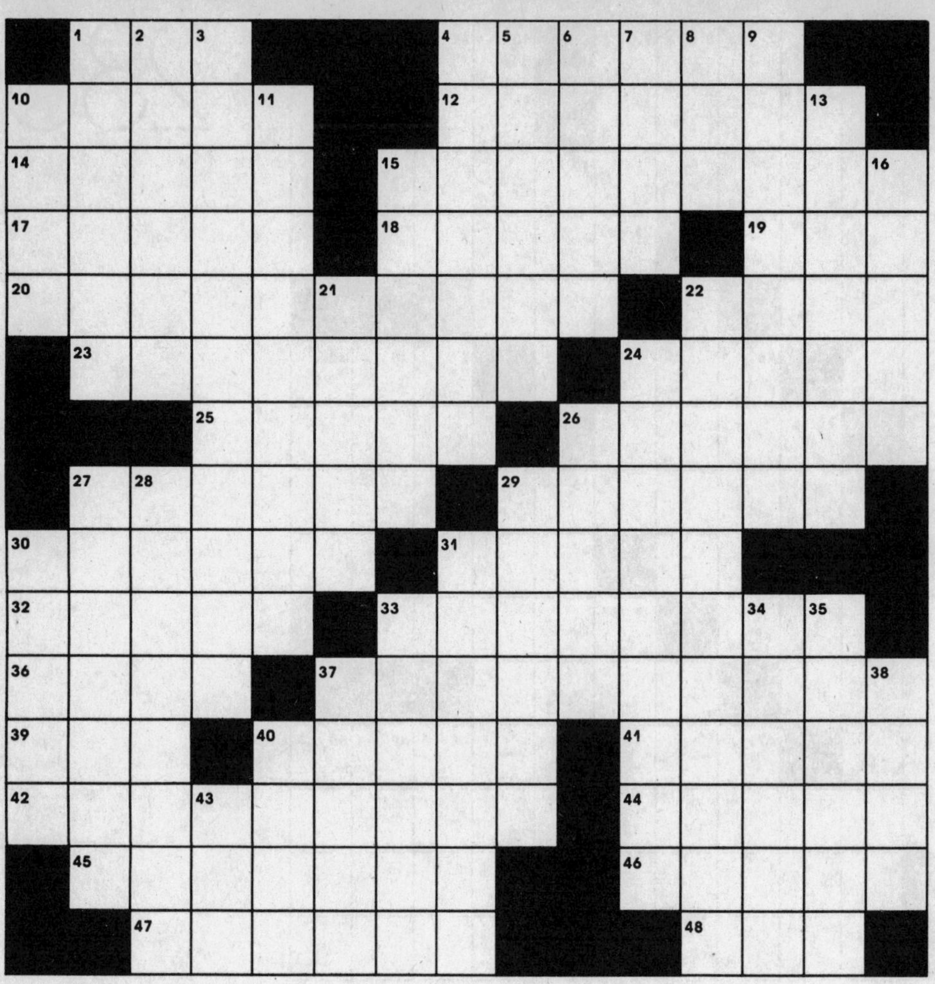

**ACROSS**

1. Abbr. after a name
4. Least menacing
10. ___-de-lis
12. In the dark
14. Spooky
15. On the road
17. Actress in "Dynasty"
18. Better qualified
19. Bikini part
20. One followed by 24 zeros
22. Quids pro ___
23. Capital of Assam
24. Dawn
25. Climbing plant
26. Actor Cotsworth
27. Legendary automatons
29. Encircle
30. Waterfront facility
31. Sub detector
32. "Adam Bede" author
33. Activity at a TV studio
36. Spotted
37. One followed by 21 zeros
39. Writer Beattie
40. Polite word for Hans
41. Actress Verdugo
42. Overfullness
44. Farmers' storage structures
45. NaCl plant
46. Singer's vocal exercise
47. Some bottom-line figures
48. Part of a keyboard's top row: Abbr.

**DOWN**

1. Nice schoolchildren
2. An angel
3. One followed by 18 zeros
4. Kind of engine
5. Kind of computer
6. Expert
7. Pitcher
8. He pitched against Pee Wee
9. Court of justice
10. Consultants' revenue
11. Elastic
13. On the way
15. Hawk's weapons
16. Sudden breaths
21. Camel's distant cousin
22. One followed by 15 zeros
24. Like some evening gowns
26. Desert or peninsula
27. Lead ores
28. Pekingese, e.g.
29. Obtained
30. Steep, flat-top hills
31. Church employees
33. Call it a day
34. Black ornamental work
35. Thieves: Slang
37. Locales
38. Space-age acronym
40. African hammerheads
43. U.N. org.

# 237

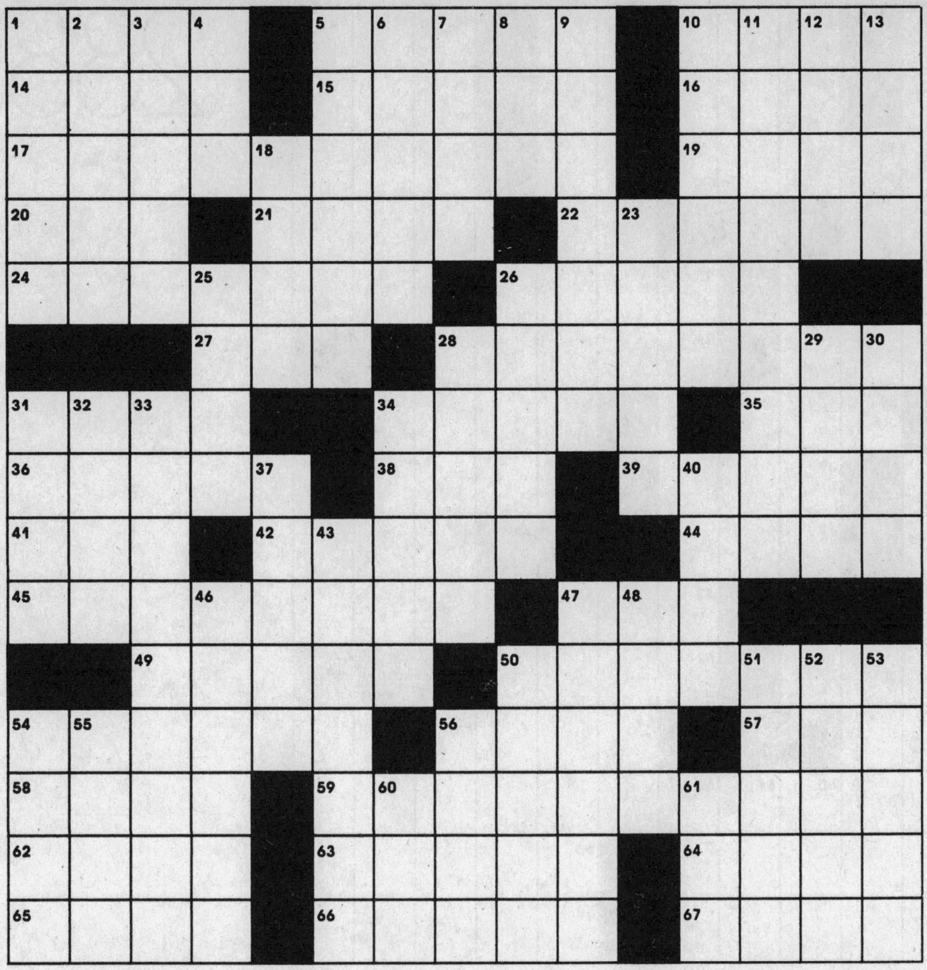


**ACROSS**

1. Elizabeth or Charles
5. Miner's stake
10. Truant type, for short
14. Buck heroine
15. "____ Lessways": Bennett
16. Hindu god
17. Large sailing ship
19. Irate fit
20. Math abbr.
21. Space monkey
22. A Nobelist for Peace: 1927
24. Tar's asset
26. Corpulent
27. Pongid
28. Wholesome
31. ____ out (reprimand)
34. Dickensian dish
35. A daughter of Cadmus
36. Crook's ruse
38. Beat it
39. Follower of Low or Vulgar
41. "Lady Windermere's ____": Wilde
42. "Riding on ____ . . ."
44. Protagonist in "God's Little Acre"
45. Cole entertainers
47. Speed unit
49. Actor Noah
50. Indonesian island
54. Cousin of kielbasa
56. Singers Armen and Starr
57. Bit for Fido
58. A son of Gad
59. Wouk work, with "The"
62. "Eye of ____": Shak.
63. Graian Alps river
64. Whale
65. Nigerian city
66. Actress Garson
67. Disagreeable chow

**DOWN**

1. Cenobites' habiliments
2. Hatter's guest
3. Ling-Ling is one
4. Last straw
5. Transfigure
6. V.I.P.'s vehicles
7. Dole
8. European carp
9. Theater awning
10. Give out, as a task
11. Chicago
12. "Heroides" author
13. Better than never
18. General Purpose Car
23. Ariz. politician
25. Refrain syllables
26. Like a boa
28. British herring measures
29. Monad
30. Certain award
31. Golf stroke
32. "Merry" in a game name
33. Like some hair styles
34. Halo
37. Scene of hysteria: 1692
40. Tamarisk tree
43. Washington wore one
46. ____ rights (red-handed)
47. Phenomenon at Yellowstone
48. "____ sprach Zarathustra"
50. Nucleus of sorts
51. High card, in euchre
52. One of the Nereids
53. Disperse
54. Foundered
55. Precinct
56. Genu
60. Rep. since 1948
61. Agcy. controlling TV

## 238

**ACROSS**

1. "____ di Lammermoor"
6. Kind of flare or furnace
11. ____ alai
14. Plant of the rose family
15. Apt
16. He rules at home
17. Celtic bunny?
19. Small antelope
20. Biblical femme fatale
21. External ear part
23. Alençon or Brussels
25. Merchants
26. Lecturers
29. Sped
30. G.I. address
31. Prefix with chord or meter
33. Spartan magistrate
36. ____-frutti
39. Forelimb
40. Stanza
41. Nobelist in Chemistry: 1922
42. Costa ____
44. Legal point
45. Like some beer
47. Surrounding
50. Rambles
52. Read the ____ act to
53. Raiment
54. Gross
58. "Ça ____," French Revolution song
59. Resort where bunnies go Dutch?
63. Number of weeks per annum
64. Martini ingredient
65. Hesitant
66. "My Gal ____"
67. Bucks, e.g.
68. Fatuous

**DOWN**

1. Nomologists specialties
2. Layer of the eye
3. Part of a honeycomb
4. Shoe part
5. Trash collector
6. Bad Godesberg, e.g.
7. Sphere
8. Tennis stroke
9. Bedouin beauty in "Peer Gynt"
10. Goes over again
11. Imprisoned bunny?
12. Love affair
13. Common bridge bid
18. Right-hand page
22. Expert
24. Cliffs
25. Colliery wagon
26. Information
27. Magnum ____
28. Bunny's follower?
32. Quang ____, Vietnamese town
34. Comeuppance place for Gretel's witch
35. Remainder
37. Round paintings
38. House phone
43. Friends, to Fabius
46. Small space
48. Increases
49. Luciano's homeland
50. Keens
51. Auricles
55. Wild leek
56. Cut
57. Mary Baker or Nelson
60. Nothing
61. Conductor Queler
62. "____, We Have No Bananas"

# 239

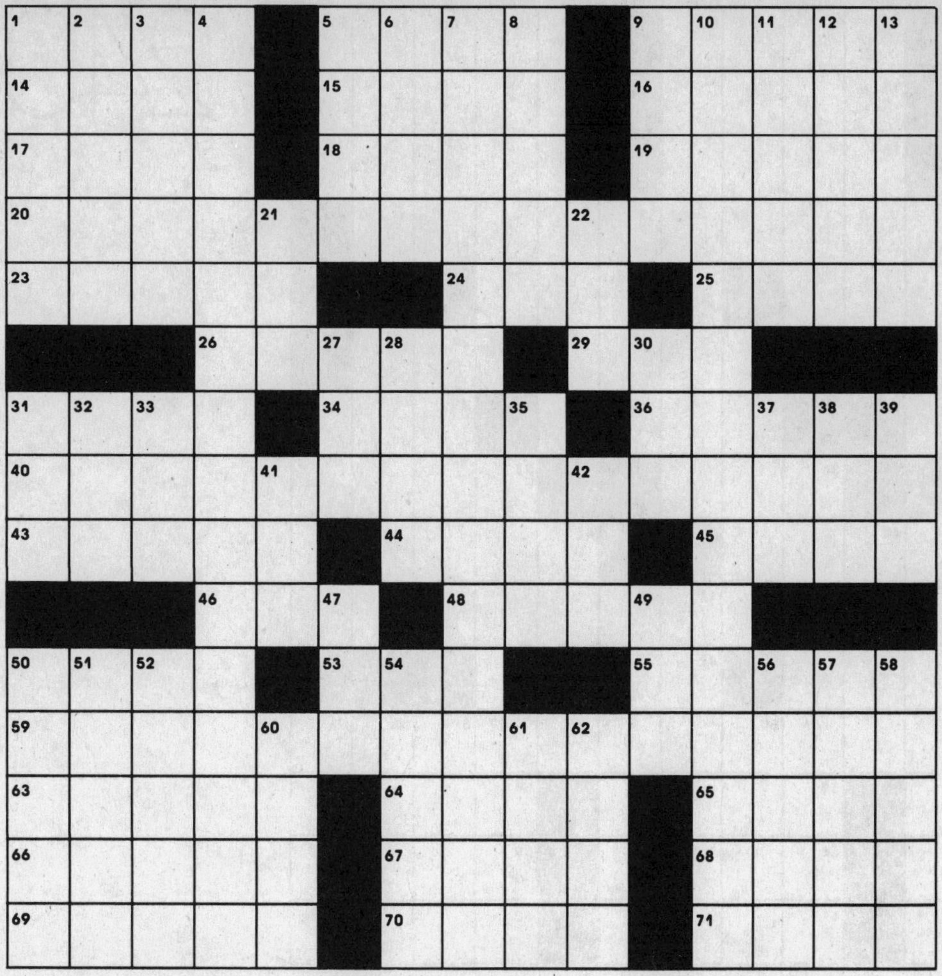

**ACROSS**

1. Ballad
5. Elevator part
9. Type of furnace
14. ". . . wing ___ prayer"
15. River into the Baltic
16. Revenue, in Rennes
17. Anatomical channel
18. Pakistani garment
19. Waterloo native
20. Statesman
23. Turkish cavalryman
24. Buddhist Thai people
25. God of war
26. Not in an undertone
29. Needlefish
31. False god
34. Hat part
36. Fully developed
40. Novelist
43. "The Velvet Fog"
44. Horne
45. "Thou ___ beguile the world": Shak.
46. White House nickname
48. Former name of Myanmar
50. Cacholong or fiorite
53. Eastern Medit. land
55. Birdlike
59. Poet
63. Hello, in Hoolehua
64. Disturb
65. Bard's negative
66. Reach effectively
67. Barely makes out
68. "Virumque" follower
69. Anthony and Clarissa
70. She, in Siena
71. Adherents

**DOWN**

1. Braces
2. Available
3. Tomato blight
4. Professor-author
5. Teapot cover
6. Garden evictee
7. Actress
8. Plant used for making pipes
9. Spirit; zest
10. Artist
11. Sadat
12. Passé
13. Looks after
21. Gallic garlic
22. Word with tag or paddle
27. Gram. case
28. Russia's ___ Mountains
30. Rhine feeder
31. Play the ponies
32. First-year Latin word
33. Demeanor
35. Preprandial reading
37. One, in Livorno
38. Inf. officers
39. Holiday in Hue
41. Word of affirmation
42. Legal profession
47. Diamond ___
49. Spoil
50. Missouri feeder
51. Was outshone
52. ". . . ___ in your eye": Lamb
54. Pile of rock debris
56. Suppositions
57. Emissary
58. Pianist Peter's kin
60. Breaks bread
61. Pure fiction
62. "Bridal Chorus" maiden

# 240

**ACROSS**

1. Rebuff
5. Fido's favorite org.
9. West Coast athlete
14. City on the Wabash
15. Mobster
16. Elimelech's wife
17. State
18. Sicilian resort
19. Beard group
20. What 25, 42 and 48 Across clarify
23. Shh!
24. Cultivate
25. "Alas! poor Yorick. I knew him, ____"
31. Wrong
32. Site of Mercyhurst College
33. Charged particle
35. Take on cargo
36. Metric-system initials
37. Swedish rock group
38. Exclamation of surprise
39. Suffix with origin
41. Hotfoot it away
42. It swallowed Amittai's son: Jonah 1:17
46. Greek letters
47. Turkish regiment
48. "Music has charms to soothe a savage ____"
54. Sans ____ (carefree)
55. Streak or stripe in Sarthe
56. Ballot
57. Indian wild sheep
58. Cold-war adversary
59. A son of Seth
60. Judges' seats
61. Sign that may stop a truck
62. Stock-exchange membership

**DOWN**

1. Mex., Hond. et al.
2. Dolly of "Hello, Dolly!"
3. Hebe's brother
4. Intent of a commercial
5. Chinese province, rich in loess
6. Blanketlike raincoat
7. Dunce-cap shape
8. Electricians' linking devices
9. "____ meet again"
10. She married Clark
11. Symbol of craziness
12. Gosden role
13. Pincer
21. Parts of innings
22. Buckwheat tree
25. Circle of light
26. Birthplace of G.R.F.
27. Free from
28. Rio ____, S.A. stream
29. Sign of the zodiac
30. Having rounded divisions
34. Title
36. Explain the sense
37. Is successful
39. What a slater does
40. "Now hear ____!"
41. Mop
43. Plant of the madder family
44. Follower of Lao-tse
45. Changes
48. Cold wind
49. Destroy
50. Space org.
51. Outstanding
52. Greek portico
53. Use a cupel
54. U-boat

# 241

**ACROSS**

1. Prime-time fare
11. Soft masses
15. Shelve
16. Word heard topside
17. Non compos mentis
18. Plant or animal part
19. Asian weight
20. Make ready, for short
21. Calendar abbr.
22. Ways: Abbr.
23. Unseal, poetically
24. Spell
27. Suffix for Roman
29. Virginia willow
30. Robert of "Quincy"
31. Saying
33. Gas: Comb. form
34. Art cult
37. Fabulous flier
38. Wave: Fr.
39. Nigerian people
40. Inventor of a glass harmonica
44. Parental palindrome
45. Rough
46. Place near Harrisburg, Pa.
49. Paper-folding art
51. "Gang ___ a-gley"
52. Reptile
54. Ocean route
55. Prehistoric tool
57. Rey's edict
58. Heron's cousin
59. Diagnostic aid
61. Track of an animal
62. Ecologist's concern
63. Layers
64. Short stories akin to fables

**DOWN**

1. Broaches
2. Robber
3. Fairy-tale figure
4. Authentic
5. Add up
6. Little piece
7. Something to do
8. Superior
9. Broad comedy
10. End: Comb. form
11. Dross
12. Of a northern people
13. Spotted
14. Castle locale
23. Aloud
25. Sawbuck
26. Roofing slate
28. In the capacity of
29. Substance used in perfumes
32. Destroy
34. Destroy
35. Charming
36. Supreme authority
38. Lennon's widow
40. Italian title
41. Tafia
42. Radical
43. Abbr. in banking
47. Bay tree
48. Looking fixedly
50. Romantic adventure stories
51. Moro and Ray
53. Fruits
56. Bombeck
57. Turkish chief
59. Fiacre
60. Eliminate the alternatives

# 242

## ACROSS

1. Petitioned
6. Geller of Tel Aviv
9. ___-Bethlehem (plants)
13. Astral
14. N.L.'s Rose
16. Set in motion
17. South Pacific kingdom
18. Treats a fever
19. Spiritual adviser
20. Leghorn's largess
21. By ___ (intermittently)
24. Ad ___ (pertinent)
25. Palmist
26. Formality
31. Dismal and Okefenokee
35. Servicewoman in Eng.
36. Become less reserved
38. Like a martinet
39. Protein hormone
40. Prepared to fire
42. Personal: Prefix
43. Ostriches' kin
45. Walesa, for one
46. Approach
47. Portions of the Torah
49. July sports event
51. Bhang or cannabis
53. NCO's bosses
54. One of the Army brass
58. Radius locale
61. Ballet's Bruhn
62. Columnist Barrett
63. Roast host
65. Hawaiian goose
66. Air apparent?
67. Shoe strips
68. Tense
69. Bellwether's mate
70. Get dazed

## DOWN

1. A goddess of fertility
2. Walk heavily
3. Alan or Peggy
4. Cardiologist's graph
5. Cause auricular malfunction
6. Parvenu
7. Guns a motor
8. Willow-family members
9. What good movies receive
10. Don't dele
11. Inning sextet
12. Speed meas. used in film making
15. Laborers in 1066
22. "___ man with . . ."
23. Moistens, in a way
24. Famed Liverpudlian
26. Box-office smash
27. Hiding place
28. Abhorred
29. Windjammer, for one
30. Mead locale
32. Jason's wife
33. Hecuba's husband
34. A 4 A.M. sound
37. Gusher
41. Reese or Street
44. Marionette maker
48. Litigious ones
50. They surprise
52. Hidden-treasure guardian
54. Had the lead
55. Rubberneck's activity
56. Sufficient, to FitzGerald
57. Craze
58. Adolescent's ailment
59. Soviet military symbol
60. Farrago
61. Compass pt.
64. Busch or West

# 243

**ACROSS**

1. Men's get-together
5. Rosita's residence
9. Where Panjim is
12. Coal-tar derivative
14. College grad
15. Confess, with "up"
16. Prickling sensation
17. As a rule
19. "Her beauty was sold for ___": A. J. Lamb
21. Printer's line on a letter
22. Destroy a Soho structure
23. Paraphernalia
26. Mario's movie
28. Batter's position
30. Middle-age problem
33. Tommy Tune musical
35. Warms up
36. Nigerian native
37. Wolf's look
40. Caught
41. Investigate intensely
43. Steelmaker's scoria
44. Bitter vetch
45. Berry trees
47. Caesar's love
49. Half: Prefix
50. Grand Duke of Muscovy
53. Within the law
57. Where she's kept (See 19 Across)
60. ___ the ground (overdoes)
62. Govt. notes
63. "Paris ___," J. Brady book
64. Table section
65. Veal for a schnitzel
66. Kay's title
67. Printer's mark
68. Adventure story of yore

**DOWN**

1. Sparkle
2. Domingo's voice
3. Of a West Germanic people
4. Bond adversary
5. Flowery tropical plant
6. At ___ (bewildered)
7. Billows
8. G.I.'s lethal supply
9. Period of prosperity
10. Pussycat's shipmate
11. Even one
12. Sch. affiliates
13. Space-vehicle unit
18. Marine plants
20. Circus feature
24. Reagan was one
25. Takes it easy
27. Naught
29. Poe mystery
30. Showed partisanship
31. A poplar
32. Clementine's pa, for one
34. Pub. series
38. Kudu's kin
39. Devil's-bones
42. Ribs of leaves
46. Ring used as a seal
48. Speak from memory
51. Curriculum ___
52. Where jets soar and roar
54. Vexes
55. Sheath on a shoelace
56. "___ we forget . . ."
58. Is indisposed
59. Sentence ending, sometimes
60. River to the Dnieper
61. Prefix for corn or form

# 244

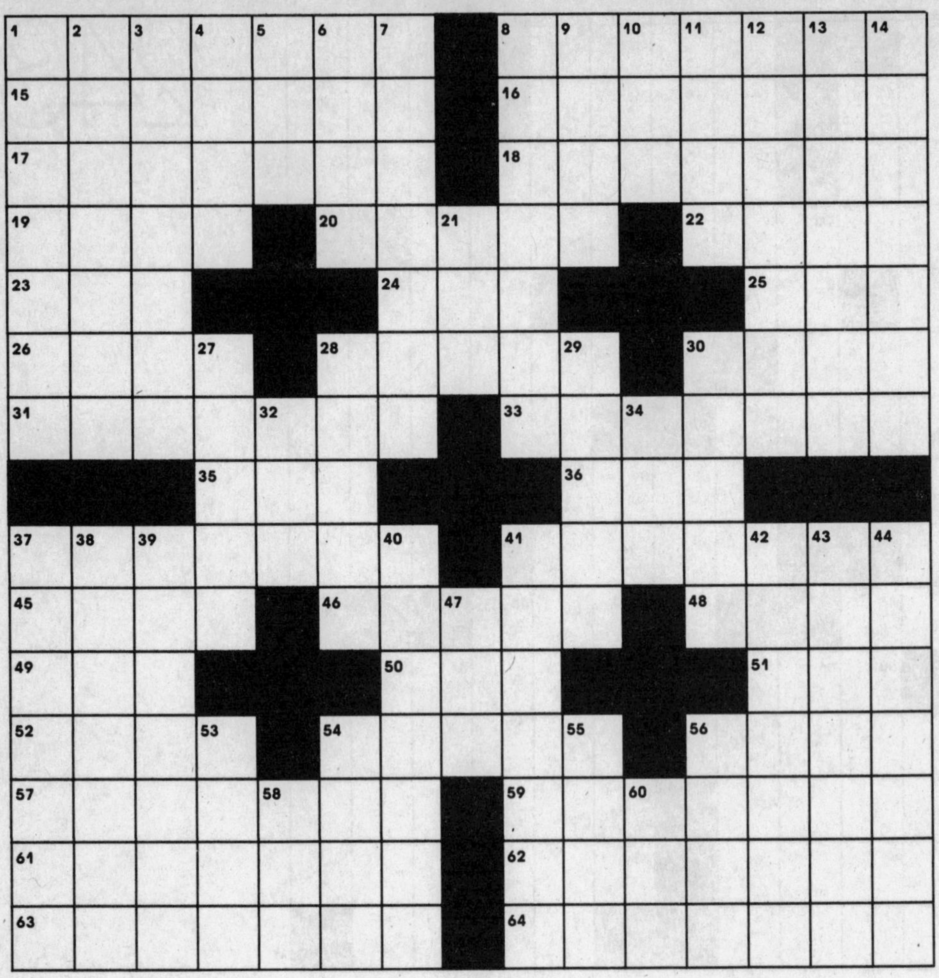

**ACROSS**

1. Jean Baptiste Poquelin
8. Type of windlass
15. Hit Broadway show: 1981
16. Semitic goddess of fertility
17. Young hare
18. Ocean channel
19. Woeful word
20. Villa for Chernenko
22. Voiceless sound
23. Part of a div.
24. Laotian neighbor
25. Wire measure
26. Object
28. Artificial conduit
30. ____ à chou
31. States
33. Altered
35. Louis XVI, e.g.
36. Repository
37. Abutting
41. Signaling devices
45. Part of HOMES
46. Pile of rock debris
48. Nautical term
49. Negative conjunction
50. Its capital is Draguignan
51. Right-angled plumbing joint
52. Capital of Fiji
54. Radio, TV, etc.
56. Football or track
57. Bellerophon's son killed by Ares
59. Vitalize
61. Old North Church signal
62. Electrical restricting device
63. Two Arthurian lasses
64. Certain roofers

**DOWN**

1. Tropical affliction
2. Western and Spanish
3. Medical washings
4. Dec. 13, e.g.
5. Suffix for musket or profit
6. Did penance
7. Demesnes
8. Dismiss with disgrace
9. On the deep
10. Sch. group
11. Yields to weakness
12. Shocks
13. Diminish by harassment
14. Ragged
21. Corvine cry
27. Amalgamate
28. Task
29. Type of puzzle
30. Noted late basso
32. Brooklyn's Preacher
34. That is to say: Abbr.
37. Like bridge cables
38. Excitation
39. Buddhist state of blessedness
40. Alehouses
41. Sepultures
42. Ennoble
43. Storyteller
44. Type of market
47. Nipper
53. Not pro
54. Scantily sufficient
55. Deep blue
56. Neglect
58. Cave, at times
60. Miss Hogg

# 245

**ACROSS**

1. West Point student
6. Drill sergeant's call
9. Role for Price
13. Century plant
14. Muscat is its capital
16. Off-key
17. Alfredo, to Baron Douphol
18. Texas city on the Brazos
19. Thin, piping note
20. Start of a message to the Met
23. "____, mi dicon venal," Puccini aria
24. "____ Rosenkavalier"
25. More of the message
34. Hophead hunter
35. Suspended
36. Moon-vehicle unit
37. I.R.S. employees
38. Bit of edelweiss
40. Albert Speer, for one
41. Satisfied sounds
42. Other, to Domingo
43. Blue dye
44. More of the message
49. Sheepish comment
50. The Flying Dutchman's milieu
51. End of the message
60. Nonclerical
61. Memorable baritone Giuseppe de ____
62. Six-Day War hero
63. "____, que le monde révère": Meyerbeer chorus
64. Six, in old dice games
65. January, to Don José
66. Hgts.
67. Sesame
68. Exudes, as charm

**DOWN**

1. "____ nome," Verdi aria
2. Not "fer"
3. Brubeck or Garroway
4. Always
5. Dravidian language
6. Elephant rider's seat
7. "Cielo ____!": Ponchielli aria
8. ". . . ____, mio Dio!": Leonora's prayer
9. Aft
10. Hawkeye State
11. Alice Miller's maiden name
12. Brother of Hebe
15. Drowsy
21. Afr. republic
22. Safecracker
25. Cuzco Indians
26. Gounod's first opera
27. Refuse
28. "Ninety-day wonder" sch. of W.W. II
29. Pulsate
30. Manon's assent
31. Chan portrayer
32. Huon's love in "Oberon"
33. Poet Dickinson
38. Wren's cathedral
39. Nose around
40. Slangy denial
42. Colorful fish
45. Earliest computer
46. Homeland of 62 Across
47. Arikara
48. Tonio's stage name in "I Pagliacci"
51. Soprano Frances of yesteryear
52. Brad or spad
53. Hint to "the fat lady"?
54. "Belle ____ . . .": Offenbach barcarole
55. First of the eighth century
56. "Là ci darem la ____," Mozart duet
57. Court cry
58. Like cerium
59. Simian space traveler

# 246

**ACROSS**

1. Ticket part
5. Good earth
9. Photographer's request
14. Screen idol
15. Drive-in sight
16. Daises
17. Hitchcock, in a way
19. Edmonton skater
20. Eyes and ears?
22. Rani's wrap
23. "The ___ Show"
24. M–S connection
27. Three-wheeler, for short
29. Resort
32. Kind of den
33. They're sold in lots
35. It blew in 1852
36. Disney and Kelly
38. Lahr role
39. Idea-to-product interval
41. What ravers don't make
42. Sixties coll. group
43. At ___ (puzzled)
45. Etonian pop
46. Hue man
47. Noun suffix
49. First looks at Mars and Venus?
55. "Exodus" actor
56. Film trailer's task
57. AMPAS award
58. Ditto, to Cato
59. Monad
60. Judges
61. Dovecote sounds
62. Educators' degs.

**DOWN**

1. Slippered
2. End: Comb. form
3. Hindustani
4. Hollywood turkey's production crew?
5. This makes engineers beam
6. Costume
7. To ___ (exactly)
8. Film censor, often
9. Emulated Moby Dick
10. Wavy silk pattern
11. At rest
12. Stretches
13. Concha
18. Tocsin
21. Cameraman's concerns
24. Carols
25. Chose
26. S.A. fruits
28. Do's and don'ts
29. Actress Eva Marie
30. Journalese
31. TV's Lou Grant
34. Edited for television?
36. Tricked
37. Like "The Blob"
40. Robert and Rod
41. Mar
44. Music lover's purchase
46. Kind of girl or boat
48. Mosque men
49. "West Side Story" director
50. Tale starter
51. Make over
52. Epicarp
53. Geraint's wife
54. Cpls.' bosses
55. London hippie

## ACROSS

1. A symbol of distinction
5. Summer drinks
9. Movie or TV program
13. New Zealander
14. "Man ___ dog!"
16. King of Norway
17. Legendary Greek hero
18. Sidestep
19. Rodomontade
20. Riviera relative?
23. Ham's word
24. "___ Meister-singer"
25. ___ decisis (legal principle)
28. Prepared for mil. inspection
31. Miles from England
35. Water buffalo
36. Deficit
38. Tokyo of old
39. High-kicker's question on the Riviera?
42. XXXIV x III
43. Millay's "Aria ___"
44. Kind of dollar
45. ". . . ___ face the world with": Browning
47. Inner: Comb. form
48. Organic compound
49. Nigerian native
51. Ice melter
53. Another Riviera relative?
59. Bossy's milieu
60. Berate
61. Score for Trottier
63. "___ homo!"
64. A Jackson Sec. of War
65. Caved in
66. Three-handed card game
67. Like a prestidigitator
68. Cancel a dele

## DOWN

1. Hit the slopes
2. Amonasro's daughter
3. Kind of song
4. Like July 4, 1776
5. ___ in the woods
6. A branching off
7. Riviera summers
8. Evening in Empoli
9. "And is there honey still ___?": Brooke
10. Turkish regiment
11. Lion's "neckpiece"
12. Triton
15. Secretariat's post-racing role
21. "___ got sixpence"
22. British Columbia group
25. Prisoner of 1920
26. Do roadwork
27. "Tomorrow" girl
29. Brainstorms
30. Threw away
32. Shorten again
33. Antarctic cape
34. Fete
36. A nucleic acid: Abbr.
37. Sgt. or cpl.
40. Pueblo brick
41. Some bank accounts
46. Slate
48. A descendant of Aaron
50. Story opener
52. Concerning
53. Name for Santa
54. Peruvian of yore
55. "If ___ a hammer . . ."
56. Call to court
57. Whitewash
58. Roof part
59. Thing, in law
62. Rent

# 248

**ACROSS**

1. A sister-in-law of Jacob
5. Zeno's "classrooms"
10. "Worms of the Nile"
14. ____ Mouse (Mickey's son?)
15. ____ von Stroheim
16. Rizzuto or Harris
17. Alberto Azzo II, e.g.
18. Hasn't a way to run away?
20. Imitation stone?
22. One phoned
23. Pouring
24. Spree in the ether?
25. In the buff
27. Spacek from Texas
28. Posed
29. Herring's relative
31. The Pentateuch
35. "____ to be born . . ."
38. The works
39. ____-trump (bridge bid)
40. Concentrate
41. Place for a carrus
43. Four bells
44. Layer
46. Lonely, in Paris
49. Religious payers or collectors
52. Texas shrine
53. Put on a pedestal
54. Original sin?
57. Firebug
59. Renovate
60. Further
61. Ignited anew
62. Corny place
63. Lacking avoirdupois
64. Jannings and Ludwig
65. Marion chaser

**DOWN**

1. City on the Skunk
2. Spode piece
3. Hill dweller's overshoe?
4. Wintry
5. Supports
6. A rival of Chris
7. Sow sound
8. I, II or III
9. Some hutches
10. Satan
11. Dolphins' coach
12. Hamelin musician
13. Glossy
19. Blames on
21. Estuary
24. Advance tentatively
25. Mil. branch
26. Western alliance
27. Piquant; caustic
30. What some quibblers split
32. Turn back
33. Jean Schopfer's pen name
34. Do a cutler's job
36. Place to bill and coo?
37. Regard well
42. Widows
45. "... bear to live, ____ to die": Pope
47. Rotating part
48. Punish via a fine
49. Cloths from mulberry bark
50. Pastoral literary work
51. Trunks
52. Thin as ____
54. Nut from a Philippine tree
55. Way in
56. Ear part
58. Thread: Comb. form

# 249

**ACROSS**

1. Section of land
5. Agatha Christie was one
9. Word before bog
13. Brown-bagger's time
14. Wang Lung's wife
15. Headdress
16. Walter Lantz creation
19. City in Pa.
20. Armor of a sort
21. Jewish title of respect
22. Skelton or Grange
23. Bern's river
24. Glaswegian's turndown
25. ___ Pete (cheap wine)
27. Rels. of villages
28. Sec. of State's aide
29. Low-caste Hindu
30. Romulus did him in
32. Sardi's and Lindy's
36. String of coral isles
37. ___ of Gilead
39. Creator of Dogpatch
42. ___ out (spend)
43. Callas and Ouspenskaya
45. Ab ___ (from the start)
46. Rep. rival
47. To be, in Barcelona
48. Prefix with cook or heat
49. Turbulent ocean phenomenon
51. Enter stealthily
53. Arthur Lake role
55. Small cases
56. She sings "O patria mia"
57. Danish architect Jacobsen
58. Parking mishap
59. Before long
60. Autocrat

**DOWN**

1. Sadat namesakes
2. Radiator additive
3. A soft drink
4. Conductor Akira ___
5. Singer Morton ___
6. Get ___ of (take a gander)
7. Double this for a honey eater
8. Bookbinder's sheet
9. Ancient inhabitant of Scotland
10. U.S. painter: 1844–1916
11. Punta ___
12. Toxophilite's prop
15. Kind of gas
17. Richard III supporter
18. Red Cross supply
26. "With ___ and a bound . . .": Coleridge
27. Yours ___
28. "Swinging on ___," 1944 song
31. Strips
33. Fine sword
34. Shaded walks
35. Certain mules
38. Tennyson poem
39. Ribbed or twilled
40. Fly
41. "Cops and robbers" weapon
43. Mythical denizen of the deep
44. A ham, sometimes
46. Creator, in Cuzco
47. Old Italian coin
50. Ridicule
52. Raison d' ___
54. Life story, for short

# 250

**ACROSS**

1. Trellis piece
5. Light brown
10. Gritty
14. Candy striper
15. Pith helmet
16. Middle name of No. 21
17. Culbertson coup
18. Whirligig of a sort
19. Skirt length for Mickey's girlfriend?
20. Middle name accidentally given to No. 18
22. Annulled
24. Prune
25. Inclusive abbr.
26. Actor Don or footballer Alan
29. Vestige
33. Kegler's org.
34. Hebrew month
36. He wrote "The Bramine's Journal"
37. Caribbean vacation spot
39. Tear
41. Liquid portion of fat
42. Picayune objections
44. At some remove
46. Hordeolum
47. Famed yacht
49. Racket for a sport
51. Winter Palace resident
52. Obsession
53. Pleats
56. Middle name of No. 37
60. Mozart's "Porgi amor"
61. End
63. Any large exhibition
64. Klinger of "M*A*S*H"
65. Play
66. Manx murmur
67. Lynn of baseball
68. Martina's ex-mentor
69. Sothern and Sheridan

**DOWN**

1. Soprano Silvia ____
2. "Hi-____, Hi-Lo," 1952 song
3. Furniture style
4. Pantheon, e.g.
5. Degeneration
6. Diving bird
7. Choose
8. "Hey, Look ____," 1960 song
9. Causes to sparkle
10. Middle name of No. 29
11. Came down
12. Leo's pride
13. Tennyson character
21. Mix at a party
23. Palma-Christi derivative
26. Middle name of No. 20
27. Purple dye
28. Unit of corn
30. Frock
31. Join
32. Counting-out word
33. Agouti's cousin
35. Narrow inlet
38. Middle name of No. 19
40. Future NCO?
43. Beveling-machine operator
45. Expert
48. Poisonous gas that smells like garlic
50. Outline
53. Fishhook
54. Ancient name of the Saône
55. Flag
56. Apollo 17 passengers
57. The yoke is on them
58. In the know
59. Plants
62. One of the Bobbsey twins

**ACROSS**

1. Where Romans routed Hannibal: 202 B.C.
5. Portal
10. Trial run, in horse-racing lingo
14. Emerald Isle
15. Crude person
16. A river of the Punjab
17. Agitate, colloquially
18. Like most X-rated films
20. Instrument for measuring distance traveled
22. Hack
23. Desserts
24. Substantive
25. Stereotype
28. Heat-removing substances
32. Lily, in Lille
33. Tryon's "The ___"
35. Gastropod mollusk
36. Indian victims of miners: 1864
38. Small inland islands
40. Broz
41. Pendants
43. Braid
45. High, rugged mountain
46. People sensitive to beauty
48. ". . . the bonnet of Bonny ___": Scott
50. Naso, the poet
51. Russian river
52. Purplish red
55. Henry Morgan's activity: 17th century
59. Meditating
61. Winged
62. Black cuckoos
63. Site of Hercules' first labor
64. "De mortuis nil ___ bonum"
65. Narrow ledge
66. Jam often created in N.Y.C.
67. Makes picots

**DOWN**

1. A memorable Mostel
2. Desiccated
3. Grain sorghum
4. Feeble
5. Upper canines
6. Nostrils
7. God with a hammer
8. Corruption
9. Call to attract attention
10. Gravid
11. Pealed
12. Lucifer's love
13. Nepalese coins
19. Ancient Celts
21. Repercussion
24. Bellini heroine
25. Warren Beatty role
26. Pseudologists
27. ". . . mercy ___ strained": Shak.
28. Basic constituents
29. R. Strauss maiden
30. Designation
31. Declivity
34. Had expectations
37. Pithy saying
39. Stellar
42. Lowest écarté card
44. Large food fish
47. Hyperion and Cronus
49. Swimming
51. A source of iron
52. Symbol for a July 4 baby
53. Crescent-shaped figure
54. Qala Nau bigwig
55. Cotton shirting
56. Pelvic bones
57. Publisher Condé ___
58. Cubist Juan
60. Lacrosse team

# 252

**ACROSS**

1. Home of more than 43 million
6. Ancient ruler of 1 Across
12. Shoulder blade
14. Sent ahead, as news
16. Loser
17. Ethiopian province
18. Hockey "trick"
19. Kind of ear or horn
20. Bishopric
21. I.R.S. mo.
22. Brother of Hebe
24. Frisbees, e.g.
26. "___ Old Cowhand"
27. Dewy
29. Cairo-to-Beirut dir.
30. Verona's river
31. Lou Grant's real-life family
33. Unevenly contested
35. Trans-Siberian railway stop
37. Kern-Hammerstein musical
41. Harsh
46. The fortunate
47. Legal thing
49. Uses a dish towel
50. Portent
51. Joe Miller joke
53. Coconut juice
54. Sapin
55. Hand holder
56. Potent compound
58. Dogfall, in wrestling
59. Omni site
61. One more
63. Nuclear-plant component
64. Set right
65. Landmark in 1 Across
66. Memorable leader of 1 Across

**DOWN**

1. Oriental
2. D.C. building
3. Mongol tent
4. Tartan design
5. Substance used by dyers
6. Symbol on the Turkish flag
7. "___ Johnny!"
8. Composer Siegmeister
9. Mare's morsel
10. Landmark in 1 Across
11. A basement problem
12. Desert partly in 1 Across
13. Mild cigars
15. Mended socks
23. That Fräulein
25. Like a tapir or anteater
26. Dec. 13 in Roma
28. Plagiarizes
30. Out of line
32. Hit sign
34. Sigmoid shape
36. "Das Kapital" author
37. Ceremonial ram's horn
38. Some natives of 1 Across
39. Extend beyond and cover part of
40. Rune equivalent to "w"
42. Vigor's partner
43. Descriptive name
44. Depends (on)
45. Glacial ridges
48. Hindu instruments
51. He wrote "What the Butler Saw"
52. Nine: Comb. form
55. Not pro
57. Jet QB
60. Cry in Bonn
62. Refrain syllable

# 253

**ACROSS**

1. Bent or shaped metal
7. Old-man ____, Mexican plant
13. Man of La Mancha
14. Laymen in monasteries
16. Usurps
17. One-time epoch of the Tertiary
18. Land measure
19. Its child is "full of grace"
21. Fishwife's cousin
22. Winter coat
24. Atrium, e.g.
25. This, to Torcuato
26. Glinka's "A Life for the ____"
27. Petrify
28. More guileful
29. Babbitt's home town
31. Chaste women
33. Mixes
35. Ring bearers of a sort
37. Sound
41. The common people
42. Competes
44. Dictator's phrase
45. Spirit
46. Actor Bruce
47. Offshoot
48. Interdict
49. Count Leo
52. Country singer Bandy
53. Source of mother-of-pearl
55. Recherché
57. Top, e.g.
58. Associates
59. Plants anew
60. Fuse

**DOWN**

1. Cockcrow
2. Magus
3. Feller's tool
4. Lecherous old man
5. And you: Lat.
6. Apostatize
7. Overlooks an offense
8. Nautical direction
9. Surfeit
10. Part of U.S.A.F.
11. Spoon, e.g.
12. Thesmothetes' milieus
13. Sand's main ingredient
15. Popeye's creator
20. Mementos
23. Vinland discoverer
25. Band often employed in offices
27. Imposture
28. Sheppard and Turpin's gun
30. Small fry
32. Biol., etc.
34. Suffragettes, e.g.
35. Scold
36. Issue
38. Vigorous
39. Columbo was one
40. Dogmas
41. Proscribe
43. Inscribes
46. "Eat to live, but ____ live to eat"
49. A load or haul
50. Londoner's marge
51. Bellow
54. ____ Palmas
56. Seventh son of Jacob

# 254

**ACROSS**

1. Grid scores
4. Former Iranian leader
8. "There is nothing like ___"
13. Freshen (up)
14. Remedy
15. Lawmaker
16. Start of a seasonal song
19. Like Amor
20. ". . . ___ Bethlehem"
21. Dickens's "Carol" boy
22. Lat. list-ender
24. Estuary
25. Jack Frost's touch
27. "Do not ___ till Dec. 25"
29. "___ boy!"
33. Elf's cousin
35. Not like the pre-ghosts Scrooge
38. Solo of "Star Wars"
39. Good health habits
41. Savage
43. Late actor Jack ___
44. Draco body
46. Oven stuffer
47. Cluster
49. Tidings
51. Body blueprint, for short
52. Uncooked
55. Wall sheathing
57. Wood sorrel
59. Start of a carol
62. Whimpers
64. See 2 Down
66. "Jerusalem" author
67. Troupe's trip
68. Tight
69. "___ Is Born"
70. Crèche site, at times
71. Opp. of ques.

**DOWN**

1. ". . . better not pout, I'm ___ why"
2. "I'm ___" (with 64 Across, start of a Berlin classic)
3. Variety-show piece
4. Prep. or elem.
5. Wheel cover
6. Small cavities
7. Ship's wheel
8. Semitic lang.
9. Slangy stocking stuffer
10. Landed
11. Prefix with plane or tone
12. Where to have a merrie hol.
13. High-school jrs.' exam
17. Whizzer's word?
18. Meadow
23. "The war ___ all wars"
26. Oahu food
28. A Christmas-shopping mo.
30. Epithet for Frosty
31. Kris Kringle
32. Tiny colonist
34. "Give ___ little kiss . . ."
36. "The ___ Noel"
37. Excessively
39. Fair Deal Pres.
40. One, in Berlin
42. Terhune canine
45. Hotel employee
48. Trinity, in Russia
50. Mustached mammal
53. Counties, in Denmark
54. Tiny
56. "___ Pinafore"
58. Aide for a D.A.
59. Hooters
60. Fireside ___
61. "___ Sanctorum"
63. Singer James
64. Desert coat
65. Leprechaun's land: Abbr.

# 255

## ACROSS

1. Lets in
7. Sound heard in a library
10. Loman portrayer
14. Shrimp's relative
15. Item on Ali's record
16. Podded plant
17. Orwell's year
19. Something often polished
20. Party song
22. Asian weight unit
25. ". . . ____ I saw Elba"
26. Yellow flags
27. Against the thing, in law
29. N.L. teams
31. Prominent Democrat
34. Certain marbles
37. Hebrew word for Lord
38. Negligent
39. Army Joe and Jane
40. ____ Fail (coronation stone)
42. Name linked with cruelty
44. Castle innovation
46. Assignation
48. "Lust for Life" author
49. Salad-bar bean
52. Morning-after cries
55. Have ____ to grind
56. Annual cry at midnight
59. "____ 'Clock Jump,'' 1938 song
60. Jan. 1 decision
64. Ending for hip or gag
65. Chemical suffix
66. Tune
67. Lewis and Fiorito
68. Nabokov novel
69. Colosseum and Circus Maximus parts

## DOWN

1. Be Little
2. "Agnus ____"
3. Periodical, for short
4. Smoked, in a way
5. Costume for Gelsey Kirkland
6. Milady's concern
7. Like some kisses
8. Jaeger
9. Kibitzer's activity
10. Be made up (of)
11. Approves
12. Pickle
13. Bundles of hay
18. H.C.H. successor
21. Lubes
22. Father ____
23. ". . . teach ____ dog new tricks"
24. A singing Ford
28. Bunkum
30. Classic villain
32. Belle of a 1935 song
33. Former spouses
35. Singer John
36. Music center in Italy
41. Twelve on the clock
43. Squiffed conditions
45. Surprise
47. Name for a dog
49. "____ of golden daffodils": Wordsworth
50. "Inferno" writer
51. Kind of trap
53. A neighbor of S.D.
54. Nobelist Lagerlöf
57. Counting-out word
58. Elman's teacher
61. Tiriac of tennis
62. Zenana area
63. Louis or Bill

# 256

## ACROSS

**1.** Health-club feature
**6.** Quebec university
**11.** Part of a boxing ring
**12.** Haunt
**13.** Darby or Hunter
**16.** First name of 63 Across
**17.** One of three emissaries in 61 Across
**19.** Verdi heroine
**20.** City SE of Firenze
**21.** Describing certain stocks
**22.** Dribble
**24.** Drumbeats
**26.** Cream-cheese companion
**27.** Psyche
**28.** Personnel manager
**31.** Hawaiian city
**34.** Orly-Dulles commuters
**37.** Chit
**38.** Second emissary
**41.** Actress Stark
**42.** A Hart
**44.** Verve
**45.** Dronelike
**47.** Small bribes
**49.** Indian chief
**50.** Mimic
**53.** Kneepan
**57.** Derrings-do
**58.** Punt propeller
**60.** Quantity in hand, sartorially
**61.** Lubitsch film: 1939
**63.** Star of 61 Across
**64.** U.S. collection agcy.
**65.** Helm direction
**66.** Dermal breakouts
**67.** Mubarak's predecessor
**68.** Hector

## DOWN

**1.** Heroic tales
**2.** Its 13th was Jefferson's birthday
**3.** Plant rust
**4.** Newsworthy
**5.** Memorabilia
**6.** Donovan's department
**7.** "Hallelujah, I'm ____"
**8.** Of palm or sole
**9.** Gen.'s aide
**10.** Jerry-built shelter
**13.** Third emissary
**14.** "____ first you don't . . ."
**15.** Mdse. producers
**18.** The south wind
**20.** Mardi Gras V.I.P.
**23.** Soprano Lucrezia
**25.** Date-setting phrase
**28.** "A Hymn to ____," from "My Fair Lady"
**29.** ____ to 1 (long shot)
**30.** Most of the people in 61 Across
**31.** Holbrook
**32.** ____ jiffy
**33.** Chaney
**35.** "____ Skylark"
**36.** Nero, to Agrippina
**39.** Musical notation
**40.** ____ accompli
**43.** ____ voce (privately)
**46.** Prolegomenon
**48.** Ditalini and cappelletti
**49.** West
**50.** Former Spanish enclave in Morocco
**51.** Golda
**52.** High priest's vestment
**53.** One-time N.Y. political boss
**54.** Blackmore's Doone
**55.** Service-sta. jobs
**56.** Cropped up
**59.** A soup basis
**62.** Figs. expert
**63.** Hood's heater

# 257

## ACROSS

1. Reject
8. Plays
14. Painter of "Battle of San Romano"
15. Scalloped
16. This might be stolen from you
17. Danish cheese
18. Role for a memorable Mae
19. Deli offering
21. Follower of Faust
22. Start of a Shakespearean title
24. Seven maids' items
25. Noun suffix
26. What Epimenides did for 57 years
28. Plant growing near the sea
30. Chain
32. Russian pastry
33. Dubbing experts
37. Devoured, as gossip
38. Cribs
40. Canceled
43. What syne means
44. "Liquor is quicker" author
45. Turkish coin
46. Mammoth man-eater
47. Contents of some wells
48. Provide the money
51. Article in a Bonn magazine
52. Draft work
54. Suggest, as associations
56. Second, and others
57. Dandelions' kin
58. Indulges in cabotinage
59. Group in a bowl

## DOWN

1. Old sailor's weapon
2. Paris was his undoing
3. Place for polishing pots and pans
4. Bo Derek film
5. Automotive name
6. Jumper in a circus
7. Town meetings
8. Racing site
9. Nice dream
10. Throughout: Prefix
11. Calif. county and water colorist
12. Join
13. French flower
15. "City Lights" hero: 1931
20. "General Hospital" is one
23. Hawes's "Fashion Is ____"
25. O'Neill, to Fellini
27. Anatomical roofs
29. Guys
31. Pod removals
34. Verdicts
35. Wood pigeon
36. Squirrel, at times
39. Cassandra was one
40. Without pattern or plan
41. "Eaters of raw flesh"
42. Pavlova was one
44. Relative
48. Dandy's partner
49. Product of a Spanish pine
50. Inner: Comb. form
53. Chickadee's relative
55. A basketball tourn.

# 258

**ACROSS**

1. Filmed a film again
7. Bikini part
10. Rizzuto or Foster
14. Exhibit
15. Corn unit
16. A Turner
17. Fast woman's dating list
20. Prophet
21. "I like ___"
22. Deeds, to Dumas
23. Author Hunter
26. Villa d'___
28. "___ body meet a body . . ."
31. "Picnic" playwright
33. Beat
36. Fast woman's benefactor
39. Between Ab and Tishri
41. Ripener
42. Quaker gray
43. Pure, in Ponce
44. ___ aut nunquam (now or never)
45. Fast woman
47. Lucy's landlady
49. Chemical suffix
50. Kennedy, to friends
51. Highlander's name
53. Prohibit
55. Mountain pools
58. Shad product
60. N.M. pueblo people
64. Seeker of fast women, sometimes
68. High flier
69. Charged particle
70. Overturns
71. Wax work
72. Gene stuff
73. Basin or 42d

**DOWN**

1. Soaks flax
2. Bacchanalian cry
3. Marceau, e.g.
4. Malraux or Previn
5. What MCCII over II equals
6. Common Market inits.
7. Chicken's prominence
8. Indian princess
9. Dull ending
10. Task for a personnel officer
11. Stag
12. Anent
13. Didion's "Play It As It ___"
18. Blackjack natural
19. Abhor
24. Man, to Manlius
25. "Ready, willing ___"
27. Foamy synthetic
28. "Life ___ end in itself . . .": O. W. Holmes
29. Musical interweave
30. Ten-percenter
32. Roman official
34. Dress feature
35. Exaggerated
37. Heavenly title
38. Transfer
40. Lady's man
46. Tennis grouping
48. Threat word, with "or"
52. Emulate Columbo
54. The ___ woman
55. Comic-strip laments
56. ". . . ___ of sympathy": Emerson
57. Pro ___
59. Charlie's widow
61. Queenly name
62. Waves on the Italian Riviera
63. Group of RR's
65. Accomplished
66. Gravy, in Grenoble
67. Pick

## 259

### ACROSS

1. Columbia Lou
7. Tom Terrific
13. Whalebones
14. Member of the work force
16. Colonizing tropical crawler
17. Historic period
18. Hgt.
19. Yarn measure
20. Rep. or Dem.
21. Bishopric
22. Stripped
24. Hornsby's sobriquet
26. Attila's men
27. Concerning
29. Pitcher Medich's nickname
30. Author Bret
31. Miss Astaire et al.
33. Like a lost cause
35. The Old Professor
37. Tiny tubers
41. Capital of Kan.
46. Nine: Comb. form
47. Molder
49. "____ of Athens"
50. Henbit, e.g.
51. Big Poison or Little Poison
53. "____-daisy!"
54. Oahu city
55. Sea eagle
56. German article
58. Prefix for metric or tonic
59. The Ten Commandments
61. Excess amount
63. Notched, as a leaf
64. Iron compound
65. Wee Willie
66. The Fordham Flash

### DOWN

1. Lei
2. Shade provider
3. Mays, The Say ____ Kid
4. Genuine
5. ____ sanctum
6. Swiss resort
7. Err
8. Our home
9. "____ Named Sue"
10. Wernher ____ Braun
11. Deletion
12. University officers
13. "Black sheep" precursors
15. Pee Wee and Rich
23. Photog's abbr.
25. The Big Train
26. Newhouser or McRae
28. U.S. electrician and inventor
30. Greek serf
32. Jeanne d'Arc, for one: Abbr.
34. Fala or Checkers
36. French alien
37. Emulates Zsa Zsa or Liz
38. Hebdomad
39. 43,560 square feet
40. Williams or Turner
42. Musical "more"
43. Experiential
44. Hungarian patriot and statesman
45. No particular person
48. Start golfing
51. Inscribed
52. Uele or Ebro
55. Israeli airline
57. St. Philip ____
60. Exist
62. B. & O. et al.

# 260

**ACROSS**

1. Black-belt sport
5. Southwest building
10. Campus gp.
14. Syria, of yore
15. Caesar, for one
16. Blow one's stack
17. "The ___ Love"
18. Spellbound
20. Overspread
22. Flattens
23. ___ account (not at all)
24. Tocsin
26. Variety of croquet
29. Region of Israel
31. Creative work
34. Obligations
36. Sire
38. End
39. Any person that
41. Decline
42. Selene's love
44. Gelid
46. Thrice: Comb. form
47. Battery feature
49. Escaped gradually
50. Lots of land
52. Of a force
54. Choristers
56. Bakes in a casserole
61. "Friend, ___": Luke 14:10
63. Jack's giant
64. Hard to find
65. What "nemo" means
66. Chela
67. Nancy or Ed
68. Durable fabric
69. Openers

**DOWN**

1. Door feature
2. Russian stream
3. Charles or Bill
4. In a threatening fashion
5. Wheyfaced
6. Orville Wright's birthplace
7. Wine flask for Socrates
8. Gauze strips
9. Tokyo, of yore
10. Carmelite, for one
11. Flashy display: Slang
12. U.S. author: 1909–55
13. Koppel and Knight
19. Crossbeam
21. Crook in a branch
25. ___ lamb (gigot)
26. Thesaurus name
27. "A linen stock ___ leg . . .": Shak.
28. Squaring process
30. Govt. security
32. Name meaning "born again"
33. Current style
35. Circe's subjects
37. 1400 hours
40. Slammer
43. Fen
45. Make turbid
48. Geologic epoch
51. Ecclesiastical mantles
53. Confronted courageously
54. Site of a famous tomb
55. Good earth
57. Loafer, e.g.
58. Stare amorously
59. Beseech
60. Runs up
62. Part of I.T.T.

# 261

## ACROSS

1. "Scotch fiddles"
6. Circle parts
10. Trumpets' kin
12. Nova-shaped
15. "All the President's Men" figure
16. Ruler of a kind
17. ___ powder (explosive)
18. Kind of gun
20. L-Q connection
21. VII minus IV
22. Ever, to Burns
23. Calibrated camera setting
24. German subs
27. Practical people
29. Chess pieces
30. "A man may kiss ___ lass": Burns
32. Heavily, to Verdi
35. Snares
39. Achieve, British style
41. Kind of sauce
42. Pilfer or mooch
45. Blue flicks, often
48. Part of D-day
49. B.&O., etc.
51. Puncture prefix
52. Feed-bag contents
53. Butt residue
54. Fundy highs and lows
57. "The ___ Room," 1962 film
60. Readily perceived
62. ___ Year Book: 1422
63. Mexicans and Brazilians
64. Some J.F.K. visitors
65. Mennonites et al.

## DOWN

1. Spore clusters
2. Mess-kit filler
3. Favorite residence of Frederick II
4. Wis. college
5. Sault ___ Marie
6. Satellite launched in 1966
7. Petition: Abbr.
8. More awkward
9. Distorts, as a newscast
10. .30-cal. rifle
11. Withered
12. Hydrocarbons used in making plastics
13. ". . . from so deep ___?": Shak.
14. Tie fabrics
19. Prefix for dynamic
23. Zip around
24. Fig. behind home plate
25. Apoidea member
26. Lucifer or Beelzebub
28. Building wing
31. Yugoslav capital
33. What reveille causes
34. Of nerves: Comb. form
36. Summa cum laude candidate
37. Virginia Clemm's bridegroom
38. A Chaplin
40. Noun suffixes
42. Sailor's wooden block
43. Narrow gorge
44. Lutheran theologian and family
46. Cassowary or ostrich
47. Like vinegar
50. Cartoonist-author Silverstein
55. Slaughter or Cabell
56. Wall and Fleet: Abbr.
58. Sump
59. Quartet in "One Sunday Afternoon"
61. Vessel for Virgil

**ACROSS**

1. Mexican snack
5. ___ Ababa
10. Pack
14. Leave out
15. Thin dress material
16. Egg on
17. Rephrasing of answer to 26 Across
20. Some
21. Pt. of a monogram
22. Rims
23. Malaria symptom
24. Achy
26. Realize a football pro's dream
33. Sacred images
34. Actress Turner
35. Popular dessert
36. Rocco's finger
37. Houston ballplayer
39. Adjective for a pittance
40. Above, to Shelley
41. Aspersion
42. Clothes-drying frame
43. Rephrasing of answer to 56 Across
47. Formerly, formerly
48. A Great Lake
49. Aver
52. Condemn
53. Refuge
56. Perform a quarterback's function
60. Merit
61. Elegant apartment
62. Roofer's item
63. Mile equivalent, proverbially
64. Suppress
65. Small merganser

**DOWN**

1. Forum garb
2. Prayer ending
3. Helena or Nancy
4. Famed Giant
5. Highway
6. Motherless calves
7. Grime
8. Seine sight
9. Ocean
10. Potential socialite, for short
11. Math. course
12. Fairy-tale character
13. Marries
18. Peaks
19. ___ cotta
23. ___ time (never)
24. Box
25. Wine: Comb. form
26. Relict
27. More frigid
28. ___ Dame
29. Extreme
30. "Aïda" or "Carmen"
31. Electrician, at times
32. Suspicious
37. Start of a Shakespeare title
38. Mutton fat
39. Rodents
41. Scatter
42. Serving with no return
44. Surgical threads
45. Leguminous container
46. Weasel of northern regions
49. Hold back
50. Siamese
51. Sched. entries
52. Cold-cuts emporium
53. Actor Tamiroff
54. Raise one's hackles
55. Recognized
57. Half an African fly
58. "2001" computer
59. Gp. honored on Nov. 1

# 263

## ACROSS

1. Grandfather of Enos
5. Englishman's trolley
9. Prior's superior
14. Musical round
15. A river at Cairo
16. Where many a Goya hangs
17. Arthur Wynne creation: 1913
19. Tiff
20. Warty critter
21. Desk job of a sort
23. "Lux Christi" composer
25. Eskimo knife
26. Veer
29. Lamb's kin
31. Gal of songdom
34. Papal cape
35. Dock support
37. An Adams
39. Maenad chaser
40. ____-de-sac
41. Limit loss risk
43. "To ____ their golden eyes": Shak.
44. Complicate
46. Delos locale
47. Uno + due
49. Abby's sister
50. Bind
51. Bombard or strafe
53. Miles from Ingatestone
55. Enigmata
59. Abridgments
63. "Paper Moon" actress
64. Devise
66. ____ decisis
67. Tunnel
68. Blackthorn
69. Nelsons, e.g.
70. Snead's needs
71. It gets pegged

## DOWN

1. Chief
2. Moneta ____, Italian's gold coin
3. Sleep like ____
4. Skillful
5. Tug's charge
6. TV's Miss Morgenstern
7. Broadcast
8. Fashion
9. ". . . glory of an ____ day": Shak.
10. Antony's adversary
11. Rumanian coins
12. God identified with Woden
13. Chinese clan
18. Fans of black-and-white squares
22. It has principals and seconds
24. Yields
26. Passable
27. Enclosed
28. Trencherman
30. Rogers or Weng
32. Confuse
33. Boston airport
35. Glance over
36. Polo's field
38. Nidus
42. Chicago suburb
45. Scruff
48. Charles of ring fame
50. Cockatoo features
52. Everything, in Essen
54. He uses the Palmer method
55. Ritzy
56. "Verily I say ____ you . . .": Matt. 26:21
57. Fervor
58. Aquarium fish
60. Army mascot
61. Greenspan's field: Abbr.
62. Marginal mark
65. Pindaric poem

# 264

**ACROSS**

1. Apparatus for emptying coal
7. Port
11. Feign
14. One of the faithful
15. Molding, by gosh!
16. Digit down below
17. Fruit (literally, seeded apple)
19. Trio in terror
20. Other
21. Shoelace tip
22. Unit for Connors
23. Potassium or sodium, e.g.
26. Detect
28. Industrial fallout
31. Media abbr.
32. Skulls
33. By way of
35. Run in neutral
38. Controller of future generations?
41. Shortly
42. Wagon follower, in Paris
43. Like the North Pole before Peary
44. Watchdog over TV
46. Parting words in London
48. ___ as a kitten
51. Van Gogh had one
52. Highway sign
53. Dominoes
55. Add liquor
59. ___ Borch, Dutch painter
60. Material for a piñata
63. Ad ___ (pertinent)
64. Verve
65. Deadly
66. Approves
67. Pealed
68. Windmill sails

**DOWN**

1. Cassette item
2. Object of one's affections
3. Mums
4. Superiority
5. Part of a journey
6. Blunder
7. "Vive le roi!"
8. Brigitte's equal
9. Honored, in a way
10. Waver
11. Town on the Salinas
12. Kitchen utensil
13. Waspish
18. Top student's foursome
24. Revise
25. Footpath
27. Sparkle
28. Mars: Comb. form
29. Kin of Pandora's box
30. Author of "This Hunger"
32. Army brass: Abbr.
34. Fevers or chills
36. Carrillo and Gorcey
37. Kind of shrew
39. Presidents' mil. rank
40. About
45. Portable room
47. Lessen the pain
48. Type of physicist
49. Polished
50. Oahu's highest peak
54. Eads, e.g.
56. Long for
57. Roughen
58. Fish dish
61. Literary initials
62. Gull's cry

# 265

**ACROSS**

1. Boundless
5. Part of B.S.A.
9. Subject of Katz's "Days of Wrath"
13. "___ of Capri," 1934 song
14. "He did not ___ button for it": Rabelais
15. Iowa city
16. ___ impasse
17. Ryan or Tatum
18. Appoint
19. Two cities in Italia
22. Soak flax
23. The goods, to a D.A.
24. Squealer
27. Pep
29. Beginnings
32. Road sign
34. Jigger contents
36. Bandleader Jones
38. Two cities in Italia
42. Rossellini classic: 1946
43. Wave's kin
44. A Cassini
45. Something to serve
48. Reporter's query
50. "___ tu," Verdi aria
51. Label
53. First biter
55. Two cities in Italia
61. River under the Ponte Vecchio
62. Rinse or dry
63. Tasso's "Rinaldo" is one
64. Perennial herb
65. Pile up
66. Saarinen
67. Steal a look
68. Cleveland's ___ Park
69. Peruse

**DOWN**

1. Drugstore container
2. Vino town
3. Czech, for one
4. Gedda, e.g.
5. Healthy, in Elba
6. Fawn
7. ___ alla Scala
8. Old West gathering place
9. Poster, in Positano
10. Muscat is its capital
11. San ___, on the Italian Riviera
12. Simple sugar
14. "Il Giardino dei Finzi-___," De Sica film
20. Gun an engine
21. Pitcher's aid
24. Invitation abbr.
25. ". . . ___ and hungry look"
26. Leoncavallo clown
28. "Mamma ___!"
30. Fulcrum for an oar
31. Frugal one
33. Columnist Pegler
35. Fixed bench
37. They followed that star
39. Democratic Republic of the Congo, once
40. Bird's crop
41. Buttercup parts
46. Moulin Rouge dance
47. Cell product
49. Breakfast in old Rome?
52. Decorative sticker
54. Fencing gear
55. Kind of enterprise
56. "Picnic" author
57. Mme. Schiaparelli
58. Cartel letters
59. Cuneo coin
60. Image
61. Viper

# 266

**ACROSS**

1. Bridge partners
6. Part of Orion
10. Western school-teacher
14. Flynn
15. Festive cry in Plato's day
16. N.A. Indian
17. Use skates
18. Son of the old sod
20. Emergency call
21. Yeats's Muse
23. Movie stars
24. Fine cigar
26. One of Sudan's southern neighbors
27. Kind of nut
29. Donahue
30. Court minutes
31. Electrician
33. Style
36. Tourist attraction near Cork
40. Stitch
41. Mole, for one
42. Can. province
43. Kiln
44. Athlete fond of combers
46. Troon aide
49. Column block
51. Takes on hands
52. Scottish proprietor
53. Absent
56. Limerick product
58. Immature seed
60. Sediment
61. Cassini
62. Forty-____
63. Reykjavik bedtime story
64. Sailmaker's triangle
65. West German sea-port

**DOWN**

1. Throws
2. Guthrie
3. Fare for Kelly
4. Dowser's tool
5. Hash-mark site
6. "Borstal Boy" author
7. LuPone role
8. Sylvan carnivore
9. Platform for Pate or Murphy
10. When Grundy was born
11. Flirt ender
12. Author Dahl
13. Table for Tiberius
19. These cause tough going
22. Not diluted
25. Gregory Peck role
26. Nobelist in Chemis-try: 1934
27. Isis's sacred pets
28. Dull pain
29. Weight allowance
31. British servicewoman
32. Boniface's concern
33. Tall canine of Erin
34. Pay to play
35. Mercury's is 88 days
37. Prodigal
38. "The African Queen" screenwriter
39. Dessert offering
43. Ukrainian seaport
44. Bors or Geraint
45. Defeated
46. Country once partly under Incan rule
47. Made known
48. Dehydrated
49. Market Square Arena player
50. Loyal
52. "Le Roi d'Ys" com-poser
54. Take off
55. Seedless plant
57. Record
59. What pompon girls display

# 267

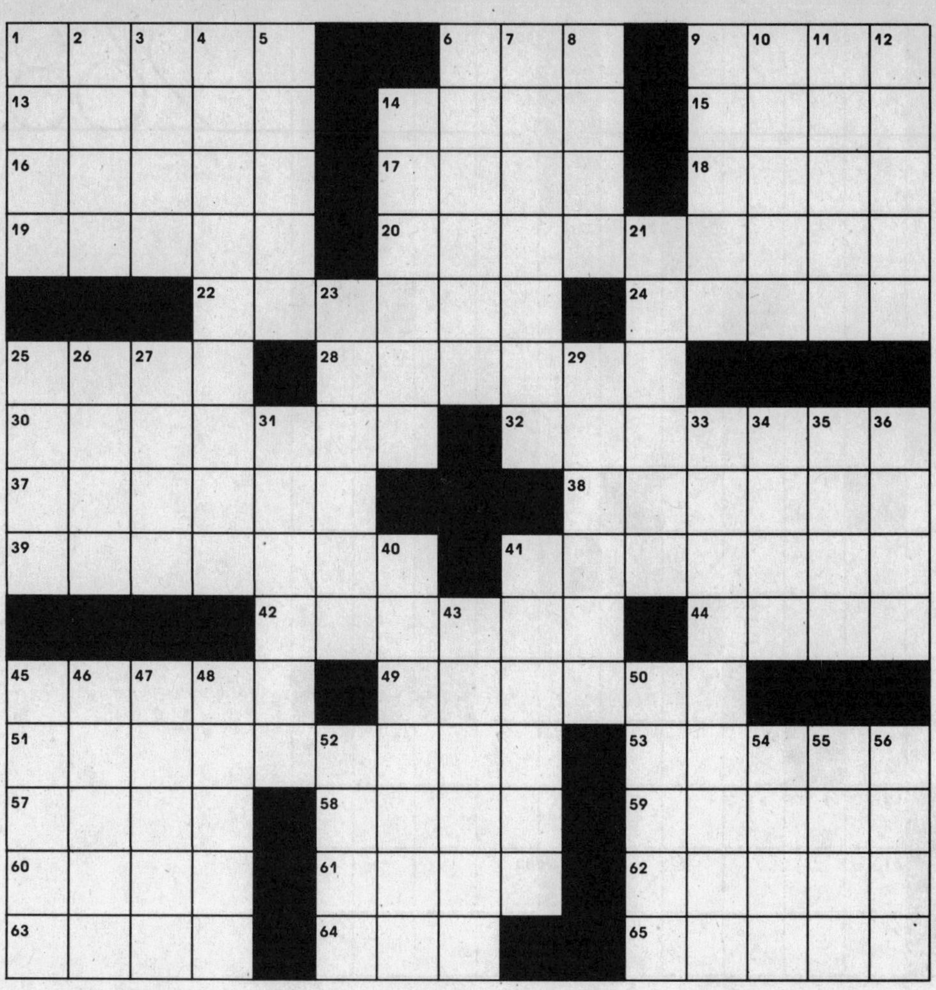

**ACROSS**

1. Brazilian dance
6. An arm of H.U.D.
9. Titubate
13. "___ of One's Own": Woolf
14. Down Under leapers
15. Part of a roof
16. Eos's time
17. It was, to Nero
18. Cliff
19. Complication
20. Defender of Rome: 1849
22. One of the Fords
24. Sports shocker
25. Foundation
28. "My Sister ___"
30. Footstool
32. Noted U.S. seismologist
37. Depended
38. Hypothesis
39. Knowing
41. "___ Tattoo," T. Williams play
42. Rootlessness
44. Bull and Rolvaag
45. Stand for de Kooning
49. Poet Aiken
51. Traveling bag
53. Sociologist's concern
57. Frost
58. Composer-singer from Ottawa
59. Ring-shaped reef
60. Black
61. Litigant
62. Home of the "Golden Hurricane"
63. Sobrinos' kin
64. Hampshire's home
65. Holm

**DOWN**

1. Lip
2. ___ for one's money
3. Actress Maris
4. Middle-class
5. Plentiful
6. "___ We Know," 1934 song
7. Magpie or pack rat
8. Italian commune
9. A summing up
10. Hyde and Grey
11. Circumvent
12. On the up and up
14. Get back
21. Nobel Peace Prize winner: 1950
23. Companion of writin' and 'rithmetic
25. Five-time Wimbledon champ
26. Egyptian symbol
27. Manche's capital
29. One or the other
31. Basic materials
33. "Father of History"
34. Dupe
35. Old tongue
36. Gypsy gentlemen
40. One source of milk
41. Chorus rejectee's problem
43. Dance of the 60's
45. Shore bird
46. Excuse of a sort
47. Group north of Tonga
48. Sir Anthony and family
50. Instrument for Perlman
52. Soviet wire service
54. Ship's motion
55. Gilbert's Lord High Everything ___
56. Lath

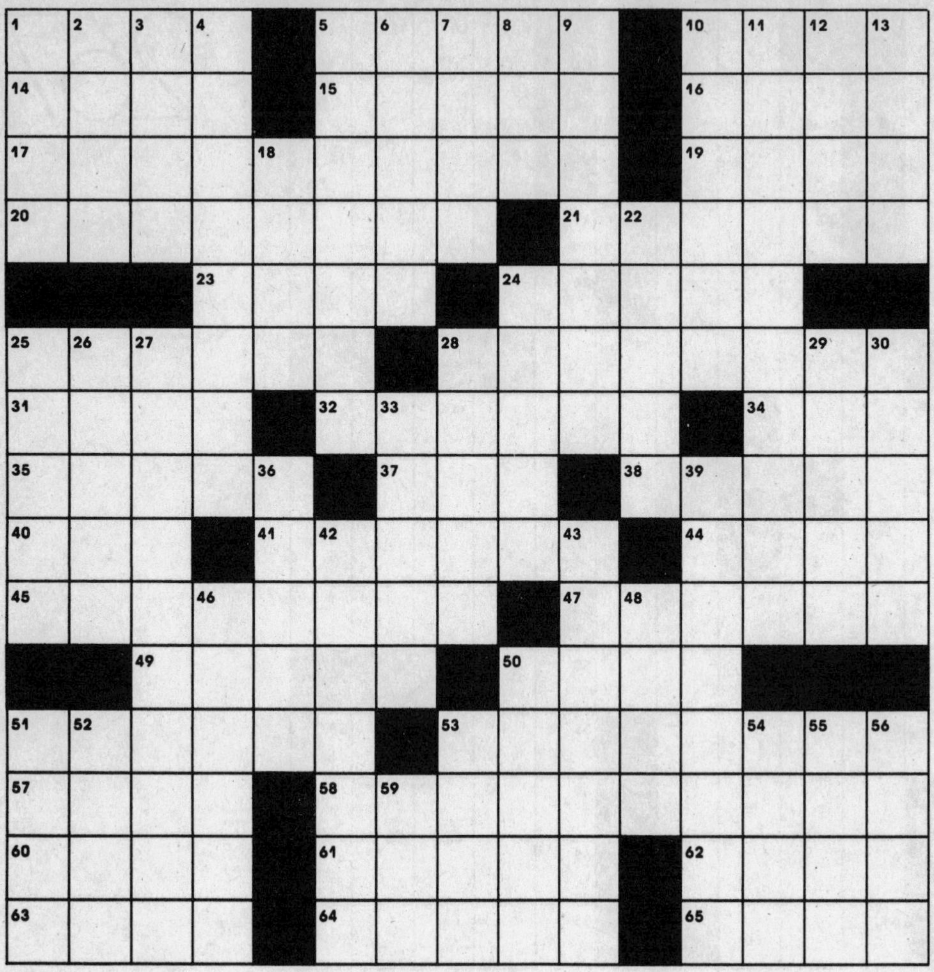

# 268

**ACROSS**

1. Where Zeno taught
5. City in Lombardy
10. Wife, to Cicero
14. All: Comb. form
15. Wazhazhe tribe
16. Anagram for rode
17. Geometer from Syracuse
19. Freshly
20. A.F.C. team
21. Transcripts
23. River in England
24. Befuddle
25. Brute
28. Wraps up
31. On the Red
32. ". . . ___ and arrows . . ."
34. Master
35. Paints
37. Follower of broad or pole
38. Mortise adjacency
40. Tokugawa shogunate's capital
41. Roundup aides
44. Declare, in pinochle
45. Celebrated dialectician
47. Approaches, with "in"
49. Lets
50. Well disciplined
51. Couple
53. Most maudlin
57. Spanish demonstrative
58. Early atomic theorist
60. Styptic
61. A sea was named for him
62. Historic caravel
63. Pry
64. Salad days
65. Haruspex

**DOWN**

1. Soda fountains in N.E.
2. Biting
3. Head of a tale
4. Plato was one
5. Twinklings
6. Grenoble's river
7. Lassies' partners
8. Golden or Gilded follower
9. Nidification
10. Father of Cronus
11. Eleatic philosopher
12. Czech-Polish river
13. Dust-ups
18. Corse and d'Yeu
22. "From whom we do ___ . . .": Shak.
24. His discoveries may be major
25. Turnover
26. ". . . I say, not ___"
27. "The Laughing Philosopher"
28. Sets
29. School, in Avignon
30. Issues
33. Vegetates
36. Novel by Jack Schaefer
39. Heartstrings
42. Draw
43. Egyptian talismans
46. Change a title
48. Respirator
50. Ricin or ptomaine
51. Genet or Gabin
52. King Harold III's creation
53. Charge
54. A "long tail"
55. Logical
56. Tolstoy's sovereign
59. "___ man can tether time or tide": Burns

# 269

**ACROSS**

1. Gathering
5. Loafer
9. Madcap
13. Parisienne's magazine
14. ___ arts
15. Yucca's cousin
16. She made a hit in '63
19. "Finlandia" composer
20. Truly
21. Shade of blue
22. Famed clinic
23. Thai or Ainu
25. Shower adjuncts
29. Give ___ (chastise)
30. Man's slipper
31. Fictitious surname
32. She made a hit in '46
36. 100%
37. A cause of errors
38. Outlet
39. Accepts with pleasure
41. Fuse thoroughly
43. Spheres
44. Author of "The Yosemite"
45. Smelter slag
48. Time of night
52. She made a hit in '29
54. Words of ken
55. Cantina fast food
56. Ford's running mate
57. The one yonder
58. Prop for Aquarius
59. Role for Sonny Shroyer

**DOWN**

1. Makes a touch
2. Et ___
3. Strike arbitrators
4. Erasure
5. Far East capital
6. Some radiomen
7. "Yes, cheri"
8. Atones
9. Unplanned
10. Helm position
11. About
12. Director or conductor
14. Actor Aherne
17. Wee circus worker
18. Regardless
22. Ike's wife
23. It hangs "thereby"
24. Noiseless
25. Set-tos
26. Clio award winners
27. ___ fro
28. Airmailed
29. What "vidi" means
30. Grandifloras
33. White, earthy powder used for optical glass
34. Thrash
35. Trample down
40. Medieval jerkin
41. Lifts up
42. Connection
44. Drive a car
45. Cabaret bit
46. Dollars and cents
47. Draft status
48. Passengers on Apollo 17
49. Pour ___ (intensify)
50. Capital of Manche
51. Sizes up
53. Corvine sound

# 270

**ACROSS**

1. Muzzles
5. Forest denizen
9. Plant pores
12. "____ Hunter"
15. U.S.N. missile
16. Pituitary secretion
17. Helpful device
18. Claude and John
20. Author Deighton
22. Sasquatch features
23. Egg follower
25. Austrian statesman
26. Lingerie item
29. Burnett tugs hers
32. Ate sparingly
35. Bestial
36. Hero of a famous chanson
37. Teed off
39. Cites
40. Homophone for owed
41. Fish dish
43. R.A.F. aircraftsman: Colloq.
44. Secretly
47. Draft initials
49. Howard and Robert W.
53. Former TV squad
55. Seize an opportunity
56. Obsequious
58. Watercraft
59. ____ stay (ship's fastening device)
60. Wimp
61. British order

**DOWN**

1. Harry and Janice
2. Early church chalice
3. Robin Williams role
4. Blue Jay twirler
5. Dinah and Larry
6. Time period, in Bayonne
7. Own
8. An earth sci.
9. Salubrious spot
10. Helot's lot
11. Have high hopes
12. Bacall movie
13. Photog. blowup
14. In medias ____
19. Kite's org.
21. Nick from Omaha
24. Cattleman's stick
26. Karen and Al
27. M. Coty
28. Appends
29. Spain's longest river
30. Hardscrabble
31. Ben and Dan
33. Augur
34. Mackles
38. Como and Mason
39. Diamond play
42. ____ Bensey, in "Tobacco Road"
44. Stone slab
45. Poe house
46. Tart
48. Horne arias
49. Radio bands
50. Motorists' org.
51. Outer layer
52. Assam silkworm
54. Ten: Comb. form
57. Tub

# 271

## ACROSS

1. Aid a felon
5. Escape
10. River in W Europe
14. Washington Square lass
15. Aegean gulf
16. Quechuan
17. Knicks' rivals
18. Frozen rain
19. Type of cloth
20. Trilogy by Aeschylus
22. List of things to be done
24. Centuries and centuries
25. Arabian gulf
26. Peasant
29. "Alcestis" dramatist
34. McDonald or Colman
36. Resident of Viborg
37. ____ Miss
38. Eleven, in Ecuador
39. Exalt
41. Phoenician seaport
42. Religious org.
43. Ma Kettle portrayer
44. President called Old Buena Vista
46. "Antigone" dramatist
49. Lady Jane and Joel
50. Plato "Symposium" topic
51. Mitchell's mansion
53. Conquered
56. Athenian comedist
60. Wheeling's river
61. "____ the Body Electric": Bradbury
63. El Bahr
64. Pious jargon
65. Zeal
66. Bearish group of stars
67. Nigerian group
68. Clamant
69. Straw beehive

## DOWN

1. Memorable cartoonist
2. Dutch South African
3. Borgia in-law
4. Musts for mosaics
5. To eat, in Emden
6. Traveling bag
7. Space
8. Female rabbit
9. Bistro; café
10. Satyrs' kin
11. Soon
12. Astringent
13. Bombay bigwig
21. User's fee
23. Stare in surprise
25. Anglo-Saxon currency
26. Charles ____, pop singer
27. John Wayne film: 1953
28. Open a bottle
30. Commune in NE Italy
31. Author of "The White Company"
32. Hirsch of football fame
33. Calchas and Mopsus, e.g.
35. Severe
40. Is infirm
41. "Oedipus ____," by 46 Across
43. "Mondo Cane" theme song
45. Taj Mahal's city
47. Slaves of Spartans
48. Members of a certain pool
52. "Twelve ____ Men"
53. Primary points
54. Whaler of fiction
55. Kind of type or cut
56. Noon, in Neuilly
57. Actor Bogarde
58. Other
59. Harvest
62. B'way message

# 272

**ACROSS**

1. Head of David's army
5. Master, in colonial India
10. R.W.R., e.g.
14. Hot-rod rod
15. Galley-proof word
16. Birth name of Hussein's wife
17. Duplicate
19. One of the Gigantes
20. Captivate
21. Soapbox spiel
23. ___ the Impaler, 15th-century Hungarian prince
25. Pineapples or mints
26. Set in a church tower
30. Whirl
33. "Our Town" girl
34. "I ___ Lassie," old song
36. Bleat
37. Rackets
38. Rank
39. Bills
40. Kin of trig.
41. ___ belli
42. "La ___ de Chaillot": Giraudoux
43. Pass on, as gossip
45. Similitudes of sorts
47. Cathode's vis-à-vis
49. Miedaner's "The ___ of Anna Klane": 1977
50. Tale tellers, sometimes
53. One of the Five Nations
57. Spicy stew
58. Big-top bigwig
60. Achilles' vulnerable spot
61. Of less than 90 degrees
62. Better this than sorry
63. Partner of ends
64. Means of support
65. Cómo follower

**DOWN**

1. Amulet stone
2. Babe and kin
3. "When I was ___ . . ."
4. Harrows
5. Helical form
6. Alder tree, in Ayr
7. On Everest
8. ". . . ___ what I say . . .": Alice
9. Blitzed
10. Flat
11. Awakes a memory
12. Name meaning "hairy"
13. ___-Altenburg, Germany
18. Sports-car event
22. Author Seton
24. Republicans Bob and Elizabeth
26. Type of waxwing
27. "A miss is as good as ___"
28. Like a raccoon
29. ___ to par (ailing)
31. Gateleg, for one
32. Slackens
35. Certain endorsements
38. Nonsense
39. Peerage
41. Plant shoot
42. Region's animals
44. Historical accounts
46. Boniface's customer
48. Heath
50. London district
51. Presented a case
52. Cold shoulder
54. Philippine group
55. Dexterous
56. Bailiwick
59. John Wilkin's hit song: 1964

# 273

## ACROSS

1. End of a counting rhyme
7. Kind of orange
12. Place for an aglet
15. Mini-poem
17. Secular or civil
18. Galveston sight
19. Lout
20. Rabble-rouser's forte
22. Malayan transportation
24. Sews up
25. Inventory
27. Rig, for short
28. Lingerie item
31. Furnish
33. Fog
36. Speech teachers
39. Broadcaster
40. Tumbler
41. Gridiron measure
42. How come?
43. Fifth-day creation
46. Cotton-spinning machines
49. In seclusion
52. Just
53. Reckless
57. Fled
58. Garland for a poet laureate
59. Neil Simon, e.g.
61. Brewer from Toledo
62. Poker pest
63. Useful plastic
64. Cantankerous

## DOWN

1. Settings for Steichen
2. What the Tin Man wanted
3. Nonsense
4. Drill sergeant's word
5. Hypothetical force
6. Breathing apparatus
7. Unwanted attention
8. Saw
9. Mother of Aeneas
10. Sommer
11. Glance from Groucho
13. Snub-nosed: Fr.
14. Buoy
16. Go for it
21. Sidney Smith's creations
23. Vinegary: Comb. form
26. Dresser need
28. Expurgate
29. Actress McClanahan
30. The "cruellest" mo.
32. Blueprint person
34. Khachaturian
35. Whey
36. Untrained
37. Presidential monogram
38. Firmly restrained
44. Torture
45. Poet-political activist Jones
47. Something to clap at school
48. Watch
49. Not so polite
50. Ancient city in Syria
51. Disneyland denizen
53. Castor or tile
54. "____ generally shammin' . . .": Kipling
55. "Ta-____-Boom-De-Ré"
56. Golda
60. Keep after sch.

# 274

## ACROSS

1. Film
5. Cosmetics applier
9. Resolute
13. Later in the text
14. Pizarro's "City of the Kings"
15. Novel of 1847
16. Avoid
17. Sleep like ____
18. Anagram for stop
19. Esteem
21. Certain fringe
23. Half of "La Gioconda"
24. Wis. establishments
26. Eleventh hour, formally speaking?
31. "Up and ____!"
32. Dash
33. Play at a formal Halloween party?
40. Ninth word of "Trees"
41. Cab tab
42. Refined W. C. Fields film?
49. Unintelligent
50. ____ Tranquillitatis
52. Din deadener
54. Tolkien's Smaug, e.g.
56. Box resident
57. Galba's successor
59. Bluish gas
60. Laborer of yore
61. Asian holidays
62. Pouting grimaces
63. Nurseryman's bane
64. Existence
65. Six-legged slaves

## DOWN

1. Was tenacious
2. Reuning group
3. Astrologer's figure
4. It holds water
5. Notorious org. of the 70's
6. Formal constitutional amendments?
7. Love affairs
8. Turkish bathing house
9. Clue for Holmes
10. Band of African warriors
11. Campus org.
12. Yr.'s dozen
13. Ship part
20. Former major-league catcher
22. Pershing's W.W. I command
25. Abba Eban's first initial
27. N.Y.C. has one
28. Kind of wind
29. West or Murray
30. Inning trio
33. Descriptive acct.
34. It precedes la-la
35. Worker or queen
36. Boarded a ship
37. Alternative to shine
38. Formed an electrical bridge
39. River in SE China
43. Fer-de-lance's kin
44. Sudan native
45. Rockne's namesakes
46. Hippolyta, e.g.
47. Seasoned dish
48. Uses a monotone
51. Chemical suffixes
52. Repose
53. High-school break-out
55. Papa's see
56. Abraham was the first
58. Malt ending

# 275

**ACROSS**

1. Gen. Bradley
5. Calumniates
10. Apricot
14. Special
15. Grable, to G.I. Joe
16. High protein source
17. U.S. Army Chief of Staff: 1972–74
20. Monitoring device
21. Cavalryman
22. City on the Oka
24. ___ Juan Hill
25. Strauss opera
29. Incite
31. "___ Pinafore"
34. "Cradle of Texas liberty"
35. I.W. of U.S.W.A. fame
36. Kind of camp
37. He captured Stony Point: 1779
40. ___ entendu (of course)
41. Elephantine group
42. Spread sunshine
43. Actress Harding
44. Calcium oxide
45. Maiden
46. Christmas tree
47. Crop crops
49. Saw-toothed
53. Jungle queen
58. Flying Tigers leader
60. Sans improvements
61. Construct
62. Orsk's river
63. Sherman, for one
64. Off the wall
65. Lomé's locale

**DOWN**

1. Grampuses
2. Playwright Connelly
3. Zone
4. Curb
5. Domain
6. One cubic decimetre
7. Número ___
8. Litter member
9. In a meager manner
10. Hangar abutment
11. Spring tide's kin
12. Equivalent
13. Security Council mem.
18. Sundial style
19. Cutter, e.g.
23. September honoree
25. Dance in duple time
26. Cote of the Nordiques
27. Burdened
28. Neighbor of South Yemen
30. Yield
31. Georgetown team
32. Hall-of-Famer Irvin
33. Kind of guitar
35. Attention-getting word
36. Salve
38. Triskaidekaphobe's fear
39. Arm
44. Perjurer
45. Delicious
46. Gambol
48. Pick out
49. "Vamoose!"
50. "Lohengrin" role
51. Precipitate
52. Raw silk color
54. Salty: Abbr.
55. Wallaroo
56. Scoria
57. War-torn town in 1944
59. ___ Meeuwtje, Minuit's ship

# 276

**ACROSS**

1. Fed. labor law: 1973
5. Communion table
10. Record
14. Maple genus
15. Zubin from Bombay
16. Tropical plant
17. Curious one in 1 Down
20. "Moonlight ___"
21. Befoul
22. Carter or Irving
23. Hawaiian goose
25. Tofu source
27. Malt kiln
30. Examine carefully
32. Cookie pan
36. Biol. is one
37. Canvas
39. Income from wealth
40. Event in 1 Down
43. Bring back
44. Units of resistance
45. Heat meas.
46. An Astaire
47. Kennedy letters
48. LL.B.
49. Loosely twisted silk yarn
51. Glinka subject
54. Morose
57. Mine passage
59. Pranks
63. Jennyanydots in 1 Down
66. To ___ (unanimously)
67. Misplay
68. Ancient people of Gaul
69. Chromosome part
70. Zola character
71. River to the North Sea

**DOWN**

1. Hit musical
2. Reflect
3. Six or seven follower
4. Notorious
5. Jordan's capital
6. Permit
7. Therefore
8. Maximally
9. Proportion
10. Label
11. Fat-choy or nostoc
12. Tone ___
13. Strange
18. An ally of Carson
19. Joyce classic
24. Noxious
26. He rebuilt Jericho
27. Purples, to Plautus
28. Hurt
29. Winnow
31. Inspirer of 1 Down
33. Perform
34. Splendor
35. TV, to a BBC fan
37. Distinct
38. Milwaukee product
39. City on the Danube
41. Fickle woman
42. French feline
47. Refugee
48. Main channel
50. Summer
52. Buffalo hockey pro
53. Violinist Kavafian
54. Male caribou
55. Verbal sigh
56. Bishop's assistant
58. Pivot
60. Frosts
61. "___ the dawn"
62. Waken
64. Song in "A Chorus Line"
65. A Stooge

# 277

**ACROSS**

1. Goddess of infatuation
4. Anticlimax
10. Follower of Joel
14. Diet abbr.
15. Troupial
16. Place for lox stocked in barrels
17. Start of a Swiftian mot on aging
20. Create
21. A daughter of Mnemosyne
22. Piques
23. Smart
26. Wharton School deg.
29. Carrottop of comics
31. Strut and fret one's hour
32. Imposture
33. Desperado
35. ____ line (conform)
37. Middle of mot
40. Living Dahl
41. Bizarre
42. Wash water
43. Some Lts.
44. Major followers
48. Daisy, to Dagwood
49. Sated
52. Caspian feeder
53. Itzak's contemporary
55. "I may command where ____": Shak.
57. End of mot
61. Arabian gulf
62. Early monk
63. Baseball toss
64. Make coffee
65. Long-Garn milieu
66. Sault ____ Marie

**DOWN**

1. Sloth
2. Spot for the old-fashioned?
3. Giants, for one
4. Father Flanagan's ____ Town
5. Like certain forces
6. Sobrina's kin
7. Judicial abbr.
8. Most venerable
9. Haruspices
10. Mine access
11. Ex ____ (of one's own accord)
12. Norwegian Bull
13. Fam. member
18. Sense of humor
19. Utter
24. Spout inanities
25. Bionomics
27. Tender of Thailand
28. It's often ground
30. Hibernia
32. Lethargy
34. Baltic or Atlantic
35. Explosive
36. Grendel, in "Beowulf"
37. Shade of blue?
38. Veteran
39. River of York
40. Cleo's little nipper
43. Humorous
45. Scout units
46. Tragus
47. Kind of hammer
49. Ash or trash follower
50. English composer: 1596–1662
51. "She ____ Say Yes"
54. Settled
56. Busy as ____
57. Teasel raises it
58. Homophone of owed
59. Seagoing inits.
60. Boss's grazing place

# 278

**ACROSS**

1. ____ cuisine
6. Misplay
11. Entry
12. Room
14. Part of London
15. Sobriquet for a liar
17. Race participant
18. Halted
20. St. Paul-to-Duluth dir.
21. Certain collections
23. Rub out
24. Enjoy
25. ____ Sound, Wash.
27. Mrs. Gynt
28. Clementine's pa
29. No-nos for an athlete
31. Beauticians' treatments
32. Lindbergh's craft
34. Samuel Clemens et al.
37. Rash fighter
41. Actor Jeremy
42. Mme., in Cádiz
43. Taste
44. Frequent wallowers
45. Peruvian Indians who sound hostile
47. Pheasant's nest
48. Suffix for a hydrocarbon
49. Garment-district employee
51. Iowa college
52. Freedom from karma
54. Unity
56. Left off
57. Author Gordimer
58. Slag
59. Shawl

**DOWN**

1. Behan's "The ____"
2. Buchwald or Carney
3. Shoshoneans
4. Aunt, in Nancy
5. Fabulous land
6. Pass
7. Adorée of silents
8. Study
9. Possess
10. Weather information
11. Item changed to axle grease by Dr. Carver
13. Rizzuto for 13 years
14. Covers
16. Daniel and Isaiah
19. Travel documents
22. Homilists' specialties
24. Utility-company employee
26. Casper's wife
28. Catnip and mad-dog skullcap
30. Parts of ft.
31. Vistula feeder
33. Illicit amours
34. Galileo was one
35. Like poetic justice
36. Demeaned
38. Unmanly
39. Knotty
40. Bumbo and gateado
42. Sam and J.C. of golf
45. English composer and family
46. Legislative body, in Paris
49. El ____, Tex.
50. Make over
53. Volt-ampere unit
55. Nothing

# 279

## ACROSS

1. Stir
6. ___ dixit
10. Randy
14. Asian capital
15. Burmese folklore spirits
16. Yours, in Tours
17. Tocsin
18. U.S. composer: 1874–1954
19. ___ tail (flee)
20. W.H. Auden book of poems
23. Native of Tallinn
24. Diamond ___
25. Plague
26. Very, in music
28. Pyramid builder
32. Sail briskly
35. Drop
37. Buccal
38. Like the Rockettes
39. Ref. book
40. Moore or Bumbry
41. Dies ___
42. What anosmic people don't sense
43. Humphrey's successor
44. Model
46. Illusory
48. Mary Todd's man
49. New Deal initials
50. "Othello" opener
54. S. Maugham novel
59. Metrical foot
60. Lexicon
61. Singapore ___ (cocktail)
62. Salinger character
63. Watcher
64. Jai alai basket
65. Light carriage, to Holmes
66. ___ égal
67. Photogs' solutions

## DOWN

1. Abrade
2. Sugarcane shoots
3. Torpid
4. Jane Austen novel
5. Kin's partner
6. O.K.'d in writing
7. Pearl Buck novel
8. Contain
9. Pith
10. J. Marquand novel, with "The"
11. Glasses case
12. Shabby
13. Talk or urge repetitiously
21. Urban railways
22. Faugh!
27. Hit a ball high
29. Port west of Algiers
30. N.Y. university
31. Raft
32. Actor Pickens
33. Elflike being
34. Gelling agent
36. Prizefighters
40. Bombast
42. Electra's brother
45. Saku garment
47. Argentina's ___ Conchas
51. Curly
52. An Apache
53. Tropical trees
54. Draws
55. ___ over (discuss)
56. Another Austen novel
57. Georgetown U. athlete
58. He wrote "The Nazarene"

# 280

**ACROSS**

**1.** Daughter of Tantalus
**6.** Theories
**10.** Israeli city
**13.** Prose piece
**14.** Out of kilter
**15.** Form of silica
**17.** Motif
**18.** First name in espionage
**19.** Lollobrigida
**20.** Gossip
**23.** Texas A&M athletes
**26.** Speak haltingly
**27.** Baronet's title
**28.** Remus or Esau
**31.** The Altar
**32.** Unit of tobacco
**34.** "I've Got ___ in Kalamazoo"
**36.** Center the football
**39.** One adept at table talk
**42.** Code word for "A"
**43.** Folded tortilla
**44.** Pause-filling sound
**46.** Formal wear, informally
**48.** Actress Hartman
**50.** Before, to Beaumont
**51.** Wound yarn
**55.** Emcees' remarks
**57.** Conversationalist
**60.** "Stole ___ and away he run"
**61.** Heroic
**62.** Postman's beat
**66.** Muscovite, e.g.
**67.** Silent one
**68.** Orbital point
**69.** Bird's bill
**70.** Withered, to Wither
**71.** For ___ (permanently)

**DOWN**

**1.** P. and L. figure
**2.** Comic Kabibble
**3.** Sugary ending
**4.** Disney film: 1942
**5.** Shoemaker's need
**6.** Poet's foot
**7.** Item on a pitcher's mound
**8.** Tiny particles
**9.** Neighbor of La Crosse, Wis.
**10.** Abnormal talkativeness
**11.** ___ War: 1839–42
**12.** Florentine poet
**16.** Bolger 1939 co-star
**21.** Egyptian dam
**22.** "Killer Dolphin" author
**23.** Venomous ophidian
**24.** Comedienne Radner
**25.** Spare fare
**29.** "___ Rhythm"
**30.** Twangy
**33.** Talent of 39 Across
**35.** Points
**37.** Jacob's eighth son
**38.** Prefix for dactyl
**40.** Prentiss from San Antonio
**41.** Affirm
**45.** Enero or febrero
**47.** Craft for corsairs
**49.** Arctic jacket
**51.** Con man's forte
**52.** Make a surprise visit
**53.** Cinched
**54.** Twofold
**56.** Rhetorical device
**58.** Pseudologist
**59.** Vertex
**63.** Expend
**64.** O'Neill from Cambridge
**65.** "Bus" terminal

# 281

**ACROSS**

1. Pinchbeck
5. Woodworkers' tools
10. Sans ___ (peerless)
14. "___ kleine Nachtmusik"
15. U.S.S.R. part
16. Aztec god of sowing
17. With, to Pierre
18. Florida bay
19. O.T. book
20. Violin virtuoso
23. Emblem of sovereignty
24. Kind of knot or stitch
25. Hood's exit
28. Fifty percent
31. Infrequently
35. Sale words
37. Gretzky score
39. Filmy fabric
40. Violin virtuoso
43. Dote on
44. "William ___," Rossini opera
45. Jolly boat
46. Striped polecats
48. Wiener topper
50. ___ Miguel, Azores island
51. Rock star Jagger
53. ___ Cliburn
55. Violin virtuoso
61. One of "The Three B's"
62. Practical
63. Bowed instrument
65. Soprano Petina
66. Facing
67. "___ music . . .": Gershwin
68. Squalled
69. A son of Boreas
70. Space-vehicle units

**DOWN**

1. Wall St. watchdog
2. "Oh, it's ___-yee . . .": Gruber
3. Jean Baptiste ___, French violinist
4. Kind of soprano
5. Swedish turnip
6. A giant of Palestine
7. Dope
8. John, Paul et al.
9. Complications
10. Model
11. Sphinx site
12. ". . . his nose was as sharp as ___": Shak.
13. Rijn branch
21. Royal monogram
22. Meuse River city
25. Bolivian seat of government
26. "Do as I say, not ___"
27. Musical scale
29. "The ___ Chord"
30. Disconcerts
32. Creator of Edmond Dantès
33. Conductor Seiji
34. Edison's ___ Park
36. Ivory carving
38. Quiet
41. Spiral: Comb. form
42. Instruments for 61 Across
47. Creator of "Peanuts"
49. U.S.A.F. auxiliary
52. Porter's "___ Went to Haiti"
54. Author Shute
55. Scandian chieftain
56. Realty unit
57. Tip-off of a sort
58. Opponent of S. Grant
59. Buster Brown's dog
60. Type of lens
61. Highchair wear
64. Inf. officers

282

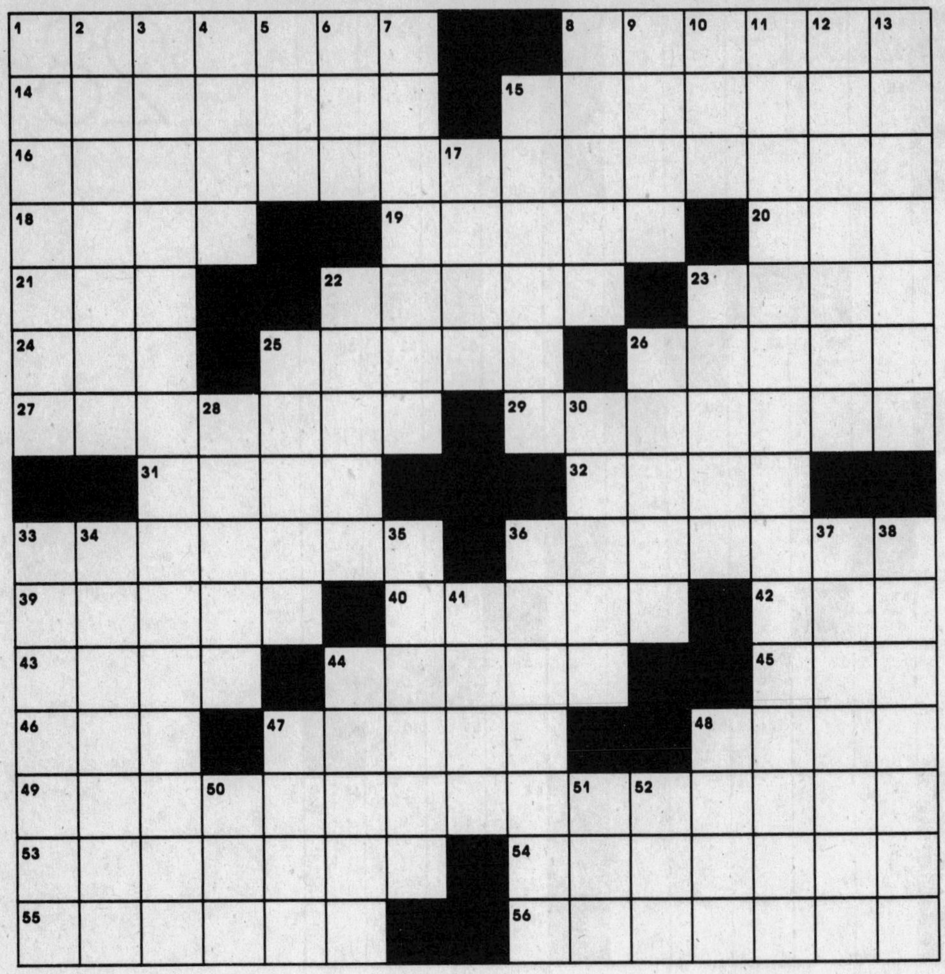

**ACROSS**

1. Part of Dobbin's foot
8. Tampa Bay Rowdies' game
14. Unconfined
15. American landscape painter
16. Canine woes
18. Seine sights
19. Hawks' antitheses
20. Yale or Whitney
21. Fiber cluster
22. Coe or Ovett
23. Barbecue item
24. Philippine native
25. Distinction
26. Ill will
27. Ham's activity
29. Made smooth and lustrous
31. Present
32. Protracted
33. Mail boats
36. Piled up
39. Afterward, at Monte Carlo
40. Fold
42. Gibbon
43. Dutch painter of "The Quack"
44. Aviates
45. Enzyme
46. Outside: Comb. form
47. Famed bag man
48. Monkshood
49. Nectar search
53. Portico
54. Underwrite
55. Lamb products
56. Removes iron oxide

**DOWN**

1. Metallic films
2. Olympian
3. Dormant volcanoes
4. Identifies
5. Assam silkworm
6. Col.'s command
7. In want
8. Morley of "60 Minutes"
9. Switch positions
10. Golfer Peete
11. Crawling critics
12. Part of the French motto
13. Moved a house
15. Romeo and Juliet
17. Alone
22. French Impressionist
23. Gyrates
25. Uredo
26. A weasel
28. Levee worker
30. Egyptian geishas
33. Board for Benton
34. Parisian gangsters
35. Item to throw in
36. Made effervescent
37. Most facile
38. Clothes
41. Wooden strip
44. Levantine ketches
47. Do in
48. ____ Ben Adhem
50. Monk's title
51. "Paris ____," Brady book
52. Drive in N.Y.C.

# 283

**ACROSS**

1. Honolulu tourist attraction
6. Alda vehicle
10. Fictional detective
14. Henry Cabot ___
15. Miss Fitzgerald
16. What disagreeable items often stick in
17. Lifeless
18. Soviet range
19. "Biggest Little City"
20. Merciful
22. Coach
24. Basketball defense
26. Deep pink
27. Pass
30. Village
32. Salad ingredient
33. Venture
35. Levant or Wilde
39. Final: Abbr.
40. Acetylsalicylic acid
42. Kimono adjunct
43. Near a part of the innominate bone
45. Tied
46. Home of the Cyclones
47. Barter
49. Garden tool
51. Absorbed with
54. Like a porcupine's quills
56. Townsman
58. Pillage
62. Wither
63. Fogy
65. Part of G.I.
66. Puzzler's lake
67. Harrow's rival
68. Abominable
69. "___ Soul," 1938 Carmichael-Loesser song
70. Allot
71. Part-song singers

**DOWN**

1. Play by Mae West: 1928
2. Whet
3. Barbara or Anthony
4. Herod ___, Judean king
5. Discourages
6. Parts of pecans and cashews
7. Every one
8. Venetian-blind part
9. Bob, e.g.
10. Stints
11. Site of conflict
12. Bisons' locks
13. Preparation
21. Requires
23. Home-run king
25. Makes a great effort
27. Needle case
28. Allay
29. Con
31. Epitaph starter
34. Mimicked
36. Search thoroughly
37. Navigator Tasman
38. Stevens of Met fame
40. Bitter
41. Ink type
44. Dressed
46. ___ zone (deep-sea realm)
48. Chaplet
50. Six outs
51. Be discouraged
52. ___ bouffe
53. Iberian nation
55. Inclined (to)
57. Memo
59. S. African fox
60. Clever or attractive
61. Limited-access social place
64. Morse symbol

# 284

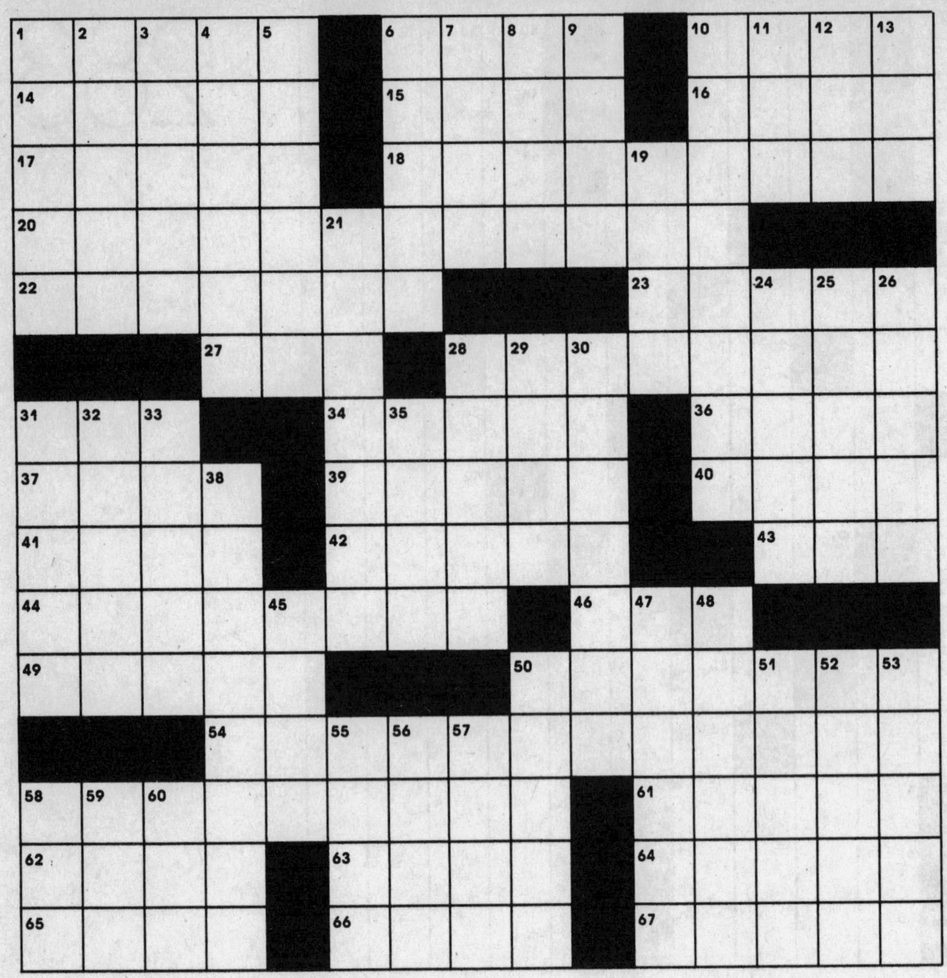

## ACROSS

1. Mythological shield
6. "___ the word!"
10. Tipster
14. Persian
15. "___ True What They Say . . .?"
16. Nimbus
17. U.S. artist-inventor
18. Arms factory?
20. Computer language?
22. ". . . like a ___ in the sky": Carroll
23. Brazilian dance
27. Weller or Gamgee
28. Sad Big Ben?
31. Keeve
34. Two-toed sloths
36. Secular
37. "To ___ and a bone . . .": Kipling
39. Gamut
40. Sicilian hot spot
41. Actress Kirk
42. Assisted
43. Complement to yang
44. Siamese followers?
46. Loc. or op. follower
49. Diaphanous
50. Gear for Steichen and Arbus
54. Yankee bull pen?
58. Circulatory system?
61. Straighten
62. Sesame and peanut extractions
63. Cassowary's cousin
64. Scatter again
65. Harvard undergrounder?
66. Rages
67. They beat deuces

## DOWN

1. Point toward
2. Wear away
3. Lake in Italy
4. Gores
5. Madre or Nevada
6. Indistinct
7. Zip-py org.
8. Bearing
9. Male caribou
10. Docile
11. Gallic affirmative
12. Samovar
13. Make lace
19. Stratagem
21. Japanese warrior
24. Thought-provoking
25. Crêpes from Natasha's kitchen
26. Noted N.A. highway
28. Troops
29. Racing sled
30. Item seen in lots of lots
31. Soapstones
32. Fictional Heep
33. Thrash
35. Brad or spad
38. Fence fixture
45. Lifeless
47. Reveal
48. Job O. Henry had
50. Whale of a constellation?
51. ___ Cain
52. Vex
53. Goulash and ragout
55. Not kosher
56. Robin Cook novel
57. Cultivated
58. His mom gave us Hope
59. Prevaricate
60. Violinist Bull

# 285

**ACROSS**

1. Actor Convy
5. Javelin
10. Not in harmony
14. Song for Sutherland
15. Hagar's wife
16. Laptev Sea feeder
17. Decathlon winner: 1968
19. "____ It Romantic?"
20. Top pitcher
21. Pisa's river
22. Mesopotamian's Urfa
24. Sympathy
25. Interlace
26. Crib adjunct
29. Boring
32. Ever's pal
33. Like crabgrass
35. Madison loc.
36. She might be called "Becky"
37. Tourn. Nicklaus won five times
38. Dispatched
39. Serbian city
40. Designer ____
42. Whenever
43. Certain college members
46. Entertains
48. Love, in Hilo
49. Center the football
50. Atoll sight
52. Tramp's friend in a Disney film
53. Lily, in Lyon
56. Galley features
57. Winner of the 800-meter run: 1980
60. Independent
61. Figure skater Brian
62. Inkling
63. It gets pitched
64. Obligations
65. Runner Decker

**DOWN**

1. An Ali
2. Heiden or Liddell
3. Vex
4. Former chess champ
5. Marathon gold medalist: 1972
6. Pink perennial
7. Old-time actor Lincoln
8. "The ____ of Reason": Paine
9. Winner of eight gold medals in track and field
10. E.T. et al.
11. Star in Berlin: 1936
12. Rutherford and Harding
13. Tat-tat predecessor
18. Follow
23. Chancy cube
24. ____ colada
25. Atlas, e.g.
26. Meaux's river
27. NBC newsman Roger
28. Pole-vault winner: 1968
29. Robes in "The Robe"
30. Kind of pie
31. Bass-baritone Simon
34. "Peter Grimes," e.g.
38. Consommé
40. Decathlon winner: 1960
41. Boxing gold medalist: 1952
44. Cupboard
45. Overly
47. Irish county
49. Socked away
50. Attic
51. Bern's river
52. ____-majesté
53. Aldous Huxley work
54. Journey, to Julius
55. Tarry
58. Before quattro
59. Get-up-and-go

# 286

**ACROSS**

1. Father: Comb. form
6. Adjusts a projector
13. Spreads
14. Linked, in a way
15. Choir parts
16. "Rosemary's Baby" star
18. To study: Fr.
20. Sticky stuff
21. Chinese pagoda
23. Win
24. Code of silence in Sicily
26. Distributor of a kind
28. Copenhagenites
30. Fried-chicken part
31. Undo
32. Metric meas. of length
35. "An' they talks a ____ lovin' . . .": Kipling
36. "We're ____ See the . . ."
38. A people of Mexico
39. She sheep
40. Concert halls
41. Sweetmeat
43. Boa
44. Win a contest for trenchermen
45. Game
48. Declaim
50. Maugham's "Cakes and ____"
51. Nigerian town
52. Shoots toward
54. Buttonwood or sycamore
57. Forster's "A Passage to ____"
60. In a contiguous line
61. Vacuum tube
62. Liberated
63. "The Apostles" composer

**DOWN**

1. Blue grass
2. Any whatever
3. Private conversation
4. Origin
5. Publishers
6. Acquaintance, perhaps
7. Whom FitzGerald translated
8. Export-contract abbr.
9. Merkel of movies
10. NCO's
11. Diamond muff
12. Mormon leader: 1862–1941
14. Moslem prince
17. New Deal org.
19. Quotidian
21. Postpone
22. Dart's big brother
24. Playground game
25. Pawns or knights
27. Part of Hawaii's motto
29. Fitting
32. Cutthroat
33. African village
34. Dull finish
37. ____-de-lance
38. Skip a class
40. Autumn mo.
42. Mere; slight
43. Stadium section
45. Lacuna
46. Straightedge
47. Foolish
49. "Pluck ____ rose . . .": Shak.
52. Exempt
53. Indigo
55. Kin of et al.
56. Chinese measure
58. Song heroine
59. Gas: Comb form

# 287

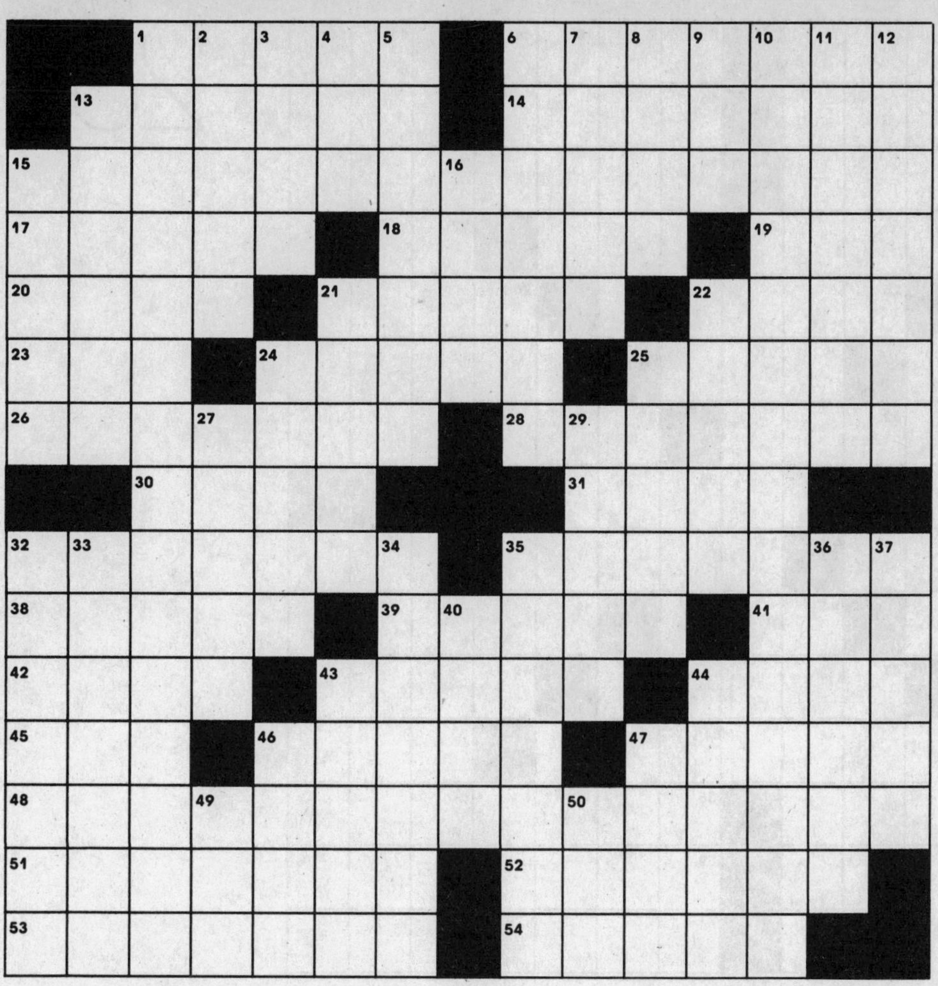

**ACROSS**

1. Greek letter
6. Went by
13. Little innocent
14. Drain access
15. Holmes memoir
17. Error generator
18. Type of protest
19. "___ ramblin' wreck . . ."
20. Spot
21. Finch
22. British weapon
23. Suffix with Adam or Eden
24. Dicer's bad throw
25. Position
26. Tenements
28. Accounts
30. Persephone
31. Sly
32. Virgin or Sandwich
35. Sets the pool balls again
38. An anagram for slate
39. "Over ___," W.W. I song
41. Bark
42. Wagnerian goddess
43. Lawn essential
44. Beige
45. Jewish teacher
46. Part of Hispaniola
47. Mohammedanism
48. Holmes story
51. Like a valid defense
52. This may be lame
53. Unceasing
54. Barbecue

**DOWN**

1. Holmes adventure
2. Built like a fullback
3. Coloratura Mills
4. Cask
5. Humblers
6. More vapid
7. Ex-Asian coin made of silver wire
8. Soon
9. Deg. for a Platonist
10. Holmes adventure, with "The"
11. Component
12. Requires
13. "As ___ as unsunn'd snow": Shak.
15. Freud's "The Ego and ___"
16. Lucre in Livorno
21. Particle
22. Roman robe
24. Darrs
25. Steeple
27. Cute marsupial
29. Some crockery
32. Battologize
33. Crusader's adversary
34. Conflicts
35. Domicile occupant
36. Kin of judo
37. Covered with foam
40. The heart, to Tut
43. British prisons
44. Ebb and flow
46. Goddess of youth
47. Orejon, e.g.
49. ___ soda
50. Outer: Prefix

# 288

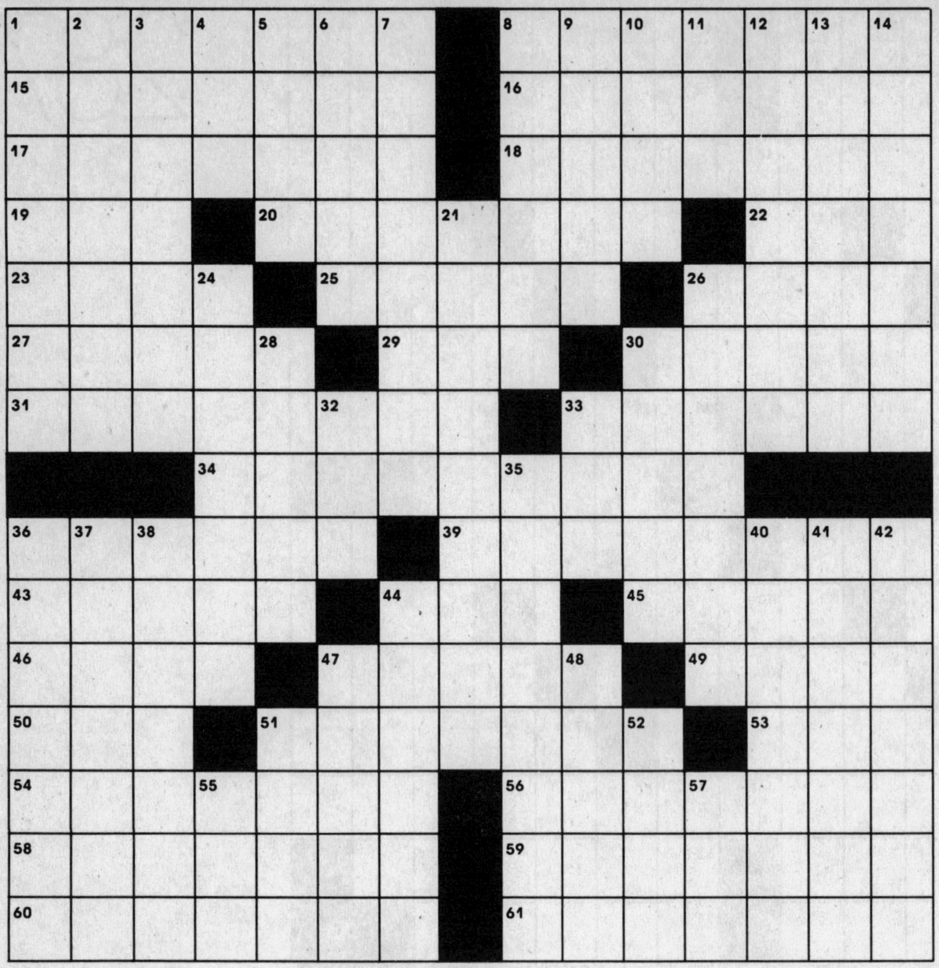

**ACROSS**

1. Peace pipe
8. Use the voice
15. Eternal
16. Home of Transylvanians
17. Italian mayor
18. Absconders
19. H.S. subject
20. Beginning of a toast
22. Where a wrestler works
23. Prevarications
25. Hoarfrosts
26. Rich source
27. ___ Soleil (Louis XIV)
29. Natalie's father
30. Hermit
31. Person from Nineveh
33. Grade-school period
34. Brazilian dance
36. Part of AWOL
39. Himalayan people
43. Rot
44. Good sense
45. Provide an embankment
46. Talk-show host Thicke
47. Ill-mannered ones
49. Palm type
50. Target for Trevino
51. Grueling test
53. Hied
54. Chains
56. White ant
58. Hillary's conquest
59. Satan, e.g.
60. Lowers an appraisal
61. Cassandra was one

**DOWN**

1. Brightest star in Auriga
2. Miseries
3. Books for Heep
4. Rubber tree
5. Interlock
6. Organic compound
7. Catherines I and II
8. Positioned in advance
9. Actors Jack and Tim
10. "Typee" sequel
11. Siesta
12. A buttercup
13. Harangues
14. Spring festivals
21. A flowing forth
24. Commodities item on Wall St.
26. Settles
28. Sarcasm of a sort
30. Pry
32. Adherent
33. "Auld ___ Morris," Burns poem
35. Fertilizer ingredients
36. Conformed
37. Suppose
38. Less abundant
40. Midas's fatal flaw
41. Nullifies
42. Pitting devices
44. Defeats
47. Scot's scholarship
48. Act component
51. Yard parts
52. Famous Russian-born artist-designer
55. Mr. in Helsinki
57. Commune in czarist Russian

# 289

**ACROSS**

1. Formally opens
10. Raised rapidly
15. Reduction
16. Book by Carole Klein
17. Count in "The Marble Faun"
18. "Cut the comedy!"
19. Sandy's single
20. What a ques. demands
21. Prevailing condition
23. Concerned with
24. Maintain
25. Word with talk or tennis
28. Dubs
30. Draft org.
33. An opposite of down
35. Strict stickler
37. Cattle calls
38. Town NE of Venice
40. First president of Angola
41. Diplomat's concern
43. U.S. Vice President: 1845–49
45. Trio joiner
46. 5.619 bushels, in Egypt
48. Evans and Robertson
49. Astaire or Waring
50. ". . . ____ in the daytime": Psalms
52. Blind alley
55. Pleasure, in Paris
56. Apt suffix for visual
59. Whey
60. Piano soundboard, e.g.
63. In harmony
64. Crossword solver's asset
65. Jampan
66. Skid-row denizens

**DOWN**

1. Tzara's art cult
2. Black
3. "The Lay of Havelok the ____"
4. Give ____ whirl
5. Petroleum ingredients
6. Catkin
7. Middle flipper of a lobster's tail
8. Photo order
9. Reagan's budget director
10. Most spirited
11. ". . . ____ unto my feet": Psalms
12. Schneider or Bawden
13. Type of factor or rule
14. Rose or Rozelle
22. Eyed wickedly
23. "____ my yellow basket"
25. Fla. port
26. Incipient oak
27. Coop group
29. Go ____ a minute
30. Fishhook fastening
31. Bristles
32. Lee's icy opposite
34. Ecuadorian dollars
36. Buhlwork
39. Moved unsteadily
42. Shell's team
44. Endocrine gland
47. Calif. resort
49. Part of the biota
51. Leroy Brown's creator
52. "The corn ____ high . . ."
53. Limit
54. Urge on
56. Ending for palm or graph
57. Jazzman Sims
58. Bald eagles' kin
61. Gelderland city
62. When many meet for lunch

# 290

**ACROSS**

1. ___ Simbel, Egypt
4. Bluish green
8. Eponym's contribution
12. Oodles
14. Abstain from
15. One-eyed god
16. Verb that reverses time
17. Almighty
19. Welch
21. Famed Mormon family
22. Immature
25. Type of jet engine
26. Schoolroom missile
28. Mercer song: 1944
31. "___ Off to Larry," 1961 Del Shannon hit
32. Come to terms
34. Tears, to Tennyson
36. Yoko ___
37. Opera's Varnay et al.
39. Textile screw pine
40. ___-de-vie
41. Morsels
42. Pianist Gilels
43. Swedish port
45. Any Jesuit, e.g.
48. Full of: Suffix
49. Early Christian theologian
50. Cannonballs
54. Noted English inventor: 1847–1908
57. The antis
60. Sport, to a guru
61. Flanges
62. "The ___," Lustbader novel
63. They may be split or tight
64. Faulkner man
65. "Cogito, ___ sum"
66. Erhard prog.

**DOWN**

1. Radio-tube stabilizer
2. Safari blind
3. Like Kilroy, once
4. Male clowder member
5. Raptor at sea
6. World Bank word
7. Askew
8. ". . . ditties of ___": Keats
9. Yemeni port
10. Obey
11. Tolkien creatures
13. Feats
14. Thin layers of rocks
18. "O tempora! ___!"
20. Composer Donald ___
23. ___ National Park, Okla.
24. Great pupil of Titian
26. Old woman's abode
27. Site of Iloilo
29. Hard
30. ___ badge
33. Perron part
35. Ridge
37. Demeans
38. Put out of action
42. Glenn Miller vocalist
44. Knobbed
46. Tropical vine
47. Per. from July 1, 1957 to Dec. 31, 1958
50. Dry, cold wind
51. Neat as ___
52. Tachometer rdgs.
53. The big house
55. Auto pioneer
56. Political cartoonist
58. Participial ending
59. Juan's eye

# 291

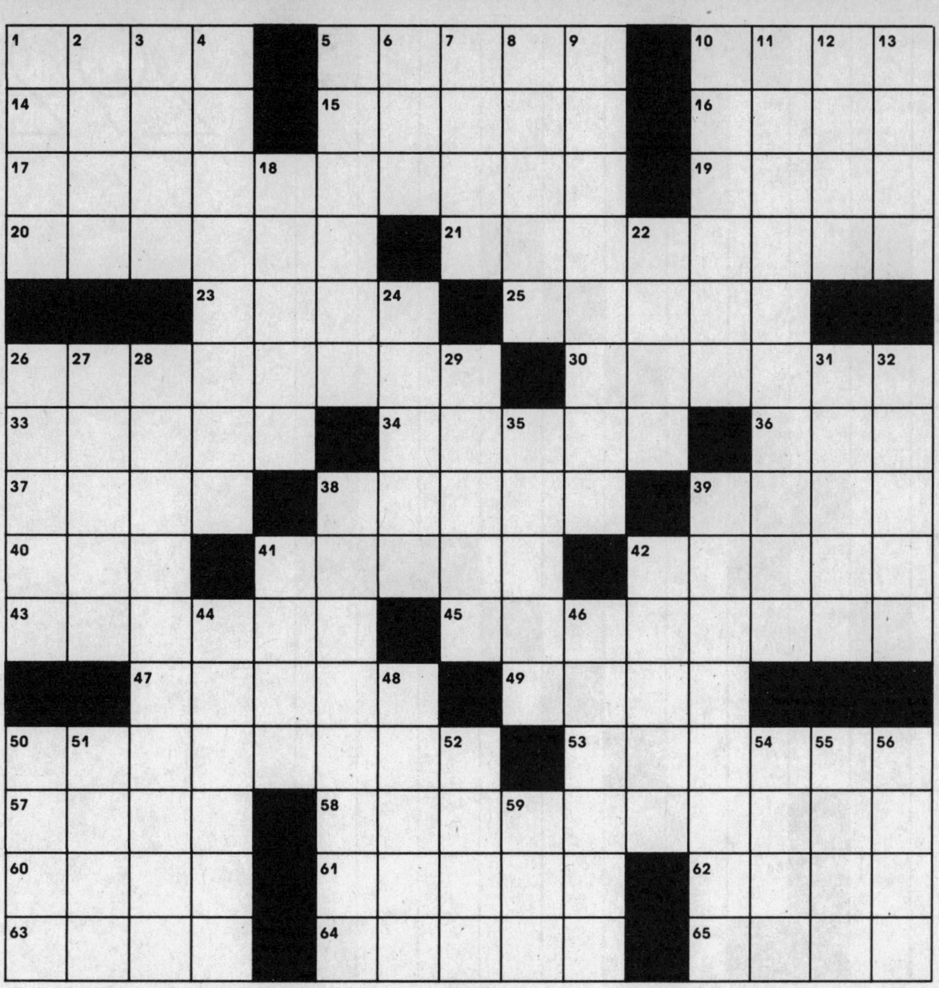

**ACROSS**

1. Napoleonic victory site in 1806
5. Kind of stitch
10. Buy ____ in a poke
14. Actor Guinness
15. A "manship"
16. Biotite
17. Relish
19. Scored on a serve
20. Igloo dweller
21. Moorish palaces
23. Campus bldg.
25. Excellent!
26. Besmirched, in a way
30. Kind of gravy
33. Ridge; crest
34. Preferable
36. Part of U.S.S.R.
37. Social asset
38. Capitol go-fers
39. Iso-
40. Have
41. Sky Whale
42. Jubilate
43. Decampment
45. Long, slender cigar
47. Belief
49. Multiflora
50. ____ with (take liberties)
53. Consolidated
57. Show-biz award
58. Circus in London
60. Merchandise
61. Felt pity for
62. River to The Wash
63. Tense
64. Downtown signs
65. Donna or Rex

**DOWN**

1. Play tricks on
2. New Havenites
3. Smooch
4. Chance
5. A country's flag
6. Cuckoo
7. Composer Bartók
8. Pacifies
9. Gastronomes
10. Surprised
11. Roguish
12. Champagne bucket
13. Runs about
18. Love, in Livorno
22. Rich Little, e.g.
24. ____-arms
26. ____ grace (clement edict)
27. Afghan
28. Alfresco enjoyment
29. Unearth
31. "____ Never Know," 1943 song
32. Hit musical
35. Actor Romero
38. Duncan role
39. Outside
41. Julia Child, e.g.
42. Relaxed
44. Rapacious
46. Wanderers
48. Thaw
50. Relocation
51. Snoozing
52. Mother of lynx
54. Hard, brittle gelatin
55. Different
56. Used henna
59. 100 yrs.

# 292

**ACROSS**

1. Ankara garment
7. Flat-bottomed boat
12. Druggist's jar
14. Column
16. Metallic element
17. Loosen, as a corset
18. An anagram for rates
19. Recumbent
21. Damone
22. An order to a helmsman
23. Pelisse
24. Exclusive
25. Hesitant sounds
26. Safe
27. Caustic
28. Chinese idol
29. Cache
31. Full-grown
33. Questionable
34. Farm-association member
36. Short distance
37. Chilean seaport
38. Used naphtha
40. Dance step
43. Ultramodern Spanish artist
44. Integrity
45. Plant of the mint family
46. Boston or Kenilworth follower
47. Author of "Wonderland"
48. Inventor of etching
49. To wit
51. Writer's concern
53. Frozen, in Fontainebleau
54. Afternoon function
55. Secures, as a vessel
56. Absorbent

**DOWN**

1. Hazan
2. Church areas
3. What some soubrettes do
4. Word with clock or bomb
5. Mil. address
6. Baffle
7. Fungus that smolders when lit
8. Cows, to Cowper
9. Unsound
10. Added vanilla, perhaps
11. Skill
12. Canadian peninsula
13. Region in Austria
15. Withdraw
20. Nose-bag contents
23. Sudra, for one
24. Discarded metal
26. Europe's longest river
27. Had the flu
28. Small gray bird
30. ___ gum, used in varnishes
31. Airport people
32. He has a cheesy job
34. Las Vegas pastime
35. Cheer
36. Flounders
39. Awkward
40. K.P. activity
41. Office
42. Twilled cloth
44. Grant's successor
45. Suffragette Anthony
47. Cassini
48. Pedestal section
50. Old French coin
52. Gab

# 293

**ACROSS**

1. Vanished creatures
6. Cries of triumph
10. Ratchet wheel part
14. Ship that carried Miss Liberty
15. Calcium oxide
16. A Met score
17. Exclusive
18. Reverse curve
19. Bank (on)
20. Sophie Tucker's theme song
23. Suffix with concert
24. Hired assassin
25. Steer clear of
28. Kind of cross
30. Falsify
34. Queen seduced by a cuckoo
35. Chichi
37. Lows
38. Sheikdom dweller
39. ____-eaters: "Odyssey" characters
41. English royal house
42. Hang laxly
43. Glitter on a TV screen
44. Homager's cousin
45. Succeeded
48. Dundee denial
49. Stingy
50. Iroquoians
52. Joker
54. Norton-Handy song: 1913
61. Superman, to Lois Lane
62. Alpaca or vicuna
63. Joyous cry of a card holder
64. Napoli's Castel Sant'____
65. ____ fixe
66. Bony predecessor of path
67. Muscat is its capital
68. Heroine of a d'Erlanger opera
69. Rose's seamier side

**DOWN**

1. Matrices
2. Plinth
3. Judge
4. Caldwell-Kern song: 1923
5. He wrote "Lives of the Hunted"
6. Myriad
7. Cahn-Styne musical comedy: 1947
8. Afghan nobleman
9. Vacillate
10. The Gershwins' last musical comedy: 1933
11. Bailiwick
12. Cunning
13. Ballads
21. Disastrous
22. Lehar work
25. Fissile rock
26. Long-billed bird
27. Asian range
29. In a line
31. Kind of step
32. John Ridd's girl
33. Glacial ridge
36. City on the Colorado
40. Ejects
46. Palindrome in a palindrome
47. Blockhead
51. Verse form
53. Cloister's director
54. Aaron Burr's daughter
55. Position of power
56. Writer Calderon
57. ____ Scilly
58. Biblical preposition
59. Elbe feeder
60. Quickly

# 294

**ACROSS**

1. Check
5. Victor at Chickamauga Creek: 1863
10. Film producer Hunter
14. Sound
15. Measuring instrument
16. Imposing
17. Rink equipment
18. One of the Pointer Sisters
19. Festivity
20. Putrescine, e.g.
22. Fanatic
24. Basic
26. Con man, at times
29. Jan Hus, to some: 1412
33. Exultant
34. Balsam
35. Author Rölvaag
36. "Breaking Away" character
37. Russian river
38. Engraver's tool
40. Hoosier humorist
41. Get-up
42. Miniaturized tree
43. Caromed
46. Teachers' college course
47. Bargain
49. Old trail or territory
52. Growing in clusters
56. Fur for Richard II's robes
57. Mennonite sect
59. Humor
60. Saladin's prize in 1187
61. "Man delights ___": Hamlet
62. Biblical scribe
63. Sordor
64. Tire mark
65. Consider

**DOWN**

1. Packet, for one
2. Savoir-faire
3. Vegetable oil spread
4. Diffuse through
5. Cooked meat in a covered pan
6. Long, narrow carpet
7. Foreign
8. Procure
9. Cattleman
10. Fete
11. Menilite, e.g.
12. Fodder fermenter
13. Vamoose
21. Dahlia's kin
23. Aural organ
25. Meager
26. Exclude
27. Suppress in speech
28. Hardens with heat
30. Trunk ___
31. A tale of Troy
32. Mont ___, Alpine pass
34. Murk
37. Queen of Carthage
38. Fencer's pass
39. Not purfled
41. Widespread
42. Aground
44. "Odalisque" painter
45. King of beasts
46. Corruptive atmosphere
48. Hackneyed
49. Face shape
50. Heavy sea
51. Gael's land
53. Mushy ground
54. Vexed
55. Kind of cheese
58. Forest humus

# 295

## ACROSS

1. "Nighthawks" artist
7. "Homage to the Square" artist
13. Hold a meeting
14. Channel to the ocean
16. Etnas
17. Urn
18. Mad. Ave. products
19. Fictitious defendant
20. Literary memorabilia
21. ____-Saud
22. TV's "Man from U.N.C.L.E."
24. ____ lazuli
26. Handout
27. Excalibur, e.g.
29. Sma'
30. Entertainer from N.C.
31. Swaddle
33. Sometime role of 25 Down
35. "Distressed Poet" artist
37. Mobile homes
41. Informal wear
46. Former Dodger pitcher
47. C.I.A. predecessor
49. British weight unit
50. Capra's "____ Wonderful Life"
51. Assigned share
53. Little or Frye
54. Smidgen
55. Chignon
56. Winslow Homer's "____ Cay"
58. Greek letter
59. Type of barometer
61. Sandy
63. Moon-shaped ornament
64. Certain promises
65. "Verbum" artist
66. "Poseurs" artist

## DOWN

1. Barn dance
2. "____ Boat to China"
3. Cpl.'s inferior
4. Equal
5. Sign up
6. Shut again
7. Aggressive one
8. Cants
9. U. east of Ole Miss.
10. Monogram of Anna Christie's creator
11. Trattoria offering
12. Mews
13. Dance step
15. Composer Chausson
23. Hockey great
25. "The Blue Room" artist
26. Hoover or Norris
28. Arlene and Roald
30. Comic Mort's family
32. "Ulalume" poet
34. Wall St. listings
36. Topped ball on a diamond
37. Like some rites
38. Court attendants
39. Novelized family at Steventon
40. Town in Nigeria
42. Alma-____, Russian city
43. Director of "Apocalypse Now"
44. Israeli parliament
45. Word on a dollar bill
48. Reins
51. Very
52. Enveloping glows
55. The two
57. Tanzania's Mount ____
60. Kind of room
62. A connective

# 296

**ACROSS**

1. Owner of a multi-colored coat
7. Spasmodic, as a muscle
13. Old French dance
14. Outer ear
16. Another dance
17. Changeable; variable
18. Debussy's sea
19. Rainbow, e.g.
20. French possessive
21. Except
22. Work of Snorri Sturluson
24. Driers for hops
26. They returned in a Lucas film
27. Makes turbid
29. Fourth Arabic letter
30. Device for preparing apples
31. Composed
33. Snarl
35. Plucked forcibly
37. About to occur
41. ". . . the ___ of gold": Keats
46. High times
47. Unite
49. Buy a round
50. Cubitus
51. Laughs, in Lille
53. Colonist with loyalty to royalty
54. Trumpery
55. Something to step on
56. Baden-Baden, e.g.
58. Zilch
59. Light cotton fabric
61. Boss, in Bari
63. Ireland's northernmost county
64. Bade
65. Dressing table
66. Proscenium drape

**DOWN**

1. Unidentified female
2. Carried to excess
3. Mayday relative
4. Cartoonist Hulme
5. Wing: Comb. form
6. "With-it" guy of the 40's
7. Anchor-hoisting machines
8. Certain flies
9. Diamonds, in Pedro's deck
10. Annual court tourn.
11. Growler
12. French diplomat, poet, dramatist: 1868–1955
13. TV's Pyle et al.
15. Complete
23. SEC member
25. A basic need
26. Hairstylist-producer Peters
28. British guns
30. Younger son or brother
32. Early pome picker
34. Dutch painter Gerard ___ Borch
36. Sans sagacity
37. Accustomed
38. Cocktail with a bang
39. Where Custer last stood
40. Actress Balin
42. Cunning or finesse
43. "Fidelio" heroine
44. NASA explorer of Mars
45. Fashioned
48. Caligula was one
51. Charged
52. Consolation for Mark Roth
55. Lerner-Loewe musical
57. Skink
60. Hands
62. Lab. work

# 297

## ACROSS

1. Songbird
8. Cupboard
15. Suppose
16. Mother-of-pearl source
17. Souvenir
18. Sea nymphs
19. A goal of NOW
20. Like the nose
22. ____ shibah (mourn in Israel)
23. An S.S.R.
25. Donna and Walter
26. Recess
27. Yearns
29. Powerful lobby in D.C.
30. Debussy opus
31. It's usually read monthly
33. One touch of Venus?
34. His motto is "To alms!"
36. Aver
39. Slaves to fashion
43. Coolers for firebugs et al.
44. About three times a diam.
45. Establish
46. Axes
47. Cornered
49. Pro ____
50. Season on the Seine
51. Made a dull sound
53. Crag
54. Joggers
56. Eye, e.g.
58. Trifling sum
59. Satellite, e.g.
60. Alternates
61. Plants anew

## DOWN

1. Interval between two related phenomena
2. "Beautiful" place
3. Broadway Joe's family
4. Mature
5. Card-game cries
6. Diarize
7. Took up again
8. Where Banff is
9. Fosters a felony
10. Denude
11. O'Neill play
12. Harmful
13. Dandelions' kin
14. Canopies
21. Scared stiff
24. Some seamstresses
26. Discoverer of the St. Lawrence
28. Haruspices
30. Puts down
32. Cause of blasphemy?
33. Varlet
35. Liked very much
36. Rises
37. Height
38. Indefinitely
40. Law
41. What a flautist in a limerick did
42. Lenient ones
44. Pie parts
47. Cast
48. Farm-implement pioneer
51. Tissue layer
52. Flounders
55. Monogram of a famed Fabian
57. Ligature

# 298

**ACROSS**

1. Pedestal part
5. Bits
10. Med. subject
14. Filipe or Jesus of baseball
15. Done for
16. Fictional Dick
17. Was crazy about
20. Climb
21. Knowledgeable
22. Pond-scum component
25. Surly, cowardly person
26. Life, according to a song
34. Jazz style
35. Viscount's superior
36. Ballet dancer Eglevsky
37. On the blue
39. Warm thoroughly
42. Native of Brno
43. Squiggles
45. Variety
47. Bengal follower
48. Shipshape
52. ___ Cruces, N.M.
53. A daughter of Phoebe
54. Sets in firmly
59. Distressed
63. "Do I ___?" (Prufrock query)
66. Parking-lot sign
67. Canary's cousin
68. Pilaf ingredient
69. Intends
70. W. German seaport
71. Large amount

**DOWN**

1. Grackles
2. A Waugh
3. Lérida lady
4. Ban
5. Alias: Abbr.
6. Thrash
7. Girasol
8. "Beer-hall putsch" site
9. Colossus of Rhodes, e.g.
10. A son of Venus
11. Kind of star
12. Incite
13. Phoenician seaport
18. Party favorite
19. Calif. missionary Junípero: 1713–84
23. Butter
24. Hair style
26. Manual computers
27. Deck hands' superior
28. "Wozzeck" is one
29. Buckle
30. Hosp. workers
31. Ran in neutral
32. Cancel
33. Cleave
38. Dom, e.g.
40. Tarnish
41. Shoe follower
44. Slapping sound
46. Add
49. Woolly
50. Prize
51. Cowboys, at times
54. Surmise
55. Ankle-length coat
56. Shrub used for hedges
57. ___ on (admits)
58. Chalcedony
60. Spanker, e.g.
61. "___ homo"
62. Muscle
64. Standoff
65. Actress Blyth

# 299

**ACROSS**

1. Wilson of baseball fame
5. National park in Alberta
10. Gabon's Bongo
14. "How now! ____?": Hamlet
15. Valence valediction
16. He painted "The Queen's Party"
17. Samovars
18. Symbol of womanly beauty
19. Red 1 and Blue 5
20. ____ sequitur
21. Hotfoot it
23. Brace
25. Tic-tac-toe winner
26. Jazz singer Simone
27. Mason's conical weight
32. Aristocratic
34. Yeas, in a way
35. Purpose
36. According to
37. Gallants
40. Novel by Kathleen Coyle
41. Angelus, e.g.
43. ____-daisy!
44. Like a sieve
46. Verbal violation
48. Frascati or Orvieto
49. Nitrous oxide, e.g.
50. Harmful
53. Famed comedienne
58. D.C. agcy.
59. Mohammed, for one
60. One of the Hours
61. Shuttlecock
62. Cartoonist Lazarus
63. Forty follower
64. Angered
65. Nabors TV role
66. Malibu museum
67. Moist

**DOWN**

1. Stay with
2. Directional signal
3. Saxophonist Adderley
4. Chess pcs.
5. Grand ____, near Great Abaco
6. Victor Hugo's wife
7. "And, will you, ____ you . . .": Shak.
8. Means of support
9. Amusement-park attraction
10. Some tasks
11. Author Angelou
12. Composer Wilder
13. Bell the cat
21. Rollers for high rollers
22. Billing time: Abbr.
24. ____ vous plaît
27. Light refractor
28. Brightly colored parrot
29. Highly energetic person
30. Migratory worker of the 30's
31. Quail quantity
32. Seizes
33. Ersatz butter
34. Whelps
38. Traitor
39. Pitchman's accomplice
42. Unlike a scribble
45. Unified
47. Lone Eagle's monogram
48. ____ Giscard d'Estàing
50. He painted "The Fife Player"
51. "____ my snickersnee!": Gilbert
52. Tea container
53. Light shedder
54. Nobel chemist in '34
55. Telephone
56. Naval battle site: 1813
57. Bowed
61. Command

# 300

**ACROSS**

1. Loud noises
5. Out front
10. Launching sites
14. "Step ___!"
15. Amazon feeder
16. One bad way to run
17. Trophies
20. Like a firearm
21. Region of ancient Greece
22. Part of Mao's name
23. Burns poem
24. Freight-car type
27. "When I was ___ . . ."
28. Tillie the Toiler's boyfriend
31. Kind of ink
32. R.b.i., e.g.
33. Roman-fleuve
34. Cups
37. Viet ___
38. Guthrie the younger
39. Exodus land
40. Unclose, to Keats
41. ___-dieu
42. "On a clear day you ___ . . ."
43. "Educating ___," 1983 film
44. ___ loss
45. Coney Island feature
47. Scolder's action
52. Bowls
54. Sarah ___ Jewett
55. Wed
56. Hurdy-gurdy
57. String, in a way
58. Solitaire stock
59. Conductor Peter ___

**DOWN**

1. Type of tube
2. Big Dipper part
3. Minute: Comb. form
4. Scary or wondrous
5. He may get the blues
6. Now's partner
7. Mild expletive
8. Gunrunning unit
9. Rule the roost
10. Kind of rice
11. Mine, in Marseille
12. Portuguese lady
13. High "measure"
18. Open and shut
19. "___ Cassius has a lean . . ."
23. Southwestern aspen
24. Great Lakes food fish (we kid you not)
25. "___ of Old Smokey"
26. ". . . more an antique Roman than ___": Shak.
27. Start of a Dickens title
28. ___ Thanksgiving Day Parade (N.Y.C. event)
29. Awestruck
30. Brahman is one
32. Mideast land
33. John Hancock
35. Truffle
36. Ropes for vaqueros
41. ___ Rivera, Calif.
42. Sway sharply
43. Assigned X or PG, e.g.
45. Yawn maker
46. Lab heater
47. Recipe word
48. This, to Pedro
49. Frankenstein's aide in films
50. Western org.
51. Fat, in France
52. Pipe material, for short
53. Gene stuff: Abbr.

1

```
RAPS#HERA##MEND
ERIC#ODIST#OVER
INTHENICKOFTIME
DECORATE#LIELOW
##HORNE#SELL###
STENO#DEPRESSOR
MODERN#LEAD#LAE
IGOR#ALIEN#BITE
TAU#PROD#TBONES
ESTUARIES#EAGRE
###SPAN#TARTS##
SOWHAT#LASTSTOP
THEELEVENTHHOUR
ONER#DANCE#ENDO
WOKS##STER#DEEP
```

2

```
STAR#ELIS#LASSO
KENO#LOCO#OREAD
ACTV#ABEL#GRADE
THEEMPERORJONES
ESDRAS##SHAG###
####LETA#IMAGES
CARPE#ANON#NODE
ABIE#TRIPE#CONE
SEND#ROMA#SEDAN
HEGIRA#ALAI####
###CEST##STAMPS
ATOUCHOFTHEPOET
SHARE#REAM#AREA
CERED#TAPA#CELL
HESSE#STEN#ESSE
```

3

```
SOCK#SCOFF#FRAU
HULA#LAVAL#LOOS
ATOP#ELEVATIONS
GROUNDFROMUNDER
SETTO###REFT###
####ODDS##FLASH
BATONROUGE#OTTO
ATIP#ARMOR#CLIO
SEEP#GRASSSKIRT
HEROD##CHET####
###RIIS###OSAKA
FEETONTHEGROUND
INDUSTRIAL#AREA
STAN#RINSE#PEEP
HOME#OATEN#SILT
```

4

```
#CETERA#ACROSS#
COMICAL#DIARIES
ADULATE#ESSENCE
SIL#DEHISCE#COP
ACAD##ONTO#TENT
LITE#MUSE#GARDE
SLEEKEST#PALEST
###POWERDIVE###
ALDERS#URGENTLY
REESE#ACES#TRIO
LACT#ALTA##SIGN
ITE#PLASMAS#BAD
SHINIER#ELOCUTE
SEVENAM#RELATER
#REDANS#SEEPED#
```

5

```
HAIL#RUTH#ADLER
ULNA#OSEE#MIAMI
MEAD#BESTWISHES
INCISORS#ATERRE
DECEITS#THIS###
##USN##ARIETTA#
MURIEL#MANSARDS
ORAN#ADAME#BART
ENTWINES#SELMAS
#SEANCES##DIP##
###ITEM#ENISLED
ELATER#ANATHEMA
ROBINSEGGS#ISER
ICONS#GALA#NOSE
SINGE#OREL#GNAR
```

6

```
OFF##KISS#ALLOT
PLUS#ERAT#GOOSE
TONI#NOVA#ETHAN
EUGENONEGIN#EKE
DRIGO##SEND#NAT
###FLEA##SARG##
BEDRAGGLE#SIREN
ATOI#GRIDS#GIRO
HONED#OVERTONES
##CDIV##NOEL###
CHA#MOLE##REVES
HER#WILLIAMTELL
ENLAI#ADDS#TRAY
SNORT#MELT#OSTE
TASKS#AREA##EER
```

7

```
#DAG##BEAM#MIST
RUML#HELGA#ITTO
ARIA#AROAR#NEAR
HORSEMEN#TREATY
###STET#VIII###
COMICS#WINGSPAN
IRISH#MAGI#HILO
DASH#SOLOS#ALIT
ELSA#PIER#PLACE
REALTORS#PUFFED
###FINE#SIZE###
INAFOG#UNCOMMON
OAHU#ECLAT#PANE
UNAL#REARS#TRUE
SAHL#SYNE##YES#
```

8

```
LIZ#TOR#USE#TBS
IRA#OSE#FOXTROT
CII#PIC#ONEHAND
ISR#REAL##TONY#
THECARPENTERS##
###HIS#NEAR#LOW
ABIES#BIEN#SAXE
HANSELANDGRETEL
ABUT#ORGY#UPEND
BEN#CARR#AMI###
##DONNYANDMARIE
#WACO##DIVA#ALL
BATHTUB#ZIG#JIM
ONESELF#ACE#AKA
XED#SOS#MED#HEN
```

9

```
HASH#FEATS#FLAP
ALEE#ONSET#AONE
CORNHUSKERSTATE
KEENER###ENAMEL
###ARTS#REEL###
BAT#BEL#ETA#CGS
AREA#EARL#KULAK
CENTENNIALSTATE
KNOLL#TOTI#EPEÉ
SAN#EWE#EGG#SST
###AVID#SHUN###
SORREL###TAILOR
THEINLANDEMPIRE
AIDS#ONION#PEAT
ROSE#WILTS#YULE
```

10

```
#SPANKS#TABLES#
ANEMONE#IDEATES
BARONET#MUNDANE
OPS#EATABLE#MAN
UPON#DEBUT#PITO
TENON#ELK#DONOR
#RATEL#ETCETERA
###IVAN#URAL###
CROCUSES#ELUDE#
HERES#ALB#SCIRE
EDDS#STARS#KARA
ODE#CONGEAL#MAS
PERCALE#ABALONE
SALUTES#SECONDS
#NYLONS#TREADS#
```

## 11

WASPS MICA CARE
ABELE ICON ELAN
DEPARTMENTALIZE
ELATERIDS BESOM
RANA PASTRY
SPA END CAST
PITA SEVER ISIS
ONES CLARA AONE
TEDS ETTES LUTE
ANNA SIP VON
VARIED TARE
ANILE SIBILANCE
DIVERSIFICATION
STER ULNA CERRO
OARS ELIS EDSEL

## 12

PACA SCAMP SEAT
AMAN ERROR ARNO
NAST NATTE CITY
THEPONYEXPRESS
ERI YEA
LAPSE ABE AMASS
AVOTRE ENTREPOT
BENJ CARGO NATE
ONTOLOGY RATITE
RAISE OLD COLON
ETA RAT
THEPANAMACANAL
OATH IMAGO ASIA
ELAM MILER PALM
SOHO ARLEN ANTA

## 13

STOMAL PSHAW
SHAPIRO ELOPES
TAKESFORTYWINKS
ONERS SAILS TEM
ITSA JETTY SOTO
CET AUNTS SHUCK
ROUNDEL TOTHE
TWODECKER
TESTA SONATAS
HALER SNAIL BPS
ISAR SHALT MILO
NIN AWAKE SOLAR
GETSSOMESHUTEYE
RETIRE COLONEL
DEANS ENURED

## 14

ASTO GAMP THAW
SHELF OKIE RAGE
TAPIR BILLSIKES
ILIVE SNOOP EST
REDEEM TIC
RSTU MELODIC
COLT ANTA EPOCH
AVOWS AIR SPREE
REDIP RASP EAST
PRESLEY HERR
TAT RIFLED
QED SCALE LILLE
URIAHHEEP LEAVE
ISNO ERNE ELMER
PEEK DOZE DARE

## 15

RELAX PEN DEREK
ABOVE ALE EMOTE
SEVEN RASPBERRY
ENERO ATTS RYES
NOBILITY
RONS FLOE SCRAM
APIN FEND ALOHA
NEVADA FROMES
CREPE ASEA TEAK
HANDS MOMS HODS
RIVULETS
ESTA ALAR KNAVE
DAUGHTERS AESIR
ARBOR TIO LATER
MIENS SAN DROSS

## 16

ASA AROMA PLOW
CALM RURAL RAVE
EFFACEMENT OMAR
DEACON SHAMBLE
ABALL ODOR
ARROW LAS STERN
LEE ENACTS EQUI
IGO BANQUET USN
BARB BOUCLE ISO
INGOT SEC XENON
AGAL ROMAN
DINGBAT INJURE
ANIL THINKSOVER
DOZE CANOE YELL
ONES HINDS AYE

## 17

GARB OLDE DAMP
ROUE TRAIN REAR
INNS HAYES ARLO
PETERANDTHEWOLF
TONTO REA
BROWSE WEIRDOS
LAVIE ANON ERIE
ABET PRONE EARN
BATH HANS OPTED
TADPOLE ABBESS
APT SAVOR
HORNSOFADILEMMA
AGOG MARIA AOUT
ILLE AMMON TRIM
LEER PASS HERE

## 18

SCRIMP TRALAS
AQUARIA PREDICT
RUBBING REDDEER
MAI ANEMONE SRI
ALCAN BOND FLOP
DOLL BORE CLOSE
AREAWAYS FLOWER
MISSESOUT
APPOSE CARESSED
PRIDE TOME ALDO
RENE RODE AMAIN
IVE TERENCE STU
LETTHEM EARSHOT
INAVALE SNIPERS
STRAWS STEADS

## 19

HALOS CATIS
RECALL ABUSED
FORTYDAYSOFRAIN
OBOES TETRA GEE
RAID STALE BASE
ELS WHERE MUTED
SOMBRERO CARESS
RAINFALLS
STRUCK GLITTERS
TRICK DRAMA MET
ROVE BRACE GENE
ACE PLICA SENTA
WATEROVERTHEDAM
REVOKE TEASEL
REFER EAGER

## 20

ROES ANNALS
ROMAIC SEABEES
COMESTOTHEPOINT
HOARY PRODS SOI
AMIS GLARY PURL
FEN PLANE MARAT
FRESHENS CARES
HANDMILLS
ALIGN INITIALS
STORE STEMS VEE
CORK AUTRE CITE
ONE UNIAT CHASM
TELLSITLIKEITIS
TREACLE AIRMEN
SINGES DOES

## 21

```
#SPAS#CLEM#SCAR
STOMP#RAVE#TAPE
LANAI#YMIR#ASOF
EIGHTISENOUGH##
PRESENT#CEN#ETH
TSE##DAME#RADIO
###ABELE#AILING
#THREESCOMPANY#
WAITED#CLUES###
ASSET#FAIL##ODS
DST#LAR#GEMSBOK
##ONEDAYATATIME
ZERO#ICER#SATIE
AVIV#MASC#OLENT
PACA#ESTH#NERO#
```

## 22

```
#EGGS#BRAD#SNUB
CLARE#RAIN#COPE
HUBERTANDADOLPH
ELEE#HYDE#ELLEN
###NAE###ORDERS
THEGREENING####
AURAE#ROLE#GREY
SLAG#ARRIS#RAVE
KATE#ROMA#BEREA
####SALADGREENS
DASSIN###RON###
OAKEN#OGEE#GRAD
GRETNAANDGERALD
MOAT#BRAG#DONAT
ANNO#ASWE#SWAN#
```

## 23

```
ARMS#GAFFS#IPSE
BEEP#AGORA#NEAR
ASTI#LOREN#SEGO
STARSANDSTRIPES
#SLIT###HOOD###
###TAMPS#STEELE
ARGONAUTS##SLUR
SELFDEPRECATING
ONUS##AUTOCRATS
POETRY#MANTA###
###LOEB###EIDE#
BROOKLYNDODGERS
OAHU#PEARS#HAVE
ALII#EASEL#TRIP
REOS#DRAGO#SENT
```

## 24

```
RESTORES#HOSMER
INTEREST#OLEATE
BRUNETTE#MIDRIB
LIP#GRAPHED#JOE
ECON#OTHER#COLL
TOROS#EER#CORAL
###SIP#NOMINATE
GENTLEMANFARMER
OVERAWED#ROI###
VAGUS#LOC#SEDER
ELAM#MOULD#DELE
RUT#CONGEAL#LIT
NAILED#LATITUDE
ETOILE#AVERAGES
DENIAL#SERENEST
```

## 25

```
HIT##AMOS#RSTUV
ASIF#BANT#INURE
TERR#ARTE#TARGE
CREE#SOAPCOPPER
HEDDAHOPPER####
###OMEN#ERNESTO
#TOPASS#STAYOUT
REPP#######ERGO
ALIENOR#SCOPES#
PLEROMA#IAGO###
####NAMEDROPPER
CLODHOPPER#POLO
LORRE#AHME#EPIC
ALTAR#GOAL#RISK
WASTO#ERNS##NEY
```

## 26

```
EARTH#SNAP#LISP
AGORA#TELE#INCA
SUPERBOWLSUNDAY
TEAMPLAY##REINE
###BOO#EMIGRATE
HARLOW#AIDES###
ALIEN#IRKED#FED
HOOD#HOSEA#MULE
APT#WINDS#CURSE
###SONIA#NASSER
SATURDAY#ARC###
ARILS##GOTEAMGO
COLLEGEALLSTARS
RIDE#ELMO#SENAT
ADEN#TIER#ELEME
```

## 27

```
#POD#AVAILS#LAG
DADA#PIGLET#ABE
ATOR#EXALTATION
HERKIMER#ABACUS
###ADEN#FLIP###
FLAGON#VIOLENCE
LABEL#DONNE#YRS
OTIS#PRIDE#BLAT
CID#CROCS#TROVE
KNEEHOLE#LEANER
###NATL#DICK###
ASCORE#LATHERED
PARLIAMENT#MORE
IGO#OSMOSE#ALSO
NOW#TEENER#NYE#
```

## 28

```
ALLI#CASED#ITSA
LOAN#OBILI#MEAN
GUSTAVEFLAUBERT
ADHERENT#GRUDGE
###RIND#ROBE###
ATLAST#LENS#SAW
HAILE#VELA#ACRE
ALAINRENELESAGE
LENA#EXIT#STRIP
FRA#EDEN#STEELY
###SUED#SEER###
ALLURE#SUNRISES
GUYDEMAUPASSANT
ANNS#EGRET#KINE
SEXY#DEERE#SLAW
```

## 29

```
COWPEN##SMELTED
UNIATE#JEOPARDY
BELTED#ANTECEDE
ISLES#SMITE#MIR
SHIN#STELE#POEM
TOW#PARSE#VERSA
STATELAW#SAN###
##WALTWHITMAN##
###COY#ICEPLANT
STEIN#ESTES#ROE
TEST#SATUP#ACTA
UNC#BURLS#BRIAR
ATABRINE#ARISTO
REPEATER#PULSES
TREATER##ONSIDE
```

## 30

```
#SPAR#ODAS#TIER
ALAMO#BELA#INTO
MODELWIVES#ATNO
BORNEO#ICECREAM
OPE##ROTA#BOAR#
###SEDATION#APE
DELIVERED#TALER
EMINENT#EARRING
AMBER#ALABAMANS
RYE#SENATORS###
##REAR#SEMI#ELI
SMALLEST#ANEMIC
TUTU#CHEESECAKE
USED#TORT#SHIED
BEDE#SOSO#SOLD#
```

## 31

SWELLS BICKER
APHASIA BALANCE
DRASTIC OCELOTS
LATE RANK WOE
AID PRAWNS CODA
INO HALLE MONET
YEAR STEELERS
HORSED SADISM
LOUVERED TACO
ELCID SEGEL WIT
ADAN SPEARS NCO
NOL PIPS AMIN
ENLACES POURING
STIPULE EARINGS
TOTELL DREADS

## 32

CHEAT CLASS
THEUSA HAVANA
THEPRIMROSEPATH
ORATE PERES ROE
PAPA LEPER MINX
ICE FORUS VANCE
CENSURED DIGGER
PERDITION
AWHILE ARCLIGHT
TROTS STIES ROW
LIME NAIAD RILE
AGE SATON MILLE
SHRINKINGVIOLET
TUREEN LANDER
NEEDY ENDED

## 33

POPE FACE LEA
LURE AMASS DUAL
AZUR CURST INTO
ZED SILO REDDEN
ALITTLELEARNING
SHEET CYST
PSHAW THEE COW
TILT BROOD SLAP
ANY COOT OHARA
SARA QATAR
ADANGEROUSTHING
DEFIED FITS FUR
ACID OFFER TIRE
GORE MOTTO REST
EYE BOSS IDEA

## 34

ABAB CALMS ALMS
GAEL URIAH MIEN
THREEPENNYOPERA
STINGRAY STENOG
DRU STAR
THREEMUSKETEERS
HEART SPIRE NAP
EARS BURRS LAZE
ITE SIRET AARON
THETHREESISTERS
HIER RYE
ACCENT TRIESOUT
THREETIMESTHREE
TEEN ARENE OGLE
AWED SENDS WYES

## 35

ELA FACTO MOB
PAS ARROW SIEVE
SUPERBOWLSUNDAY
OREN INN PANELS
MANDATE WAVE
ORE SIDEWALK
CONFERENCE OLAN
ANETO LAK ARTIE
ETAH FIRSTPLACE
NOTEBOOK HIE
REST REGALED
ATBATS SAN NEMO
NFLCHAMPIONSHIP
TRIES PASSE ALE
ESP STEED RED

## 36

EARTO RAJAS
INSEAM ALECTO
INTHENICKOFTIME
SAWED CLIFF MEN
TWIN FROST PULE
LAN SLOSH BELEM
EYESTONE LENITY
CROSSROAD
ABROAD HERDSMAN
BEERY JASEY AVO
OLDE RAVEN STER
MAT HAREM START
BYAHAIRSBREADTH
SPARSE LINGOS
ENDED EATER

## 37

LOPE ERLE OWED
EVIL LOONY HOPE
WILLIAMFAULKNER
DDE DIET LOADER
RENO REDYE
OBESE MILO RWE
ICON ATOR LEA
SCOTTFITZGERALD
AUK ERNE ENTS
NRA NINO DANDY
GOOGS GALE
SIENNA SARA ASK
ERNESTHEMINGWAY
CATA EERIE IRAN
TEST MANN EYRE

## 38

OFALL LACED
PILEUP SALAMIS
PERPETUALMOTION
ARE RETREAT NCO
LAMP SOBER BEER
STAID NOV TENSE
ENSUE REPEATED
MOVIESTAR
REGIMENS ARDOR
ENERO ACU SEVER
VANE AMENS DEVI
AME ANENDTO RID
MOVINGSTAIRCASE
PRANCES ENGAGE
SNEER TYPED

## 39

OBIE COAST COME
VIOL RILLE OBED
ANTEBELLUM ULNA
LEAVES EMPORIUM
ANTE EAST
SPITTER ESTEEMS
TAME DRAFTS RAT
ASPS ORF CANE
ITO FIRMER ATOP
RASCALS TEETERS
SAIL ETCH
STIRRUPS AROMAS
CUBE MANIPULATE
ABLE ERODE ISLE
TEEN SEWED CHER

## 40

PELF MEAD GREET
UXOR ACRO LUCIE
PICA SANG OCHRE
ATOUGHROWTOHOE
DOIT AHME
CAP REENTRY DAB
ARETE ICE CAPE
RAKEDINTHECHIPS
IGOT DAR RILLE
BEE SIROCCO YET
AMOR ARUM
VEGETABLEPATCH
DEVIL TOLA JURA
ATALL EDOM OBOL
MONEY DEWY RACE

41

```
CALF#MEANS#DAMP
ALII#ANNUL#OLEO
TARN#ZANTE#LOIN
TREASURE#ELLENS
###NAME#SPCA###
GARCIA#DISTRACT
ORIEL#MILOS#TAR
ORAS#SIMON#PARA
DAL#BONES#RILES
SYSTOLES#WEALTH
###ENVY#TRIS###
GRANDE#TWENTIES
LOON#NORIA#EDGE
ERNE#CHECK#REAP
EYER#YOKES#SALT
```

42

```
RIIS#SKEIN#BACH
ACCENTUATE#AROO
THECOURSEOFTIME
EON#BATES#LOSES
DRIVER###AORTA#
###ALTEREGO#OBS
ABCS##RULED#TOO
ALAE#DINAR#ALUM
RUB#TACIT##PETE
EER#EVANESCE###
#SILLY###LASSOS
STOOL#STEIN#ARC
HOLDSONESCOURSE
INEE#CONTENTION
PETS#ABNER#ESNE
```

43

```
REGALIA#HAMELIN
EVADING#ANIMATE
MIRANDA#RECITES
ALD#TIRED#ALERT
TEED#CAVES#ERAL
CYNIC#GENES#ATE
HEARHEAR#WELLES
###GEAR#PERI###
AGREES#HARIKARI
BEE#RETAG#CEDED
ANTE#SILOS#DUPE
STILL#PAPER#LEA
HIREOUT#ADAMANT
ELECTRO#GAZETTE
DESTINE#ONENESS
```

44

```
#HEARST#BRONTES
#EQUATE#RACCOON
#MULTIPLECHOICE
SLID#PIECES#LEA
KIN#JUDAHS#MINK
INA#ALIST#PONES
DELICATE#CLOGS#
###KATY#VOID###
#SAONE#TENNYSON
WANNA#WORST#HUA
APTS#WARMTH#RTS
GPO#DANCER#HILT
NONEOFTHEABOVE#
ERITREA#RILLET#
RONSARD#SNEERS#
```

45

```
CALM#DEVIL#EGER
ALOU#OVERA#XENO
PASS#WARMS#INDY
PITCHEDBATTLE##
###LURE###SERFS
PAPER##PAPA#ALA
ATRI#TAILOR#LOU
POINTINQUESTION
ANN#INTUIT#EZRA
WAC#OKIE##PRESS
SLING###ADAM###
##PEANUTGALLERY
ZOLA#AXIAL#EXES
OYER#HORNE#SIDE
OLDS#AREAS#STER
```

46

```
AROW#SHORE#DUEL
PALO#POKER#IPSO
BRAE#ASIAN#ASST
#EFFECTED#AMIES
###UKE###AGED##
#IDLE#OUTDATED#
ADO#DAMPED#EDEN
SEWS#TEPEE#ROPE
PANE#AGENDA#WOO
#LANDLADY#TENT#
##NODE###IOR###
CADRE#OUTSMART#
AMOI#ANNIE#SORE
LOUT#CODER#EVEN
ASTA#ERODE#REED
```

47

```
ARAP##THAIS#JAB
CORE#WRASSE#EGO
CATSWHISKER#RUN
TRYTHE##SEVERED
####ETC###ERY##
#TRANSEPTS#ABO#
CRECY#NIOBE#UVA
WITHOUTQUESTION
OAR#USEUP#KELLY
#LOB#CREEPINTO#
##GOO###ELM####
VERANDA##OODLES
EVA#EASTBYSOUTH
RED#ODIOUS#AGUA
ORE#FASTS##SEXY
```

48

```
#HOPING#ALGER##
MARINER#COLLEGE
AVENGER#TROUTER
RAGGED#DINGDONG
SNAP#EPI##GETTO
HANO#DENIM#SALT
ASONE#AGNES#LES
###GNOLAGNIS###
TRS#STELE#DICED
HEIM#ODIST#NOVE
ELGAS##NTH#GLEN
KINGKONG#EASERS
INANAME#GAVOTTE
DELETES#PRINTER
##STENT#STAGED#
```

49

```
FRIAR#ROCS#ELLS
LADLE#AVOW#REIN
ARIEL#CEREBRATE
GEO#ALERTER#SHE
##MIXEDMETAPHOR
FRAMES#AGANA###
LUTIST#NESTLERS
EDIT#######MAUI
DECAPODS#TRIVET
###TENET#MUSERS
LITERACYTESTS##
IRE#SPIRANT#DON
LIPREADER#LARGO
ASEA#SENT#ECOLE
CHEW#SRES#REPEL
```

50

```
SLATS#PROM#TRES
TOTHE#ROMA#HEXA
ACRID#OVERRIGID
GOING#MENNONITE
###KEPI##ELKS##
ADDS#ANAS#ETTES
TERN#RESH#SHEET
OLIO#ANTIC#ERLE
LIFTS#CABA#WEEP
LATHE#EBBS#ODDS
##FITS##OSAR###
IDENTICAL#BLOWS
TANGERINE#ADMIT
ALCO#ETAT#BOISE
LIEF#SETH#AFTER
```

## 51

```
GODWIT#FALL#PGA
ORIOLE#UVEA#RAB
STORKS#LIMPKINS
HOCK#LIMA#PANNE
ALE#CANARY#STEN
WASPY#ARYAN#ETC
KNEECAPS#HOARSE
###GLUT#ZOOS###
CHASER#WOODCOCK
RAM#SAPOR#LITHE
ERNE#SHRIKE#TIS
EVERS#OSLO#WONT
PARAKEET#DORMER
ERI#ELBE#ATEASE
RDS#PIED#KENNEL
```

## 52

```
SEAS#PEAK#SCARE
ECRU#LACE#THEIR
ROOM#ACHY#ORONO
FLAM#THREEKINGS
SERENE#IDLES###
###ROSES#ISTHMI
FIRST#ATTA#MUIR
EDINA#SMU#GAMMA
LOCO#VEAL#ASPEN
SLOWTO#SARDI###
###FOLIC#ASSIST
HOLLYSTALK#LOLA
ATEAM#ARIE#ANIL
SHAKE#LOTI#NINO
POSEN#OLAN#DAKS
```

## 53

```
YAP#ARAM#ALLIN#
ECU#CELA#SUEDE#
STRONGBROWNGOD#
MILIEU##MATA###
EVIL#LORAN#LEAK
NEE#SAVER#SNARE
###CITES#SPAVIN
#SULLENUNTAMED#
HERALD#MOORE###
OTARY#BERLE#SAG
TALE#TORME#BONY
###NAIL##NORMAN
#ANDINTRACTABLE
#PRONG#OPAH#ROC
#TANTE#TORO#EGO
```

## 54

```
AVON#JAMES#EDAM
RITE#OXEYE#LENA
ATIC#CODEX#AMIN
BACKBONE#ORIOLE
###LOSE#GLANCES
SQUARESHOOTER##
OUNCE##INGE#ARF
LIRE#SANDY#STIR
EPI#ACED##GUILE
##VICIOUSCIRCLE
CHASTEN#HAZE###
HELLIN#GIRAFFES
AXLE#CARNE#IRAQ
FEET#ELATE#ROSY
EDDS#SIMON#EMYD
```

## 55

```
RAPT#MATH#BASIE
INRE#ATHE#ENATE
OVEN#KEEN#LEGAL
DISTRESSSIGNALS
ELI#OTTO#NIT###
##DASH#URDU#SKI
APERY#PNEUMATIC
ZINC#CODES#GALE
ONTHEHOOF#ERROR
VAS#GAFF#SCAR##
###TAR#MUIR#YIP
SLOWLYBUTSURELY
TORII#ASIT#OYER
APART#MILE#MEDE
BELLE#ACER#ADES
```

## 56

```
CATCH#MIRE#FEAR
AGREE#AMEX#OLLA
ROAST#LAMEBRAIN
ARC#ADAGE#IMBED
TATTERDEMALION#
###ARAY#BIGCRAB
RIPSAW#HERE#ATO
ENOS#BIERS#STOW
AFR#PODS#CHEERS
REPTILE#SOON###
#COUNTERCULTURE
STIRK#FOOTS#SUM
HISTORIAN#THANE
EVEL#AXLE#EIGER
MEDE#WEDS#REEDY
```

## 57

```
##FRANC#AGLOW##
#BOOBOO#BAABAA#
CARDING#UNDERGO
ORBIT#NASTY#REF
ATAN#SIXES#LINT
SED#SIZED#DIODE
TRESTLES#GIBRAN
###COED#SALE###
BIJOUX#SHILLING
ONEUP#COALS#NEO
AFAR#BALLY#SHED
SOL#MOTEL#SHADE
TROJANS#OFHOLLY
#MUUMUU#PEEWEE#
##STAMP#SWAYS##
```

## 58

```
SIZED#SPED#EVIL
ADIME#CERO#NILE
GENUSIRRITABILE
SAC#EROSE#SLIER
###CREDO#ASO###
DEPOT##NODICAL#
OLES#ALARMS#ROT
OMNIAVINCITAMOR
ROC#SAMOAN#MOTE
#SESSION##PERSE
###AIL#GOTIN###
LIMPS#ORDER#ABA
ACAPITEADCALCEM
DASH#RITE#CALLA
INTO#ALAR#YOUTH
```

## 59

```
ISNT#PEACE#AMIS
STER#URBAN#NOSE
LUXEMBOURG#IZAR
ENTAIL#TEAMMATE
###SKIS##GEUM##
INQUEST#GETSBY#
TOUR#HOARSE#IOR
OBEY##ODO##EQUI
NEZ#RAGOUT#DULL
#LOCATE#SITWELL
##NEST##EMMA###
DECLARED#BARELY
AXIL#ALEXANDRIA
NITA#CIVIL#VAMP
STYR#TEASE#ILES
```

## 60

```
GRAZ#SEAT#AMBER
RENO#ANDA#LOOSE
ANNOUNCERSBOOTH
STAMPER#THELMA#
###LOSER#ARA###
ADVENT#EARTHMAN
SAONE#BARI##ALI
SCISSORLIFTUNIT
ACC##SAID#APACE
MAEWESTS#FOSTER
###ILE#MERIT###
#DANITE#MISRULE
HANDHELDCAMERAS
ADIEU#KIER#ASIS
MOLDS#OBEY#MADE
```

## 61

```
APOC#SHUTS#ADAY
SOUL#LOPAT#COBO
PLEASANTJOURNEY
SANMATEO#PRESTO
###SHED#TOSS###
#JIHAD#GEVA#ADO
CODER#AONE#TBAR
HAILANDFAREWELL
IDOL#ADAM#GOLLY
PST#CZAR#KELLY#
###FLAX#SIRE###
APPEAR#DELIGHTS
TILLWEMEETAGAIN
ICAL#THANE#ERDA
PONS#HONOR#DEEP
```

## 62

```
EFS##FACE#MACHU
ORT##AGHA#ATLAS
LOOP#LIES#ROUTE
UNWELCOME#IMBED
STEREO#IRANI###
###IONIC#SECRET
DEMON#TASK#WORE
AVID#PALES#ELIA
DECI#ILEX#OILER
ORACLE#LYING###
###TERSE#REHASH
STOAS#IMPORTUNE
COMBS#LEAN#STOW
UTILE#ONCE##ORE
DETER#STER##SER
```

## 63

```
SLOTH#ANT###NAB
NAPES#LURK#BOLO
IDEST#IRONSIDES
PERT#OBSTETRICS
#NATALIE#SAT###
##TUNE#RESTHOME
ORIBI#PYLE#OBEY
LEVELER#STUFFER
PLEB#POSE#SAUTE
ESSAYIST#MENS##
###BES#AIRSACS#
PEDIATRICS#TATE
UNDERLINE#SITAR
SOAS#EVER#TOEIN
SLY###EDS#ANDRE
```

## 64

```
LATER#SPA#RIATA
AMUSE#KOS#ONTAP
CONTRAILS#ETHOS
ELI#OUTLET#ESSE
RECALL#STARR###
###LLD###SEABED
POETS#PROTECTOR
ORLE#LEASE#TUNA
SCARRINGS#SISSY
TANNER###AHO###
###ABACA#MANORS
WAIT#SALTED#HAT
ASTIR#PARSONAGE
SIEVE#ETA#WIRER
PARED#REM#SPADE
```

## 65

```
APTERAN#BIRETTA
TERRANE#ANTARES
TRANSCENDENTALS
URN#PENATES#NEE
NISI#SAPID#ASSN
ENIDS#HEM#ARMET
SELECT#SELLOUTS
##LAURA#SALUT##
STUTTERS#DESACS
LAMES#SEC#RABAT
AVIS#MONET#LIRA
TEN#PINATAS#LII
TRANSLITERATION
ENTAILS#RETITLE
DEEPSET#ASSAYED
```

## 66

```
ELLAS#URAL#ACRE
GUANTANAMO#TROD
ANZIOBRIDGEHEAD
DAY#CLINT#REEDY
###SKEG##SAN###
TARES##CLASSICS
AGUE#SALUTE#NUT
MISSIONARYRIDGE
ALE#NOSIER#VEAL
RESENTER##PASTA
###VIS##DARN###
ADMAN#HAILE#BUD
BRIDGEATCONCORD
ANNE#WHITESANDS
DOER#EATA#ARGUS
```

## 67

```
HABITAT##ISABEL
APATCHOF#NOSALE
MARSHALLISLANDS
SIR##BLEATED###
#LIST#SANE##SAR
##EERO###PISANO
#BRIAREUS#CEROS
BERMUDATRIANGLE
ABEAM#RAILROAD#
SEESAW###OURS##
ELF##ESCE#SASS#
###SATIRES##OTT
FRENCHPOLYNESIA
IODINE#PENITENT
ROSTER##REPEATS
```

## 68

```
BOSC#DISC#ALBEN
AROC#IDEO#NOLAN
LAHR#MEAN#HOUSE
IDONTWANTTOSET#
###BAIL#RENE###
DOCENT#FILEDOFF
ACRE##PAVES#LUI
THEFIRENEXTTIME
ERA#DONGS##OVER
DEMILLES#ELLERY
###CELT#ARIL###
#THEWORLDONFIRE
SWAMI#AVID#ROUE
RIVAL#TOME#ETTE
ONEND#EVES#EASE
```

## 69

```
ARCA#DIVA#FACTS
SOIE#ERIN#OPERA
HANSELANDGRETEL
ENDIVE#ERIE#EKE
##ERATO#EDIT###
TOR#SERB#ERODED
ORES#SEED#OPINE
SILLS#AAR#NEEDS
COLIC#DREG#SWAK
ANANAS#SARI#ASS
###GMEN#MORAL##
ALA#PAIL#MARKOF
GOTTERDAMMERUNG
ESTER#ALOE#ARAT
STUDS#LOOT#YENS
```

## 70

```
MARINES##CRAVAT
ALANALDA#AIRIER
RAYCHARLESPERCY
AREAS##DATE####
TEDS#SHORE#SPAT
####PEARL#STALE
ALOPECIA#SPARTA
ROBERTRYANONEAL
KROCKS#BOARDERS
INLAY#COURT####
NEIN#HALLE#TALC
####BORG##SOLAR
PETEROSEKENNEDY
ANORAK#RIDICULE
LENITY##DEBATER
```

## 71

| | | | | | | | | | | | | | | |
|---|---|---|---|---|---|---|---|---|---|---|---|---|---|---|
|S|H|O|O|■|O|T|H|O|■|R|I|A|L|S|
|T|A|L|C|■|T|R|O|T|■|E|N|S|U|E|
|A|R|A|T|■|1|0|0|0|I|S|L|A|N|D|
|G|I|V|E|1|0|0|P|E|R|C|E|N|T|■|
|■|■|■|T|B|S|P|■|■|O|U|T|■|■|■|
|S|R|A|■|E|E|S|■|O|N|E|■|D|A|B|
|P|O|L|A|R|■|■|L|U|I|■|P|I|N|A|
|1|0|L|I|T|T|L|E|I|N|D|I|A|N|S|
|E|M|I|R|■|A|I|D|■|■|E|N|N|U|I|
|S|Y|N|■|E|K|E|■|S|A|N|■|A|L|L|
|■|■|■|A|C|E|■|■|A|N|I|L|■|■|■|
|■|1|0|C|O|M|M|A|N|D|M|E|N|T|S|
|1|0|0|0|L|E|G|G|E|R|■|G|O|R|E|
|D|U|P|R|E|■|R|U|S|E|■|A|V|E|R|
|A|S|S|N|S|■|S|E|T|S|■|L|A|K|E|

## 72

| | | | | | | | | | | | | | | |
|---|---|---|---|---|---|---|---|---|---|---|---|---|---|---|
|H|&|L|E|■|S|T|P|S|■|F|A|S|T|S|
|A|M|E|X|■|T|A|R|A|■|L|I|T|H|E|
|R|E|A|P|■|A|T|O|M|■|A|M|&|A|S|
|I|N|P|&|O|R|A|S|B|O|X|■|I|T|T|
|■|■|■|■|V|E|R|&|A|H|■|A|N|G|E|
|B|E|S|T|I|S|■|■|■|S|P|I|G|O|T|
|A|R|C|I|■|A|U|R|A|■|A|R|R|■|■|
|G|R|&|F|A|T|H|E|R|S|C|L|O|C|K|
|■|■|I|F|Y|■|F|L|A|P|■|A|O|N|E|
|W|A|N|I|N|G|■|■|■|L|O|W|M|A|N|
|I|V|A|N|■|O|B|T|A|I|N|■|■|■|■|
|L|I|V|■|C|L|&|E|S|T|I|N|E|L|Y|
|F|A|I|R|&|■|S|L|O|T|■|A|R|I|A|
|U|R|A|I|L|■|T|A|K|E|■|M|I|L|L|
|L|Y|N|D|E|■|&|E|A|R|■|E|N|T|E|

## 73

| | | | | | | | | | | | | | | |
|---|---|---|---|---|---|---|---|---|---|---|---|---|---|---|
|O|F|F|S|E|T|■|C|A|F|E|■|P|R|E|
|M|O|R|O|S|E|■|A|M|O|S|■|R|E|A|
|E|P|I|C|P|R|O|P|O|R|T|I|O|N|S|
|■|■|E|L|Y|■|R|T|E|■|E|M|M|E|T|
|C|A|N|E|■|D|A|U|B|■|■|P|E|G|O|
|A|N|D|■|■|O|C|R|A|C|Y|■|T|E|N|
|S|T|L|O|■|C|L|E|■|R|E|S|H|■|■|
|K|E|Y|N|O|T|E|S|P|E|A|K|E|R|S|
|■|■|R|E|N|O|■|T|O|E|■|Y|U|A|N|
|A|R|I|■|A|R|C|H|E|D|■|■|S|K|I|
|S|E|V|E|■|■|L|E|M|S|■|A|B|E|T|
|A|P|A|R|A|■|U|F|O|■|F|L|O|■|■|
|B|A|L|A|N|C|E|O|F|N|A|T|U|R|E|
|A|I|R|■|N|O|I|R|■|A|T|O|N|E|S|
|T|R|Y|■|S|E|N|T|■|B|A|N|D|I|T|

## 74

| | | | | | | | | | | | | | | |
|---|---|---|---|---|---|---|---|---|---|---|---|---|---|---|
|A|V|A|L|■|F|A|L|A|■|■|■|W|A|Y|
|N|A|P|A|■|E|L|A|M|■|P|L|A|N|E|
|E|L|I|S|■|L|I|S|A|■|R|A|I|S|A|
|A|U|N|T|■|L|I|T|T|L|E|S|T|A|R|
|R|E|G|I|N|A|■|B|O|A|S|T|■|■|■|
|■|■|■|N|E|H|R|U|■|M|A|S|C|O|T|
|G|A|F|F|E|■|E|T|R|E|■|C|O|U|R|
|A|R|O|I|D|■|N|N|E|■|P|E|A|C|E|
|M|E|I|R|■|M|O|O|N|■|I|N|T|H|E|
|A|D|E|S|T|E|■|T|E|P|E|E|■|■|■|
|■|■|■|T|O|N|A|L|■|A|R|O|M|A|S|
|R|E|S|O|L|U|T|E|L|Y|■|F|A|T|E|
|A|W|F|U|L|■|R|A|M|S|■|A|R|O|W|
|M|E|A|T|S|■|I|S|N|O|■|L|I|N|E|
|A|R|X|■|■|■|A|T|O|N|■|L|E|E|R|

## 75

| | | | | | | | | | | | | | | |
|---|---|---|---|---|---|---|---|---|---|---|---|---|---|---|
|■|■|S|E|E|P|■|■|■|P|A|R|S|I|■|
|A|L|I|G|N|E|D|■|R|E|T|I|T|L|E|
|D|O|M|E|S|T|I|C|A|N|I|M|A|L|S|
|O|G|P|U|■|■|V|O|I|D|S|■|M|U|T|
|V|O|L|S|■|F|I|N|N|S|■|A|P|S|E|
|E|N|E|■|C|A|N|T|Y|■|A|R|I|E|S|
|■|E|F|F|A|C|E|R|■|A|M|E|N|D|■|
|■|■|R|E|S|T|R|I|C|T|I|N|G|■|■|
|■|M|A|T|E|O|■|V|O|L|T|A|G|E|■|
|D|A|C|E|S|■|P|A|N|A|Y|■|R|M|A|
|O|R|T|S|■|R|E|N|T|S|■|F|O|E|S|
|F|L|U|■|M|I|N|C|E|■|■|L|U|R|K|
|F|O|R|E|I|G|N|E|X|C|H|A|N|G|E|
|S|W|E|A|R|B|Y|■|T|R|E|N|D|E|D|
|■|E|S|S|A|Y|■|■|■|I|N|K|S|■|■|

## 76

| | | | | | | | | | | | | | | |
|---|---|---|---|---|---|---|---|---|---|---|---|---|---|---|
|C|A|R|E|■|S|C|A|L|P|■|S|S|T|S|
|A|M|O|R|■|T|O|P|E|R|■|O|T|O|E|
|P|A|W|N|T|O|Q|U|E|E|N|F|O|U|R|
|E|T|A|■|A|L|A|S|■|F|I|A|C|R|E|
|■|I|N|L|I|E|U|■|M|I|N|S|K|■|■|
|■|■|■|A|W|N|■|L|U|X|E|■|A|I|L|
|A|O|R|T|A|■|F|A|T|E|■|E|D|D|A|
|Q|U|E|E|N|T|A|K|E|S|Q|U|E|E|N|
|U|S|S|R|■|O|W|E|D|■|U|R|S|A|E|
|A|T|E|■|P|I|N|S|■|M|A|O|■|■|■|
|■|■|R|A|I|L|S|■|S|E|I|S|M|S|■|
|A|L|V|I|N|S|■|W|A|R|N|■|O|H|M|
|R|O|O|K|T|O|K|I|N|G|T|H|R|E|E|
|A|L|I|E|■|M|A|T|T|E|■|A|S|E|A|
|B|A|R|N|■|E|T|H|O|S|■|T|E|N|D|

## 77

| | | | | | | | | | | | | | | |
|---|---|---|---|---|---|---|---|---|---|---|---|---|---|---|
|■|T|E|A|M|E|N|■|P|L|A|N|E|T|■|
|■|O|R|I|O|L|E|■|E|A|T|O|N|E|S|
|S|P|U|R|O|F|T|H|E|M|O|M|E|N|T|
|T|I|D|E|D|■|T|O|P|E|R|■|M|A|R|
|A|C|I|D|■|S|L|U|E|S|■|G|I|B|E|
|F|A|T|■|S|H|I|R|R|■|D|U|E|L|S|
|F|L|E|S|H|I|N|G|■|I|R|I|S|E|S|
|■|■|■|L|O|N|G|L|I|V|E|D|■|■|■|
|I|S|S|U|E|S|■|A|N|I|S|E|T|T|E|
|S|T|E|M|S|■|E|S|T|E|S|■|R|I|D|
|A|E|A|S|■|E|S|S|E|D|■|B|I|B|I|
|I|N|T|■|R|I|S|E|N|■|N|O|B|E|L|
|A|T|T|H|E|L|A|S|T|M|I|N|U|T|E|
|H|O|L|I|D|A|Y|■|L|A|P|U|T|A|■|
|■|R|E|M|I|T|S|■|Y|E|S|M|E|N|■|

## 78

| | | | | | | | | | | | | | | |
|---|---|---|---|---|---|---|---|---|---|---|---|---|---|---|
|D|A|W|S|■|I|S|T|E|■|J|A|W|S|■|
|A|L|I|M|E|N|T|A|L|■|A|N|I|L|E|
|C|A|T|S|C|L|A|W|S|■|P|O|L|E|S|
|E|D|H|■|T|A|R|N|■|P|A|L|L|E|T|
|■|■|D|R|A|Y|■|I|N|U|N|D|A|T|E|
|C|O|R|A|L|■|B|E|O|N|E|■|■|■|■|
|A|R|A|M|■|S|E|R|I|N|S|■|H|A|E|
|P|A|W|P|A|W|S|■|S|E|E|S|A|W|S|
|A|N|S|■|D|A|S|H|E|D|■|T|W|A|S|
|■|■|■|■|O|G|E|E|S|■|T|O|K|Y|O|
|H|O|T|S|P|E|L|L|■|C|H|A|S|■|■|
|A|R|R|E|T|S|■|I|R|A|E|■|H|O|E|
|F|R|E|R|E|■|S|C|O|F|F|L|A|W|S|
|T|I|M|O|R|■|H|O|M|E|T|O|W|N|S|
|■|S|A|W|S|■|Y|N|E|S|■|A|S|S|E|

## 79

| | | | | | | | | | | | | | | |
|---|---|---|---|---|---|---|---|---|---|---|---|---|---|---|
|A|F|R|I|C|A|■|■|■|H|A|L|A|S|■|
|U|R|A|N|U|S|■|A|M|E|R|I|C|A|S|
|G|O|C|A|R|T|■|T|I|M|E|N|O|T|E|
|U|N|I|■|T|I|T|A|N|I|A|■|M|U|T|
|S|T|A|G|■|R|O|B|I|N|■|H|I|R|T|
|T|A|L|U|S|■|G|A|M|■|D|E|A|N|E|
|■|G|L|A|C|I|A|L|■|M|E|L|■|■|■|
|■|E|Y|R|I|E|S|■|P|O|N|I|E|S|■|
|■|■|■|D|O|R|■|R|A|D|I|C|L|E|■|
|A|S|H|E|N|■|H|U|R|■|M|E|D|A|L|
|R|E|A|D|■|H|O|S|E|A|■|S|O|F|A|
|O|M|S|■|T|A|U|T|E|S|T|■|R|A|Y|
|M|I|S|S|O|U|R|I|■|S|O|R|A|R|E|
|A|T|L|A|N|T|I|C|■|E|L|U|D|E|R|
|■|E|E|R|I|E|■|■|■|T|A|B|O|R|S|

## 80

| | | | | | | | | | | | | | | |
|---|---|---|---|---|---|---|---|---|---|---|---|---|---|---|
|C|A|B|A|N|A|S|■|A|M|I|S|S|■|■|
|O|R|E|G|A|N|O|■|N|O|M|A|N|S|■|
|M|O|N|E|Y|O|F|F|C|O|U|P|O|N|S|
|M|U|D|■|■|S|T|I|E|D|■|S|O|A|K|
|U|S|E|■|B|E|A|N|S|■|■|■|P|I|E|
|T|E|R|R|A|■|S|E|T|H|■|Y|E|L|P|
|E|S|S|A|Y|S|■|B|O|O|T|E|R|S|■|
|■|■|■|C|E|L|L|A|R|E|R|S|■|■|■|
|■|S|E|E|D|I|E|R|■|S|E|N|O|R|A|
|P|E|N|D|■|D|I|G|A|■|S|O|R|E|R|
|L|A|C|■|■|■|S|A|I|L|S|■|E|D|T|
|A|G|O|G|■|Q|U|I|R|E|■|■|I|D|I|
|N|O|R|E|T|U|R|N|B|O|T|T|L|E|S|
|■|D|E|A|R|I|E|■|A|N|N|U|L|E|T|
|■|■|D|R|I|P|S|■|G|E|T|T|E|R|S|

## 81

DOUBTS LEAGUES
ENTREAT INTERNE
CLOUDCUCKOOLAND
KEPIS THERM NOG
LAIN STEAM JIBE
OVA WHISP GOALS
GENERA HIPLINE
MARDIGRAS
GRIPPER ISTHMI
FEELS HEWES AIM
OHMY COCAS CLOP
LEI ARRAS SLICE
INSEVENTHHEAVEN
ONENAME YEAREND
SADDLED STORES

## 82

SERT MAT DECKS
TIER ECHO ILONA
ALDA AHEM SALON
RACIAL KEEPSATA
STAND FERRET
REALLY ANIMAL
HOPE OATH SCARY
ORE SCROOGE YEN
MATCH ETTE SFAX
ENSURE HALLEL
RIDGES SPOTS
ROMANTIC OUTWIT
ALICE GIZA AERO
FILAR STET TREK
TODOS YES ESSE

## 83

RECLAME GELATI
EPAULET ALSORAN
DINNEROCCASIONS
SCOT SWATS SUTE
TUN ANISE SAT
ARID CHIN APERS
RECEDE NIAGARA
FIREEATER
OVEREAT IRISES
SPARK REGS SERE
TIM SOLER LAD
RAPT METES ELSA
ATEONESHEARTOUT
TERRORS CLOTURE
ASSETS ESTATES

## 84

JACKANAPES TAFT
EQUIVALENT OSLO
TURNEDINTO STAB
SAL RENTS PARTY
DARE YOYO
TELEG MABEL LSU
APACE EPONYMOUS
MONO NNW OGPU
EXTRACTED STEER
DYE BASAL KERRY
RHUM EGIS
ORNOT FERAL HEW
FIJI SIMILITUDE
ALAS PRIZEFIGHT
NEWT RELENTLESS

## 85

AMAS ABIG FLASH
HOTPOTATO LORCA
ANTIPODAL ENTAL
BOATING FRAGILE
LIENEE CATHEAD
WONDERS LIRA
AGE UNAIMED
NURSING BYPROXY
DESIRER BCE
NOVA DARBIES
TAKENIN ORIOLE
RUNCOLD CYANIDE
ODOUR ALKALIZES
LITRE MUENSTERS
LOSES SITS OSSA

## 86

NOSECONES AFAR
OPERATIVE RIGOR
RUMINATED ANGLO
ASIN RENUMBERED
SURELY SESS
PISA DONUTS
ARNESS UAR SAC
CATCHER SHAPING
EYE ENE SNOOTS
REDSEA URNS
WELL EMBERS
INEVIDENCE LOGO
STAID RELEGATED
HAVRE GRAVAMINA
LEAS ESTERASES

## 87

HISS SPA RAMBLE
IMPERIAL AMORAL
EMINENCE MINIMA
DARING WHODUNIT
TILT MIEN MENE
CUTE SAFE CEDAR
ARE HIREDMAN
BEDROCK LOTTERY
ONESTEPS SEA
SHAME MASS SCUP
LAVA VANS LOAN
AVENGING PULPIT
TARTAN EMACIATE
ENTITY LAVENDER
RASCAL OWE GERM

## 88

WAFT DOZE SCAD
AMOR SILEX TOGA
DEPARTMENT ENOL
ENSNARES ORANGE
SMA DRAKE
PROPINQUITY CPD
HERO DUNE EATER
AVAR SECTS MINE
SETTS SLEY BOCA
ETO AFTERBURNER
REARS APO
DMITRI ACROSTIC
RICH JARDINIERE
IRAE ODORS ALOE
BELL LADS LENS

## 89

JUDE ROPED TOMS
ETAL ABEAR ARIA
WAVE MONTYSHALL
SHIVERED CHILDE
DAVOS ALIT
FASTED AMERICAN
ARSON HOAR AGO
DOOR SKEIN CRIS
EMU KOLA HOYLE
SALAAMED TENSES
CREE CHANG
BEARER SEAPORTS
ORSONSBEAN TAIL
WITS ERASE ENTE
LEIS TALES STOW

## 90

MACHINA LAROSA
ACHERON AUGUSTI
THEBOYSOFSUMMER
HEM NEWGATE ORI
EVIL SELLS ASIE
WASAN REL EMILS
SLEIGHED PRESET
GAUD RUER
ITALIA CENTIMOS
METOO NAP SCANT
PAIN MOLES AREA
ERN LAVINIA CVI
DOGDAYAFTERNOON
EULALIE ENTENTE
STENOS RASPIER

## 91

OPT SCRAP SNOW
TOE POOCH CONE
ILE CONSTITUTES
CONSORTS ALERT
TIER RCMP
RECONSIDERATION
ENOW VOCAL CUE
BEV ANAGOGE IST
ERE LENIN ANET
CONDESCENDINGLY
ETTE OENO
SLANT BICONVEX
CONSECRATOR OAR
ANTE OILED TRA
BEAR NOIRE ELY

## 92

PARIS ATTAR
ARIOSO AMOEBA
NORTHUMBERLAND
RITES NILES STA
AMES ADDER SHIN
GAS DREAR SPEND
ALTRUISM STODGY
EASTERNER
ACHENE REENTERS
CHIDE SIDES NEO
AERY RACER ITCH
DRS RECAP ASIAN
SOUTHERNLIGHTS
OTIOSE OTOOLE
TENSE YENTE

## 93

CAROLED DISEASE
OVERAWE INERTIA
RENAMED SCREAMS
ORE BRUSQUE VII
NAGS SCOUR RILE
AGEES TAI MASER
SEDATE RESORTS
TOED TETE
ESTONIA COBALT
SPELL RUR RISER
LIVE DENOF TAXI
ATE FACTUAL RID
TORRENT TRADUCE
EMANATE ECHELON
RELATED SERPENT

## 94

MAGENTA ABNER
PICAROON POOPER
INTROMIT TOLIVE
SNOBS LED BAGEL
MONO MERITS ANA
OWE AROAR AMAT
ENNS DECLINE
LOFTED MULCTS
ABLUTED POLY
PLAN LAMER CSA
PIN SALONS PHIS
EVERY ERA PEONY
TIRANA ANSERINE
SAIGON SCILICET
LEEDS SETTLER

## 95

CRAFT TABAC
TRALEE ALIGHT
THEMARXBROTHERS
HEAPS TERR ARIL
ENTS FINES OUI
ICE AILED DIONE
RESIGNED SITTER
SENSITIVE
MASERS CREAMERY
ARLES STAGS MOO
RIA WAIVE LEAK
AGTS ANNE LORRE
THETHREESTOOGES
TREATS TOSSED
SWEAT YESES

## 96

PARR SARGE BALM
ASEA ARENA EMIA
SIAM MINUTEHAND
STRAPPED CRATER
DILL PROVIDE
INSANE PROSE
CANNERYROW SLAW
EMU ION ORE
DEBS SEWERPIPES
TOLLS ERNEST
ASSUMED ANAT
SHADED ANEMONES
TAKINGABOW NEST
ALEE ELIDE EASE
BESS SPEED DREW

## 97

DELI TENB STAID
OXEN HEUR HARPO
OPHTHALMOLOGIST
MOREEN ICER DEE
RAE SCAN
SCALDS MOD ISLE
AURAE ALI NCAA
PROCRASTINATORS
OISE RHO RINGO
REED GAL CAMEON
NAPO ORI
SAT OLEG PADANG
PRESTIDIGITATOR
AGAPE USEE TORE
NOMAD PTER EMMY

## 98

BOAR SLUB PROP
ALTOS EARL RAGE
LETUP MINUTEMEN
LONGHAIR ERASE
HENS ENOCH
APART BLOWHARD
IMAGE FLOSS COY
RUNE SLOPE SKUA
ASH PHONE AILED
SEABOARD OGDEN
NORMA ALEE
ADDER CLANKING
BULLDOZER DIRER
ELEE COLO ACARI
GARY KATY KEAN

## 99

POST CTS OILS
TRIPE SATURNIAN
RELAX ABUNDANCE
OPERA AES OKE
TARES ARA LLD
SYST PASTRY EIS
ISLES TALUK
MERCUROCHROME
ALEUT REEDS
ARE POTTED ARTS
RAP COS ALOHA
ISH CRO GABON
EMACIATED AMEND
SUNYATSEN PORGY
STLO YEA ESTS

## 100

TALC PFC SPAT
AGIO SCALY PELE
MANN IDLER ORAN
PRESERVATIONIST
ELS ECLAT
SPRY FOH KAPUT
SPIV ERA LUNATE
PREARRANGEMENTS
TITTER TOE ONES
STAID RHO AUER
OILER GPS
GRANDILOQUENTLY
LEVI PAPUA ERIE
ABES IDIOM SORA
DART DEC STAR

## 101

GRUNTS MOTTO
PRONOUNS APIECE
RUNOUTON RUNNEL
ANT SERAPIS SAD
NIGH EERIE EINE
COEUR REE ELLIS
ENNEADS REFLECT
RNA ARI
CASTING CRESTED
OLLAS ACU MORTE
RIOS DRATS NEAT
AMB TAPROOM AGE
LEBRUN RUNAFTER
SNEERS STIRRERS
TRINE SALADE

## 102

BAWL AMASS PAUL
ASIA BANTU OPRY
HELM ALOUD CHAR
SALE DAN AWHILE
INLAY KNEEL
PLATEN HIER ICS
ROMEO DENSE PRO
ICED DIRGE PROP
MAB TOADS GUANO
OLD HUNS TURNER
USAGE MUTED
ONBAIL CAB NOPE
POOR ALARM ELLA
ALIA SEPIA SPEC
LASH SUSAN SHAH

## 103

ANALYSES TRIPOD
CAMOMILE RELIVE
AMERICAN ENAMEL
DIRER MATED IRA
INCS SITES HELM
AGE ACTON GENOA
GOER TARTAR
CAESARS TETRODE
ASTUTE POPE
KOINE COPES VAS
ENOS SALLE BERN
SEL PAREE POLLO
AMATOL MANEUVER
LATENT ISOPRENE
ENERGY CEMENTED

## 104

TOFF SOWED OPAL
OARS QUIVA NERO
SHOTPUTTER ODIN
HUMORISTS SMAZE
PARTY FLAN
MAD MER JOISTS
IBIS SEQUENTIAL
CISCO TUX GIZMO
ADJUDICATE CEBU
EOLITH AXE SAT
ILUS SPARK
DENIM CHOCOLATE
ALTO BURSTSUPON
WIEN AREEL TEND
NEDS REDDY EXES

## 105

SCRAM TSHIRT
TSQUARE BAITER
OCURSED OTTOMAN
ORAL NINNY RODE
TAL TATERS TIT
EPICS THS OLENT
DEDUCTED ENERGY
GUIDELINE
ATTARS GENERATE
PAYTV ARA TYPED
ARN EDGERS RES
CADA ARENA COTE
ETAMINE IMPANEL
ALETTE NOOSERS
SENSED GAPED

## 106

JAPE TEMPT FESS
ADEN AMOUR IRAK
MARIAMONTESSORI
BREGMATA EATSIN
MILE EFTS
ARIANE CREE PAW
SANTO SOIR MALA
CLAIRECHENNAULT
OLIC ERAS OSSET
TYR GLEN IBSENS
LOGE SNEE
EDGIER OCCLUDES
BERTRANDRUSSELL
OMAR SORAS ESSA
NINE SHAPE SKEW

## 107

TICS CRAPE FACS
OMOO HORUS ACHE
PARLIAMENT SCAR
IMPORTANT ACERB
SIENA QRIN
RAF SAE QUANTA
UFOS USQUEBAUGH
SORTS QUI STALE
SOBRIQUETS ETES
LEAGUE CHR ETA
ANNA CLEAT
FORGE HEARKENED
AXIL DELIBERATE
MENE PRIME MIRE
ENGS TOAST SLED

## 108

TRAVIS OFFER
EREMITE NIEPAS
DEFENSIVEDRIVER
DARNS DALE CANA
IDAS CECIL GIG
ELI ALLAN STELE
SENORA TEETERED
REPAIRMAN
SARGASSO ITSELF
OBEYS CNOTE TAR
PES PEENS ROTI
OLEO INRE LINEN
RECKLESSDRIVING
STRATO AUREATE
SATYR YEARNS

## 109

RELY CRY DOGEA
AQUA THEE AROAR
FUNK RESPONSIVE
TAG CAST ATONED
LEARNTO TENG
RES RAH WHET
SEDATIVES LEONE
AVIGATE STELMOS
POSEN STAINLESS
SETT CTR NNE
IOWA INCISED
CALLAS VIAE XYZ
OBLIGATION MILO
REEVE CABS ELAN
NERED ULE NENE

## 110

RURAL GELS SNAP
IRANI ERAT TOPO
SINGLETREE AVEC
ELIA VACCARO
TUAREG SOLACE
EPHS HAH SBA
ETO ATRIA ATREE
THRESHINGFLOORS
HEADS DEALS BOT
WIT ORO BODE
CASHON ROOTER
FARRIER PINT
ACID BRAINSTORM
DREI EIRE ELDER
SERV SSTS TESTS

## 111

ODER AFTER ATTU
CEDE BLARE VAIN
SAID BARNS ANNO
NTOZAKESHANGE
LACE TASTE
STEELY PAIRED
MILNE ASPEN ILE
ABET EDGES GNAT
SIC LASTS ARETE
HATTER CLOSER
ROANE GILA
NIKKIGIOVANNI
MACE NAMBE IONA
AMAN GLOAT NERI
EELS SENDS GLIM

## 112

BATED CHER ACME
ASIDE HIDE GAIT
SHRINKINGVIOLET
TEES INDEED ONE
ENDOWS REAR
NASH SEEDIER
AMP TEETH AFRO
COUNTRYBUMPKINS
EINE ESNES CEE
SLIMMER SWIG
SOON ISOLDE
ICH ADDSON OIES
FLIBBERTIGIBBET
FINE REEL VERDE
YOGA SINS ERASE

## 113

CHAFF LPS BASS
RADII ARAM OMIT
ONOFF WOVE WAXY
AGRITTYPEARL
TON IREST ASSAD
DEER IMP ESE
COYOTE AMO CIII
ISIGHTTHEWRONGS
GOES OHO DECENT
ALL APE HOUK
REDDY KNOWN OWN
WRINGINTHE
LIZA LEAS TOTEA
OVER ALIT EVERT
BEEF LOS DARES

## 114

GELB CARS MARCO
ODOR HEAT AMOUR
AGRA INVINCIBLE
TEDIUM IGOR ELL
SONNET MOON
LYDIALANGUISH
RIA ENNA RICKY
ACTOR GMC ATEUP
NEROS ALOP BAO
GLYPTOGRAPHER
SURE WHINES
SPA DANA ECLAIR
CAUSIDICAL IKMO
AGREE ATRI SEBO
BEATS LIMA TRAM

## 115

BASE TILED ABAS
OSIS ONINE FAST
CINCINNATI RSTU
CACAOS MOCCASIN
INERTIA MIAMI
GALLS DRENCH
ATWO SLICED ELA
SUIT ERA PTAH
IRS STEERS USNA
ANCHOR SOLAR
OASAL MARCHER
SYNCOPES SAHARA
HUSK CATCHBASIN
ILIE ASALE SACK
NENE REBUS ETAS

## 116

FADS CACHE GABS
ABAT OTHER AHOY
NEMO REIGN MEIN
STAIRS DII MATE
SCHEHEREZADE
MAC OTO ASI
AGED EOS PLANE
SINBADTHESAILOR
SNELL ETC PLUG
ETE TAA ENS
THEFISHERMAN
SHOP PTA CANTOS
NOVA PELEE VANE
ALEC LEVEL ITER
PERT EMERY LEST

## 117

PEDRO BOMA FDR
ENROL EMIR LOUT
STALL GALL AMMO
TAKEITORLEAVEIT
LIE EAT END SNA
ELSA STATED TAL
BASES SLITS
HOBSONSCHOICE
RIVET TRANS
USE ODDSON PITS
CTR ROE WOK SIT
HORNSOFADILEMMA
ERIE MALO ALIBI
SIPS EMEU NINER
CET DEFT SEERS

## 118

MAAS ABEAM MCCL
ALLA TIARA AHOY
RAINSTORMS NEAR
INITIALLY DICTA
ARCOS BECK
CTR EKG SUBURBS
AAAA SIDESTREET
PRINT CIA SEINE
RANCHHANDS SNEE
ASCHOOL APB SSR
HOLE CHLOE
SIEVE ALLIANCES
ASCI BRAINSTORM
PEKE CARAT ERIE
SESS DROSS RAKE

## 119

ASTA AJAR BET
CLEFT GENE JOSH
TAMER AREA ULNA
IMPAIR UNRIDDEN
SPA STELA
POST PEA DISMAL
ALTO IDLE OMEGA
LIEF DIETS ATOM
EVILS TMEN CARE
DENIES TSE CLAD
GENRE ERA
BATHROOM RABBLE
OMIT UMPH PERIL
LENS TALI SUAVE
ANT SNEE STEM

## 120

OMAR IAMB AWNS
WASHINGTON BRET
NOBELPEACEPRIZE
URI SUR AFOOT
PIGLETS LATIN
ESS STRIDENT
OFA STOUT NAH
MENACHEMBEGIN
PAL GOOEY ENE
ENLARGED DIA
RIODE REDROOT
WHELP ESE UNO
JAMESEARLCARTER
APAR ANWARSADAT
GENE ESPY MOTE

## 121

WARP WAIF RABID
ALAR ASTI ENOLA
TOPO CHINAPINKS
CHINASYNDROME
HADON SERACS
UNDER ATTHAT
CHINABLUE SEINE
EEN LETME NET
NADIR CHINAWARE
TRONAS STOMA
ACTFOR ARABY
HEATHENCHINEE
CHINESEPEA EZRA
HANDL TEAS SILT
AMASS TETH TOES

## 122

DRAG SPARS
PRIVET SEAWEED
TRIPOLI HERNANI
HAVEN NAOMI STS
ADEN ARRAS DOIT
WON SPOIL DONNE
PAROS BALEEN
ONTOPOFTHEWORLD
BERLIN OILER
SPIED ATLAS MOB
CASS SILLY CERA
ULE CADET TONAL
RECEIVE OPERATE
ESTATES PALACE
ESTES MALE

## 123

GROOVE SPASM
BEESWAX QUICKIE
INCONSEQUENTIAL
DELLS QUITE PSI
ERIE DUETS SOMA
DAN ARIES SALAS
LEAGUER SOLES
GLISSANDO
SCROD TROOPER
SHREW BROOM QED
TRUE ALEUT SUVA
OID OBIES ALAIN
UNEXCEPTIONABLE
PESETAS NETTLES
STRAD GRAYED

## 124

SPACE MISS OMIT
UTURN IOWA VADE
BARED STAMMERED
HAMILCARBARCA
EVE MAS
CASSETTE STARCH
ASK URNS ISERE
PHILIPOFMACEDON
REMIT DIEM DON
INSEAM NEBRASKA
LEA OAR
PEPINTHESHORT
DEDICATED RUERS
ODDS GANG ASTOR
GOYA ERSE HEATS

## 125

BEAD CADIZ ACES
ALSO ASIDE GOAT
JOHNPHILIPSOUSA
ANY RIAL PAUPER
WOE PELT
ARTHURSSULLIVAN
BARED CURIE IBO
ATAN BURIN BLOB
SIL TUBES SOLVE
HOAGYCARMICHAEL
APOS SUR
SHOVEL TAAL ETO
MEREDITHWILLSON
URAL CARLA UPTO
GELS SLOSH DYER

## 126

POMP LAST HERO
EVIL TUTTI ODOR
GETAMOVEON PILE
REYES NITRATES
HACK CYCLO
LAPIDARY PSORIC
ABIDE OOZE NINO
RAGE ANDES GASP
ASIA NEER ACLES
SENNET LOWCASTE
ADLIB SITS
TOPSIDES MOSES
OBOE OVERPRIZED
LIKE TANEY DRAY
LEEK ENTO YALE

## 127

COMPS ASP NOSIR
INERT THE ALERT
TENOR TORTILLAS
YOUBETYOURLIFE
AER IDE
HATTER COO CPA
SARI SILO WARES
HUGOZHACKENBUSH
ATONE TIER DEKE
HEN PWA SANITY
SHA SOC
ADAYATTHERACES
STAIRCASE ETAGE
POLLO MAR SOFIA
AMESS PRO TRESS

## 128

OSTE CREE BONA
MOOT HORS SITAR
ANTHROPOPATHISM
HAE ARES TRASH
ARMADA HER
MALAPROPISMS
TIBER SLAM LEI
ADOS SHAME SAAR
ROW TETE TABLE
ALLITERATION
TAP STATUS
DICTA SARA RNA
PATHETICFALLACY
AMBER RARE IDLE
SEED ENOL PEER

## 129

PAIR ACEY SOS
MISSA NOSE SHAH
MOTET TRAS TITO
INAETERNUM ANEW
ALAI EATERY
FARINA CONNU
LOOP NEER OSAGE
OUTSIDE BANQUET
ETHEL RASP UTAH
DECOY SPOORS
PARISH ETES
ALEX INABSENTIA
NISI MAYO TOAST
SNIT EVEN TITLE
YEN SESE ARIA

## 130

VANE MANET GEMS
ITAL ONICE IXIA
SQUEEZEBOX OCTA
OUTCLASS TETHER
RESTART SIETE
ITT COLLOQUY
REVE MONEY UNO
LUXE ORG MEIN
ESQ TANKS TART
STUDENTS ORR
IRATE TRAILED
ASSISI SOLITARY
COIF QUIXOTICAL
MATT UNZIP META
EKES EDENS ETON

131

| | | | | | | | | | | | | | | |
|---|---|---|---|---|---|---|---|---|---|---|---|---|---|---|
|D|E|B| | |C|O|S|T| |S|T|E|E|L|
|O|N|E|S| |A|J|A|R| |H|A|L|V|E|
|O|R|A|L| |S|O|L|E| |A|L|I|E|N|
|N|O|M|A|N|I|S|A|N|I|S|L|A|N|D|
|E|L|E|V|E|N| |D|O|N|T| | | | |
| | | | |H|O|I| | |D|A|C|R|O|N|
|S|M|E|A|R| |C|O|S|I| |L|O|R|E|
|L|E|A|G|U|E|O|F|N|A|T|I|O|N|S|
|O|T|R|O| |A|N|T|I| |H|O|M|E|S|
|T|E|N|N|E|R| | |P|R|O| | | | |
| | | | |S|T|O|A| |E|N|T|I|C|E|
|L|O|V|E|T|H|Y|N|E|I|G|H|B|O|R|
|A|B|I|D|E| |E|V|A|N| |A|E|R|O|
|W|I|L|D|E| |R|I|S|E| |I|R|E|D|
|S|T|E|A|M| |S|L|E|D| | |T|S|E|

132

| | | | | | | | | | | | | | | |
|---|---|---|---|---|---|---|---|---|---|---|---|---|---|---|
|L|E|A|P| |F|A|R|O| | |R|A|C|A|
|A|N|D|I| |A|B|O|U|T| |A|Q|U|I|
|D|O|R|E| |C|U|T|T|H|E|M|U|★|D|
|S|L|A|P|D|A|S|H| |R|E|M|A|D|E|
| | | |L|O|D|E| |D|E|R|E| | | |
|S|C|R|A|P|E| |B|R|A|I|D|I|N|G|
|T|H|A|N|E| |B|R|I|D|E| |R|U|R|
|A|I|N|T| |J|E|E|P|S| |C|E|R|E|
|F|L|O| |B|E|N|E|S| |M|A|N|S|E|
|F|I|N|G|E|R|E|D| |C|A|R|E|E|N|
| | | |E|A|S|T| |R|A|I|L| | | |
|C|R|A|D|L|E| |H|E|L|D|O|V|E|R|
|D|A|★|D|L|Y|D|E|E|D| |T|O|N|Y|
|E|R|I|E| |S|E|N|S|E| |T|I|N|A|
|F|E|S|S| | |Y|S|E|R| |A|D|E|N|

133

| | | | | | | | | | | | | | | |
|---|---|---|---|---|---|---|---|---|---|---|---|---|---|---|
|W|A|N|D| |R|A|T|A| |C|A|N|D|Y|
|A|R|I|A| |E|G|O|S| |A|W|A|R|E|
|C|O|N|N| |N|E|R|I| |R|I|T|A|S|
| |N|A|T|I|O|N|O|F|I|S|L|A|M| |
| | | |E|N|I|D| | |R|O|L|L|S| |
|P|R|E| |T|R|A|D|E|I|N| | | | |
|E|E|L|E|R| | |A|M|S| |R|A|C|E|
|W|A|L|L|A|C|E|M|U|H|A|M|M|A|D|
|S|L|A|M| |E|V|E| | |S|N|O|R|E|
| | | | |P|L|A|S|T|I|C| |S|E|N|
| |A|R|I|E|L| | |E|R|O|S| | | |
| |M|A|L|C|O|L|M|L|I|T|T|L|E| |
|I|O|N|I|A| |O|I|L|S| |A|O|N|E|
|O|R|G|A|N| |A|L|I|E| |I|B|O|S|
|N|E|E|D|S| |D|O|T|S| |N|E|S|T|

134

| | | | | | | | | | | | | | | |
|---|---|---|---|---|---|---|---|---|---|---|---|---|---|---|
|C|A|M|P| | |N|A|G| | |T|R|O|T|
|A|L|O|E| |S|O|F|A|S| |R|U|B|E|
|T|E|R|R| |A|N|A|N|T| |A|N|O|N|
|T|A|K|E|S|F|O|R|G|R|A|N|T|E|D|
| | | |G|E|E|S|E| |A|S|S| | | |
| |C|O|R|A| | |W|I|T|H|C|A|R|E|
|S|A|T|I|N| |P|E|R|U| |E|R|A|S|
|T|R|A|N|S|I|L|L|U|M|I|N|A|T|E|
|L|O|R|E| |T|A|L|S| |O|D|D|E|R|
|O|L|Y|P|H|A|N|T| | |N|E|A|R| |
| | | |I|U|S| |O|F|T|I|N| | | |
|S|T|O|C|K|C|H|A|R|A|C|T|E|R|S|
|H|A|R|K| |A|U|R|A|S| |A|R|I|A|
|O|P|A|L| |S|I|M|M|S| |L|I|S|I|
|D|E|L|E| | |E|S|E| | |S|E|E|D|

135

| | | | | | | | | | | | | | | |
|---|---|---|---|---|---|---|---|---|---|---|---|---|---|---|
|D|E|P|T| |A|C|R|E|S| |C|A|M| |
|I|V|A|H| |T|R|U|R|O| |O|D|E|S|
|S|E|V|E|N|T|E|E|N|A|C|R|O|S|S|
|C|L|O|S|E|U|P|S| |K|A|N|S|A|S|
| | | |H|O|N|E| |C|E|R|E| | | |
|R|E|L|I|N|E| |O|R|D|N|A|N|C|E|
|E|M|E|R| | | |P|A|T|A| |O|R|S|
|S|E|V|E|N|T|Y|T|W|O|C|L|U|E|S|
|E|E|E| |O|I|S|E| | | |A|N|D|E|
|T|R|E|M|O|R|E|D| |S|A|M|S|O|N|
| | | |A|D|E|R| |E|A|S|E| | | |
|U|N|R|O|L|L| |A|N|T|O|N|Y|M|S|
|F|I|F|T|E|E|N|X|F|I|F|T|E|E|N|
|O|L|D|S| |S|I|T|I|N| |E|T|T|E|
| |E|S|E| |S|T|O|N|Y| |R|I|S|E|

136

| | | | | | | | | | | | | | | |
|---|---|---|---|---|---|---|---|---|---|---|---|---|---|---|
| |G|R|A|S|S|O| |A|S|S|U|R|E| |
| |R|O|B|E|R|T| |S|T|O|K|E|R|S|
|C|A|M|E|L|O|T| |F|O|R|E|M|A|N|
|U|D|A|L|L| |O|L|I|V|E| |A|S|A|
|R|I|I|S| |S|M|O|T|E| |L|I|M|P|
|I|N|N| |S|C|A|N| | |P|I|N|U|P|
|A|G|E| |T|O|N|E| |C|L|A|S|S|Y|
| | | |H|O|R|S|E|H|A|I|R| | | |
|D|A|M|O|N|E| |A|I|R|E| |B|M|E|
|O|V|A|R|Y| | |G|L|A|D| |R|A|M|
|G|E|T|S| |S|P|L|A|T| |S|I|R|E|
|T|R|I| |S|K|I|E|R| |F|A|G|I|N|
|A|R|S|E|N|A|L| |I|R|E|L|A|N|D|
|G|E|S|T|A|T|E| |T|I|R|A|D|E| |
| |D|E|E|P|E|R| |Y|O|N|D|E|R| |

137

| | | | | | | | | | | | | | | |
|---|---|---|---|---|---|---|---|---|---|---|---|---|---|---|
|A|S|K|S| |A|B|R|I|L| |S|M|U|T|
|C|H|I|C| |H|A|A|S|E| |P|O|L|O|
|H|U|L|A|D|A|N|C|E|R| |E|V|E|N|
|S|T|O|L|E| |D|I|E| |A|L|I| | |
| | | |P|L|U|M|E| |P|E|T|E|S| |
|R|A|S| |I|N|A|S|P|O|T| |Q|U|A|
|A|D|A|M| |A|S|T|R|O|N|A|U|T|S|
|S|O|L|I|C|I|T| |O|R|A|T|E|U|R|
|P|R|E|S|I|D|E|N|T|E| |M|E|R|E|
|Y|E|S| |E|E|R|I|E|S|T| |N|E|D|
| |S|P|E|N|D| |A|S|T|E|R| | | |
| | |I|L|O| |S|G|T| |N|O|R|S|E|
|A|S|T|A| |T|R|A|I|N|S|T|O|P|S|
|S|E|C|T| |H|O|R|N|E| |O|M|A|N|
|A|C|H|E| |O|S|A|G|E| |R|A|R|E|

138

| | | | | | | | | | | | | | | |
|---|---|---|---|---|---|---|---|---|---|---|---|---|---|---|
|S|I|T| | |B|A|S|I|C| |S|P|R|Y|
|P|R|O|W| |E|V|I|T|A| |C|R|E|E|
|Y|E|T|I| |S|E|D|E|R| |O|I|L|S|
| |D|O|N|T|T|R|E|A|D|O|N|M|E| |
| | | |S|O|O|T| | |I|N|E|P|T| |
|F|A|L|L|O|W| |W|A|G|E|S| | | |
|A|C|O|O|T| |S|I|V|A| | |A|T|T|
|R|E|D|W|H|I|T|E|A|N|D|B|L|U|E|
|E|S|E| | |N|U|L|L| |R|E|A|T|A|
| | | |S|P|E|N|D| |P|O|D|I|U|M|
| |A|S|T|E|R| | |S|A|I|L| | | |
| |T|H|I|R|T|E|E|N|S|T|A|R|S| |
|I|R|O|N| |I|N|L|E|T| |M|O|I|L|
|D|I|R|T| |A|D|L|A|I| |S|A|L|E|
|O|P|T|S| |L|O|A|D|S| | |N|O|G|

139

| | | | | | | | | | | | | | | |
|---|---|---|---|---|---|---|---|---|---|---|---|---|---|---|
|T|W|I|T| |M|A|M|A| |B|L|U|R|B|
|R|A|S|H| |E|R|O|S| |R|O|L|E|O|
|O|G|D|E|N|N|A|S|H| |I|R|V|I|N|
|D|E|U|C|E| |G|E|O|R|G|E|A|D|E|
| |R|E|A|M|S| |S|T|O|A|T| | | |
| | | |R|E|A|R| | |E|N|T|A|I|L|
|A|N|I|T|A|L|O|O|S| |D|A|N|C|E|
|L|Y|S| | |T|O|R|O|S| | |N|E|T|
|P|E|E|P|S| |M|I|L|T|G|R|O|S|S|
|S|T|E|A|K|S| | |E|L|I|A| | | |
| | | |R|A|S|P|S| |O|R|D|E|R| |
|M|A|R|K|T|W|A|I|N| |T|I|R|E|S|
|A|D|A|M|E| |B|R|E|T|H|A|R|T|E|
|S|I|T|A|R| |L|E|A|K| |N|O|R|A|
|S|T|E|N|S| |O|N|T|O| |T|R|O|T|

140

| | | | | | | | | | | | | | | |
|---|---|---|---|---|---|---|---|---|---|---|---|---|---|---|
|S|H|O|D| |S|A|M|O|S| |A|C|I|D|
|T|A|R|E| |P|R|O|V|O| |L|A|N|E|
|R|I|G|A| |H|A|R|E|S| |A|R|A|T|
|E|T|A|L| |E|F|O|R| |C|R|O|N|E|
|W|I|N|T|E|R|A|N|D|S|U|M|M|E|R|
| | | | |L|E|T| |O|A|R| | | | |
|C|A|M|E|L| | |A|N|I|S|E|T|T|E|
|A|L|A|S| |A|C|T|E|D| |R|O|A|N|
|P|E|R|S|O|N|A|L| | |A|N|O|D|E|
| | | | |N|O|V| |A|A|S| | | | |
|A|U|T|U|M|N|A|N|D|S|P|R|I|N|G|
|S|N|I|P|Y| |L|O|O|S| |A|L|A|R|
|S|L|A|P| |N|I|T|R|E| |N|I|C|E|
|E|I|R|E| |F|E|R|N|S| |G|A|R|E|
|S|T|A|R| |C|R|E|S|S| |E|D|E|N|

## 141

CAPEK LATIN
SAVAGE ERASES
ATDAGGERSDRAWN
DOGIE PESOS SUN
OREL DETER ERGO
SED SARAN ELEGY
TIMOR STEELE
SWORDOFDAMOCLES
LESION AVANT
ADMEN ATOSS TUB
CLAD TRICH WIRE
KON SAMOA RANGE
CLOAKANDDAGGER
KILLED OUZELS
SEENA SEEDY

## 142

CAREER CHAOS
OPENTO ELECTOR
MONTHINMONTHOUT
ESTE OPS SETSA
STA FLIER RITE
ALL SIERRAS ELL
TESTCASE MITRES
ARCS PERE
COSTAR BASELESS
ABC PETERED MET
REAL SORAS BAA
ORNES FED PATS
MONTHAFTERMONTH
NEGATES TINKLE
DOGIE SASSED

## 143

SPHERE SPARES
TRADERS STORAGE
RIVIERA PASSION
ANET SLOUGH STA
UTA TUNE BEIT
SECT DISK GOOSE
DORMANT FRONT
NOONE CRATE
SNIDE LOOSEST
SPIKE MING EDOS
NAPA NAPS ANT
OCT BESSIE INTO
OKINAWA STANDIN
PLOESTI TERRENE
SENSES SCORED

## 144

PACT SMEAR POET
ALAR PASSE ALDO
SARI ASSES WEIR
TIPSYCHIATRIST
EEE YIN
OSCARDIOLOGIST
SCATS OBIE SHE
EEN ABELS OER
EAT SIRE ABLER
SNOBSTETRICIAN
ITE STS
WAGERIATRICIAN
MING INDIA UNTO
ESNE STILE ICON
LEAR MOTEL TAME

## 145

GROVE TWIT SLD
PROLIX EIDO CII
ROOMATARLES IVA
IOTA VELASQUEZ
EVEN SINES URI
DER STACY AITS
REINE ACINUS
APPEAL SALEPS
ERRANT DROPS
SOOT PRONE SIC
PTA CRUDE NINA
HORSEHIDE ALAS
USA DIEGORIVERA
LAC ANSE URANUS
ALT MATS GILET

## 146

ALUM APES ROSY
RANA CANA RETIE
ATTRITION OMITS
HOBSONSCHOICE
ETRE TATS
SPILLS SILESIAN
MACLE SCOLD RIO
ELIA THINS SEMI
LEN SAROS TUNES
LOGCABIN REMEDY
AVON BERT
BYHOOKORCROOK
FLAIR IMITATION
RALLY NONO ALLY
ABEL GOER LYNX

## 147

ASPIC PIPS PREP
POONA AGRA RIAL
ELECT NOON OLGA
DEMONSTRATIVELY
NAIS ABIDES
CLASPS BRAIN
LAPIS MOONSCAPE
AMIS AORTA IRON
MASTODONS CANTO
EMOTE VALETS
SINNER MINI
PROCRASTINATION
RAVI BEAM SINGE
INEE LAVE TENET
TILS ENID ASSES

## 148

SOCCER STY AGRA
EDERLE III IRAN
REREAD AMPERAGE
BROWNBOMBER YAW
SERVER AMS
PAL TEASE SUER
AMES ALE BELLES
RIMLESS ULSTERS
ANOINT GNU IGET
ONED SATES YES
CRO PRICES
OAR WHITEHEADED
DRESSAGE INVITE
DIAS TOR POOKAS
SAME STS STRATI

## 149

PARADISE ETAGES
ABALONES KANAWA
PANAMINT ENVIED
ESE TOES GINS
REEFS RETOOLS
LYS MADS AIM
MAKESWASTE SYNE
ONESTEP UNSTEEL
MOTH DIMESTORES
ANT DECA EEL
EMANATE MEADE
ARAM LITB NIS
SPIRIT SHIMMERS
HINDER SABOTAGE
ENGINE ENSNARES

## 150

PAR PANE SCAPE
AUDACIOUS CABER
GRIMALKIN ITALO
RETIRE TEMPESTS
AES TAP SOIR
BETEL DOWSES
ACCELERATE AARE
ROLLS SWA PURGE
URAL TENMILLION
MANTLE SEMIS
HALS SIC ALP
CATENATE TATTOO
ABACA ARMATURES
MURAT KITTENISH
STATE ESSE GAS

## 151

JAW WHAM QUARK
URI HULA BUNCHE
MINTAGES EASTER
BEGSTHEQUESTION
OSSA UNTIE
RAMMED MANGY
AFI COOS MODULO
BRUSQUE LADYBUG
BARQUE POLO SEA
ENNUI LEGIST
ATTAR APSE
TWENTYQUESTIONS
HARDER SQUILLAS
DINERO AULD ARE
STERS LIKE REX

## 152

CAFE GALBA EDDA
AXIL ONEAT QUOD
LENA NADIR UNTO
KLEPTOMANIYAKS
SAT BAIL
CALEB FOR PILAR
ODA ATOMIC TENO
HYPOCHONDRIYAKS
OTIC ELEGIT RLS
SANTA SSE TONES
ALEC EAR
MEGALOMANIYAKS
GOZO LAIRD XIII
EARN ITAGO EDNA
ETAS ESSOR SEEM

## 153

LISA HASAT
TRISTE ARREAR
THEMORNINGAFTER
HOLE ENDO TIE
IRED MIDST PONE
REA RADIO COOED
DARIEN FUROR
SUNDAYAFTERNOON
ERASE GROOVE
SORAS TREAS LEW
ELIS AREAL WORE
WEN RONS ANTS
NIGHTAFTERNIGHT
CURARE LAOTSE
PENAL SPTS

## 154

LIBRAS PEA MAD
OTOOLE WANS ABA
BONBON OLDSAXON
ENGENDERS ANIMA
REALLY MAMIE
CENT LOD TIN
ALEFS ICH MOLAR
LEGIT SHE ALIBI
FALSE AAR BYALL
TIC MBA KNEE
MIGHT SPARTA
ICIER OILCARTEL
LIBRETTO TIPULA
ISL NEON IRONIC
AME TAL CAVEAT

## 155

TATA NAVAL DRUG
AGOG ICILY RARE
BEGINTHEBEGUINE
SATIRES OILS
ASIS REED
STATIC SEAT SPA
ERLE RANCH LED
MIDDLEOFTHEROAD
IKE ALBEE ESSE
SEN YSER ARCHER
WOES TRUE
PIAF BUDDING
GOOFFTHEDEEPEND
NINE EATON TRAY
USSR START SOWS

## 156

RASED APRES
SETTLE NOUGAT
STLOUISMISSOURI
TREND TAMES RUD
EINE SITAR TIDE
APT PANEL RAGS
DESERTER SPINET
LAODICEAN
BOLEYN ALACARTE
OPEC FLARE AHS
REGT BLISS AVES
ENA TRUSS SLATE
DETROITMICHIGAN
DENUDE CRAVES
SATED SOWED

## 157

AMA CANTO AMAS
CELA ANEAR NICK
HODDINGANDBILLY
WOODCUT ISSUE
PEAS ROTE
HASTEN TILT ASP
ABIE WEDGE VOA
HURRICANEANDAMY
ASE DONOR RIME
SEN ITER MAILER
TOSS SERB
ATTIC EATABLE
JIMMYANDLILLIAN
ALEE REEVE ESSE
REND MANOR ATE

## 158

BID LILA HELP
OBEY WISED ASEA
SALE HULADANCER
CRIMEA AFINGER
NEWTS ISTO
SCENE TAN OFART
CHAIRPERSON NEA
OATS RATED PTAS
OSE COMICSTRIPS
PEDAL SET HESSE
SASH SHAVE
BUSSTOP ADAPTS
DERISIVELY ITON
SANS FELIS LIDO
OUST FLEE COW

## 159

THEATRE SALTED
RANGIER TROUPES
UNDERGO ARABIAN
IDO EATER METRE
SORT LIARS ROSA
MUSIC CRIES MIK
STEELS SNAPPERS
RAPT GLUE
SCISSORS SNORTS
CAB STIES KNEEL
ONER SPEWS YARE
TAROT PROWL MEN
EPICURE REAREND
REACTOR DELANCE
SNOUTS STANDER

## 160

ROPED WIPE ACTS
OBOTE ATEN RARE
CORAL NERA ORAN
KETTLEDRUM MOWS
REASONABLE
TEAM ARTERY
ALLOTTEE LAPIN
CAMPHOR PRONATE
ISSEI CRINKLES
GLORIA HEAT
INCOHERENT
ROLL APOCALYPSE
AMID NILE EARNS
TAME ONES SWAIN
EDEN NESS SLYPE

## 161

```
EROS REMIT RASP
ROVE ARIAS ERNE
ALAR COMMERCIAL
TELEVISE HEDGE
NINE AMOS
SALINE SPONSORS
CRATE PHASE VIA
AERY BLURT TENT
MAG MEANT TERSE
PRODUCTS BOLTED
ELKE LANE
OPINE DIRECTOR
MADISONAVE AIDA
AREA RITES SMIT
REAL SLANT TENS
```

## 162

```
ALDA SUPS ALIVE
SOUL AGEE RAVEL
STRAIGHTTICKETS
UTURN SEAS ESSA
ROMMEL REMAP
ZINC STOMPS
PIUS MOOR TEARY
USSCONSTITUTION
REARS ETCH SAWS
REFUSE OHIO
MARIN STROBE
ROAM GATE TAPED
OKLAHOMASOONERS
SIEGE BIAS CREE
YESES SLUE HEAL
```

## 163

```
TRUED DATES
COUPLE IRONIC
COOLOFF SMUGGLE
ELLEN EMMET NAY
ROOD BROAD PEUR
ANN CARLY BURSA
MYGALSAL CURSES
POLLIWOGS
STROVE FILLETED
NIECE WILDE WAR
INFO PEELS LESE
FEE WALDO PIETA
FAREAST TWITTER
REMISE HITHER
EULER ETHER
```

## 164

```
TAMS OLDS SOME
ALAI RIRE QUIZ
BAST ACQUA USSR
USQUEBAUGH ETTA
UPTO OSOLE
HEE OVER GAGGED
AGRA ERIS REINE
IRAQI ISO DEANS
FEDUP EQUI SNIT
ATEASE ULNA TSE
ROSSI UPAS
QUOI PICARESQUE
URSA ANKLE KURD
ADIN NOES JIBE
RUSS AFRO ADEN
```

## 165

```
REBEL SHEARS
FIREDUP HOSTILE
EPITOME RUSTLER
ETTA PRAISE LAR
DIR VINE LEVO
ODES LADE BETEL
NEAPTIDE GLASS
ROME GIAN
WHINE HIGHTIDE
SHOTS TAGS OVER
TIGE LUNG ORA
OTT KINDLE URIS
STIPEND EBBTIDE
SLEEPER SERENER
EDWINA ROSES
```

## 166

```
CHAD BUS AFFORD
HAIR ELA POINTE
AYLI ATL PORTER
ORE AURA ELSA
TIRED ADIN TRUE
IDONOTMINDLYING
CENT RANT OOOOO
EWER ESAU
WORRY INRE CHIP
IHATEINACCURACY
ZOLA NETH BYNER
LING TAVI STA
AFINAL INI NORM
BREEZE LGE ALAI
MORRIS YEW BOYD
```

## 167

```
LAIC BAILS SEWS
IGOR AGLET EDAM
BETA LIANA TILE
RAYFLOYDLITTLE
FOES LEE
ALIST CAIRENES
CRASS USO OXY
RICHARDBENJAMIN
EAT ELI ELATE
ESOTERIC RUDDS
ILO SANE
FRANKLINPIERCE
LINK LOUIS MAXI
ACNE ELITE AVES
BEER DATED NEST
```

## 168

```
SAPS HOED SCRIP
OBOE ONLY PROVE
IOOCLOCKSCHOLAR
EXPLODES RECENT
UFO CARK
HASTO FATE BBA
MOVIE PORE LEAP
IOOODOLLARBILLS
SPIN BAIT EVOKE
SSR VETO CHEWY
TIRE HEW
STEREO GOESINTO
IODOWNINGSTREET
DRIVE SALT EMIT
ENTER EWES SOLO
```

## 169

```
OOZE SAWS BOLO
PRES ALEUT ALIA
EARP LONER NDAK
CLOAKANDDAGGER
LIME NEO
HAITI RESTRAIN
PAREE AERO IRE
SWORDOFDAMOCLES
ISM RAIL GHENT
SEABOARD GLIDE
ANN BOER
ATDAGGERSDRAWN
AGOG EATUP UREY
GENE STONE PURE
ODER ENOL STET
```

## 170

```
BREEDERS ICECAP
RONDELET PAGANO
EASTSIDE ADORNS
ADO COMPASS TAT
STUD TAPES COME
TOLES NEG SHOER
PAW DISPENSE
BYLOVEPOSSESSED
REINEDIN TET
AMBER ETS DEPOT
SEES ACHED RORY
SNR SNEERAT TAP
HIATUS GENERATE
ATTIRE ANTEATER
TEETER SEEDPODS
```

## 171

ATTA EBBED CPI
BORN LAYTO SURD
LOUD SWEETIEPIE
ETERNAL LARVA
LEAS TALLBOYS
CLOAK RAMOSE
LUV ENAMOR EVAN
ACE DISTURB AMA
MESA SCARER LOB
BREAMS USERS
TOENAILS JINN
ALLEN TINYTIM
HEARTTHROB DICE
OATS RAISE ENOL
ENE AMASS RENT

## 172

NET FAST BAABAA
IRE IBAR ARSENE
KAN VACILLATING
ISSUED FAKIR
TEENS ALS SOAVE
ADDITIVES INSET
VASES ANOINT
AMPERES CLIMATE
GEORGE IRANI
ANISE PAINTCANS
RESIN APB HALEY
TERRE MELBAS
ADMIRALTIES ART
CAVEAT URDU NBE
ENISLE SKIN SYM

## 173

SMITH ELMS RAMS
TOTIE QUIT IMAN
ADELE UNCA GORE
BIRTHRIGHT HULA
AITS INTROD
HALFWAY BOUT
OMOO ANNULET
OUTRAGE ASCRIBE
FRITTER NEON
HENS GLASSES
STERNE AEON
TALI RIGHTANGLE
OLEG ADAR DONUT
RICH LONI ERASE
MATT SLAG MARTS

## 174

ANTE HALO THAW
BOOM OMITS SONE
ACTI PINTO ENNA
STANDINGOVATION
HOLER ENS
NAME ARTEMIS
POSTMEN LEI OSE
LOT ATT TIP DEW
ONA TRE AGONIES
WARRIOR INDO
USN ANGER
BURSTOFAPPLAUSE
ANET MISER GIST
ETAL ENERO ODER
RODE SAUD NEXO

## 175

BONE AGAM TRUER
AMEN TRIO RUNNY
JEST RANT ASIDE
ANTIPASTOMISTO
CLIP ELI
SIMIAN HAD AIRY
ANENT OLEA NIO
SPAGHETTIALRAGU
SUN SAIL TENOR
OTTO SOY LASERS
TSE WAIT
VITELLOARROSTO
TENET ARTE RAIN
AGORA ICED ETRE
CANST TARO DEER

## 176

ITCH RIDS STAY
ROLE FERRY PALE
AGAR AMOUR OBIT
NOWSPRINGISDUE
AIT NEE
STAIN CAGE PGA
TISNATURESPLAN
DOLT IRA OATS
PLEASETELLITTO
SAD ENOS INTER
TNT AGR
THATWEATHERMAN
COUP INGOT EASE
URGE STEMS ARIA
DYER TOES LEST

## 177

PAIR DARED PALL
ECCE ONINE ARIA
THEMANOFDESTINY
SERENADE RHODES
MOLE SPUN
RABID SWAN LAW
SEVEN PEER COSH
HEARTBREAKHOUSE
AVIS RANT OVINE
GEL DEMO DRESS
PEAS BOAR
STREAK ALACARTE
TOOTRUETOBEGOOD
ABLE PROWL EMMA
BEER SEINE SEEM

## 178

TAEL GODS DAMES
ALDA REEL ENATE
VIGILANCE PASTE
AKIN ADMITTED
HERALDRY ACHE
ATL AME ESTERS
SHE CAVEAT MOCK
ANES SENSE AFAR
TIME TAVERN SRO
CANCEL UPI CEN
STAR SPITFIRE
PATERSON ERLE
AMENT VISCOUNTS
CIRCE IDEE ICON
EDSEL DEWS DENY

## 179

WEB SLAKE ASHE
HAIR WIRER SWAT
ACTIVITIES SALT
THEDEVILTAKEYOU
GREG STEM
COLESLAW ZEBRAS
AZO TETES LLAMA
NORM DEILS ENID
SNEAK DRAYS ERA
TENNIS DUMPIEST
INCA GMAN
SPEAKOFTHEDEVIL
TALC FLATTERING
OLLA FACER TAKE
WEAL STORY LYS

## 180

RADIANS YARDS
ANECDOTE ALERTS
JEREMIAD REPEAT
AMI SLIDING AMA
HOVE SNAG ADIM
SNEAK SOB MENE
ESSENE RAMADAN
IRON OBAN
EMPEROR TULIPS
PARS NOM OTOES
INIT LAPP ARCH
CAM TILLERS TRA
AGATES TAILORED
LETHAL ACAUDATE
DEERE EMBAYED

181

TIFFS ALACK
THREAT NOBLER
THEODOREDREISER
WARNS EXEAT TVA
ILAY SATAN FRIT
LIP HEMEN BREVE
LAYWOMEN POOLED
ACIDULOUS
TRAGUS AESTHETE
RAVES STIES LIB
ODOR RUINS CERO
NOW LAGOS PAVAN
AMERICANTRAGEDY
ERASER EUGENE
SHADY REEDS

182

ARIAS AGORA PSS
GEMMA DECOLLETE
APPAL INHABITED
STATE TEAS TANG
IRISH RST ELSE
ALF ERA PAR
GIACOMOLEOPARDI
RAILROADSTATION
INTERPRETATIONS
ASH GET GAT
AJAR IRA OFART
MUSS LAUD INAIR
INFUSIBLE GENOA
STOPPABLE HADNT
SAR ACIER TRESS

183

PERM RASP LOOK
ODEA ELIA DERMA
EDAM MOTHERSDAY
MAMACASS NATURE
BOIS FAME
MABELL MABARKER
ARRAS HAIL EVA
DOER GENRE MEAT
AMA ELSE WILDE
MAKETTLE PASSES
TITO FORT
ORACLE MATERNAL
MOTHERLODE EASE
EPEES AMEN SPIN
NEED PSST SEAS

184

VANESSAREDGRAVE
ITALIANAMERICAN
SAMSONAGONISTES
OLEINE OTITIS
RASE QUES OBS
NEUT EARFUL
DEFEATIST MITRE
ALLSTAR REACHED
RUECA KHAMSEENS
ITSELF ACUS
NEH ERNE SAAR
PAYNES MOUSSE
LEONARDODAVINCI
ARTERIALIZATION
WESTERNOMELETTE

185

ADAMS WILSON
OTTOMAN ELAINES
BROMINE LINEAGE
LON DIE LAD GAL
APES CROWD FETE
TERSE SRO SOREN
ESSENE BRICUSSE
SEMINAR
CHOCOLAT MIRIAM
LONER CAT MORSE
ATEE MALIC TOSS
ITO GAS ROC NIN
RENTERS IDOLIZE
ESTONIA NEMESES
TAYLOR GRANT

186

PAWS MEGA RADIX
SLOT ODER ERODE
ADUE SHEEPFACED
LONERS SPOUT
MUDDYBREAST MRS
SSE MAE HEROIC
DIECUTS SOUSA
ELKO KNOTS STEM
SANTA EYEWASH
SHEATH EAR PAT
ERE HIPANDTHIGH
ALEUT DEVERE
FINGERNAIL ICER
AFOOT ILSE TEAM
RIDGE CARD ASTO

187

EDIT ACLAP SOLD
LEDA SHIRR UNIO
SLOUGHOFDESPOND
ALL ROUE STEREO
AAR PAAR
FLIBBERTIGIBBET
EINES OILER AWE
DANE CATOS STEN
UNE NADAS BAILS
PEREGRINEPICKLE
NAES INK
CALAIS SHEA MAT
CLYMOFTHECLOUGH
CERO ORALE ISEE
VEER RAMPS DADE

188

MAZE BABA ASSET
ADIM EBAN UNTIE
RANI FORT GOODS
MCLEODBETHUNE
ETRE OTTER
MER HESTERS
ACUTE ADS CRAM
SHIRLEYCHISHOLM
TONY LEI HASTE
FEATHER SOS
STEAM AQUA
HARRIETTUBMAN
HIRAM RATA OPES
EROSE ABET REST
METER SURE ERSE

189

SMEARER BEGRIME
MALDIVE ELAPSES
ONESTEP TENSORS
LAG ERLKING LIE
DCI STIGMAS ANN
ELA ESE TOE
RECTORS SUCCESS
IRE ARA
SABERED GRINDER
CIO EER EXE
ANA GABFEST CPL
RTS AMATEUR REI
ARTEMIS TAUTENS
BEELINE EVEREST
SERINES DERIDES

190

SWAP LAIC SHOOT
AIDA ITMO CARPE
KNAR GRAM OLEAN
IDRATHERBERIGHT
SEDATER AID
EBO ISRAELIS
ASTRO KETO ALE
THESOUNDOFMUSIC
LES REAP UNSET
ESTROGEN IFS
EVE AINTITA
HIGHERANDHIGHER
OSLER OGEE NOSE
PLEAD NEAR ELON
SEETO ELLE DEPT

## 191

LETT CRACK SEA
ACHED AUGIE TAW
THELASTBEST AGA
SOULMATE TOOTER
NASTY DENTURE
BAILEE CERISE
UNTIL FRANC OER
SKEE DOORS AFRO
TAD FERNY GELID
STRAKE NARINE
DETAILS CAROB
ORANGS THINNEST
PAT HOPEOFEARTH
ESE TURNS TUTEE
YES STONE TYPE

## 192

ABUT SCRAP ADIT
ROSA ERASE TODO
ERSKINECALDWELL
SERENITY LEASED
SHOE AMER
HEATER FLED SIP
ERROR MULL NOLO
JOYCECAROLOATES
ADAK HIRT RIODE
ZEN DENY GALLED
HIVE SOTS
APPEAR STOODOUT
CHARLOTTEBRONTE
TITO NOONE WEAN
SLED SAPOR NAHA

## 193

ADRUM SCAR POPS
LEONE HALO EBOE
ACTORSARECATTLE
ROO MADRE HAREM
MYRNALOY PERUSE
INTWOWORDS
AZIL NEON INA
BONEDUP SHEAVED
COS EDIE BETZ
IMPOSSIBLE
GENIUS TREATISE
EXULT CHEVY RIM
READYWHENYOUARE
MATE HATE UTTER
STEW OWES TEENY

## 194

ETAS NIPA ASKEW
VAMP AMES BOONE
OMOO PENTHOUSES
KILOWATTHOUR
ELENA AER IDA
EGGED NOUN
HOURGLASSFIGURE
ENG EUR AIM SIT
FIGURESOFSPEECH
TOIL METAL
NAY RBI ILANG
SPEECHWRITER
BALSAMTREE OSSE
ARIES TOME TETE
GESSO ENID TASK

## 195

WRITE IMAGE
CAUSAL NOCENT
DRSAMUELJOHNSON
AUTRY GAUDY LIE
KIRK MARRY GALE
ASE BINGE PAVED
RELIANCE LIVERY
VIDEOTAPE
PARITY REPEATER
OGEES ADAPT RUE
DADS USERS DULL
ITE INTRO CANOE
AHARMLESSDRUDGE
ALTAIR EVENLY
TENTS SIETE

## 196

GRACES THEIST
CREMONA RATTER
HOLIDAY INTERIM
EVADES DANE PEA
LETE HULA BEST
ALE YEN DANTE
ESSAYED BLISTER
ROAD AINT
VENTURA LATERAN
APAIR HEM EVE
PERE SPED AVES
OER STOP LATENT
RIALTOS DIVERGE
STEELE DRESSED
TENSER TARTER

## 197

BOARS ATTU FRIT
AMBIT URIS RASH
BALDERDASH IDLE
ANY LEIS EASIER
BLATHERSKITE
SPIRALS TIP
CIDER NONSENSE
ANEW CLUNG LOUT
TEASPOON BONER
ANN ADIPOSE
BILLINGSGATE
ORIOLE PART ANA
SEND CHATTERBOX
KNEE TORE REEVE
YENS SEES NATAL

## 198

FLED SETUP ASIA
RUDE PARGO SOLA
ANDSMOTEHIMTHUS
TAKEOUT AROSE
ALP ARMA
DECALS ATOM ILE
EELY CRITO NOT
CRIESHOLDENOUGH
RIP TEPEE ERIE
YES RATS ARREAR
FADS ASA
STREW PRINTER
WHATSHOULDISTAY
AONE ALLEE ACRE
NUTS TEENS RHEA

## 199

CORK DART
DARING VARIES
RIVETER INCOMES
AVE ZEALOTS PRO
SEMI STYLE COIL
PRANK ERI THREE
SNEER ENTRIES
RATE SEAM
MITTENS ACERB
TUNIS DOT TREED
ESTA QUART ASHY
LIE SURREAL ION
LARAMIE SPANGLE
LIMITS SECOND
MITE REDS

## 200

EGGED WREST
QUITO AURORAS
QUARTERFINALIST
UINTA EAVES THO
INAS LAZES TOOL
ROC MOLE MUNRO
EXOTICISM OLSEN
BROZ EONS
TAHOE EJECTABLE
ELAND OKAY EAT
ELSE DUKES INTO
TDS PIKES DOZEN
HALFHEARTEDNESS
EYELETS SAINT
DOWSE SYCES

## 201

| | | | | | | | | | | | | | | |
|---|---|---|---|---|---|---|---|---|---|---|---|---|---|---|
| B | O | G | | A | M | A | T | A | | C | O | P | A | L |
| A | R | R | | S | I | M | O | N | | O | H | A | R | E |
| N | E | E | | S | N | O | U | T | | N | O | L | A | N |
| J | A | C | Q | U | E | S | L | I | P | C | H | I | T | Z |
| O | D | O | U | R | | | O | S | T | E | | | | |
| | | | A | E | I | O | U | | A | R | C | A | N | E |
| S | T | A | R | | A | L | S | O | | T | O | X | I | N |
| W | I | L | L | E | M | D | E | K | O | O | N | I | N | G |
| A | E | D | E | S | | S | L | I | P | | T | S | A | R |
| G | R | A | S | P | S | | A | E | T | N | A | | | |
| | | | | R | A | G | U | | | I | C | K | E | S |
| R | O | Y | L | I | C | H | T | E | N | S | T | E | I | N |
| A | B | O | U | T | | A | R | R | I | S | | E | G | O |
| M | O | U | N | D | | N | E | A | L | E | | N | E | W |
| S | E | R | G | E | | A | C | T | O | N | | E | R | Y |

## 202

| | | | | | | | | | | | | | | |
|---|---|---|---|---|---|---|---|---|---|---|---|---|---|---|
| C | R | A | B | | E | G | G | E | R | | B | O | M | B |
| H | O | L | E | | A | R | E | T | E | | A | J | A | R |
| I | T | A | L | | S | I | T | A | R | | C | A | N | I |
| C | H | I | C | K | E | N | A | L | A | N | K | I | N | G |
| | | | A | U | L | D | | | N | O | T | | | |
| S | H | A | N | E | | S | A | T | | T | O | A | S | T |
| T | E | X | T | | S | T | R | A | D | A | | P | T | A |
| O | N | I | O | N | S | O | U | P | Y | S | A | L | E | S |
| O | I | L | | E | R | N | I | E | S | | S | E | A | T |
| D | E | E | R | E | | E | N | S | | S | T | Y | L | E |
| | | | E | D | H | | | T | I | E | R | | | |
| S | I | D | C | A | E | S | A | R | S | S | A | L | A | D |
| A | G | E | E | | A | P | A | I | L | | L | I | F | E |
| S | L | E | D | | R | A | R | E | E | | L | E | A | N |
| H | U | M | E | | D | R | E | S | S | | Y | U | R | T |

## 203

| | | | | | | | | | | | | | | |
|---|---|---|---|---|---|---|---|---|---|---|---|---|---|---|
| S | O | A | P | | S | T | U | B | | | | S | A | L |
| A | T | M | O | | H | O | R | U | S | | E | R | G | O |
| D | I | A | L | | A | S | A | F | E | | N | A | R | C |
| | C | H | A | G | R | I | N | F | A | L | L | S | O | H |
| | | | N | E | E | R | | A | P | I | A | | | |
| | O | R | D | E | R | | C | L | O | V | I | S | N | M |
| S | H | I | M | S | | A | L | O | R | S | | W | O | E |
| L | A | V | E | | A | L | O | S | T | | R | E | N | E |
| O | R | A | | C | I | C | A | D | | V | I | D | O | R |
| P | A | L | M | E | R | A | K | | C | O | P | E | S | |
| | | | A | N | I | L | | C | A | L | L | | | |
| S | P | O | T | T | E | D | H | O | R | S | E | W | Y | |
| T | I | M | E | | S | E | A | L | E | | Y | O | U | R |
| A | C | E | Y | | T | N | U | T | S | | O | R | L | E |
| D | A | N | | | | M | L | S | S | | H | E | E | P |

## 204

| | | | | | | | | | | | | | | |
|---|---|---|---|---|---|---|---|---|---|---|---|---|---|---|
| S | E | M | I | N | A | R | | C | E | R | A | M | I | C |
| C | L | O | S | U | R | E | | A | L | A | B | A | M | A |
| H | U | N | T | I | N | G | | N | E | B | U | L | A | R |
| E | S | S | | T | E | R | R | A | C | E | | A | G | E |
| M | I | T | T | | L | E | A | S | T | | T | R | E | E |
| E | V | E | R | T | | S | E | T | | C | H | I | R | R |
| R | E | R | E | A | D | S | | A | I | R | W | A | Y | S |
| | | | S | S | E | | | | M | E | A | | | |
| T | R | E | S | T | L | E | | A | P | P | R | O | V | E |
| R | A | R | E | E | | N | O | D | | E | T | N | A | S |
| I | D | E | S | | A | A | R | O | N | | S | A | L | T |
| P | I | C | | A | R | M | O | R | E | R | | T | E | A |
| L | A | T | T | I | C | E | | E | R | O | D | E | N | T |
| E | T | E | R | N | A | L | | R | A | T | R | A | C | E |
| S | E | D | A | T | E | S | | S | C | O | U | R | E | D |

## 205

| | | | | | | | | | | | | | | |
|---|---|---|---|---|---|---|---|---|---|---|---|---|---|---|
| | | T | O | P | I | C | | S | C | O | N | C | E | |
| S | P | I | N | A | C | H | | C | A | B | B | A | G | E |
| M | A | L | A | C | H | I | | O | M | I | C | R | O | N |
| O | P | T | | T | O | M | | R | U | E | | B | T | U |
| K | A | E | L | | R | E | A | P | S | | N | O | I | R |
| E | Y | R | I | E | | S | C | I | | S | E | N | S | E |
| R | A | S | P | E | D | | C | O | N | T | E | S | T | S |
| | | | | L | A | C | O | N | I | A | | | | |
| L | A | S | V | E | G | A | S | | T | U | R | N | I | P |
| O | T | T | E | R | | L | T | D | | B | E | A | N | S |
| C | H | I | T | | R | I | S | E | S | | T | U | B | A |
| A | L | L | | L | A | P | | R | T | E | | S | O | L |
| L | E | T | T | U | C | E | | M | I | D | T | E | R | M |
| S | T | O | U | T | E | R | | I | N | D | I | A | N | S |
| | E | N | T | E | R | S | | S | T | O | R | M | | |

## 206

| | | | | | | | | | | | | | | |
|---|---|---|---|---|---|---|---|---|---|---|---|---|---|---|
| B | E | A | R | D | E | D | | S | C | R | A | P | E | S |
| L | A | B | O | R | E | R | | T | H | O | R | E | A | U |
| O | R | A | T | O | R | Y | | R | I | P | C | O | R | D |
| O | L | D | | P | I | S | C | I | N | E | | N | N | E |
| D | O | D | O | | E | A | R | N | S | | D | I | E | T |
| E | B | O | N | Y | | L | U | G | | G | E | E | S | E |
| D | E | N | T | I | S | T | S | | B | E | A | S | T | S |
| | | | R | E | T | S | | W | A | N | D | | | |
| S | I | C | I | L | Y | | C | I | S | T | E | R | N | S |
| T | R | E | A | D | | V | A | R | | S | N | O | O | T |
| R | O | L | L | | C | E | R | E | S | | D | A | N | A |
| I | N | E | | C | A | N | D | L | E | S | | N | U | T |
| P | O | S | T | U | R | E | | E | N | C | L | O | S | E |
| E | U | T | E | R | P | E | | S | N | O | O | K | E | R |
| S | T | A | L | L | E | R | | S | A | W | Y | E | R | S |

## 207

| | | | | | | | | | | | | | | |
|---|---|---|---|---|---|---|---|---|---|---|---|---|---|---|
| P | A | N | A | C | E | A | | | C | R | A | S | S | |
| A | M | A | Z | O | N | S | | I | R | I | D | I | U | M |
| M | O | R | O | N | I | C | | M | E | M | E | N | T | O |
| E | R | R | | E | D | O | M | I | T | E | | C | U | D |
| L | O | A | F | | S | T | A | T | E | | H | E | R | E |
| A | U | T | O | S | | S | S | A | | M | I | R | E | S |
| | S | E | I | N | E | | S | T | E | E | P | E | S | T |
| | | | B | A | S | E | M | E | N | T | S | | | |
| C | A | R | L | I | S | L | E | | G | A | T | O | R | |
| A | R | E | E | L | | E | D | O | | L | E | P | E | R |
| M | M | E | S | | S | M | I | R | K | | R | A | Z | E |
| E | O | N | | F | L | E | A | B | A | G | | L | O | W |
| O | R | T | O | L | A | N | | A | S | I | N | I | N | E |
| S | E | R | V | A | N | T | | C | H | A | I | N | E | D |
| | D | Y | I | N | G | | | H | A | P | L | E | S | S |

## 208

| | | | | | | | | | | | | | | |
|---|---|---|---|---|---|---|---|---|---|---|---|---|---|---|
| R | A | J | A | H | | I | V | E | S | | E | T | T | E |
| A | L | O | N | E | | D | I | N | T | | S | H | U | L |
| P | I | E | T | A | | A | S | T | A | | D | E | L | I |
| | | T | A | R | T | | A | I | R | S | | H | A | T |
| B | A | H | | T | H | E | G | R | E | A | T | O | N | E |
| A | V | E | C | | A | L | E | E | | T | U | N | E | |
| N | E | B | O | | W | A | S | | P | Y | R | E | | |
| K | R | A | M | D | E | N | | H | U | R | R | Y | U | P |
| | | R | E | E | D | | H | U | R | | E | M | M | A |
| | S | T | U | N | | P | U | G | S | | T | O | P | S |
| T | H | E | P | O | O | R | S | O | U | L | | O | S | S |
| R | I | N | | F | R | A | T | | E | A | R | N | | |
| A | I | D | A | | B | I | L | K | | P | I | E | C | E |
| S | T | E | W | | I | S | E | E | | A | P | R | I | L |
| H | E | R | E | | T | E | R | N | | Z | E | S | T | Y |

## 209

| | | | | | | | | | | | | | | |
|---|---|---|---|---|---|---|---|---|---|---|---|---|---|---|
| V | O | N | | | P | A | S | S | | S | P | A | T | E |
| A | L | E | C | | E | L | A | N | | M | A | Y | A | N |
| M | E | A | L | | D | A | T | A | | I | L | E | D | E |
| P | O | P | O | C | A | T | E | P | E | T | L | | | |
| | | | S | A | N | E | | | S | T | O | L | E | S |
| | S | P | U | R | T | | W | A | T | E | R | I | S | H |
| H | O | A | R | D | | S | I | R | E | N | | O | T | O |
| E | I | R | E | | S | O | L | E | S | | P | N | E | U |
| A | R | I | | S | P | A | T | S | | S | L | E | E | T |
| R | E | A | C | T | O | R | S | | R | E | A | L | M | |
| D | E | N | I | R | O | | | S | A | M | S | | | |
| | | | T | E | N | O | C | H | T | I | T | L | A | N |
| V | I | S | I | T | | P | O | O | H | | E | A | S | E |
| A | Z | T | E | C | | T | A | R | E | | R | I | T | E |
| L | E | A | S | H | | S | T | E | R | | | N | O | D |

## 210

| | | | | | | | | | | | | | | |
|---|---|---|---|---|---|---|---|---|---|---|---|---|---|---|
| A | R | N | O | | B | A | S | E | R | | D | A | L | E |
| R | E | A | P | | I | N | U | R | E | | A | L | O | W |
| M | I | N | I | M | M | I | N | I | M | | R | I | L | E |
| | D | O | U | A | I | | S | C | I | M | I | T | A | R |
| | | | M | I | N | A | | A | T | E | E | | | |
| A | V | I | D | D | I | V | A | | T | A | N | T | R | A |
| W | A | D | E | S | | A | L | B | E | N | | R | U | G |
| A | G | O | N | | C | R | I | E | D | | C | A | M | E |
| R | U | N | | R | O | S | S | A | | S | A | L | O | N |
| D | E | T | O | U | R | | T | R | A | M | M | A | R | T |
| | | | R | I | P | E | | D | R | A | B | | | |
| A | V | O | N | N | O | V | A | | A | L | I | A | S | |
| H | E | R | A | | R | E | G | A | L | L | A | G | E | R |
| E | R | A | T | | A | R | I | R | E | | T | A | R | O |
| M | A | L | E | | L | Y | O | N | S | | A | R | A | M |

## 211

| | | | | | | | | | | | | | | |
|---|---|---|---|---|---|---|---|---|---|---|---|---|---|---|
| M | I | S | C | ■ | M | A | G | I | C | ■ | S | C | O | T |
| A | R | E | A | ■ | A | R | A | R | A | ■ | C | A | S | E |
| C | A | R | P | E | N | T | E | R | S | ■ | A | S | I | A |
| R | E | T | I | R | E | S | ■ | ■ | C | A | N | T | E | R |
| ■ | ■ | ■ | T | A | G | ■ | C | O | A | S | T | E | R | S |
| S | T | J | O | S | E | P | H | S | D | A | Y | ■ | ■ | ■ |
| O | R | A | L | E | ■ | L | A | T | E | N | ■ | W | A | D |
| L | E | N | S | ■ | C | A | R | L | S | ■ | M | A | R | Y |
| E | Y | E | ■ | S | A | N | T | E | ■ | P | A | S | T | E |
| ■ | ■ | ■ | F | O | S | T | E | R | F | A | T | H | E | R |
| S | T | R | E | S | S | E | D | ■ | A | I | T | ■ | ■ | ■ |
| H | O | O | D | O | O | ■ | ■ | M | I | N | E | R | A | L |
| E | N | T | O | ■ | C | A | P | I | S | T | R | A | N | O |
| A | T | O | R | ■ | K | R | O | N | A | ■ | E | M | I | R |
| F | O | R | A | ■ | S | P | I | E | L | ■ | D | A | L | E |

## 212

| | | | | | | | | | | | | | | |
|---|---|---|---|---|---|---|---|---|---|---|---|---|---|---|
| A | B | U | G | ■ | ■ | A | L | B | S | ■ | ■ | J | F | K |
| M | E | N | U | S | ■ | N | O | R | T | E | ■ | U | L | E |
| P | E | L | I | C | A | N | T | O | R | S | ■ | D | A | Y |
| S | P | I | N | E | S | ■ | S | O | U | P | C | O | N | S |
| ■ | S | T | E | N | C | H | ■ | D | C | I | I | ■ | ■ | ■ |
| ■ | ■ | ■ | A | T | H | O | S | ■ | K | E | V | E | L | S |
| P | O | M | P | ■ | A | M | O | S | ■ | D | I | V | O | T |
| A | L | I | I | ■ | M | E | L | O | N | ■ | L | E | D | A |
| R | I | N | G | S | ■ | R | I | L | E | ■ | W | R | E | N |
| R | O | D | E | O | S | ■ | D | O | R | I | A | ■ | ■ | ■ |
| ■ | ■ | ■ | O | L | A | F | ■ | S | U | T | R | A | S | ■ |
| P | R | E | N | A | T | A | L | ■ | D | A | B | B | E | D |
| I | A | L | ■ | C | I | N | E | M | A | L | L | A | R | D |
| X | Y | L | ■ | E | R | N | S | T | ■ | L | E | T | U | S |
| Y | E | S | ■ | ■ | E | Y | E | S | ■ | ■ | R | E | M | S |

## 213

| | | | | | | | | | | | | | | |
|---|---|---|---|---|---|---|---|---|---|---|---|---|---|---|
| D | E | M | I | ■ | P | L | A | T | E | ■ | T | I | P | S |
| I | C | A | N | ■ | R | O | S | I | N | ■ | S | N | E | E |
| C | H | I | C | K | E | N | I | N | T | H | E | C | A | R |
| E | O | N | ■ | A | S | E | A | ■ | R | O | T | A | T | E |
| ■ | ■ | T | A | T | E | R | ■ | S | A | S | S | ■ | ■ | ■ |
| H | E | A | R | S | T | ■ | W | H | I | T | E | S | O | X |
| A | L | I | T | ■ | ■ | M | I | E | N | ■ | ■ | A | R | E |
| I | G | N | S | ■ | P | A | N | E | S | ■ | S | I | A | N |
| T | I | E | ■ | ■ | A | D | D | N | ■ | ■ | I | N | T | O |
| I | N | D | U | S | T | R | Y | ■ | F | A | T | T | E | N |
| ■ | ■ | ■ | N | I | C | E | ■ | R | A | N | U | P | ■ | ■ |
| F | A | M | I | S | H | ■ | H | A | L | T | ■ | E | O | S |
| A | N | D | T | H | E | C | A | R | C | A | N | T | G | O |
| D | O | L | E | ■ | R | O | D | E | O | ■ | A | E | R | O |
| E | N | I | D | ■ | Y | E | A | R | N | ■ | B | R | E | N |

## 214

| | | | | | | | | | | | | | | |
|---|---|---|---|---|---|---|---|---|---|---|---|---|---|---|
| O | C | C | U | R | ■ | A | T | O | M | ■ | B | A | J | A |
| M | O | R | R | O | ■ | B | O | L | O | ■ | O | V | A | L |
| A | M | O | N | G | ■ | H | Y | D | R | O | X | I | D | E |
| N | E | W | ■ | U | F | O | S | ■ | A | B | I | D | E | S |
| ■ | ■ | Q | U | E | E | R | ■ | K | I | L | N | ■ | ■ | ■ |
| C | O | U | R | S | E | ■ | M | O | N | O | G | R | A | M |
| A | V | I | S | ■ | D | E | E | P | E | N | ■ | A | B | E |
| P | I | L | A | F | ■ | A | T | E | ■ | G | A | Z | E | R |
| E | N | L | ■ | E | U | R | E | K | A | ■ | C | Z | A | R |
| R | E | S | E | N | T | E | D | ■ | S | H | I | M | M | Y |
| ■ | ■ | ■ | I | C | E | D | ■ | R | H | O | D | A | ■ | ■ |
| W | O | O | L | E | N | ■ | V | I | E | W | ■ | T | A | W |
| I | M | M | E | R | S | I | O | N | ■ | A | M | A | T | I |
| N | O | N | E | ■ | I | R | I | S | ■ | R | A | Z | O | R |
| G | O | I | N | ■ | L | A | D | E | ■ | D | A | Z | Z | Y |

## 215

| | | | | | | | | | | | | | | |
|---|---|---|---|---|---|---|---|---|---|---|---|---|---|---|
| C | U | R | I | A | E | ■ | ■ | T | R | U | S | T | S | ■ |
| A | T | O | N | C | E | ■ | S | E | A | S | C | A | P | E |
| T | O | T | T | E | R | ■ | I | N | T | E | R | C | O | M |
| A | P | T | E | R | ■ | A | N | T | ■ | ■ | A | T | O | M |
| L | I | E | N | ■ | E | G | G | S | ■ | O | M | I | N | E |
| P | A | R | T | E | R | R | E | ■ | G | I | B | L | E | T |
| A | N | S | ■ | T | R | E | ■ | C | A | L | L | E | R | S |
| ■ | ■ | ■ | S | H | O | E | ■ | A | L | I | E | ■ | ■ | ■ |
| C | U | S | T | A | R | D | ■ | I | L | E | ■ | S | C | I |
| A | N | T | O | N | S | ■ | A | M | E | R | I | C | A | N |
| T | R | A | P | S | ■ | S | W | A | Y | ■ | T | O | R | T |
| S | A | M | P | ■ | ■ | T | I | N | ■ | S | H | O | V | E |
| U | T | I | L | I | Z | E | S | ■ | P | L | A | T | E | N |
| P | E | N | E | L | O | P | E | ■ | P | A | C | E | R | S |
| ■ | D | A | D | O | E | S | ■ | ■ | S | P | A | R | S | E |

## 216

| | | | | | | | | | | | | | | |
|---|---|---|---|---|---|---|---|---|---|---|---|---|---|---|
| ■ | L | I | V | ■ | M | A | N | ■ | ■ | S | C | O | L | D |
| M | I | C | A | ■ | A | H | A | B | ■ | L | E | V | E | E |
| A | D | E | N | ■ | C | O | T | A | ■ | O | D | E | T | S |
| J | O | S | E | P | H | P | A | S | T | E | R | N | A | K |
| ■ | ■ | ■ | S | O | O | ■ | L | I | E | ■ | I | S | T | S |
| E | R | A | S | E | ■ | P | I | C | N | I | C | ■ | ■ | ■ |
| L | A | M | A | ■ | F | R | A | ■ | A | S | H | C | A | N |
| S | H | I | R | L | E | Y | M | A | C | L | A | I | N | E |
| A | S | N | E | A | T | ■ | A | L | E | ■ | R | I | N | D |
| ■ | ■ | ■ | D | R | I | N | K | S | ■ | A | D | I | O | S |
| S | L | A | G | ■ | S | E | A | ■ | P | E | W | ■ | ■ | ■ |
| H | A | R | R | Y | H | E | R | S | H | F | I | E | L | D |
| A | U | R | A | S | ■ | D | O | P | A | ■ | C | L | U | E |
| G | R | O | V | E | ■ | Y | V | E | S | ■ | K | I | L | O |
| S | A | W | E | R | ■ | ■ | A | W | E | ■ | ■ | E | A | U |

## 217

| | | | | | | | | | | | | | | |
|---|---|---|---|---|---|---|---|---|---|---|---|---|---|---|
| G | R | A | T | A | ■ | A | T | I | C | ■ | M | A | S | S |
| N | A | M | E | D | ■ | B | O | M | A | ■ | A | L | T | A |
| A | N | I | T | A | ■ | R | U | P | P | ■ | D | I | O | R |
| R | E | C | O | N | C | I | L | E | R | ■ | R | E | I | D |
| L | E | O | N | A | R | D | O | D | A | V | I | N | C | I |
| ■ | ■ | ■ | ■ | ■ | A | G | U | E | ■ | O | V | A | ■ | ■ |
| R | B | I | ■ | A | V | E | S | ■ | T | I | E | T | H | E |
| E | U | G | E | N | E | D | E | L | A | C | R | O | I | X |
| L | Y | N | X | E | S | ■ | L | I | M | E | ■ | R | E | O |
| ■ | ■ | I | C | A | ■ | S | A | L | E | ■ | ■ | ■ | ■ | ■ |
| P | E | T | E | R | P | A | U | L | R | U | B | E | N | S |
| E | L | A | S | ■ | A | R | T | I | S | T | I | C | A | L |
| R | I | B | S | ■ | C | A | R | P | ■ | I | G | L | O | O |
| D | O | L | E | ■ | A | P | E | U | ■ | C | H | A | M | P |
| U | T | E | S | ■ | S | E | C | T | ■ | A | T | T | I | S |

## 218

| | | | | | | | | | | | | | | |
|---|---|---|---|---|---|---|---|---|---|---|---|---|---|---|
| P | A | C | T | ■ | S | O | S | O | ■ | B | A | C | O | N |
| A | L | O | E | ■ | E | R | A | L | ■ | A | L | O | S | E |
| S | L | U | E | ■ | C | A | N | D | Y | S | P | O | T | S |
| T | E | N | T | ■ | T | N | T | ■ | A | I | S | L | E | S |
| E | N | T | E | R | ■ | T | A | C | K | S | ■ | ■ | ■ | ■ |
| ■ | ■ | F | R | A | U | ■ | A | R | S | ■ | A | B | A | B |
| A | W | L | ■ | I | N | O | N | E | ■ | A | R | U | B | A |
| T | H | E | F | L | O | R | I | D | A | D | E | R | B | Y |
| L | E | E | R | S | ■ | S | T | O | N | E | ■ | G | A | S |
| I | N | T | O | ■ | G | O | A | ■ | U | P | T | O | ■ | ■ |
| ■ | ■ | ■ | ■ | S | E | N | D | S | ■ | T | R | O | P | E |
| S | P | I | D | E | R | ■ | E | T | A | ■ | A | K | I | N |
| W | A | R | A | D | M | I | R | A | L | ■ | L | I | N | D |
| A | R | E | N | A | ■ | A | B | R | I | ■ | E | N | T | E |
| N | I | S | A | N | ■ | N | Y | E | T | ■ | E | G | A | D |

## 219

| | | | | | | | | | | | | | | |
|---|---|---|---|---|---|---|---|---|---|---|---|---|---|---|
| C | R | A | S | H | ■ | K | O | C | H | ■ | ■ | H | A | P |
| R | E | C | T | O | ■ | A | L | O | U | ■ | K | A | R | L |
| O | C | H | L | O | C | R | A | T | S | ■ | A | R | T | A |
| S | R | I | ■ | ■ | O | A | F | ■ | K | U | N | L | U | N |
| S | E | L | ■ | A | C | T | ■ | W | I | N | ■ | E | R | E |
| W | A | L | E | S | A | ■ | T | H | E | I | D | I | O | T |
| O | T | E | L | O | ■ | Q | U | E | S | ■ | R | A | T | A |
| R | I | S | I | N | ■ | U | T | A | ■ | S | E | N | O | R |
| D | O | T | H | ■ | M | O | T | T | ■ | P | A | L | S | Y |
| P | N | E | U | M | A | T | O | ■ | M | E | D | I | C | S |
| U | R | N | ■ | I | S | H | ■ | J | A | W | ■ | B | A | Y |
| Z | O | D | I | A | C | ■ | V | E | X | ■ | ■ | R | N | S |
| Z | O | O | S | ■ | L | I | E | S | I | N | W | A | I | T |
| L | M | N | O | ■ | E | D | I | T | ■ | H | O | R | N | E |
| E | S | S | ■ | ■ | S | O | N | S | ■ | G | O | Y | I | M |

## 220

| | | | | | | | | | | | | | | |
|---|---|---|---|---|---|---|---|---|---|---|---|---|---|---|
| ■ | ■ | M | A | I | N | E | ■ | K | A | N | S | A | S | ■ |
| S | T | O | I | C | A | L | ■ | I | N | C | I | T | E | S |
| K | E | N | N | E | D | Y | ■ | N | E | O | C | E | N | E |
| O | A | T | ■ | S | I | R | ■ | D | Y | S | ■ | L | S | T |
| A | P | A | S | ■ | R | I | F | L | E | ■ | C | I | A | O |
| L | O | N | E | R | ■ | A | L | I | ■ | P | O | E | T | S |
| S | T | A | T | O | R | ■ | O | N | A | S | P | R | E | E |
| ■ | ■ | ■ | ■ | G | E | O | R | G | I | A | ■ | ■ | ■ | ■ |
| S | O | B | I | E | S | K | I | ■ | L | L | O | Y | D | S |
| A | V | E | R | T | ■ | A | D | M | ■ | M | O | O | R | E |
| D | E | L | E | ■ | C | L | A | U | S | ■ | F | R | O | G |
| A | R | I | ■ | R | O | O | ■ | S | U | F | ■ | U | V | A |
| T | R | E | V | I | N | O | ■ | C | A | L | I | B | E | R |
| S | A | V | A | G | E | S | ■ | A | V | A | T | A | R | S |
| ■ | N | E | V | A | D | A | ■ | T | E | X | A | S | ■ | ■ |

## 221

PARES ELOGES
ALPACA EPIGRAM
TREASUREMEASURE
ROACH AIMER ELA
OUSE ACRES ASOR
OSU SLEET GLOBE
PERTAIN STEAMED
EURE ALTE
SILTING ARIETTA
PNEUS RACED WIG
ASIS SERES NOTA
NUS SPEAR SISAL
GLUTTONSBUTTONS
LARIATS INARMS
ERECTS CANOE

## 222

ROVER AVES PPPP
ALIKE DADO EEEE
NIGEL ALAN PATS
GOODYUMAMAN LET
OVEN TIGERS
ACHENE CRAZY
BAAL ASEA ARISE
UNHORSE HOMERUN
GASPE EAST NORD
ELAND AMENDS
SORDID RAVE
III COMEDIENNES
ELLA RANA SANTA
VEER ELAN ETNAS
ERSE STLO SENSE

## 223

DORSALS ARCADES
EPAULET FURNISH
CARBINE EMANATE
OLIVEDRAB TUBAL
RITE LORRE MOTT
UNARM LAIRS LEI
MENTAL BLUENOSE
ERIN ECRU
SPARKLET TURBOT
AEC STAUB MELBA
META STREW MUTT
PRIMA ENGELBERT
LANOLIN GLEEFUL
EGALITE ASTRIDE
DELETED REIGNED

## 224

IMET ANEW SITES
TORE COPE WHERE
SAMMYCAHN ARNIE
TABOO STET DEN
LURI TAHOE
AFFORDS OVERRAN
FLARE HOWE ATMO
TOC CODAS REO
ORES RUES SCANS
NATURAL TRAIPSE
ONEND EARN
REF TECS FADES
AMATI ALLTHEWAY
RICER RACE RENO
ALENE EMIR SNOW

## 225

CACTUS ACH FAST
ILLUSE BOA UNTO
STABAT ENLARGER
TOPE ADVISORS
TRAM KEEL LEO
SHROVE ENDS ASS
SEASONERS
EXPENDS ESTATES
CASTANETS
ICS ARAN ABDUCT
MAW BALK SUIT
PRIMEVAL ROME
APPOSITE ATONER
LEES NOT RUNINS
ADDS ERS FESCUE

## 226

MATH LAMBS
CATION AVIATE
DOUBLEORNOTHING
AURAL TACIT PAL
TRET NOTED LEMA
ESE COPTS BONER
SENTINEL DOODLE
ONONESOWN
SABRES SELLSFOR
IMAMS GNATS OLA
TIDE ORALS ARIZ
EGG BRAKE STEVE
DOUBLENEGATIVES
SYRIAN SHAMES
SANDY AGER

## 227

MICA AMIS CAP
LAGOS ADANO ONA
AXONS AIRFORCES
CIRCUMLOCUTIONS
ERA SOS GATE
LIONESS ETH
ETAT OWED ATRIA
ASTRONAVIGATION
POSIT BEAR ROTA
COS SALINAS
AMBI EST NIA
QUATERCENTENARY
ASSYRIANS OGLED
BET MEDOC FLANS
ASE ASSN FEST

## 228

HARP ROMA SAG
AMIR PICAS CPAS
LIMELIGHTS OPTS
LESSEE SCUTTLES
SACK HARTE
CATERER GEYSER
ADORN IDLES ARE
POPS SOL TURN
ORB PASTA PICOT
SEAMAN MOLDERS
NOUNS ALAI
EPAULETS DIETED
BONN TARGETDATE
BRAT TITAN UPON
ESS ERAS PENS

## 229

SHAY SPEC RAMS
MOVE TORSO EMIT
OLEO ALIEN TORE
GERWOMAN WEAKEN
ODER GOBI
SHAMES WOMANAGE
TOMES KORAN SEA
RUIN WIDEN STES
ASS DOTES WHOSE
YESWOMEN SHARES
EGAD SPEW
FALLEN SHEWOMAN
ALOT FELON MADE
DOSE UPEND ANEW
SEER LADE NESS

## 230

ASTA AROSE TICK
DEATHCOMESASTHE
EVILUNDERTHESUN
LEW BEEN ETAT
ERAS IDAS
SENIORS REDEEMS
SWEETEN MAH
PERILATENDHOUSE
ONE LITERAL
SAVARIN SINATRA
LESS FROM
ANUN CASE ICI
THEMIRRORCRACKD
AMONGTHEPIGEONS
JENA SODAS STET

## 231

TAMP■VET■ELTORO
ODAY■IDO■MEAGER
FARR■NIP■CAMELS
FLYINGTIGER■■■■
SEPTET■■RENAMED
■■OES■NCO■STOLA
SIP■SNOOPY■ENID
TOPS■IMMIE■ETTA
UNIT■LAPUTA■YES
NINER■DOS■LAP■■
GASPERI■■EASYST
■■■■WICKEDWITCH
SAUCER■LOU■THOR
RUTILE■ENC■IOTO
OREADS■ESE■SNOB

## 232

CLEF■ACTED■PRAM
HALO■PARTY■RAGA
ICAO■IRATE■OVER
CENTRALPARKWEST
■■■RENO■■SEL■■■
SLEET■MAI■ESTEE
HISS■CATNAP■ANT
EASTEIGHTYSIXTH
ENE■TENORE■MIRO
PASTY■OSA■APSES
■■■AMA■■MMCL■■■
PARKAVENUESOUTH
ATOI■APORT■DREI
CLAN■SETAE■ESNE
TING■TEALS■DANS

## 233

■■RACER■DEBASE■
■DONATE■ELECTRO
LITTLECABLECARS
AVAIL■OTTER■GAM
BITS■SIMON■CITO
ONE■DOLOR■SHEIS
REDWINES■BIERCE
■■■HANDPRESS■■■
LATELY■HOLSTERS
IDEAS■DECAY■NEA
PART■LARKS■ORAL
AME■SERIF■SCOTT
SANFRANCISCOBAY
ENCLAVE■SKATES■
■TEASEL■HIRED■■

## 234

CLUB■ATE■FALLEN
RASE■TRY■ORIOLE
OVERSHOE■EMBOSS
PARAMOURS■ARMET
■■■TEST■EDDA■■■
STAEL■■PARASOLS
CANDLE■ITA■■REO
RIG■YELLOWS■CAR
AGE■■LEE■SPOUSE
PARAPETS■■OUSTS
■■■PERU■COOT■■■
DUPED■PARAFFINS
ANIMAL■CORSICAN
MANANA■ROE■TOPI
PLENTY■END■SNAP

## 235

BRAC■BASED■WIMP
RICO■EMILE■OOOO
ATHOUSANDCLOWNS
DEEPNESS■IODATE
■■■EWES■ASPS■■■
■SCRIM■AVIS■BSA
ATLAS■SHOO■PRIS
LAUGHCLOWNLAUGH
DINE■RAYS■OPINE
ARK■SETS■TWINS■
■■■JADE■OREL■■■
ASSURE■SPILLAGE
SENDINTHECLOWNS
STAG■ZAIRE■TRAM
TAPE■ANNAS■EYRE

## 236

■ESQ■■■TAMEST■■
FLEUR■■UNAWARE■
EERIE■TRAVELING
EVANS■ABLER■BRA
SEPTILLION■QUOS
■SHILLONG■SUNUP
■■■LIANE■STAATS
■GOLEMS■GIRDLE■
MARINA■SONAR■■■
ELIOT■RETAPING■
SEEN■SEXTILLION
ANN■BITTE■ELENA
SATIATION■SILOS
■SALTERN■■SOLFA
■■LOSSES■■■NOS■

## 237

CAPE■CLAIM■AWOL
OLAN■HILDA■SIVA
WINDJAMMER■SNIT
LCD■ENOS■QUIDDE
SEALEGS■PUDGY■■
■■■APE■CLEANCUT
BAWL■■GRUEL■INO
ALIAS■LAM■LATIN
FAN■APONY■■TYTY
FIDDLERS■GAL■■■
■■BEERY■CELEBES
SALAMI■KAYS■ORT
AROD■WINDSOFWAR
NEWT■ISERE■CETE
KANO■GREER■CROW

## 238

LUCIA■SOLAR■JAI
AVENS■PRONE■UMP
WELSHRABBIT■GOA
SALOME■■■TRAGUS
■■■LACE■TRADERS
DOCENTS■RACED■■
APO■■OCTA■EPHOR
TUTTI■ARM■STAVE
ASTON■RICA■■RES
■■ONTAP■AMBIENT
WANDERS■RIOT■■■
ATTIRE■■■COARSE
IRA■CONEYISLAND
LII■OLIVE■TIMID
SAL■MALES■SAPPY

## 239

POEM■CAGE■BLAST
ANDA■ODER■RENTE
ITER■SARI■IOWAN
RAMSAYMACDONALD
SPAHI■■LAO■ARES
■■■ALOUD■GAR■■■
BAAL■BRIM■ADULT
EMILYJANEBRONTE
TORME■LENA■DOST
■■■CAL■BURMA■■■
OPAL■ISR■■AVIAN
SAMUELCOLERIDGE
ALOHA■ROIL■NEER
GETAT■EKES■CANO
EDENS■ESSA■ISTS

## 240

SLAP■SPCA■UCLAN
PERU■HOOD■NAOMI
AVER■ENNA■TROOP
MISCONCEPTIONS■
■■■HUSH■TILL■■■
HORATIONOTWELL■
AMISS■■ERIE■ION
LADE■■CGS■■ABBA
OHO■ATOR■■SCRAM
■AFISHNOTAWHALE
■■■PSIS■ALAI■■■
■BREASTNOTBEAST
SOUCI■RAIE■VOTE
URIAL■USSR■ENOS
BANCS■EATS■SEAT

## 241

```
SPORTSCAST#WADS
PIGEONHOLE#ALEE
IRRATIONAL#SETA
TAEL#PREP##TUES
STS#OPE#STRETCH
#ESQUE#ITEA#ITO
###UTTERING#AER
DADA##ROC##ONDE
EDO#FRANKLIN###
MOM#RUDE#ENOLA#
ORIGAMI#AFT#ASP
LANE##CELT#AUTO
IBIS#CARDIOGRAM
SLOT#ATMOSPHERE
HENS#BEASTTALES
```

## 242

```
ASKED#URI##★SOF
★LIKE#PETE#★TUP
TONGA#★VES#★ETS
EGG#FITSAND★TS#
###REM##SEER###
★CHINESS#SWAMPS
WAAC#THAW#STERN
ACTH#AIMED#IDIO
RHEAS#POLE#NEAR
SEDRAS#ALL★GAME
###DRUG##LTS###
#★★★GENERAL#ARM
ERIK#RONA#EMCEE
NENE#SMOG#RANDS
EDGY##EWE#SEE★S
```

## 243

```
#STAG##CASA#GOA
PHENOL#ALUM#OWN
TINGLE#NORMALLY
ANOLDMANSGOLD##
SERIF#RASE#GEAR
###CINE##STANCE
SAG#NINE##HEATS
IBO#GLADEYE#GOT
DELVE##SLAG#ERS
ELDERS##AMOR###
DEMI#IVAN#LEGAL
##INAGILDEDCAGE
RUNSINTO#TBILLS
ONE#LEAF#CUTLET
SIR#STET##GEST#
```

## 244

```
MOLIERE#CAPSTAN
AMADEUS#ASTARTE
LEVERET#SEAGATE
ALAS#DACHA#SURD
REG###TAI###MIL
ITEM#SEWER#PATE
ASSERTS#REVISED
###ROI###BIN###
TANGENT#BUZZERS
ERIE#TALUS#ALEE
NOR###VAR###ELL
SUVA#MEDIA#OVAL
ISANDER#ANIMATE
LANTERN#LIMITER
ELAINES#SLATERS
```

## 245

```
CADET#HEP##AIDA
AGAVE#OMAN#SOUR
RIVAL#WACO#TWEE
ONEHUNDREDYEARS
####GIA##DER###
ISTOUGHTOIGNORE
NARC###HUNG#LEM
CPAS#SPRIG#NAZI
AHS#OTRO###ANIL
SOHAPPYBIRTHDAY
###BAA##SEA####
ANDAHUNDREDMORE
LAIC#LUCA#DAYAN
DIEU#SICE#ENERO
ALTS##TIL#OOZES
```

## 246

```
STUB#LOAM#SMILE
HERO#AUTO#PODIA
OLDMASTER#OILER
DOUBLEFEATURES#
###SARI#LATE###
NOPQR#TRIKE#SPA
OPIUM##USEDCARS
ETNA#WALTS#LION
LEADTIME##SENSE
SDS#ALOSS#PATER
###DYER#TION###
#WORLDPREMIERES
MINEO#HERALDING
OSCAR#IDEM#UNIT
DEEMS#COOS#PDDS
```

## 247

```
SASH#ADES##FAME
KIWI#BITES#OLAF
IDAS#AVERT#RANT
#ANTIBESAUNTIE#
###OVER##DIE###
STARE#GID#SARAH
ARNI#REDINK#EDO
CANCANNESCANCAN
CII#DACAPO#EURO
ONETO#ESO#ESTER
###IBO##SALT###
#NICENICENIECE#
RINK#CHIDE#GOAL
ECCE#EATON#GAVE
SKAT##DEFT#STET
```

## 248

```
ADAH#STOAS#ASPS
MINI#ERICH#PHIL
ESTE#CANTALOUPE
SHAMROCK#CALLEE
##RAINY#SKYLARK
UNCLAD#SISSY###
SAT##SHAD#TORAH
ATIME#ALL#ONENO
FOCUS#ITER##TEN
###STORY#ECARTE
TITHERS#ALAMO##
ADORED#PRIMEVAL
PYROMANIAC#REDO
ALSO#RELIT#CRIB
SLIM#EMILS#ETTE
```

## 249

```
ACRE#DAME##PEAT
NOON#OLAN#TIARA
WOODYWOODPECKER
ALTOONA#PLATING
RAB#RED#AAR#NAE
SNEAKY#TPS#ASST
#TELI##REMUS###
##RESTAURANTS##
###ATOLL##BALM#
CAPP#LAY#MARIAS
OVO#DEM#SER#PRE
RIPTIDE#CREEPIN
DAGWOODBUMSTEAD
ETUIS#AIDA#ARNE
DENT##SOON#TSAR
```

## 250

```
SLAT#ALOMA#GAME
AIDE#TOPEE#ALAN
SLAM#ROTOR#MINI
SIMPSON#VACATED
###LOP##ETAL###
#AMECHE#RESIDUE
PBA#IYAR#STERNE
ARUBA#RIP#OLEIN
CAVILS#AFAR#STY
AMERICA#CROSSE#
###CZAR##TIC###
GATHERS#MILHOUS
ARIA#FINIS#EXPO
FARR#ENACT#MEOW
FRED#RENEE#ANNS
```

## 251

ZAMA ENTRY PREP
ERIN YAHOO RAVI
RILE EROTOGENIC
ODOMETER HAGGLE
ICES NOUN
CLICHE COOLANTS
LIS OTHER SNAIL
YANA HOLMS TITO
DROPS PLAIT ALP
ESTHETES DUNDEE
OVID LENA
CLARET PIRATING
RUMINATIVE ALAR
ANIS NEMEA NISI
BERM SNARL TATS

## 252

EGYPT CHEOPS
SCAPULA RELAYED
ALSORAN ERITREA
HAT TIN SEE APR
ARES DISCS IMAN
RORIC NNE ADIGE
ASNERS ONESIDED
IRKUTSK
SHOWBOAT SEVERE
HAVES RES WIPES
OMEN OLDIE MILK
FIR ARM TNT TIE
ATLANTA ANOTHER
REACTOR REDRESS
SPHINX SADAT

## 253

SWAGED CACTUS
QUIXOTE OBLATES
UNSEATS NEOCENE
ARE TUESDAY NAG
RIME ROOM ESTA
TSAR STUN SLIER
ZENITH VESTALS
COALESCES
BESTMEN INTACT
DEMOS VIES INRE
ELAN DERN CION
BAN TOLSTOY MOE
ABALONE ELEGANT
ROTATOR RELATES
RESETS SOLDER

## 254

TDS SHAH ADAME
PERK CURE SOLON
SLEIGHBELLSRING
ALATE COMEYETO
TIM ETAL ARM
NIP OPEN ITSA
GNOME SOFT HAN
HYGIENE VIOLENT
SOO ADIB ROAST
TUFT NEWS DNA
RAW LATH OCA
OCOMEALL MEWLS
AWHITECHRISTMAS
BLAKE TOUR TAUT
ASTAR APSE ANS

## 255

ADMITS SSH COBB
PEANUT TKO OKRA
EIGHTYFOUR NAIL
AULDLANGSYNE
TAEL ERE IRISES
INREM NINES
MONDALE AGATES
ELI LAX GIS LIA
DESADE ONESTEP
TRYST STONE
ADSUKI OWS ANAX
HAPPYNEWYEAR
ONEO RESOLUTION
STER ENE MELODY
TEDS DAR ARENAE

## 256

SAUNA LAVAL
APRON ABODE KIM
GRETA BULJANOFF
AIDA ROMA NOPAR
SLOBBER RATTATS
LOX SOUL
HIRER HILO SSTS
IOU IRANOFF KOO
MOSS ELAN APIAN
SOPS MIR
IMITATE PATELLA
FEATS POLE FOUR
NINOTCHKA GARBO
IRS APORT ACNES
SADAT TEASE

## 257

CASTOFF DRAMAS
UCCELLO CRENATE
THUNDER HAVARTI
LIL SAUSAGE IAN
ALLS MOPS ENCE
SLEPT SALTBUSH
SERIES PIROG
SYNCHRONIZERS
ATEUP PONIES
RECALLED SINCE
NASH LIRA OGRE
INK FINANCE DER
EDITING CONNOTE
COMINGS ENDIVES
EMOTES ROOTERS

## 258

REMADE BRA PHIL
EVINCE EAR LANA
TOMDICKANDHARRY
SEER IKE ACTES
EVAN ESTE
IFA INGE TEMPO
SUGARDADDY ELUL
AGER ACIER NETO
NUNC BELLESTARR
ETHEL EINE TED
ALEC VETO
TARNS ROE TAOS
STAGEDOORJOHNNY
KITE ION UPENDS
SEAL DNA STREET

## 259

GEHRIG SEAVER
BALEENS LABORER
ARMYANT IRONAGE
ALT LEA PTY SEE
BARE RAJAH HUNS
ANENT DOC HARTE
ADELES HOPELESS
STENGEL
ROOTLETS TOPEKA
ENNEA ROT TIMON
WEED WANER UPSY
EWA ERN EIN ISO
DECALOG OVERRUN
SERRATE FERRITE
KEELER FRISCH

## 260

JUDO ADOBE FRAT
ARAM SALAD RAGE
MANI HYPNOTIZED
BLANKETED RAZES
ONNO ALARM
ROQUE NEGEV ART
ONUSES BEGETTER
GOAL WHOSO WANE
ENDYMION FROZEN
TER ANODE OOZED
ACRES ODIC
ALTOS ESCALLOPS
GOUPHIGHER OGRE
RARE NOONE CLAW
AMES TWEED KEYS

## 261

```
■SCABS■■■ARCS■■
CORNETS■STELLAR
BRADLEE■TSQUARE
NITRO■RAY■■MNOP
■■III■EER■FSTOP
UBOATS■REALISTS
MEN■■ABONNIE■■■
PESANTE■ENTRAPS
■■■REALISE■■SOY
SCROUNGE■XRATED
HHOUR■RRS■ACU■■
OATS■■ASH■TIDES
LSHAPED■EVIDENT
EMELINE■LATINOS
■■SSTS■■■SECTS■
```

## 262

```
TACO■ADDIS■STOW
OMIT■VOILE■URGE
GETTHEGREATBIRD
ANY■INIT■■EDGES
■■■AGUE■SORE■■■
WINTHESUPERBOWL
ICONS■■LANA■PIE
DITO■ASTRO■MERE
OER■SLUR■■AIRER
WRESTLEAPECCARY
■■■ERST■ERIE■■■
STATE■■DAMN■ARK
THROWTHEPIGSKIN
EARN■SALON■TILE
MISS■ELIDE■SMEW
```

## 263

```
ADAM■TRAM■ABBOT
ROTA■OHIO■PRADO
CROSSWORD■RUNIN
HOPTOAD■EDITING
■■■ELGAR■ULU■■■
SWERVE■EWE■SAL■
ORALE■STILT■DON
SATYR■CUL■HEDGE
OPE■SNARL■ELLAS
■TRE■ANN■CEMENT
■■■ZAP■SARAH■■■
PUZZLES■RESUMES
ONEAL■CONSTRUCT
STARE■ADIT■SLOE
HOLDS■TEES■TENT
```

## 264

```
TIPPLE■LEFT■ACT
ADORER■OGEE■TOE
POMEGRANATE■ARS
ELSE■■AGLET■SET
■■■METAL■DESCRY
■ACIDRAIN■RCA■■
CRANIA■VIA■IDLE
GENETICENGINEER
SOON■LIT■UNTROD
■■FCC■CHEERIOS■
ASWEAK■EASEL■■■
SLO■MASKS■■LACE
TER■PAPIERMACHE
REM■ELAN■LETHAL
OKS■RANG■SWEEPS
```

## 265

```
VAST■■SCTS■MORO
ISLE■CAREA■AMES
ATAN■ONEAL■NAME
LIVORNOETORINO■
■■■RET■PROOF■■■
RAT■VIM■ONSETS■
SLOW■NIP■■ISHAM
VENEZIAEMANTOVA
PAISA■■WAC■OLEG
■NOTICE■WHO■ERI
■■■BRAND■EVE■■■
■FIRENZEENAPOLI
ARNO■CYCLE■EPIC
SEGO■AMASS■EERO
PEEK■NELA■■SCAN
```

## 266

```
PAIRS■BELT■MARM
ERROL■EVOE■OTOE
GLIDE■HIBERNIAN
SOS■ERATO■IDOLS
■■HAVANA■UGANDA
CASHEW■■TROY■■■
ACTA■WIRER■■WAY
THEBLARNEYSTONE
SEW■AGENT■■ALTA
■■■OVEN■■SURFER
CADDIE■PLINTH■■
HIRES■LAIRD■OFF
IRISHLACE■OVULE
LEES■OLEG■NINER
EDDA■GORE■EMDEN
```

## 267

```
SAMBA■■FHA■REEL
AROOM■ROOS■EAVE
SUNUP■ERAT■CRAG
SNARL■GARIBALDI
■■■GERALD■UPSET
BASE■EILEEN■■■■
OTTOMAN■RICHTER
RELIED■■■THEORY
GNOSTIC■THEROSE
■■■■ANOMIE■OLES
EASEL■CONRAD■■■
GLADSTONE■MORES
RIME■ANKA■ATOLL
EBON■SUER■TULSA
TIAS■STY■■ISLET
```

## 268

```
STOA■MILAN■UXOR
PANT■OSAGE■REDO
ARCHIMEDES■ANEW
STEELERS■TENORS
■■■NENE■MIXUP■■
SADIST■FINISHES
ASEA■SLINGS■ACE
LIMNS■AXE■TENON
EDO■HAZERS■MELD
SOCRATES■CLOSES
■■RENTS■TAUT■■■
JOINER■CORNIEST
ESTA■ANAXAGORAS
ALUM■CARIB■NINA
NOSE■TEENS■SEER
```

## 269

```
BAND■■SHOE■RASH
ELLE■BEAUX■ALOE
GIRLFROMIPANEMA
SIBELIUS■INDEED
■■■TEAL■MAYO■■■
■ASIAN■BATHMATS
ITTO■■ROMEO■DOE
SAINTLOUISWOMAN
ALL■HASTE■■VENT
WELCOMES■BLEND■
■■■ORBS■MUIR■■■
SCORIA■MOONRISE
KANSASCITYKITTY
ISEE■TACOS■DOLE
THAT■EWER■■ENOS
```

## 270

```
■■GAGS■■■STAG■■
STOMATA■THEDEER
POLARIS■HORMONE
AID■PEPPERMILLS
■LEN■BIGFEET■■■
■■NOG■RAAB■■BRA
EARLOBE■NIBBLED
BRUTAL■■■ROLAND
RILEDUP■ADDUCES
ODE■■EELS■ERK■■
■■■SUBROSA■SSS■
FASTSERVICE■MOD
MAKEHAY■SERVILE
SAILERS■TRIATIC
■■NERD■■■BATH■■
```

## 271

ABET■EVADE■SAAR
ROSE■SAROS■INCA
NETS■SLEET■LOIN
ORESTEIA■AGENDA
■■■EONS■OMAN■■■
CHURL■EURIPIDES
RONALD■DANE■OLE
ONCE■RAISE■TYRE
SDA■MAIN■TAYLOR
SOPHOCLES■GREYS
■■■EROS■TARA■■■
FALLEN■MENANDER
OHIO■ISING■NILE
CANT■ARDOR■URSA
IBOS■NOISY■SKEP

## 272

JOAB■SAHIB■PRES
AXLE■PRIMA■LISA
DEADRINGER■ANAX
ENDEAR■HARANGUE
■■■VLAD■NANAS■■
CARILLON■GYRATE
EMILY■LOVEA■BAA
DINS■FETID■NEBS
ALG■CASUS■FOLLE
RETAIL■PARABLES
■■ANODE■SOUL■■■
SPINNERS■ONEIDA
OLLA■RINGMASTER
HEEL■ACUTE■SAFE
ODDS■LABOR■ESTA

## 273

FATHEN■■■NAVEL■
SHOELACE■ODELET
TEMPORAL■TANKER
OAF■DEMAGOGUERY
PROA■SUTURES■■■
STOCK■SEMI■■BRA
■■LEND■■PEASOUP
RHETORS■STREWER
ACROBAT■■YARD■■
WHY■■FOWL■MULES
■■■RETIRED■MERE
HARUMSCARUM■RAN
ANADEM■COMEDIST
TERESA■KIBITZER
■SARAN■■■ORNERY

## 274

■HAZE■SWAB■FIRM
BELOW■LIMA■OMOO
ELUDE■ALOG■OPTS
ADMIRE■LUNATIC■
MONA■DAIRIES■■■
■NICHOLASOFTIME
■■■■ATEM■■■ELAN
ROBERTFORAPPLES
POEM■■■FARE■■■■
THEBANKRICHARD■
■■■ASININE■MARE
■EARPLUG■DRAGON
JACK■OTHO■OZONE
ESNE■TETS■MOUES
WEED■ESSE■ANTS■

## 275

OMAR■SLURS■ANSU
RARE■PINUP■PEAS
CREIGHTONABRAMS
SCANNER■TROOPER
■■■■OREL■SAN■■■
SALOME■ABET■HMS
ALAMO■ABEL■BOOT
MADANTHONYWAYNE
BIEN■HERD■ELATE
ANN■LIME■DAMSEL
■■■FIR■REAP■■■■
SERRATE■LIONESS
CLAIRECHENNAULT
ASIS■ERECT■URAL
TANK■NUTTY■TOGO

## 276

CETA■ALTAR■TAPE
ACER■MEHTA■ALOE
THERUMTUMTUGGER
SONATA■SOIL■AMY
■■■NENE■SOYA■■■
OAST■■VET■SHEET
SCI■SAIL■USANCE
THEJELLICLEBALL
REVIVE■OHMS■CAL
ADELE■ETA■■ATTY
■■■TRAM■TSAR■■■
SAD■ADIT■ANTICS
THEOLDGUMBIECAT
AMAN■ERROR■REMI
GENE■RENEE■YSER

## 277

ATE■BATHOS■AMOS
CAL■ORIOLE■DELI
EVERYMANDESIRES
DEVISE■■ERATO■■
IRES■DRESSY■MBA
ANNIE■ACT■■HOAX
■■■BRAVO■TOETHE
■TOLIVELONGBUT■
ARLENE■OUTRE■■■
SUDS■■JGS■ETTES
PET■CLOYED■URAL
■■ISAAC■■IADORE
NOMANWOULDBEOLD
ADEN■ESSENE■PEG
PERK■SENATE■STE

## 278

■■HAUTE■ERROR■■
■PORTAL■LEEWAY■
WESTEND■ANANIAS
RAT■STOPPED■NNE
ANAS■ERASE■LIKE
PUGET■ASE■MINER
STEROIDS■SINGES
■■■MONOPLANE■■■
PILOTS■OINTMENT
IRONS■SRA■SAPOR
SOWS■ANTIS■NIDE
ANE■PRESSER■COE
NIRVANA■ONENESS
■CEASED■NADINE■
■■DROSS■STOLE■■

## 279

CLINK■IPSE■LEWD
HANOI■NATS■ATOI
ALERT■IVES■TURN
FORTHETIMEBEING
ESTH■LIL■NAG■■■
■■■ASSAI■CHEOPS
SPANK■LOSE■ORAL
LEGGY■ENC■GRACE
IRAE■ODOR■AGNEW
MIRROR■FALSE■■■
■■■ABE■WPA■ACTI
THEBISHOPSAPRON
IAMB■TOME■SLING
ESME■EYER■CESTA
SHAY■SANS■HYPOS

## 280

NIOBE■ISMS■LOD■
ESSAY■ALOP■OPAL
THEME■MATA■GINA
■■■BLABBERMOUTH
AGGIES■■STAMMER
SIR■TWIN■ARA■■■
PLUG■AGAL■SNAP■
■DEIPNOSOPHIST■
■ALFA■TACO■AHEM
■■■TUX■LISA■ERE
SPOOLED■■INTROS
CONFABULATOR■■■
APIG■EPIC■ROUTE
MICA■CLAM■APSIS
■NEB■SERE■KEEPS

## 281

SHAM RASPS EGAL
EINE UNION XIPE
CHEZ TAMPA EZEK
ITZHAKPERLMAN
ORB SLIP
LAM HALF SELDOM
ASIS GOAL GAUZE
PINCHASZUKERMAN
ADORE TELL YAWL
ZORILS SLAW SAO
MICK VAN
JASCHAHEIFETZ
BACH UTILE VIOL
IRRA LINER IGOT
BLEW ZETES LEMS

## 282

PASTERN SOCCER
ATLARGE LAFARGE
THEBITESOFFLEAS
ILES DOVES ELI
NEP MILER SPIT
ATI HONOR SPITE
SENDING SATINED
GIVE LONG
PACKETS AMASSED
APRES PLEAT LAR
LAAR SOARS ASE
ECT SANTA ATIS
THEFLIGHTOFBEES
TERRACE ENDORSE
ESSAYS DERUSTS

## 283

♦ HEAD MASH SAM ♠
LODGE ELLA CRAW
INERT ALAI RENO
LENIENT TRAINER
PRESS DAMASK
ELAPSE THORP
TUNA DARE OSCAR
ULT ASPIRIN OBI
ILIAC EVEN AMES
TRADE DIBBLE
LOSTIN SPINY
OPPIDAN RANSACK
SEAR DODO ISSUE
ERIE ETON NASTY
♥ AND METE GLEE ♣

## 284

AEGIS MUMS TOUT
IRANI ISIT AURA
MORSE SPEARMINT
ADDERSTONGUE
TEATRAY SAMBA
SAM BLUEBELL
TUB UNAUS LAIC
ARAG RANGE ETNA
LISA AIDED YIN
CATTAILS CIT
SHEER CAMERAS
PITCHERPLANT
BLOODROOT ALINE
OILS EMEU RESOW
BEET FADS TREYS

## 285

BERT SPEAR AJAR
ARIA HELGA LENA
BILLTOOMEY ISNT
ACE ARNO EDESSA
PITY TWINE
MOBILE TIRESOME
ANON ROOTY WIS
REBA PGA SENT
NIS JEANS ONCE
ELECTORS AMUSES
ALOHA SNAP
LAGOON LADY LIS
OARS STEVEOVETT
FREE ORSER IDEA
TENT NEEDS MARY

## 286

PATRI FOCUSES
OLEOS ARMINARM
ALTOS MIAFARROW
ETUDIER GOOP
TAA EARN OMERTA
ARTERY DANES
BREAST OPEN DKM
LOTO OFFTO CORA
EWE ODEA NOUGAT
SCARF OUTEAT
GRITTY RANT ALE
AUNA FIRESAT
PLANETREE INDIA
ENDTOEND DIODE
RESCUED ELGAR

## 287

THETA ELAPSED
CHERUB MANHOLE
THEFINALPROBLEM
HASTE SITIN IMA
ESPY SERIN STEN
ITE THREE STAND
DECKERS REPORTS
KORE WILY
ISLANDS RERACKS
TAELS THERE YAP
ERDA GRASS ECRU
RAB HAITI ISLAM
ACASEOFIDENTITY
TENABLE EXCUSE
ENDLESS ROAST

## 288

CALUMET PHONATE
AGELESS ROMANIA
PODESTA ELOPERS
ENG HERESTO MAT
LIES RIMES LODE
LEROI NAT LONER
ASSYRIAN RECESS
BOSSANOVA
ABSENT TIBETANS
DECAY WIT REVET
ALAN BOORS SAGO
PIN FURNACE RAN
TETHERS TERMITE
EVEREST ENTICER
DERATES SEERESS

## 289

DEDICATES RANUP
ABATEMENT ALINE
DONATELLO CANIT
ANE ANS CLIMATE
INTO KEEP
TABLE NAMES SSS
ACROSS MARTINET
MOOS UDINE NETO
PROTOCOL DALLAS
AND ARDEB DALES
FRED ICRY
IMPASSE GRE IZE
SERUM RESONATOR
ATONE EDUCATION
SEDAN DERELICTS

## 290

ABU TEAL NAME
GOBS FORGO ODIN
EMIT OMNIPOTENT
RAQUEL OSMONDS
UNRIPE ION
SPITBALL DREAM
HATS AGREE DEW
ONO ASTRIDS ARÀ
EAU BITES EMIL
YSTAD CELIBATE
OSE ORIGEN
BARRELS AYRTON
OPPOSITION LILA
RIMS NINJA ENDS
ANSE ERGO EST

## 291

```
JENA#CABLE#APIG
ALEC#ONEUP#MICA
PICCALILLI#ACED
ESKIMO#ALCAZARS
###DORM#SUPER##
ASPERSED#REDEYE
CHINE#NICER#SOV
TACT#PAGES#EQUI
OWN#CETUS#EXULT
FLIGHT#PANATELA
##CREED#ROSE###
MAKEFREE#MERGED
OBIE#PICCADILLY
VEND#ACHED#OUSE
EDGY#NEONS#REED
```

## 292

```
#CAFTAN##SKIFF#
GALLIPOT#PILLAR
ANTIMONY#UNLACE
STARE#PRONE#VIC
PORT#CLOAK#SOLE
ERS#VAULT#ACRID
###JOSS#SECRETE
#ADULT###SHADY#
GRANGER#STEP###
ARICA#OILED#PAS
MIRO#HONOR#SAGE
IVY#OATES#DURER
NAMELY#PHRASING
GLACEE#TEADANCE
#SNUGS##SPONGY#
```

## 293

```
DODOS#AHAS#PAWL
IRENE#LIME#ARIA
ELECT#OGEE#RELY
SOMEOFTHESEDAYS
###INA#BRAVO###
SHUN#TAU#WANGLE
HERA#ARTY##MOOS
ARAB#LOTUS#YORK
LOLL##WOMP#ESNE
ENSUED#NAE#NEAR
###ERIES#WAG###
THEMEMPHISBLUES
HERO#WOOL#BINGO
ELMO#IDEE#OSTEO
OMAN#TESS#THORN
```

## 294

```
STOP#BRAGG#ROSS
HALE#RULER#EPIC
ICER#ANITA#GALA
PTOMAINE#ZEALOT
###ESSENTIAL###
DEBATER#HERETIC
ELATED#FIR##OLE
BIKER#DON#BURIN
ADE##RIG#BONSAI
RESILED#METHODS
###NEGOTIATE###
OREGON#RACEMOSE
VAIR#AMISH#MOOD
ACRE#NOTME#EZRA
LEES#TREAD#DEEM
```

## 295

```
#HOPPER#ALBERS#
CONVENE#SEAGATE
HEATERS#SAMOVAR
ADS#ROE#ANA#IBN
SOLO#LAPIS#DOLE
SWORD#LIL#SALES
ENWRAP#CERAMIST
####HOGARTH####
TRAILERS#SLACKS
REUSS#OSS#STONE
ITSA#QUOTA#APER
BIT#BUN#RUM#PSI
ANEROID#ARENOSE
LUNETTE#PAROLES
#ESCHER#SEURAT#
```

## 296

```
#JOSEPH#CLONIC#
GAVOTTE#AURICLE
ONESTEP#PROTEAN
MER#ARC#SES#BUT
EDDA#OASTS#JEDI
ROILS#THA#CORER
SEDATE#ENTANGLE
####EVULSED####
IMMINENT#REALMS
NOONS#WED#TREAT
ULNA#RIRES#TORY
ROT#GAS#SPA#NIL
ETAMINE#PADRONE
DONEGAL#ORDERED
#VANITY#TEASER#
```

## 297

```
TANAGER#CABINET
IMAGINE#ABALONE
MEMENTO#NEREIDS
ERA#SEPTATE#SIT
LITH#REEDS#COVE
ACHES#NRA#LAMER
GASMETER#CARESS
###MENDICANT###
ASSERT#FADDISTS
STIRS#CIR#SETUP
CANS#TREED#RATA
ETE#THUDDED#TOR
NUDGERS#FEATURE
DRIBLET#ORBITER
SEESAWS#RESEEDS
```

## 298

```
DADO#ATOMS#ANAT
ALOU#KAPUT#MOBY
WENTBANANASOVER
SCALE##LITERATE
###ALGA#CUR####
ABOWLOFCHERRIES
BOP#EARL##ANDRE
ASEA#TOAST#SLAV
CURLS##SORT#ESE
INAPPLEPIEORDER
####LAS#LETO###
IMPLANTS##UPSET
DARETOEATAPEACH
EXIT#SERIN#RICE
AIMS#EMDEN#SLEW
```

## 299

```
HACK#BANFF#OMAR
ARAT#ADIEU#DALI
URNS#HELEN#DYES
NON#BALLTHEJACK
TWOSOME##OOO###
##NINA#PLUMBBOB
NOBLE#PROS#SAKE
ALA#SQUIRES#LIV
BELL#UPSY#HOLEY
SOLECISM#VINO##
###GAS##MALEFIC
LUCILLEBALL#FDA
ARAB#IRENE#BIRD
MELL#NINER#IRED
PYLE#GETTY#DEWY
```

## 300

```
BAMS#AHEAD#PADS
ONIT#NEGRO#AMOK
OSCARGRAMMYTONY
BARRELED#IONIA#
###TSE##ANNA###
COALER#ALAD#MAC
INDIA#STAT#SAGA
STANLEYAMERICAS
CONG#ARLO#EGYPT
OPE#PRIE#CANSEE
###RITA##ATA###
#BEACH#BERATING
COTTONROSESUGAR
ORNE#UNITE#ROTA
BEAD#TALON#EROS
```